VILLAS

Superb Residential Style

Des Résidences Superbes de Grand Style

Sibylle Kramer

VILLAS

Superb Residential Style

Des Résidences Superbes de Grand Style

BRAUN

CONTENTS
INHALT
SOMMAIRE

PREFACE
VORWORT
AVANT-PROPOS

Since ancient times, the term "villa" has been infused with a special aura. Villas described by Cicero and Pliny, which also included a few owned by the proverbial grandeur-loving Lucullus, provide insights into the concepts of Roman villa architecture. Some of these principles remain in application to this day; others were enhanced and expanded in line with the modern architectural style spirit, including the use of new materials. The selection of an elevated and exposed location is certainly a criterion that has remained valid through the ages. Roman summer palaces, in particular, were preferably erected near the sea and located on slopes, which ensured special views of the surrounding landscape, an advantage that was highly in demand by villa owners in those times and remains so today. The interior room structure centers on these views, and the visual axes of a villa often combine rooms with a view, terraces or large panoramic windows to create the desired spatial effect. While in ancient times the proximity to running water used to constitute a major location advantage, today a generously sized pool must be included in any individualized oasis.

This book presents 85 exclusive projects in which international architects implemented the dreams of the owners. Despite the vastly different designs and applied materials of the presented villas, they all represent the spectacular implementation of individual and luxurious desires for space, prestige and luxury. Today, the term villa denotes a noble detached house that represents a unique expression of an elevated standard of living and a distinguished lifestyle. Having at least two floors ensures the ideal living comfort of the demanding owners, for many of which the villa is no less than a built expression of their individual life script. Two basic concepts can be observed that are shared by almost all projects. The first is the use of large glass façades, windows or panoramic panes, which provide the villa with breathtaking views while also ensuring sufficient illumination for the rooms that often are exceptionally deep and open. The second is the fact that many building sites are situated in exclusive slope locations or in attractive landscapes, which necessitates finding planning solutions that position the building sustainably and organically its environment without making it appear like an imposed foreign body. Many villas have two faces, such as *Casa X* and *Lakeside Villa* – to ensure privacy, they present closed façades towards the public side, while opening up transparently and generously towards the secluded nature side. Sometimes, existing structures can be incorporated in projects that combine old and new architectural styles into a particularly enthralling mix, such as the *Home in Extremadura* or *Astley Castle*. The *Home in Extremadura* in particular, exhibits a very unique character based on the interaction of the old materials of stone and timber with the new materials of steel and concrete, which makes it stand out from mainstream palaces and their all-round glazing. Several villas vertically divide their spatial functions, reserving the top floor for private use, while the ground floor contains public or social rooms. The design freedom provided by the large available space is exemplified, for example, in the flight of steps inside the organic *Shell*.

Thus, villa owners can count themselves lucky that architects implement projects for them that often remain mere childhood dreams for others. Join us in exploring the elegant dream world of villas!

Seit der Antike ist das Wort Villa von einer besonderen Aura umgeben. Aus den Beispielen, die Cicero und Plinius geben und die neben anderen auch die diversen Villen des sprichwörtlichen Genussmenschen Lukullus beschreiben, lassen sich Erkenntnisse über die römische Villenarchitektur gewinnen, von denen einige Prinzipien bis heute Bestand haben. Andere wurden durch die moderne Architektursprache und den Zeitgeist sowie um neue Materialien ergänzt und erweitert. Gewiss zeitlos ist die Wahl des exponierten Bauplatzes. Gerade die römischen Sommerpaläste wurden gerne in der Nähe des Meeres errichtet und jene Hanglagen, die einen besonderen Ausblick in die Landschaft eröffnen, waren damals wie heute von den Villenbesitzern gefragt. Das innere Raumprogramm orientiert sich nach wie vor an diesen Ausblicken, sodass die Sichtachsen einer Villa häufig Aussichtsräume, Terrassen oder große Panoramafenster miteinander verbinden um ein entsprechendes Raumerlebnis zu kreieren. War in der Antike die Nähe zu fließendem Wasser ein wichtiger Standortvorteil, so ist es heute der großzügig angelegte Pool, der in der individuellen Oase nicht fehlen darf.

Der vorliegende Band vereint 85 exklusive Projekte, in denen internationale Architekten die Träume ihrer Bauherren verwirklichen. So unterschiedlich die Gestaltung und die verwendeten Materialien der präsentierten Villen auch sind, es vereint sie stets die spektakuläre Umsetzung individueller und luxuriöser Wünsche von Raum, Repräsentanz und Individualität. Unter einer Villa versteht man heute ein vornehmes, frei stehendes Haus, das einen einzigartigen Ausdruck von gehobenem Lebensstandard und distinguiertem Lebensstil repräsentiert. Mindestens zwei Stockwerke sorgen dabei für den idealen Wohnkomfort der anspruchsvollen Bewohner, für viele ist die Villa nicht weniger als der gebaute individuelle Lebensentwurf. Dabei lassen sich zwei grundsätzliche Strömungen beobachten, die beinahe allen Projekten gemeinsam sind. Zum einen kommen großflächige Glasfassaden, Fenster oder Panoramascheiben zum Einsatz, die der Villa atemberaubende Ausblicke ermöglichen, zum anderen aber natürlich auch dafür sorgen, die häufig besonders tiefen und offen gestalteten Räume angemessen zu belichten. Weiterhin befinden sich viele Bauplätze in exquisiter Hanglage oder an landschaftlich reizvoller Stelle und machen es so notwendig, eine Planungslösung zu finden, dass sich der Baukörper nachhaltig und organisch in die Umgebung einfügt und nicht wie ein aufgesetzter Fremdkörper wirkt. Dabei hat die Villa oftmals zwei Gesichter, wie die Beispiele *Casa X* und *Lakeside Villa* zeigen: Sie verschließen sich mit geschlossenen Fassaden zugunsten der Privatheit zum öffentlichen Raum und öffnen sich großzügig und transparent zur nicht einsehbaren Natur. Manches Mal kann dabei noch auf bestehende Bausubstanz zurückgegriffen werden, bei diesen Projekten verbinden sich die alte und neue Architektursprache zu einer ganz besonders spannenden Mischung, so etwa beim *Home in Extremadura* oder beim *Astley Castle*. Gerade ersteres entwickelt aus dem Aufeinandertreffen der alten Materialen Stein und Holz mit den neuen Materialien Stahl und Beton eine ganz eigene Qualität, die direkt aus der Masse der rundumverglasten Paläste hervorsticht. Viele Villen nehmen eine vertikale Teilung des Raumprogramms vor und behalten das Obergeschoss einer privaten Nutzung vor, während im Erdgeschoss auch öffentliche oder gesellschaftliche Räume angesiedelt sind. Wie frei und weitläufig hier aufgrund des verfügbaren Platzes gestaltet werden kann, verdeutlicht beispielsweise die Freireppe innerhalb der organischen *Shell*.

Und so kann sich jeder Villenbesitzer glücklich schätzen, dass die Architekten das erbaut haben, wovon andere seit der Kindheit nur träumen dürfen. Werfen Sie mit uns einen Blick in die elegante Traumwelt der Villen!

Le mot « villa », dont l'origine remonte à l'Antiquité, a de tout temps été entouré d'une aura particulière. Cicéron et Pline l'utilisaient déjà, notamment pour décrire la résidence du célèbre Lucullus, et certaines des caractéristiques architecturales mentionnées par ces auteurs restent valables à notre époque, même si les villas modernes se distinguent par l'utilisation d'une gamme plus vaste de matériaux. Ce qui reste inchangé au travers des siècles, néanmoins, c'est la prédilection pour les sites remarquables : aujourd'hui comme hier, les villas sont de préférence construites au bord de la mer ou sur des terrains en pente offrant des vues panoramiques sur le paysage. De plus, l'agencement des pièces, le percement des fenêtres et la disposition des terrasses sont souvent conçus pour mettre en valeur ces perspectives sur l'environnement. Mais tandis que la proximité d'un cours d'eau était jadis un critère d'implantation déterminant, ce rôle d' « oasis rafraîchissante » échoit aujourd'hui à une piscine.

On trouvera dans le présent ouvrage quatre-vingt-cinq villas d'exception conçues par des architectes du monde entier afin de réaliser les rêves de leurs clients. En dépit de la grande variété de styles et de matériaux qu'elles illustrent, toutes ces réalisations ont en commun de refléter un certain goût du luxe, du prestige et de la personnalisation. Le terme « villa » s'applique de nos jours à un bâtiment indépendant, de grande classe et sur deux niveaux ou plus, qui intègre un confort maximal, reflète un style de vie distingué et constitue souvent rien de moins qu'un achèvement architectural personnalisé pour le maître d'ouvrage. Par-delà ces caractéristiques communes, la quasi-totalité des villas modernes partagent deux éléments d'architecture typiques : d'une part des fenêtres panoramiques ou des murs entièrement vitrés qui ouvrent largement les pièces sur l'extérieur et leur assurent un bon éclairage naturel ; d'autre part une implantation sur un terrain en pente ou dans un site de qualité exceptionnelle, ces deux dernières particularités exigeant de l'architecte qu'il conçoive un bâtiment capable de s'intégrer à son environnement de manière organique afin d'éviter qu'il n'y apparaisse comme un corps étranger. Par ailleurs, la villa moderne est souvent une entité à deux visages, comme le montrent les réalisations *Casa X* et *Lakeside Villa*, des bâtiments fermés et intimistes d'un côté, transparents et largement ouverts sur la nature environnante de l'autre. Les architectes peuvent également choisir de développer leur projet sur la base d'un bâtiment préexistant, comme dans le cas d'*Astley Castle* ou du *Home in Extremadura*, deux réalisations où l'ancien et le moderne se complètent de manière spectaculaire. Les édifices de ce type, dans lesquels des matériaux traditionnels comme le bois et la pierre s'associent au béton et à l'acier, acquièrent une qualité particulière qui les distingue des villas de grand standing entièrement vitrées. Notons également que la plupart des réalisations modernes répartissent les pièces de manière verticale en réservant le rez-de-chaussée aux espaces publics et à la vie sociale, tandis que les chambres et autres espaces strictement privés se trouvent au niveau supérieur. L'escalier assurant la liaison entre les différents étages offre alors à l'architecte une liberté de conception proportionnelle à l'espace disponible, comme on peut le voir dans la villa *Shell*, un bâtiment aux formes organiques.

Grâce à son architecte, le propriétaire d'une villa a ainsi le bonheur de vivre dans un cadre de prestige dont d'autres rêvent depuis leur enfance. En feuilletant ce livre, vous aurez le plaisir de jeter un œil dans le monde élégant des villas.

BRUGES, BELGIUM **HOUSE ROCES**

ARCHITECTS: GOVAERT & VANHOUTTE ARCHITECTS
COMPLETION: 2010_**PROPERTY SIZE:** 2,219 M²
GROSS FLOOR AREA: 532 M²_**NUMBER OF ROOMS:** 4
PHOTOS: TIM VAN DE VELDE

Villa Roces is integrated into an oblong terrain in the forest surrounding Bruges, Belgium. The concept consists out of a wooden wall flanking a wide glass box. The house is made of glass built along the wall to counter the lack of light and to reflect the forest. Functioning as a background for this glass box, the wall is constantly visible both inside and outside. Similar to the box design of the transparent volume, the inside space contains clearly defined boxes and volumes that incorporate the structural elements. Inside, the house contains a split level with the lower half located underground. This reduces the total built height above ground level, creating a distinguished contrast to the verticality of the trees.

Die Villa Roces liegt auf einem länglichen Waldgrundstück nahe der belgischen Stadt Brügge. Der Entwurf setzt sich aus einer Holzwand und einem offenen gläsernen Kubus zusammen. Glas ist das vorherrschende Material. So wird dem Mangel an Licht begegnet und die Atmosphäre des Waldes einbezogen. Die hölzerne Wand dient dem Glaskubus als Kulisse und ist von innen wie außen stets präsent. Im Innern wiederholt sich das Design des transparenten Baukörpers in klar definierten Kuben und Volumen, die die strukturellen Elemente verbinden. Eine Hälfte des terrassierten Hauses liegt unterirdisch, was die Gesamthöhe reduziert und einen deutlichen Kontrast zur Vertikalen der Bäume schafft.

Cette villa se trouve sur un terrain boisé des environs de Bruges. Son concept de base est un mur en bois flanqué d'une boîte en verre, le bois renvoyant à la forêt environnante, tandis que l'usage intensif du verre vise à compenser une faible luminosité. Visible quel que soit l'endroit où l'on se trouve à l'intérieur ou à l'extérieur du bâtiment, le mur fonctionne comme un écran masquant la boîte en verre. On retrouve le concept de boîte à l'intérieur du bâtiment, puisque les éléments structurels sont eux aussi intégrés à des espaces et volumes clairement définis. Un niveau semi-souterrain a permis de réduire la hauteur de l'ensemble, ce qui met en évidence l'horizontalité de la villa, qui s'affirme ainsi en contraste par rapport à la verticalité des arbres.

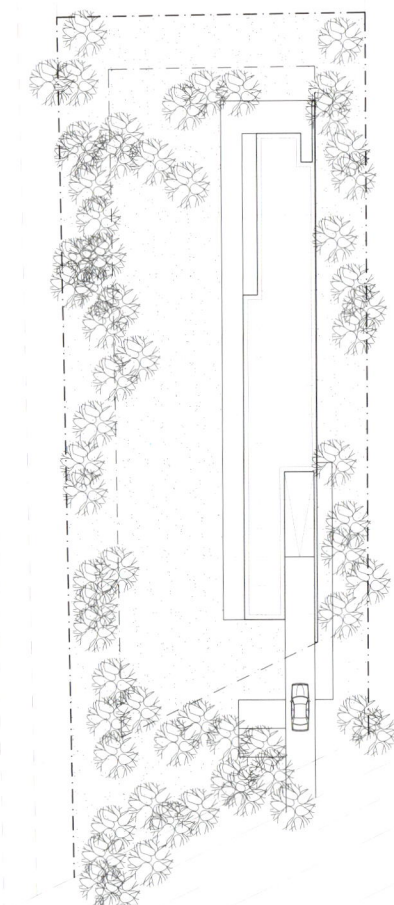

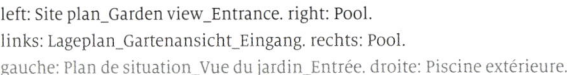

left: Site plan_Garden view_Entrance. right: Pool.
links: Lageplan_Gartenansicht_Eingang. rechts: Pool.
gauche: Plan de situation_Vue du jardin_Entrée. droite: Piscine extérieure.

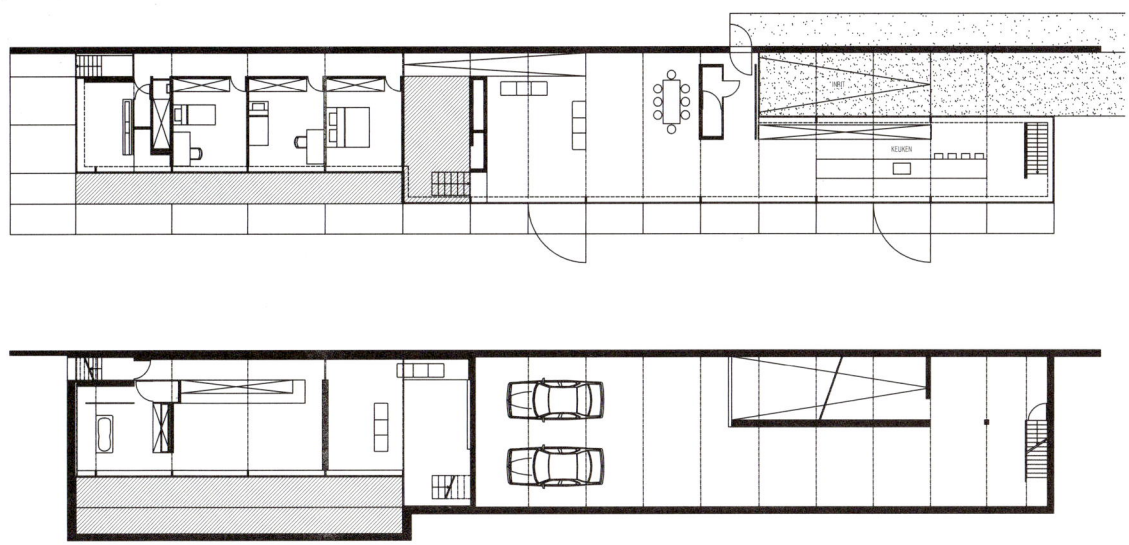

left: Exterior view. right: Floor plans_Living room_Room sequence.
links: Außenansicht. rechts: Grundrisse_Wohnraum_Raumsequenz.
gauche: Vue de l'extérieur. droite: Plans_Séjour_Enfilade.

STERZING, ITALY **HOUSE IN STERZING**

ARCHITECTS: BERGMEISTERWOLF ARCHITEKTEN
COMPLETION: 2011_**PROPERTY SIZE:** 37,000 M²
GROSS FLOOR AREA: 245 M²_**NUMBER OF ROOMS:** 8
PHOTOS: GÜNTHER RICHARD WETT

A group of buildings in combination with a historic chapel is being created near a mountain. The desired space for living, sauna and the garage was developed in three building sections that are integrated into the existing landscape and incorporate the remnants of the former building, such as the stone walls and the shingles of the chapel. These three sections were inserted into the terrain without affecting the existing topography. Terraces located in front of them incorporate the outside space, while the exterior façade features decorative letters by artists Lois and Franziska Weinberger. The buildings are separate in terms of their function, shape and materials, yet create a single unit due to their positioning.

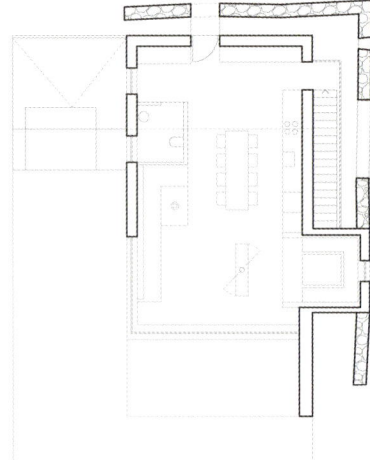

Gemeinsam mit einer historischen Kapelle entsteht ein Ensemble am Berg. Die gewünschten Anforderungen von Wohnen, Sauna und Garage wurden in drei Gebäudeteilen geschaffen, welches sich in die bestehende Landschaft integrieren und mit den Überresten des Bestandes, den Steinmauern und den Schindeln der Kapelle arbeiten. Diese drei Gebäudeteile wurden so ins Gelände hineingesteckt, dass die bestehende Topographie unverändert bleibt. Ihnen werden Terrassen vorgelagert, die den Außenraum mit einbeziehen und zudem erhalten sie an der Aussenfassade Schriftinstallationen von den Künstlern Lois und Franziska Weinberger. Die Gebäude sind nach ihrer Funktion, Form und Materialität getrennt und dennoch ergeben sie durch ihre Positionierung in der Landschaft eine Einheit.

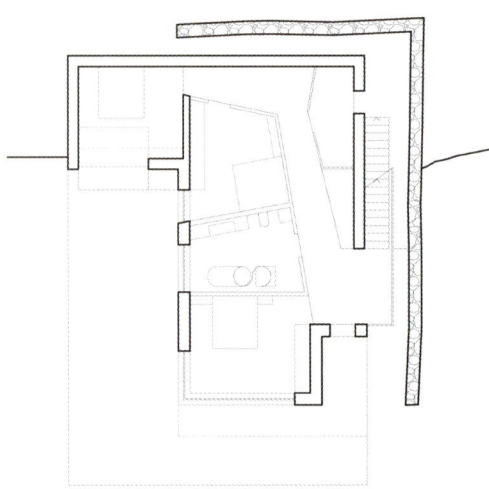

Cette maison est construite à flanc de montagne près d'une vieille chapelle. Trois volumes distincts, en harmonie avec les ardoises de la chapelle et de vieux murs en pierres, sont disposés de manière à s'intégrer à la topographie sans la bouleverser. Ils abritent le garage, le sauna et les pièces d'habitation, se complètent par des terrasses et s'agrémentent à l'extérieur par des installations dues aux artistes Lois et Franziska Weinberger. Bien que séparés les uns des autres, présentent des formes différentes et réalisés avec divers matériaux, les trois volumes qui composent le bâtiment forment un ensemble grâce à leur positionnement dans le paysage.

left: Top floor plan_Ground floor plan_Exterior view. right: Outdoor area.
links: Grundriss OG_Grundriss EG_Außenansicht_Terrasse. rechts: Außenbereich.
gauche: Plan niveau 1_Plan RdC_Vue de l'extérieur. droite: Extérieur.

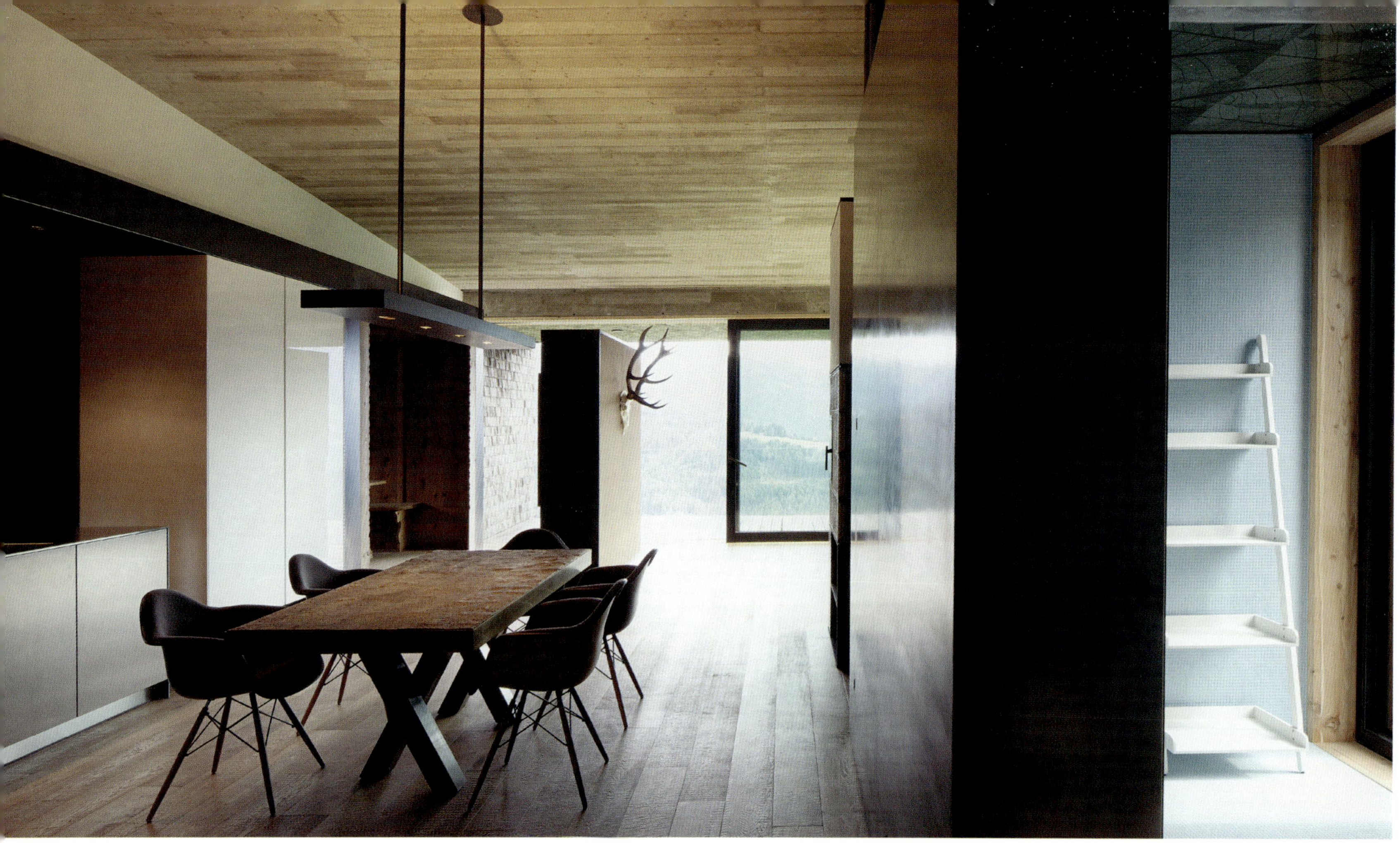

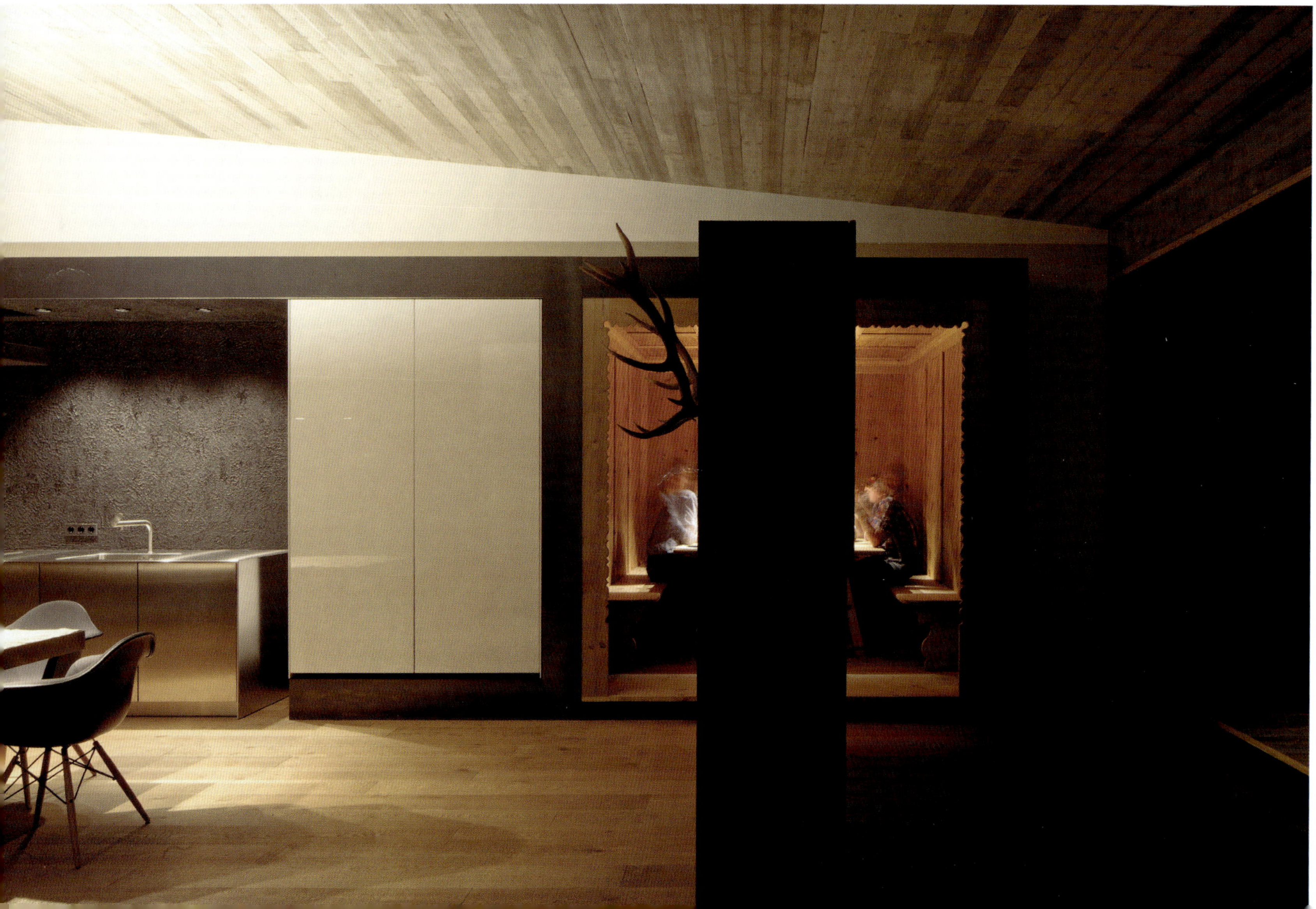

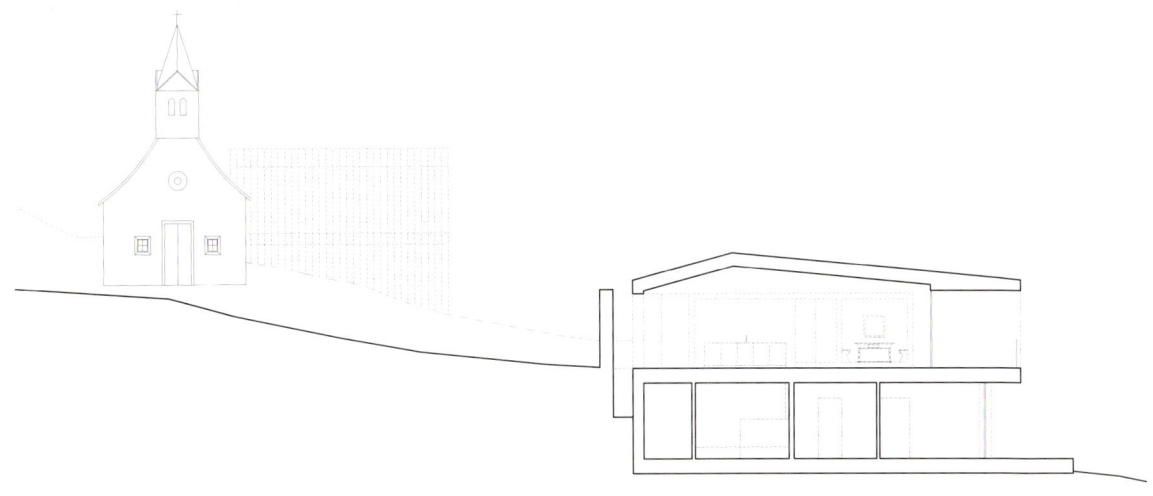

left: Dining area_Living area. right: Section_Bathroom_Kitchen_Stairs.
links: Essbereich_Wohnbereich. rechts: Schnitt_Bad_Küche_Treppe.
gauche: Salle à manger_Séjour. droite: Vue en coupe_Salle de bains_Cuisine_Escalier.

POTSDAM-MITTELMARK, GERMANY **HOUSE O**

ARCHITECTS: PETER RUGE ARCHITEKTEN
DESIGN TEAM: PYSALL RUGE ARCHITEKTEN
COMPLETION: 2011_**PROPERTY SIZE:** 867 M²
GROSS FLOOR AREA: 360 M²_**NUMBER OF ROOMS:** 10
PHOTOS: WERNER HUTHMACHER

The plot is situated in a magnificent hilly location with view of the lake. It sur-roundings are dominated by villa-style historical and new residences. The large number of old trees was kept mostly intact. The layouts of this three-family house are open and unconstrained, occasionally extending across several floors. Understated materials, such as exposed concrete, glass, wood and natural stone underline the simple and modern architectural style. The top floors are accessed by an external stairwell. The open southern and northern façades render the interior of the building bright and cheerful.

Das Grundstück liegt in einer landschaftlich traumhaften Hanglage mit Blick über den See. Die Umgebung wird dominiert durch villenartige historische und neue Wohnhäuser. Der umfangreiche alte Baumbestand wurde weitestgehend erhalten. Die Grundrisse dieses Dreifamilienhauses sind offen und frei gestaltet und erstrecken sich teilweise über mehrere Geschosse. Zurückhaltende Mate-rialien, wie Sichtbeton, Glas, Holz und Naturstein unterstreichen die schlichte moderne Architektursprache. Alle Obergeschosse werden über eine Außentrep-pe erschlossen. Durch die offene Süd- und Nordfassade gibt sich das Gebäude im Inneren hell und freundlich.

Cet immeuble situé dans une zone résidentielle où abondent les villas an-ciennes et modernes bénéficie d'une implantation de rêve avec vue sur un lac. Construit en respectant autant que possible les grands arbres présents sur le ter-rain, le bâtiment abrite trois logements, dont un duplex, chacun d'entre eux se caractérisant par des plans modulables. Des matériaux sobres (verre, bois, pierre naturelle et béton brut de coffrage) soulignent le style résolument moderne de l'architecture. Un escalier extérieur dessert tous les étages. Les façades nord et sud entièrement vitrées confèrent à l'intérieur un bon éclairage naturel et une atmosphère chaleureuse.

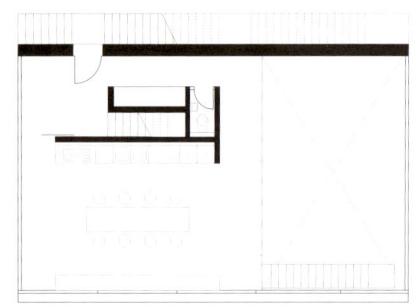

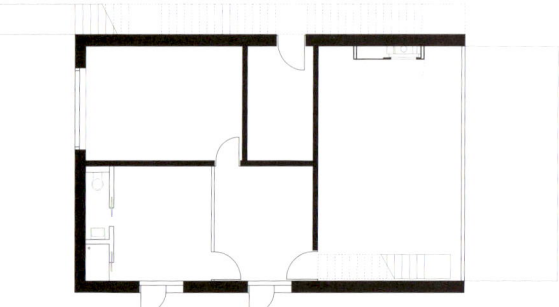

left: First and ground floor plans_Bathroom_Living area. right: Garden view.
links: Grundrisse 1. OG und EG_Bad_Wohnbereich. rechts: Gartenansicht.
gauche: Plan niveau 1 et RdC_Salle de bains_Séjour. droite: Vue du jardin.

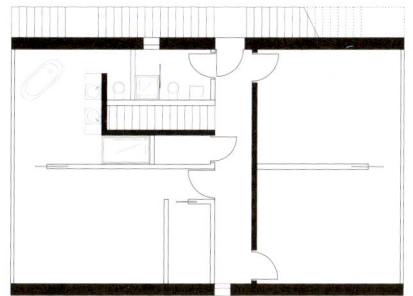 

left: Street view. right: Second and top floor plans_Kitchen and dining room.
links: Straßenansicht. rechts: Grundrisse 2. OG und 3. OG_Küche und Essbereich.
gauche: Vue de la rue. droite: Plan niveau 2 et niveau 3_Cuisine et salle à manger.

THORPENESS, UK **THE DUNE HOUSE**

ARCHITECTS: JARMUND/VIGSNÆS AS ARKITEKTER MNAL
COMPLETION: 2010_**PROPERTY SIZE:** 1,200 M²
GROSS FLOOR AREA: 250 M²_**NUMBER OF ROOMS:** 8
PHOTOS: NILS PETTER DALE

To get a planning permission it was important to relate to the existing typical British seaside strip of houses. The rooftop of the bedroom floor somehow plays with the formal presence of these buildings, and also brings to mind a romantic remembrance of holidays at bed and breakfasts while traveling through the UK. The ground floor contrasts with this by its lack of relationship to the architecture of the top floor. The living area and the terraces are set into the dunes to protect them from the strong winds, opening equally in all directions to offer wide views. The corners can be opened by sliding doors, which emphasizes the floating appearance of the top floor.

Eine Anlehnung an die traditionellen Häuserreihen englischer Küstenlandschaften war Voraussetzung für die Baugenehmigung. So spielen Dach und Obergeschoss des Dune House mit der formalen Präsenz britischer Küstenarchitektur und erinnern an einen romantischen Urlaub in einem „Bed & Breakfast". Das Erdgeschoss bricht jedoch mit der Architektur des oberen Stockwerks. Wohnbereich und Terrassen sind in die Dünen eingebettet, um sie vor starkem Wind zu schützen. Gleichzeitig sind sie zu allen Seiten hin offen und bieten einen Blick ins Weite. Die Ecken lassen sich über Schiebetüren öffnen, was den schwebenden Eindruck des Obergeschosses noch verstärkt.

La condition pour obtenir le permis de construire de cette villa située sur la côte du Suffolk, en Angleterre, était de respecter le style local. Le niveau supérieur, qui abrite les chambres, satisfait à cette exigence, tout en évoquant des souvenirs de vacances romantiques passées dans les Bed & Breakfast britanniques. Le rez-de-chaussée, par contre, se distingue par son architecture volontaire : entièrement vitré, il offre des vues panoramiques dans toutes les directions, tandis que les angles sont pourvus de portes coulissantes qui, lorsqu'elles sont ouvertes, viennent renforcer l'impression de légèreté qui se dégage du niveau supérieur. La terrasse et le séjour sont à demi-enterrés dans la dune de manière à les protéger du vent.

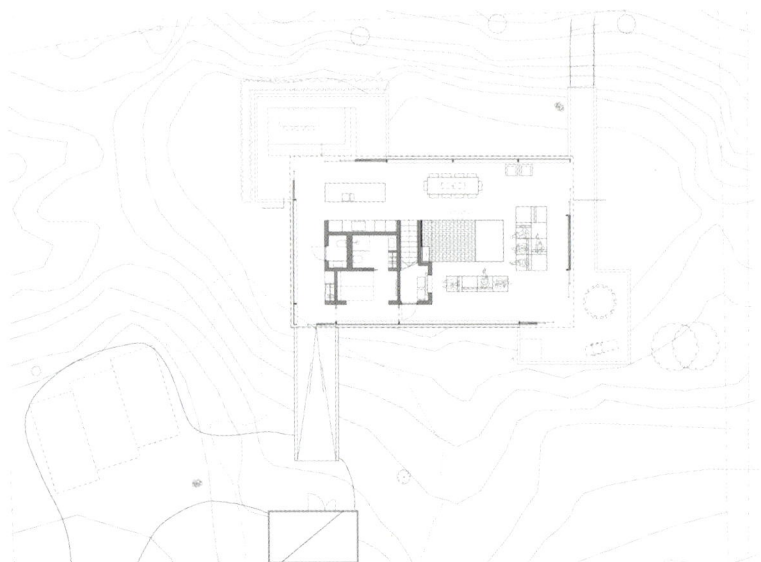

left: Ground floor plan_General view_Exterior view. right: Bedroom.
links: Grundriss EG_Gesamtansicht_Außenansicht. rechts: Schlafzimmer.
gauche: Plan RdC_Vue générale_Vue de l'extérieur. droite: Chambre.

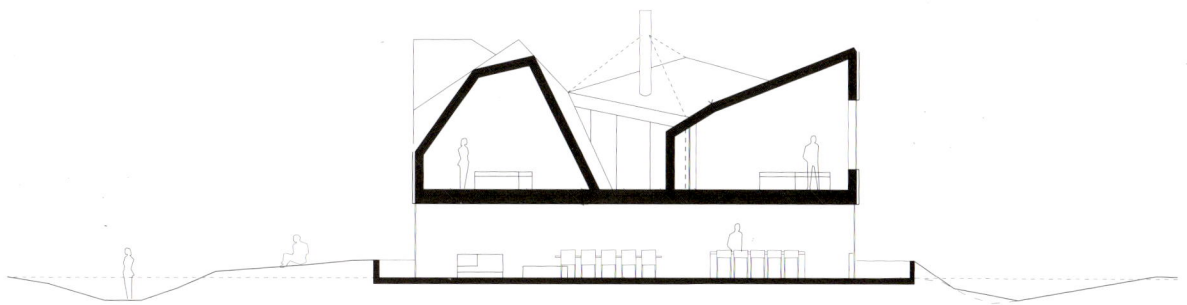

left: Interior view. right: Section_Bathroom_Kitchen_Living and dining area.
links: Innenansicht. rechts: Schnitt_Bad_Küche_Wohn- und Essbereich.
gauche: Vue de l'intérieur. droite: Vue en coupe_Salle de bains_Cuisine_Séjour et salle à manger.

ROCAFORT, SPAIN J HOUSE

ARCHITECTS: BBLAB. ANA BONET. LUCA BRUNELLI
COMPLETION: 2010_**PROPERTY SIZE:** 500 M²
GROSS FLOOR AREA: 354 M²_**NUMBER OF ROOMS:** 4
PHOTOS: RICARDO ESPINOSA

Adequate privacy is coupled with a straight relationship with the outdoors in a small urban plot. The partitioning defines the public and private areas of the house. As the sunny, open and transparent ground floor dissolves into the garden, a secretive, cagey and bright first floor introduces a more nuanced interior-exterior relationship. The desired privacy is achieved by several patios enclosed by round-shaped lattice walls. The suspended iron staircase acts as a transition between the two floors. The spatial layout on both levels creates further visual depth through several interior-exterior sequences. This house is characterized by topology rather than function. The distinct and qualified spaces allow its residents to enjoy their daily life.

Auf einer kleinen innerstädtischen Parzelle gelegen, verbindet das J House durch seine klar definierte Raumstruktur Offenheit und Privatsphäre. Während das transparente Erdgeschoss in den Garten übergeht, präsentiert sich das Obergeschoss hermetischer, Innen und Außen gehen hier eine subtilere Beziehung ein. Die gewünschte Privatheit wird über mehrere Atrien erreicht, die mit kreisförmig-perforiertem Gitterwerk verkleidet sind. Eine schmiedeeiserne Treppe verbindet die Stockwerke. Durch die Abfolge von Innen- und Außenbereichen gewinnen diese an optischer Tiefe. So ist es weniger die Funktion der Räume, die den Charakter der Villa prägt, sondern vielmehr deren Topologie. Die unterschiedlichen Raumqualitäten können die Bewohner Tag für Tag genießen.

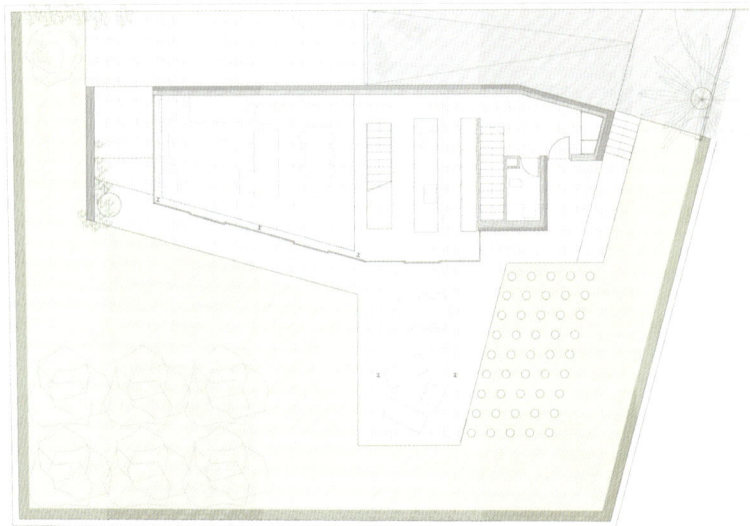

Les architectes devaient construire, sur un terrain minuscule, un bâtiment qui offrirait aux occupants l'intimité nécessaire, tout en leur permettant d'apprécier divers espaces de plein air. Le rez-de-chaussée, ouvert, transparent et ensoleillé, a vocation à se dissoudre dans le jardinet. Le premier étage, lumineux bien que plus secret, introduit un rapport particulièrement subtil entre l'intérieur et l'extérieur. Quant aux patios, ils sont entourés de murs dont les perforations circulaires permettent de voir sans être vu. Un escalier suspendu en acier assure la liaison entre les différents niveaux, auxquels plusieurs séquences intérieur/extérieur confèrent une profondeur spatiale accrue visuellement. D'une manière générale, cette maison se caractérise moins par la fonction que par la typologie.

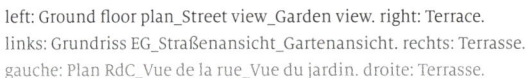

left: Ground floor plan_Street view_Garden view. right: Terrace.
links: Grundriss EG_Straßenansicht_Gartenansicht. rechts: Terrasse.
gauche: Plan RdC_Vue de la rue_Vue du jardin. droite: Terrasse.

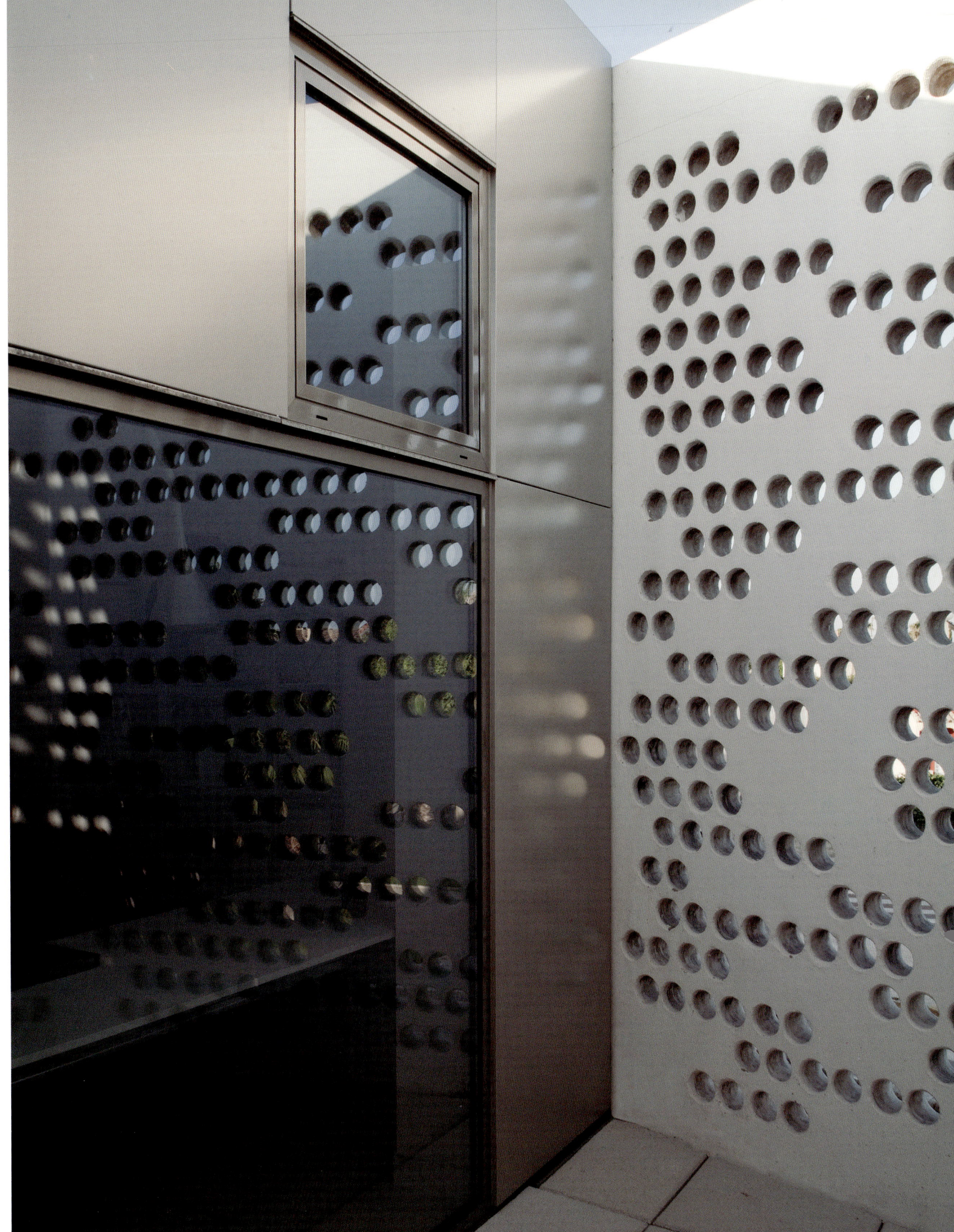

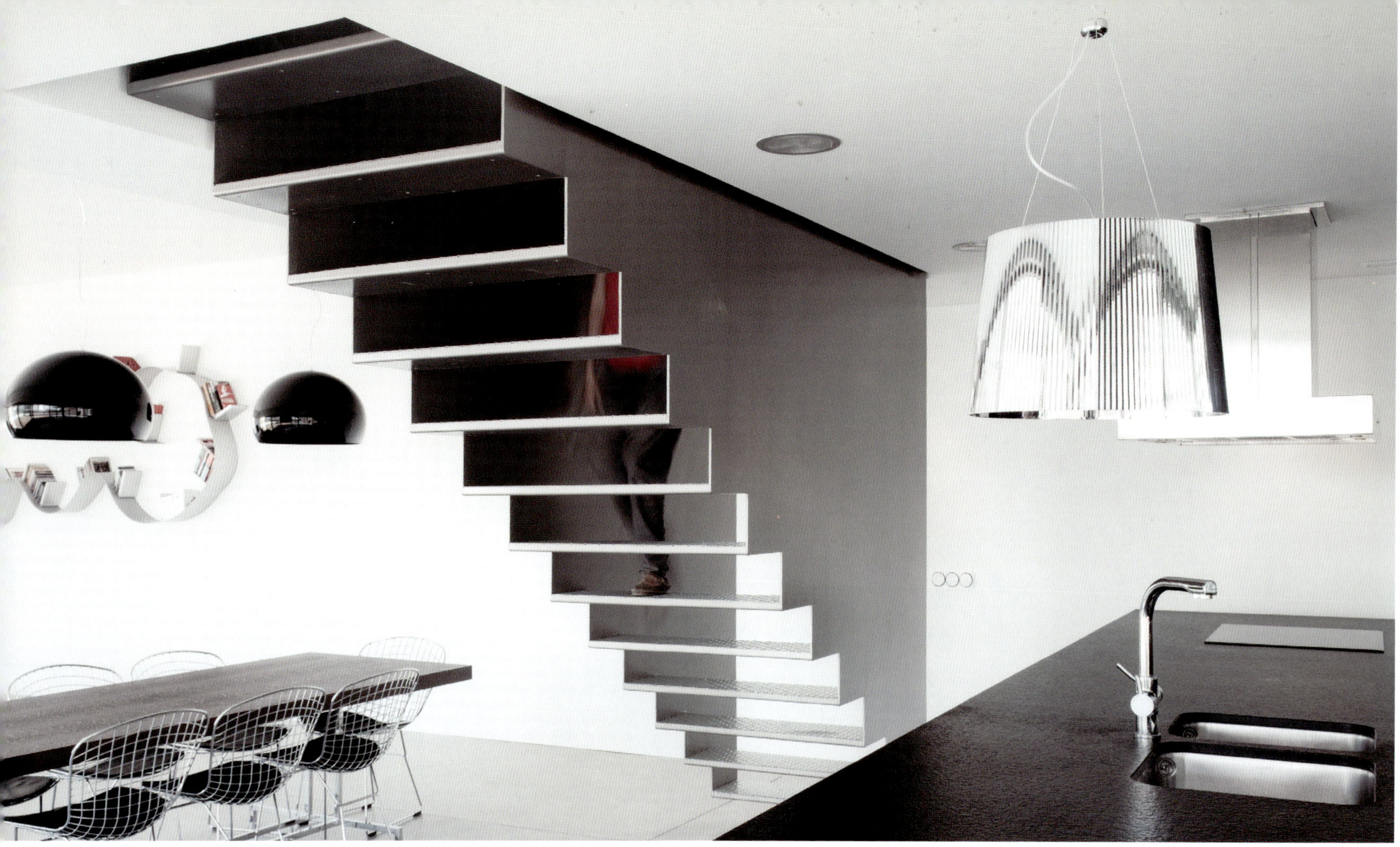

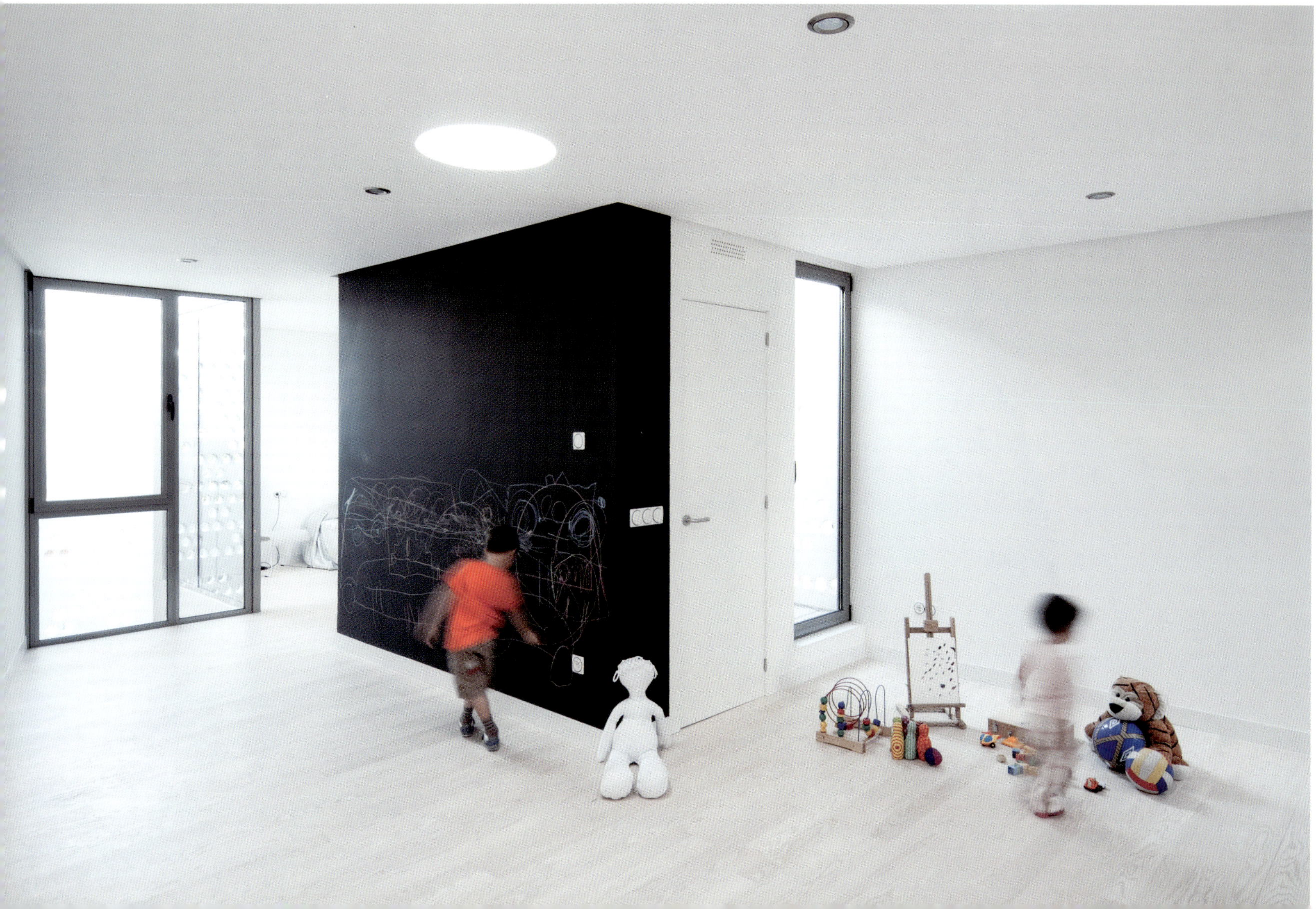

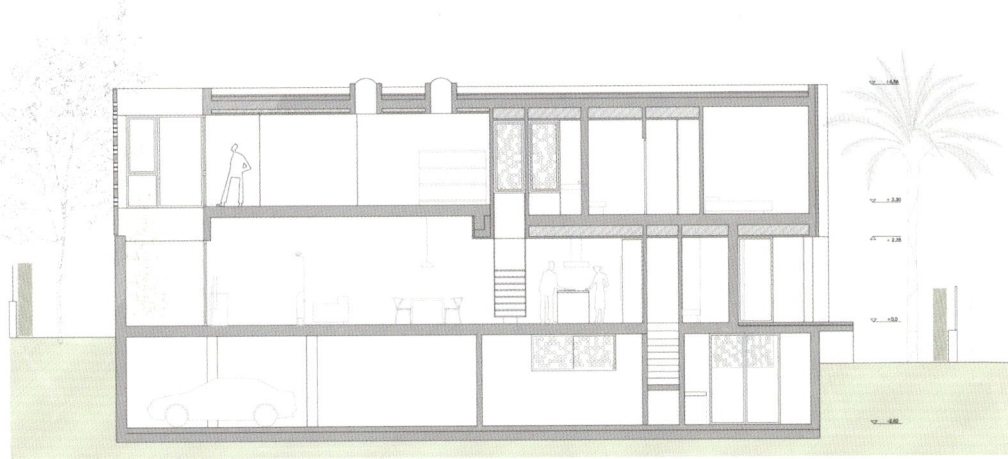

left: Dining area and stairs_Children's bedroom. right: Section_Stairs_Dining area_Exterior view.
links: Essbereich und Treppe_Kinderzimmer. rechts: Schnitt_Treppe_Essbereich_Außenansicht.
gauche: Salle à manger et escalier_Chambre d'enfant. droite: Vue en coupe_Escalier_Salle à manger_Vue de l'extérieur.

BAD HONNEF, GERMANY **HOUSE WOLKENBURG**

ARCHITECTS: DÖRING DAHMEN JOERESSEN ARCHITEKTEN
COMPLETION: 2010_**PROPERTY SIZE:** 758 M²
GROSS FLOOR AREA: 515 M²_**NUMBER OF ROOMS:** 8
PHOTOS: MANOS MEISEN

The home of the family of four in the immediate vicinity of the Rhine and Drachenfels region was demolished except for a 60qm two-floor part in the rear section of the plot to which new elements were added. The cubature of the new building reflects the original proportions, adding an intermediate section. This contains the living room on the ground floor, the entrance hall with a staircase and the children's bathroom with dressing room on the top floor. The displacement of the volumes results in a southern terrace. The large cooking area faces the street, while the dining room faces the terrace, similar to the living room. On the top floor, the rooms are arranged around the air space of the stairway.

Das Haus der vierköpfigen Familie in direkter Nähe von Rhein und Drachenfels wurde bis auf einen 60qm großen, zweigeschossigen Teil im hinteren Bereich des Grundstücks rückgebaut und ergänzt. Die Kubatur des Neubaus spiegelt die Proportion des Bestandes wieder und schiebt einen Zwischenteil ein. Dieser beherbergt das Wohnzimmer im Erdgeschoss, die Eingangshalle mit Treppenhaus und das Kinderbad mit Kinderankleide im Obergeschoss. Durch das Verschieben der Volumina ergibt sich eine Terrasse nach Süden. Zur Straße hin liegt der großzügige Kochbereich. Der offene Essbereich öffnet sich wie das Wohnzimmer zur Terrasse. Im OG arrangieren sich die Räume um den Luftraum der Treppe.

Cette villa conçue pour une famille de quatre personnes se trouve à proximité immédiate du Rhin et des ruines du château de Drachenfels. C'est le résultat de la modernisation et de l'agrandissement d'un bâtiment préexistant situé à l'arrière du terrain. Les proportions de l'extension sont similaires à celles du bâtiment d'origine. Les deux volumes sont reliés entre eux par une structure intermédiaire qui accueille un séjour au rez-de-chaussée ainsi que l'entrée, la salle de bain et le vestiaire des enfants au premier étage. Le décalage entre les deux volumes principaux a permis l'aménagement d'une terrasse qui vient prolonger au sud l'espace séjour/salle à manger. La cuisine est pour sa part située du côté rue. Les pièces du niveau supérieur s'organisent autour de la cage d'escalier.

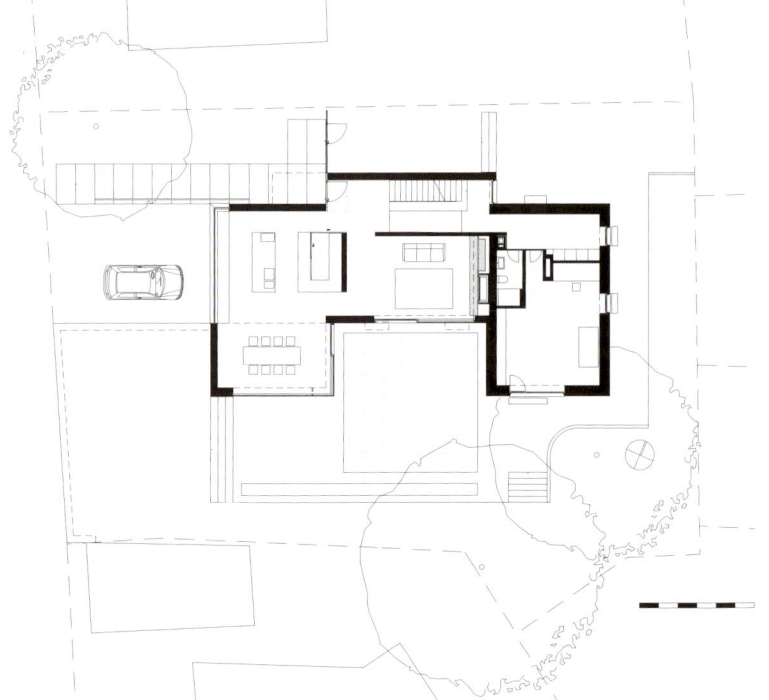

left: Ground floor plan_Living room_Bathroom. right: Street view_View from south-west_Terrace.
links: Grundriss EG_Wohnraum_Bad. rechts: Straßenansicht_Südwestansicht_Terrasse.
gauche: Plan RdC_Salle de séjour_Salle de bain. droite: Vue de la rue_Façade sud-ouest_Terrasse.

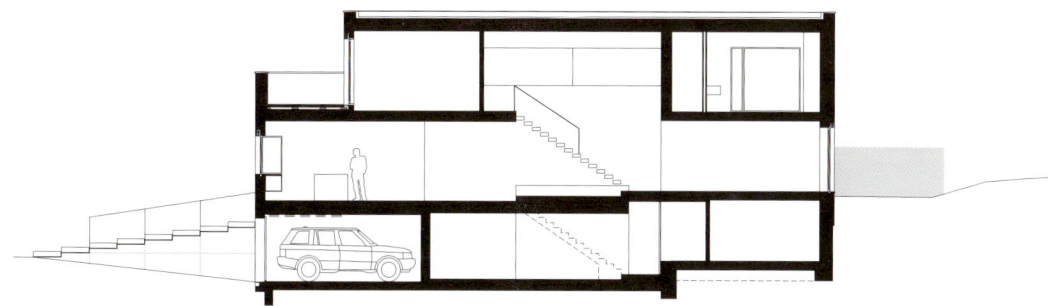

left: Bathroom. right: Section_Stairs_Kitchen_Bathroom.
links: Bad. rechts: Schnitt_Treppe_Küche_Bad.
gauche: Salle de bains. droite: Vue en coupe_Escalier_Cuisine_Salle de bains.

MADRID, SPAIN **VIVIENDA 1001**

ARCHITECTS: A-CERO, JOAQUIN TORRES ARCHITECTS
COMPLETION: 2011_**PROPERTY SIZE:** 1,400 M²
GROSS FLOOR AREA: 9,400 M²
PHOTOS: LUIS H. SEGOVIA

A single family house located in a development in the outskirts of Madrid. Besides its sculptural features, the front side of the facade furthers the integration of the building in the surrounding environment. A wide stone path, with water sheets on both sides, leads to a huge black glass door that gives access to the property. The garden contains palms, pomegranate trees and Middle Eastern vegetation. The entire building is covered in "black villar granite stone". In the back section of the building, big windows with hidden woodwork open up, introducing a great amount of light to the inside. On the porch, the window of the main living room can be automatically hidden to connect indoors and outdoors.

Die freistehende Familienvilla liegt in einem Neubaugebiet am Rande von Madrid. Ihre skulpturale Front trägt zur Einbindung des Gebäudes in die Umgebung bei. Der breite Steinweg, eingerahmt von Wasserbecken, führt zu einer imposanten Tür aus schwarzem Glas, durch die man das Anwesen betritt. Im Garten wachsen Palmen, Granatapfelbäume und nahöstliche Vegetation. Der gesamte Bau ist in Villar gehalten, einem feinkörnigen schwarzen Granit. Der hintere Teil öffnet sich über große Fensterfronten mit nahezu unsichtbaren Holzrahmen, die viel Licht ins Innere strömen lassen. Das Fenster zwischen dem zentralen Wohnbereich und der Veranda lässt sich automatisch ausblenden, sodass ein nahtloser Übergang vom Innen- zum Außenbereich entsteht.

Les formes sculpturales de cette villa des environs de Madrid contribuent à l'intégration du bâtiment dans son environnement. L'accès se fait par une allée empierrée flanquée de plans d'eau qui traverse un parc planté de palmiers, de grenadiers et d'espèces du Moyen-Orient, pour arriver à une porte monumentale pourvue d'une vitre teintée. L'ensemble du bâtiment est revêtu de plaques en granite « Negro Villar ». La face arrière de la villa s'ouvre par de grandes baies vitrées aux boiseries invisibles qui assurent un bon éclairage naturel de l'intérieur. La vitre du séjour principal peut être entièrement escamotée de manière à interconnecter l'intérieur et l'extérieur.

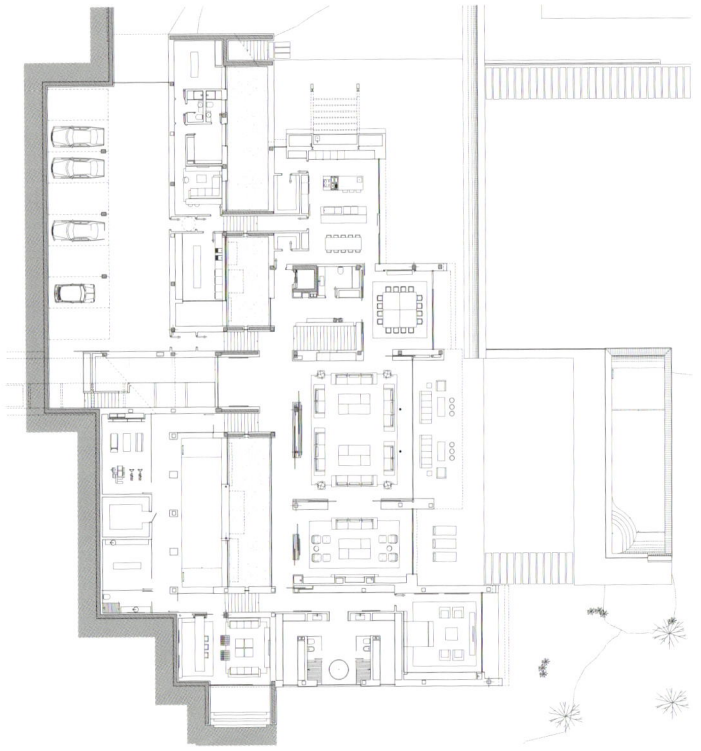

left: Ground floor plan_Main view_Exterior view. right: Terrace.
links: Grundriss EG_Hauptansicht_Außenansicht. rechts: Terrasse.
gauche: Plan RdC_Façade principale_Vue de l'extérieur. droite: Terrasse.

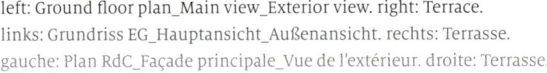

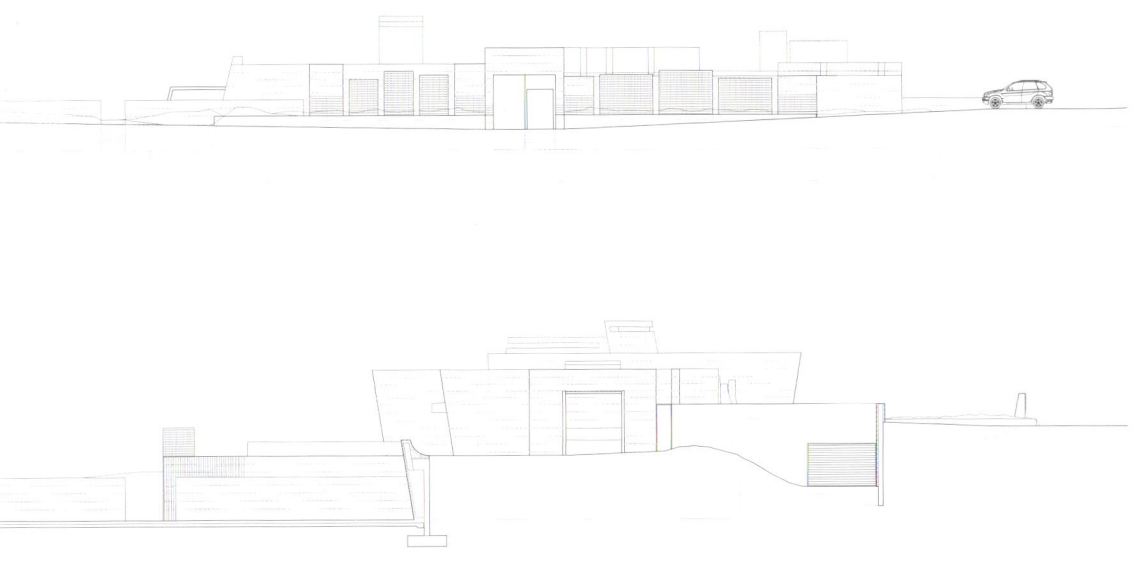

left: Pool. right: Sections_Entrance area_Exterior view_Terrace.
links: Pool. rechts: Schnitte_Eingangsbereich_Außenansicht_Terrasse.
gauche: Piscine extérieure. droite: Vues en coupe_Entrée_Vue de l'extérieur_Terrasse.

BRAUNSCHWEIG, GERMANY **VILLA M**

ARCHITECTS: AHAD ARCHITEKTEN
COMPLETION: 2010_**PROPERTY SIZE:** 600 M²
GROSS FLOOR AREA: 340 M²_**NUMBER OF ROOMS:** 5
PHOTOS: KLEMENS ORTMEYER

Together with its neighboring buildings, Villa M is situated around a central meadow, the green heart of the quarter. Its interior and exterior spaces are interwoven by linking the living area via a large terrace with the garden to the west. The breakfast terrace and the home office face the Schunteraue landscape. The air space above the dining area connects the lower with the upper living space, whose rooms are accessed by a gallery. The clear structure of the rooms is highlighted by the used materials – plaster, screed flooring, exposed concrete, and oak wood. This way, the space, light and proportions become the major architectural players.

Mit den Hauskörpern der Nachbarschaft gruppiert sich die Villa M um einen Anger, der grünen Mitte des Quartiers. In einer Verschränkung von Innen- und Außenraum verbindet sich der Wohnbereich über eine große Terrasse nach Westen mit dem Garten, die Frühstücksterrasse und das Arbeitszimmer orientieren sich zur Landschaft der Schunterauen. Der Luftraum über dem Essbereich verbindet den unteren mit dem oberen Wohnbereich, dessen Räume über eine Galerie erschlossen werden. Die Klarheit des Raumgefüges wird unterstrichen durch die Materialien Putz, Estrich, Sichtbeton und Eichenholz. So werden Raum, Licht und Proportion die Hauptdarsteller der Architektur.

La Villa M et les bâtiments voisins sont regroupés autour d'une zone verte. Du côté de l'ouest, le séjour est interconnecté au jardin par l'intermédiaire d'une grande terrasse. Le bureau se prolonge quant à lui par la « terrasse du petit déjeuner » faisant face aux prairies bordant la rivière Schunter. La salle à manger, une nef s'élevant sur deux étages, est bordée au niveau supérieur par une galerie desservant les chambres. Les matériaux (enduit, béton et chêne) ont été choisis de manière à mettre en valeur la clarté d'un concept dans lequel l'espace, la lumière et les proportions s'affirment comme les principaux acteurs de l'architecture.

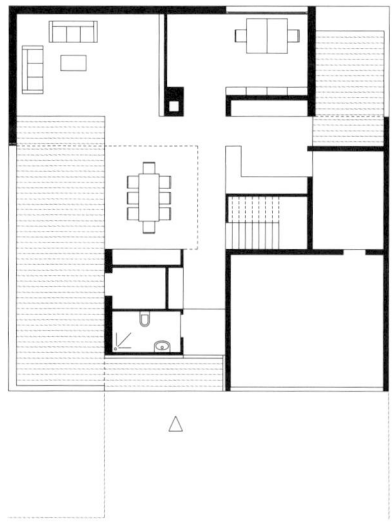

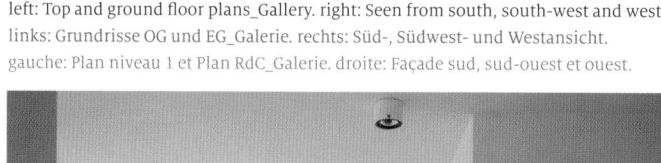

left: Top and ground floor plans_Gallery. right: Seen from south, south-west and west.
links: Grundrisse OG und EG_Galerie. rechts: Süd-, Südwest- und Westansicht.
gauche: Plan niveau 1 et Plan RdC_Galerie. droite: Façade sud, sud-ouest et ouest.

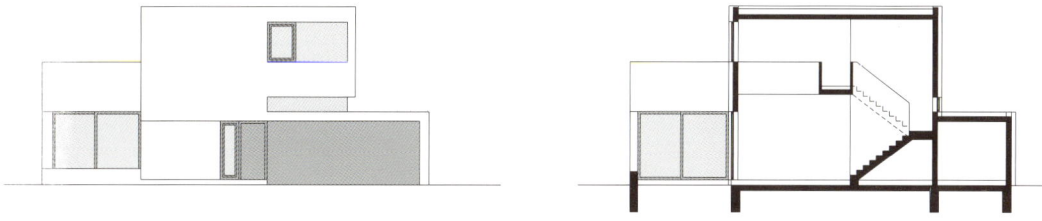

left: Dining area. right: Elevation_Section_Bathroom.
links: Essbereich. rechts: Ansicht_Schnitt_Badezimmer.
gauche: Salle à manger. droite: Élévation_Vue en coupe_Salle de bains.

MORZINE, FRANCE **VILLA SOLAIRE**

ARCHITECTS: JKA – JÉRÉMIE KOEMPGEN ARCHITECTURE,
FUGA – J. AICH & M. RECORDON DESIGNERS
COMPLETION: 2012_**PROPERTY SIZE:** 900 M²
GROSS FLOOR AREA: 620 M²_**PHOTOS:** JULIEN LANOO

A uniform cladding wraps the whole farm. The challenge of the project was to preserve its appearance, while introducing light into the heart of the building. The traditional technique of decorative wood cutouts was used to create specific perforations within the planks. The pattern was designed to respond to the path described by the shadows and light on the façade, which gave the project the name "solar house". The house is exposed on its four façades to the path of the sun, acting as a sundial. Conserving the overall appearance of the existing interior structure was another key aim that motivated the restoration efforts. To clear the room of the nave while meeting the needs of the rental house, the utility functions were integrated into the four angular volumes.

Eine einheitliche Holzverkleidung umhüllt das gesamte Gehöft. Das äußere Erscheinungsbild zu bewahren, war eine der Herausforderungen des Projekts. Gleichzeitig sollte Tageslicht ins Innere geleitet werden. Hierfür griff man eine traditionelle Technik auf: Dekorative Aussparungen in den Holzbrettern perforieren die Fassade und erlauben ein Spiel von Licht und Schatten. Alle vier Seiten der „Villa Solaire" sind, wie eine Sonnenuhr, dem Lauf der Sonne ausgesetzt. Eine weitere Zielsetzung war, das Gesamtbild im Innern zu bewahren. Dementsprechend erfolgte die Restaurierung. Um den zentralen Raum frei zu halten und gleichzeitig den Anforderungen eines Mietshauses gerecht zu werden, ist die Haustechnik in den äußeren Winkeln untergebracht.

Un bardage uniforme enveloppait autrefois cette ancienne ferme. L'un des enjeux du projet consistait à conserver l'aspect extérieur du bâtiment, tout en laissant filtrer la lumière à l'intérieur. Une technique traditionnelle – la découpe décorative des lattes de bois – a été mise en œuvre sur la façade sous forme d'ajourage. Le dessin des ajours répond aux jeux d'ombre et de lumière, ce qui explique le nom de « villa solaire » donné à la réalisation : une maison exposée sur quatre façades, qui fonctionne comme un cadran solaire. L'architecte s'est également efforcé de conserver la structure intérieure. Il a pour cela localisé les chambres et leurs servitudes dans des blocs situés aux quatre coins de la bâtisse, libérant ainsi une vaste nef centrale abritant les espaces communs.

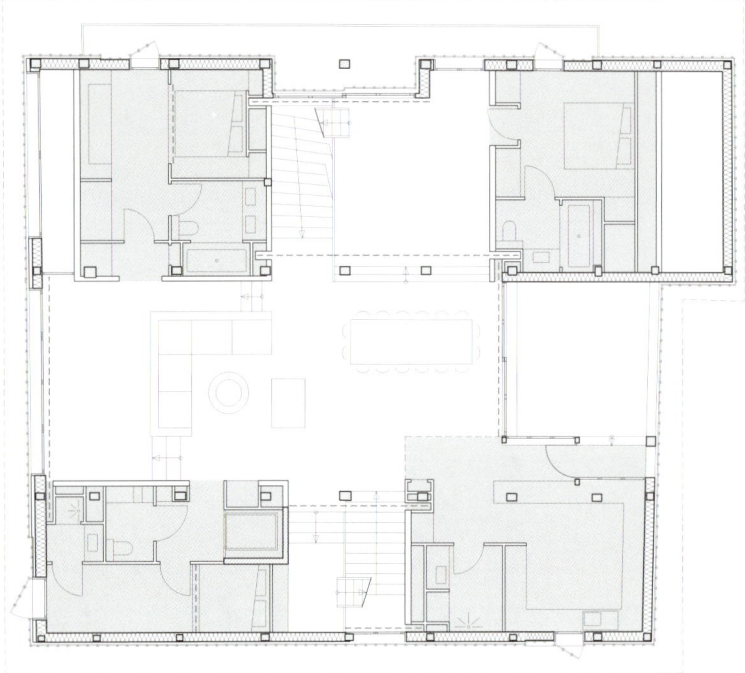

left: Top floor plan_Seen from south-east_Façade detail. right: Outdoor area_Stairs_Living area.
links: Grundriss OG_Südostansicht_Fassadendetail. rechts: Außenbereich_Treppe_Wohnbereich.
gauche: Plan niveau 1_Façade sud-est_Détail de la façade. droite: Extérieur_Escalier_Séjour.

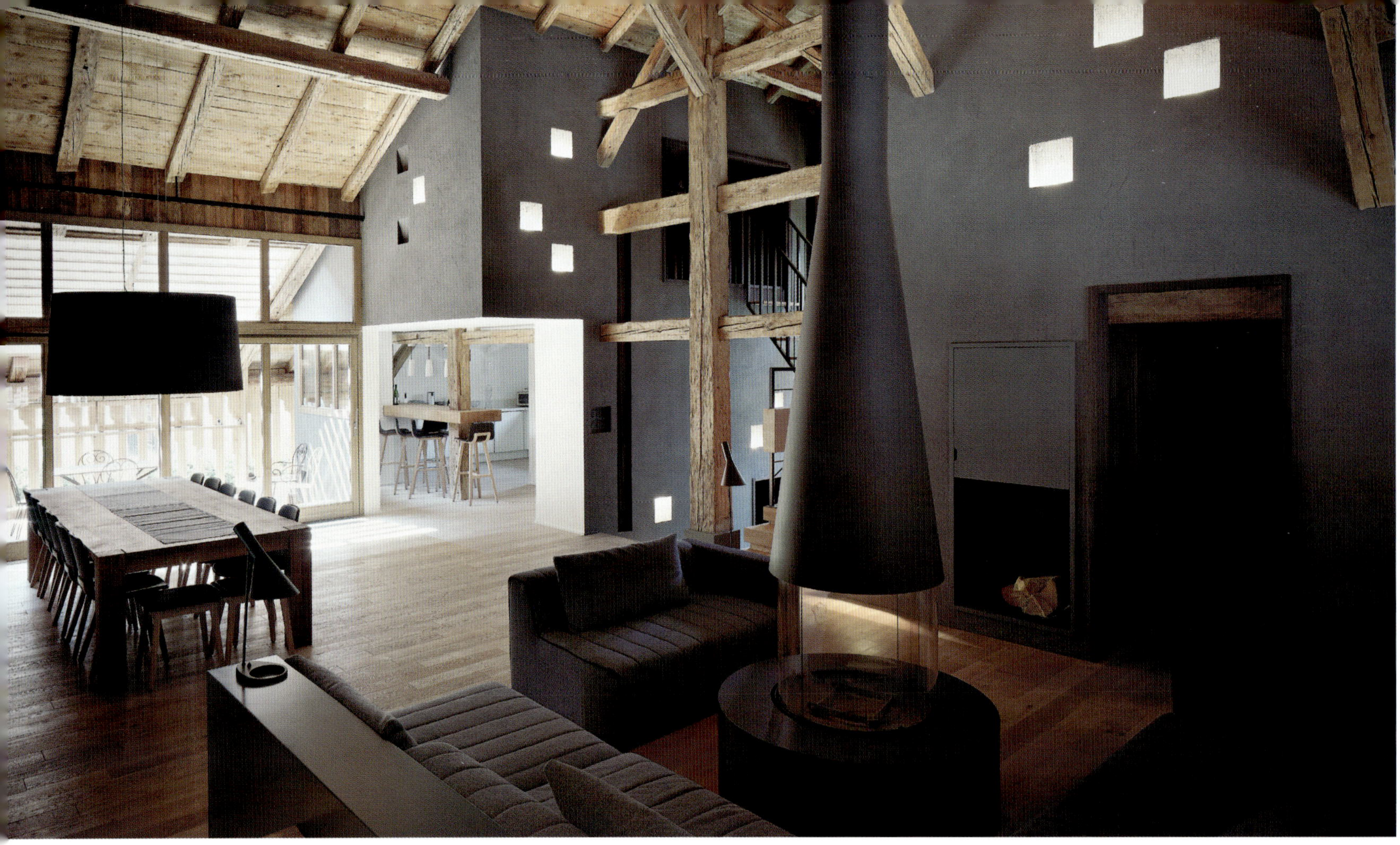
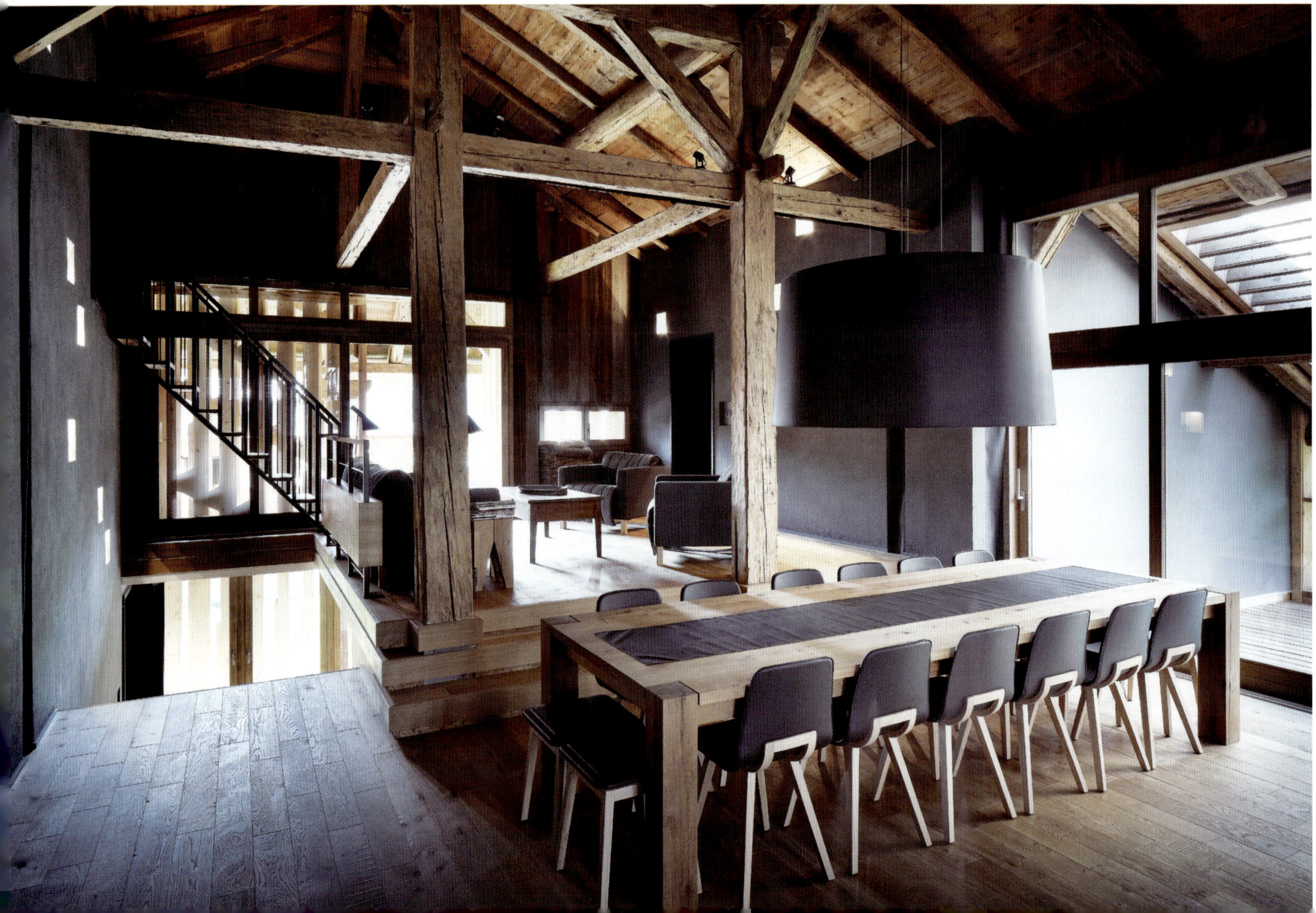

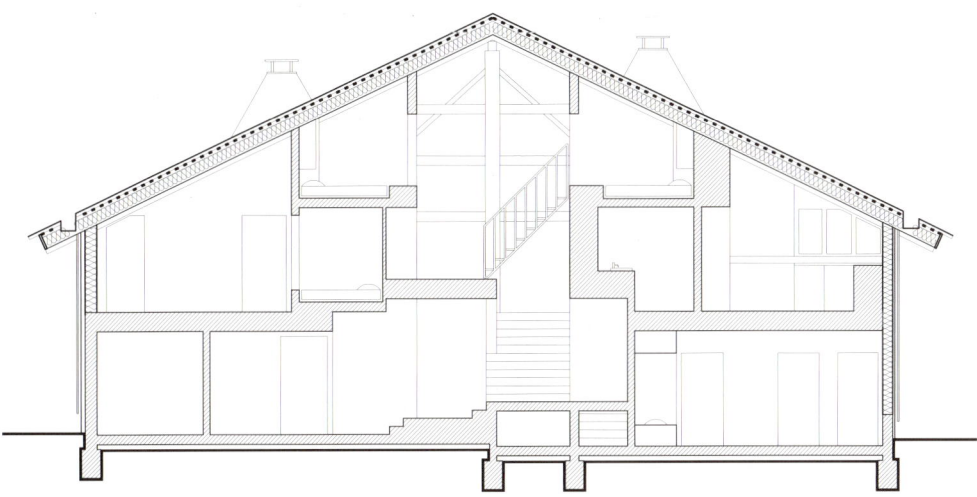

left: Living area_Dining area. right: Section_Bathroom_Indoor pool_Bedroom.
links: Wohnbereich_Essbereich. rechts: Schnitt_Bad_Hallenbad_Schlafzimmer.
gauche: Séjour_Salle à manger. droite: Vue en coupe_Salle de bains_Piscine intérieure_Chambre.

RÜTIHOF, SWITZERLAND **TWO-FAMILY RESIDENCE**

ARCHITECTS: HÄFELE SCHMID ARCHITEKTEN
COMPLETION: 2008_**PROPERTY SIZE:** 998 M²
GROSS FLOOR AREA: 2 X 347 M²_**NUMBER OF ROOMS:** 2 X 7.5
PHOTOS: TOM BISIG

The polygonal layout of this duplex villa is based on the location and the floor plan geometry. Janus-faced, the building has two main alignments, which both comprehensively incorporate all key aspects such as the sunset and the view. The entrance is from the ground floor, which is only partially inserted in the topography. A single flight concrete stairway, which is cut out of the façade, leads to the top floor. A steel stairway inserted in the wall connects the lounge and roof terrace. The cascading ceiling design creates a progressive room height. The static support is provided by two wall discs and a bearing core, which allow a mostly open layout of the building.

Der polygonale Grundriss dieser Doppelvilla entwickelt sich aus den örtlichen Gegebenheiten sowie der Grundrissgeometrie. Janusköpfig, verfügt der Baukörper über zwei Hauptwohnrichtungen, wobei die situativen Qualitäten wie Sonnengang und Aussicht vollumfänglich einbezogen sind. Der Zugang führt über das nur teilweise in die Topographie eingelassene Erdgeschoss. Eine einläufige Betontreppe, welche in der Fassade tief ausgeschnitten ist, führt in das Obergeschoss. Über eine in die Wand eingelassene Stahltreppe gelangt man in die Lounge und auf die Dachterrasse. Durch eine kaskadenartige Deckenkonstruktion wird eine progressive Raumhöhenentwicklung erzielt. Die Statik erfolgt über zwei Wandscheiben und einen tragenden Kern, was eine weitgehend offene Gestaltung des Baukörpers ermöglicht.

Le plan en forme de polygone irrégulier de cette double villa résulte de la configuration du terrain. Entité « bicéphale », le bâtiment tire entièrement profit des avantages liés à son implantation, que ce soit en matière d'éclairage naturel ou de vues sur les alentours. L'accès se fait par le rez-de-chaussée à demi-souterrain. Un escalier en béton à simple volée, éclairé par une large échancrure dans la façade, mène au niveau supérieur, où un escalier en acier conduit au foyer et au toit en terrasse. La hauteur des pièces varie progressivement grâce à une conception des plafonds « en cascade ». Deux murs porteurs et un noyau de soutènement assurent la rigidité statique de l'ensemble et permettent de largement ouvrir l'enveloppe du bâtiment sur l'extérieur.

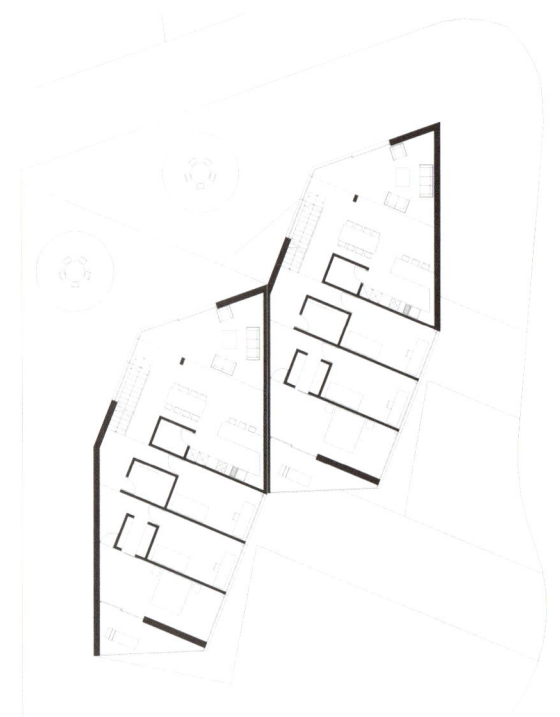

left: Top floor plan_Seen from north. right: General view_Seen from south.
links: Grundriss OG_Ansicht Nord. rechts: Gesamtansicht_Ansicht Süd.
gauche: Plan niveau 1_Façade nord. droite: Vue générale_Façade sud.

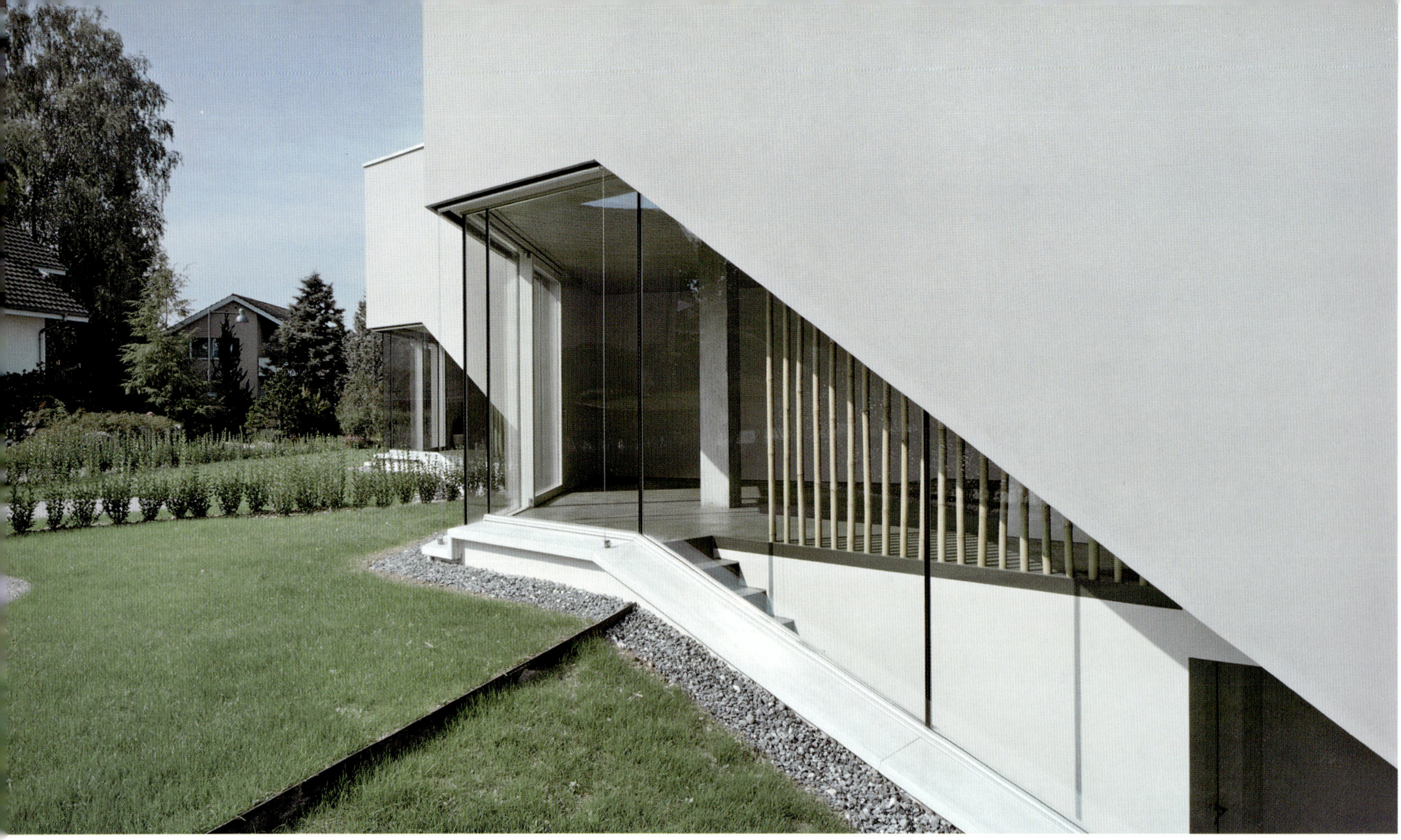

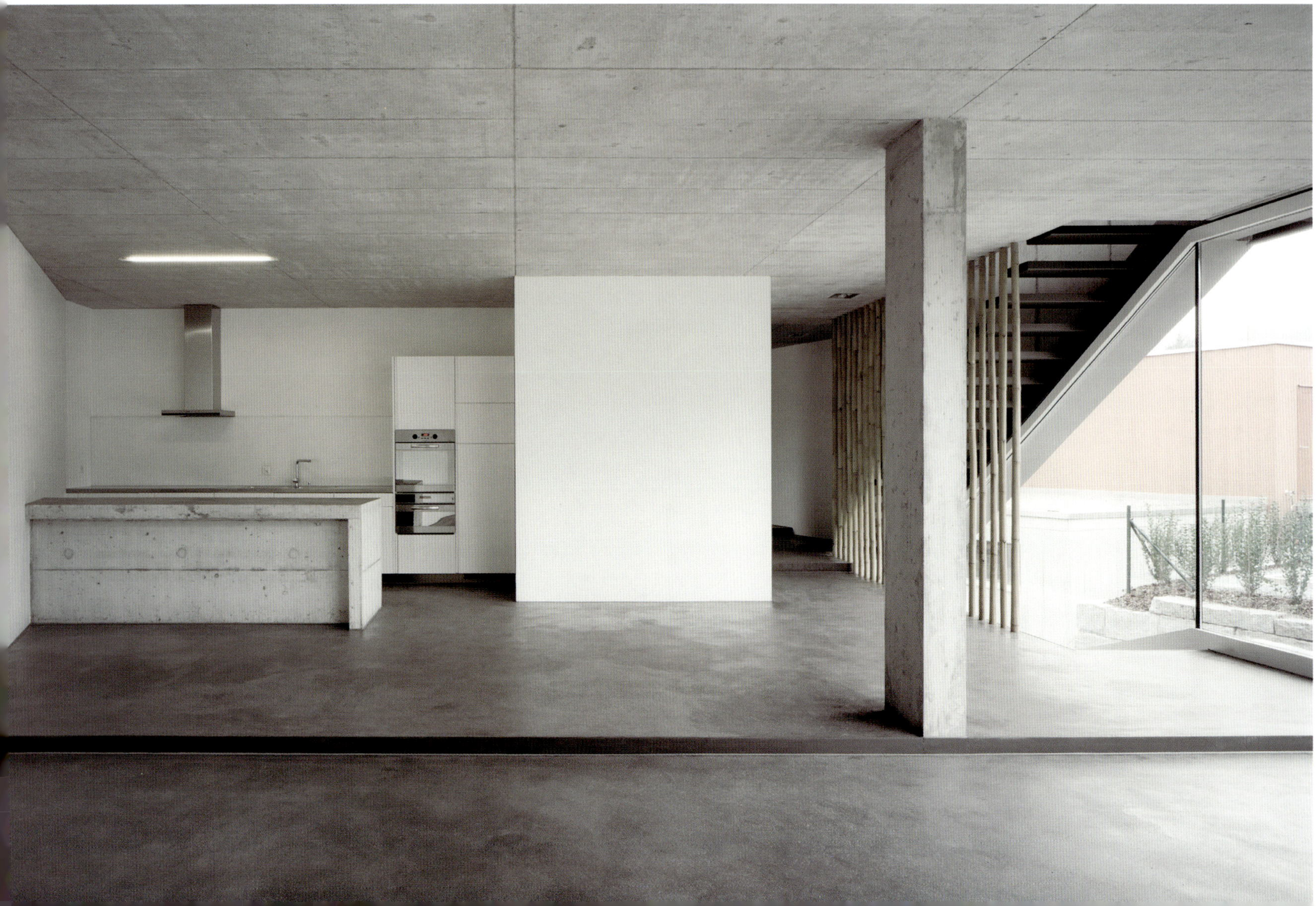

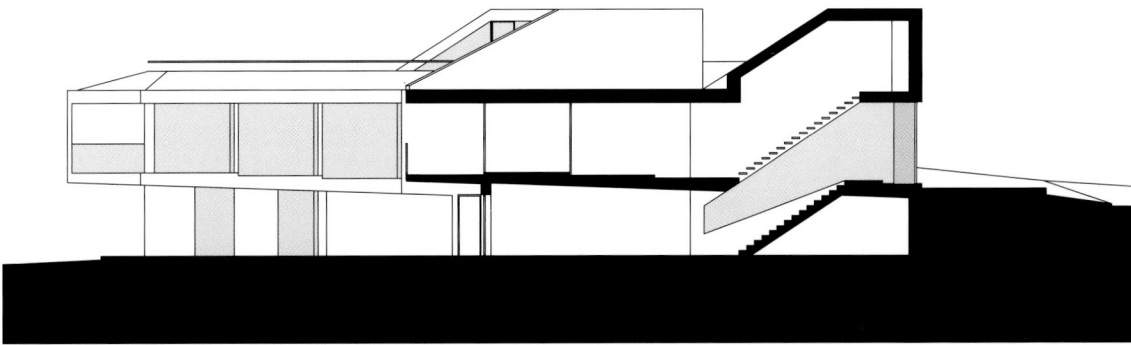

left: Seen from south_Living and dining area with kitchen. right: Section_Roof lounge and terrace.
links: Südfassade_Wohn- und Essbereich mit Küche. rechts: Schnitt_Dachlounge mit Terrasse.
gauche: Façade sud_Séjour et salle à manger avec cuisine. droite: Vue en coupe_Lounge et terrasse.

ARBEL, ISRAEL **BEAM HOUSE**

ARCHITECTS: URI COHEN ARCHITECTS
COMPLETION: 2010_**PROPERTY SIZE:** 5,059 M²
GROSS FLOOR AREA: 180 M²_**NUMBER OF ROOMS:** 5
PHOTOS: DAVIA ADIKA

The site is located in the rural landscape of Israel. The design explores the beam construction typical of country homes. The inspiration is translated to the defining lines and materials of the house as well as to the façades. The house is divided into three sections. The living room faces north with views of the backyard. Concrete walls enclose the southern section to enhance its privacy. The roof beams rest on the central wall and serve as cantilevers to the roof of the living area. The circular external lines affect the interior design, creating a resting bench in the living room and unique spaces. The area between the private and public sections of the house provides a shaded 'outside public space,' which is also the entrance axis to the house.

Im ländlichen Raum Israels gelegen, greift das Beam House die typische Balkenkonstruktion dortiger Landhäuser auf. Diese Inspiration spiegelt sich in der maßgeblichen Linienführung, den Materialien und Fassaden wider. Die Villa ist in drei Bereiche unterteilt. Gen Norden liegt der Wohnbereich mit Blick auf den Garten. Den südlichen Bereich schließen Betonmauern ein, um die Privatsphäre zu erhöhen. Die Dachbalken ruhen auf der tragenden Wand und kragen über dem Wohnbereich aus. Die geschwungenen äußeren Linien gehen ins Interior über und schaffen im Wohnbereich eine Ruhebank sowie einzigartigen Stauraum. Zwischen den Privat- und Gemeinschaftsräumen liegt ein schattiger Außenbereich, der als Eingangsachse dient.

Construite en Israël dans une zone rurale, cette villa réinterprète un modèle architectural traditionnel de la région faisant un large usage des poutres, tant pour la toiture que pour les façades. L'intérieur se divise en trois espaces distincts, le principal étant le séjour vitré disposé derrière la façade nord avec vue sur la cour. La façade sud en béton garantit quant à elle l'intimité des chambres. Les poutres du toit reposent sur un mur central et se prolongent en porte-à-faux au-dessus du séjour. Les bandeaux semi-circulaires des façades affectent la conception des intérieurs, puisqu'ils accueillent notamment un « divan intégré » dans le séjour. L'espace entre les chambres et le séjour constitue une « zone publique extérieure » qui abrite en particulier l'entrée.

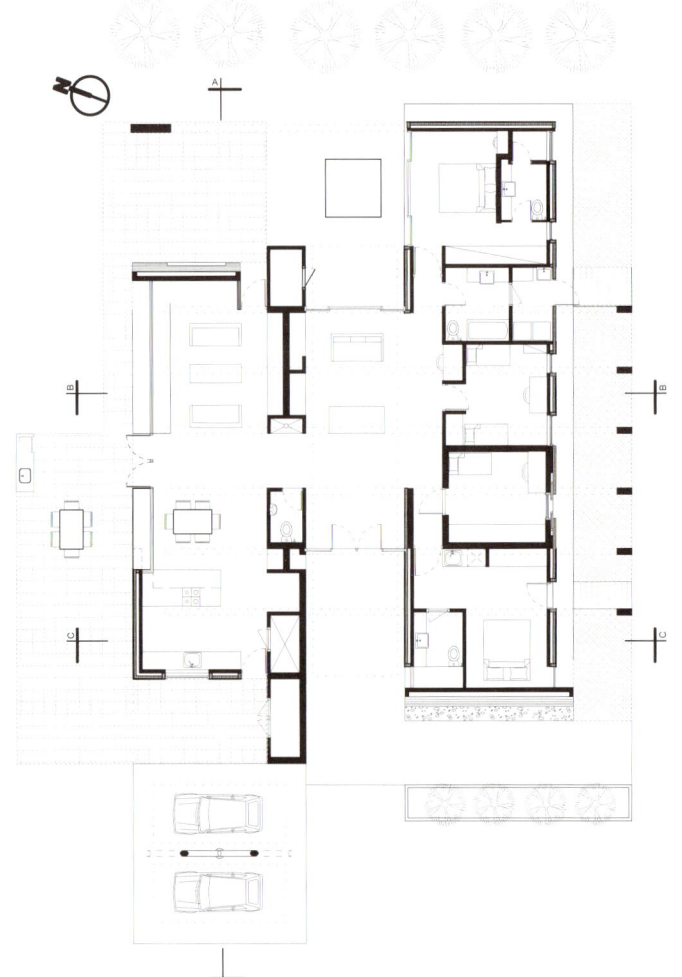

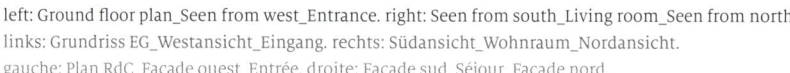

left: Ground floor plan_Seen from west_Entrance. right: Seen from south_Living room_Seen from north.
links: Grundriss EG_Westansicht_Eingang. rechts: Südansicht_Wohnraum_Nordansicht.
gauche: Plan RdC_Façade ouest_Entrée. droite: Façade sud_Séjour_Façade nord.

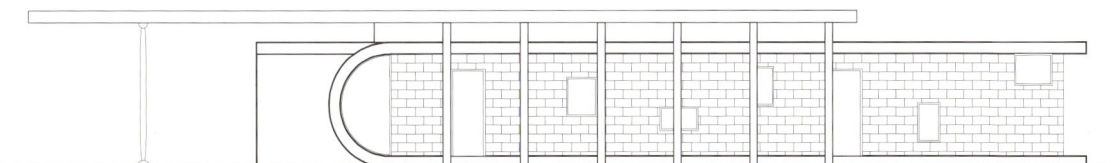

left: Entrance area. right: Elevation_Entrance_Bedroom_Living room.
links: Eingangsbereich. rechts: Ansicht_Eingang_Schlafzimmer_Wohnraum.
gauche: Entrée. droite: Élévation_Entrée_Chambre_Séjour.

MAUR, SWITZERLAND **HOUSE AESCH**

ARCHITECTS: M3 ARCHITEKTEN
COMPLETION: 2011_**PROPERTY SIZE:** 1,128 M²
GROSS FLOOR AREA: 280 M²_**NUMBER OF ROOMS:** 7.5
PHOTOS: BRUNO HELBLING

Located on an elevated plane, the plot offers excellent location qualities – a view of the landscape, lake and the alps. The tract of land has a sharp drop at its center and the building is situated precisely on this edge. The ground floor and basement are square-shaped. The attic floor is aligned by vast projections. Its counterpart is a pergola terrace on the ground floor that freely extends over the steep decline. The projections generate a fascinating structural layout that interacts with the topography. Every floor has its own floor plan. The finishing is done with raw materials, for example exposed concrete for walls and ceilings. The house has a compact façade and some of the windows are fitted on the outside with a bench on the inside.

Auf einem Hochplateau gelegen, verfügt das Grundstück über hervorragende Lagequalitäten – Landschaft-, See- und Alpensicht. Die Parzelle bricht in der Mitte steil ab. Exakt an dieser Bruchkante liegt das Gebäude. Erd- und Untergeschoss sind quadratisch. Das Attikageschoss ist durch die weite Auskragung gerichtet. Als Gegenpol ragt im Erdgeschoss eine Pergola-Terrasse frei über den steilen Hang hinaus. Die Auskragungen generieren einen spannenden Baukörper, der mit der Topografie im Dialog steht. Alle Geschosse sind unterschiedlich organisiert. Der Ausbau ist roh gehalten – so sind die Wände und Decken in Sichtbeton. Das Haus ist mit einer Kompaktfassade versehen. Die Fenster sind teilweise außenbündig angeschlagen mit innen liegender Sitzbank.

Cette villa est merveilleusement située sur un plateau avec vue sur les Alpes et un lac. Le bâtiment se trouve à l'endroit précis où le terrain, tout d'abord relativement plat, part soudain en pente. L'attique, caractérisé par un grand porte-à-faux, a pour pendant au rez-de-chaussée une terrasse en surplomb couverte d'une pergola. Ces deux protubérances établissent un dialogue avec la topographie du terrain, conférant ainsi un certain dynamisme à la villa. L'architecte a privilégié ici les matériaux simples, réalisant par exemple les murs et plafonds en béton brut de coffrage. La façade, qui présente pour sa part un aspect compact, s'ouvre par des fenêtres dont certaines ne sont pas en retrait et se complètent à l'intérieur par un appui pouvant servir de banc.

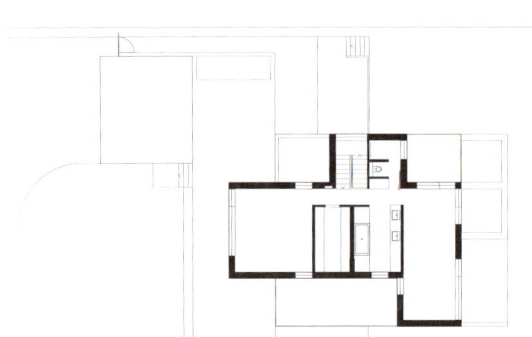

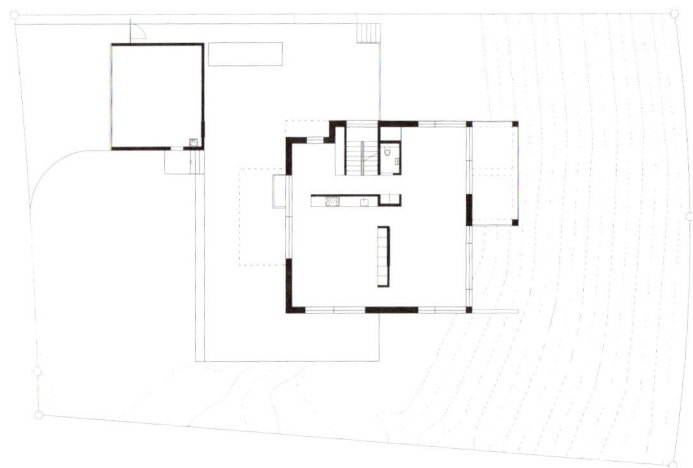

left: Attic floor and ground floor plans_Main view_ Loggia. right: Sleeping area_Living area_Bathroom.
links: Grundrisse Attika und EG_Hauptansicht_Loggia. rechts: Schlafbereich_Wohnbereich_Bad.
gauche: Plan des combles et du RdC_Façade principale_Loggia. droite: Chambre_Séjour_Salle de bains.

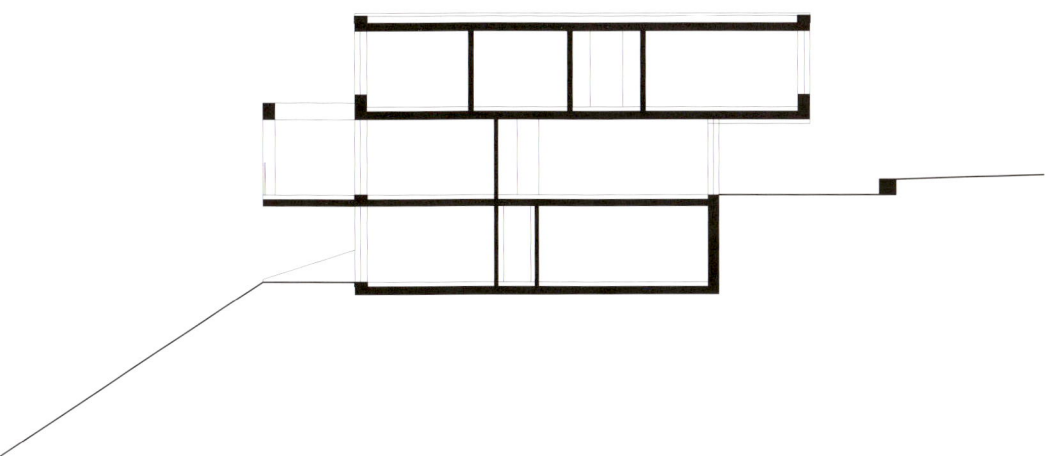

left: Stairs. right: Cross section_Kitchen and dining room_Room sequence_Living area.
links: Treppe. rechts: Längsschnitt_Küche und Essbereich_Raumsequenz_Wohnbereich.
gauche: Escalier. droite: Coupe longitudinale_Cuisine et salle à manger_Enfilade_Séjour.

MORCIANO DI LEUCA, LECCE, ITALY **HOUSE IN AN OLIVE GROVE**

ARCHITECTS: LUCA ZANAROLI ARCHITECT
COMPLETION: 2011_**PROPERTY SIZE:** 5,000 M²
GROSS FLOOR AREA: 130 M²_**NUMBER OF ROOMS:** 3
PHOTOS: LUCA ZANAROLI

The new building is surrounded by beautiful olive trees. To reduce its environmental impact, the designer focused on volumes and materials. The volume was first divided into several blocks corresponding to the functional spaces of the house (both interior and exterior) then re-assembled to obtain the optimal use based on the overall ratio between the masses. At the same time, the individual parts of the building were defined by traditional and local (literally found at the site) materials, such as the stones obtained from the excavations to build the swimming pool that were used to coat the exterior walls of the building. White lime plaster defines the simple volumes and minimal interior and exterior living spaces.

Der Neubau liegt inmitten eines schönen Olivenhains. Um den baulichen Eingriff in die Umgebung abzuschwächen, konzentrierte sich der Architekt auf Proportionen und Materialien. Er unterteilte den Bau zunächst entsprechend der Funktionen in Blöcke (innen wie außen), die er dann neu anordnete. So konnte auf Basis des proportionalen Gleichgewichts eine optimale Nutzung erreicht werden. Gleichzeitig definieren sich die individuellen Bereiche des Gebäudes über traditionelle Materialien. So sind die Außenwände des Pools beispielsweise mit Naturstein verkleidet, der beim Ausheben geborgen wurde. Dagegen kennzeichnet weißer Kalkputz die klaren Volumen und minimalistischen Wohnbereiche.

L'architecte a soigneusement conçu les volumes et sélectionné les matériaux afin de limiter l'impact environnemental de cette villa construite dans une magnifique oliveraie. Il a tout d'abord envisagé différentes unités intérieures et extérieures correspondant aux diverses fonctions du bâtiment, qu'il a ensuite rassemblées afin d'optimiser la relation entre les masses. Parallèlement, l'architecte a privilégié les matériaux locaux, et cela au sens strict, puisque les pierres de parement de la façade ont été extraites du sol lors du creusement de la piscine. Ces murs en pierres naturelles se complètent de surfaces lisses et blanches qui définissent les volumes simples de la villa et confèrent un certain minimalisme aux intérieurs.

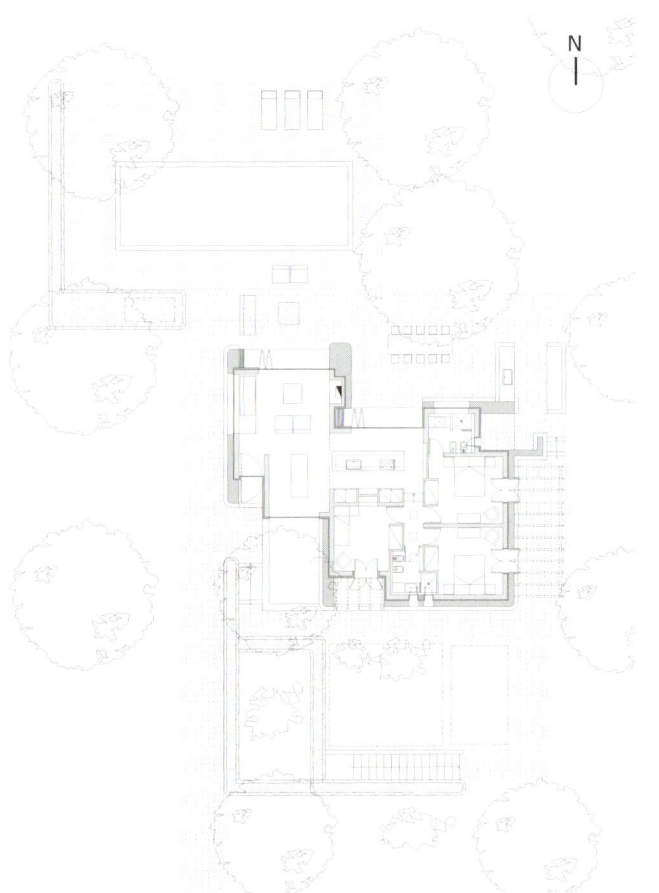

left: Ground floor plan_Entrance_Pool. right: Detail of the façade.
links: Grundriss EG_Eingang_Pool. rechts: Fassadendetail.
gauche: Plan RdC_Entrée_Piscine extérieure. droite: Détail de la façade.

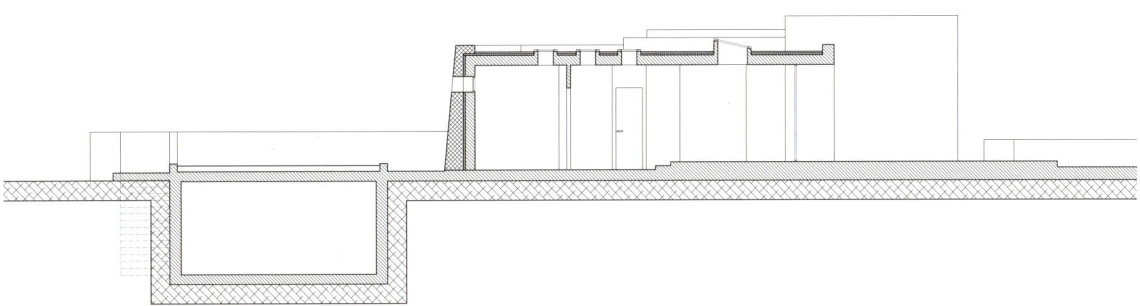

left: Terrace. right: Section_Kitchen_Living room_Dining room.
links: Terrasse. rechts: Schnitt_Küche_Wohnzimmer_Esszimmer.
gauche: Terrasse. droite: Vue en coupe_Cuisine_Séjour_Salle à manger.

ALBERSCHWENDE, AUSTRIA **HOUSE HF**

ARCHITECTS: ARCH. DI HELENA WEBER
COMPLETION: 2010_**PROPERTY SIZE:** 898 M²
PHOTOS: PABLO F. DIAZ-FIERROS

The hillside location of this villa presents magnificent views of the Bregenz Forest region. Inserted into the slope and freely projecting at the same time, the room sequence of the house is related to its topography. In line with the inclination of the slope, the ground floor entrance leads into the living zone. An open spatial sequence of interior and exterior spaces integrates the expansive landscape into the building, while the three different terraces allow experiencing it directly. Only two materials were used throughout – untreated local silver fir timber and exposed concrete. The contrast between them gives the building its special character.

Die Hanglage dieser Villa eröffnet herrliche Ausblicke in den Bregenzerwald. Eingeschoben in den Hang und frei auskragend zugleich, bezieht sich die Raumfolge des Hauses auf die Topographie. Entlang der Hangneigung gelangt man vom ebenerdigen Eingang in die Wohnzone. Hier entsteht eine offene Raumfolge von Innen- und Außenbereichen, die das Bild der weiten Landschaft in das Gebäude integriert und durch die drei Terrassen unterschiedlicher Qualität direkt erlebbar macht. Die Materialauswahl begrenzt sich auf zwei Materialien: unbehandelte heimische Weißtanne und Sichtbeton. Der Kontrast zwischen beiden gibt dem Raum seinen speziellen Charakter.

Cette villa construite à flanc de colline offre des vues magnifiques sur le massif de Bregenzerwald. Partiellement enterrée et présentant plusieurs porte-à-faux, elle organise ses différentes pièces en fonction de la topographie. En descendant la pente, l'accès se fait par une entrée qui donne sur un espace de séjour largement ouvert sur le paysage se prolongeant par trois terrasses de caractère différent. L'architecte a privilégié ici deux matériaux : le béton brut de coffrage et le sapin blanc non traité d'origine locale. Leur aspect contrasté confère à l'ensemble un charme particulier.

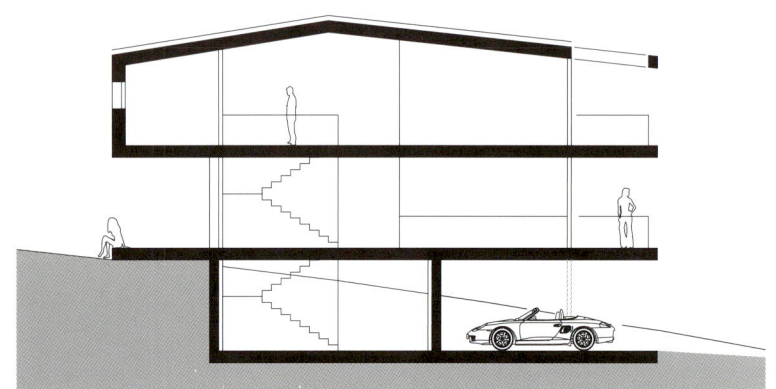

left: Section_Seen from south_Panoramic view. right: Dining area_Terrace_Retreat area.
links: Schnitt_Südansicht_Ausblick Bregenzerwald. rechts: Essplatz_Terrasse_Rückzugsbereich.
gauche: Vue en coupe_Façade sud_Vue panoramique. droite: Salle à manger_Terrasse_Zone de repos.

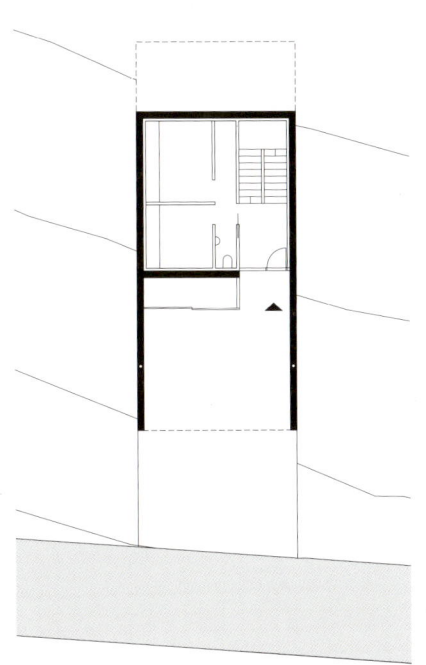

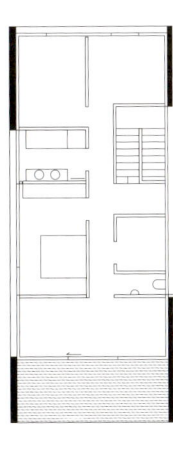

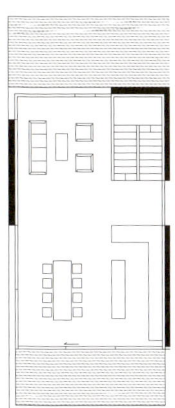

left: Stairs. right: Floor plans_Staircase_Stair vestibule.
links: Treppe. rechts: Grundrisse_Treppenaufgang_Vorbereich Treppe.
gauche: Escalier. droite: Plan _Cage d'escalier_Accès escalier.

BARCELONA, SPAIN **CASA X**

ARCHITECTS: EDUARDO CADAVAL & CLARA SOLÀ-MORALES
COMPLETION: 2012_**PROPERTY SIZE:** 500 M²
GROSS FLOOR AREA: 350 M²_**NUMBER OF ROOMS:** 4
PHOTOS: SANDRA PEREZNIETO (64–66), SANTIAGO GARCÉS (67)

The X House project aims to solve a number of issues that arise from the specific site – how to protect and include an impressive pine located on the top of the site, which makes access to the house extremely complex from the street; how to avoid deciding between views of the sea and of the mountains that are located in opposite directions; how to neutralize the presence of the contiguous constructions through the building`s shape by building a fake isolation from the neighbors; how to double the main views, permitting quality views from the front and the rear of the house. The result focused on all these priorities with a simple concept that complies with all of the previous aims without prioritizing nor explicitly formulating a response to any of them.

Das X House stellte die Architekten vor eine Vielzahl von Herausforderungen, die sich aus der besonderen Grundstückslage ergaben: wie ließe sich die imposante Kiefer auf der Spitze der Klippe schützen und neben der Zufahrt in den Entwurf integrieren; wie könnte man Ausblicke sowohl aufs Meer als auch auf die gegenüberliegenden Berge schaffen; inwieweit könnten Form und künstliche Isolation des Neubaus die Wirkung der benachbarten Bauten neutralisieren; und wie wäre es möglich, die Qualität der Ausblicke zu verdoppeln, sowohl an Vorder- als auch Rückseite? Die Lösung ist ein schnörkelloser Entwurf, der all diese Anforderungen gleichermaßen erfüllt, ohne Verzicht oder Schwerpunktsetzung.

Les architectes chargés de construire cette villa étaient confrontés à divers problèmes liés au site : comment conserver et intégrer au projet un magnifique pin parasol, bien qu'il complique l'accès au bâtiment à partir de la route ? Comment ménager à la fois des vues sur la mer et sur la montagne, deux entités situées dans des directions opposées ? Quelle forme donner au bâtiment pour neutraliser au mieux la présence des constructions voisines ? Comment optimiser les vues principales vers l'amont et l'aval ? Un concept simple – un plan en X – a permis de prendre en considération tous ces critères sans accorder la priorité à l'une ou l'autre des questions posées — et sans même y répondre de manière explicite.

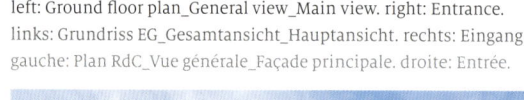

left: Ground floor plan_General view_Main view. right: Entrance.
links: Grundriss EG_Gesamtansicht_Hauptansicht. rechts: Eingang.
gauche: Plan RdC_Vue générale_Façade principale. droite: Entrée.

left: Dining area_Bedroom_Panorama. right: Section_Living area_Stairs.
links: Essbereich_Schlafzimmer_Panorama. rechts: Schnitt_Wohnbereich_Treppe.
gauche: Salle à manger_Chambre_Panorama. droite: Vue en coupe_Séjour_Escalier.

ASTLEY, WARWICKSHIRE, UK **ASTLEY CASTLE**

ARCHITECTS: WITHERFORD WATSON MANN ARCHITECTS
COMPLETION: 2012_**GROSS FLOOR AREA:** 285 M²
PHOTOS: PHILIP VEIL (68 L., 69–71), PHILIPP EBELING (68 R.)

Astley is a site rich in historic resonance – a moated castle, lake, church and the ghost of pleasure gardens. The castle walls decayed and collapsed after a fire in 1978 and a series of rescue attempts failed. A new house was constructed within the oldest part of the castle, building new walls directly onto existing remains, and retaining wings from the fifteenth and seventeenth centuries as walled external courts. The structure occupies roughly half the footprint of the ruins, while new construction elements extend over the courts to link the buttress and the retained fragments. Witherford Watson Mann opted to maintain the open character of the ruin rather than attempt to recreate the castle's former completeness. Every room is a dialog of construction across the centuries.

Auf dem geschichtsträchtigen Astley-Anwesen liegt eine Wasserburg mit See, Kirche und stimmungsvollen Lustgärten. Die Burg verfiel 1978 durch ein Feuer endgültig, mehrere Rekonstruktionsversuche scheiterten. Witherford Watson Mann entschieden sich gegen einen Wiederaufbau und bewahrten stattdessen den offenen Charakter der Ruinen. Im ältesten Teil der Burg setzt ein Neubau unmittelbar auf den historischen Bestand auf. Auch die verfallenen Seitenflügel aus dem 15. und 16. Jahrhundert wurden konserviert und begrenzen nun die Höfe. Etwa die Hälfte der Ruinen liegt innerhalb des Neubaus, während sich moderne Bauelemente bis in die Höfe erstrecken, um Mauerstreben und Fragmente zu verbinden. So setzt sich der architektonische Dialog zwischen den Jahrhunderten fort.

Le château d'Astley, jadis entouré de douves et d'un jardin d'agrément, avec un lac et une église à proximité, était tombé en ruines après qu'un incendie l'eut dévasté en 1978. Plutôt que de lui rendre son aspect d'origine, les architectes ont choisi de le reconstruire en conservant certaines ruines. La partie la plus ancienne a donc été restaurée en bâtissant de nouveaux murs en retrait des anciens, tandis que des espaces délimités par des murs construits entre le XVe et le XVIIe siècle étaient transformés en cours intérieures. La surface de ces cours correspond à la moitié de celle des ruines et les nouveaux appartements intègrent d'anciens pans de murs, certains renforcés par les contreforts d'origine. Chaque pièce entre ainsi en dialogue avec les siècles passés.

left: Ground floor plan_Exterior view_Interior view. right: Dining area.
links: Grundriss EG_Außenansicht_Innenansicht. rechts: Essbereich.
gauche: Plan RdC_Vue de l'extérieur_Vue de l'intérieur. droite: Salle à manger.

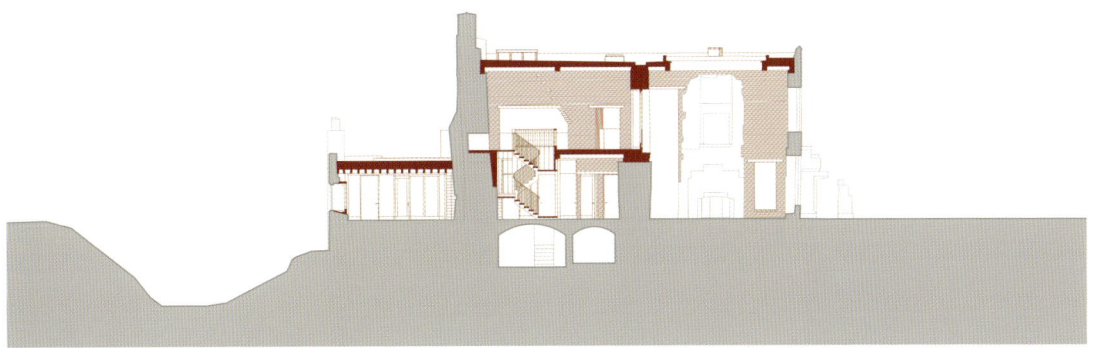

left: Stairs. right: Section_Kitchen_Living room_Bedroom.
links: Treppe. rechts: Schnitt_Küche_Wohnraum_Schlafzimmer.
gauche: Escalier. droite: Vue en coupe_Cuisine_Séjour_Chambre.

STUTTGART, GERMANY **SU HOUSE**

ARCHITECTS: ALEXANDER BRENNER ARCHITEKTEN
COMPLETION: 2012_**PROPERTY SIZE:** 2,125 M²
GROSS FLOOR AREA: 964 M²_**PHOTOS:** ZOOEY BRAUN

Located on a plot directly next to the forest, in an elegant residential district in the southern part of Stuttgart, a meticulously planned villa was created for an art lover and her family. Homage is paid to the special location by the breathtaking view from the roof terraces. The ground floor contains many diverse room situations that are equally suited for large festivities and the daily life of the family. Skylights and air spaces create expansive, light-flooded rooms. At the same time, more exclusive and intimate areas such as the living room offer retreat possibilities. The largest part of the garden level is taken up by the spa and pool area whose floor-to-ceiling glazing opens it up towards the lower southwestern section of the garden.

Auf einem Grundstück direkt am Waldrand, in einem Villenviertel im Stuttgarter Süden, entstand eine bis ins Detail durchgeplante Villa für eine Kunstliebhaberin und deren Familie. Der besonderen Lage wird durch einen atemberaubenden Blick von den Dachterrassen Rechnung getragen. Das Erdgeschoss verfügt über viele differenzierte Raumsituationen, die sich sowohl für größere Feste als auch für das tägliche Leben in der Familie eignen. Oberlichter und Lufträume schaffen großzügige, lichtdurchflutete Räume. Aber auch gefasstere, intimere Bereiche wie der Wohnbereich bieten hier Rückzugsmöglichkeiten. Der größte Teil des Gartengeschosses ist der Spa- und Poolbereich, der sich raumhoch verglast zum unteren, im Südwesten gelegenen Gartenteil öffnet.

Pour la villa où elle souhaitait habiter avec sa famille, une amie des arts a choisi un terrain de la banlieue sud de Stuttgart situé en bordure d'une forêt. Les toits en terrasse permettent d'apprécier la beauté du site. Les divers espaces du rez-de-chaussée abritent la vie quotidienne des occupants tout en étant parfaitement compatibles avec de grandes réceptions. Des puits de lumière, alliés à la multiplication de l'éclairage zénithal, font que toutes les pièces sont particulièrement claires. On trouve également à l'intérieur des espaces de séjour et de repos d'un caractère nettement plus intime. Le niveau qui donne sur le jardin, doté d'une façade entièrement vitrée orientée au sud-ouest, abrite quant à lui la piscine et le spa.

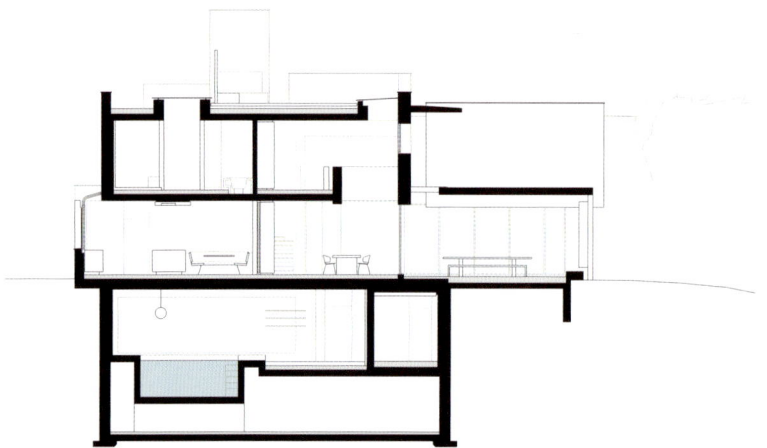

left: Section_Seen from south-west_Indoor pool_Spa. right: Exterior view_Terrace_ Piazza.
links: Schnitt_Südwestansicht_Hallenbad_Spa. rechts: Außenansicht_Terrasse_Piazza.
gauche: Vue en coupe_Façade sud-ouest_Piscine_Spa. droite: Vue de l'extérieur_Terrasse_Piazza.

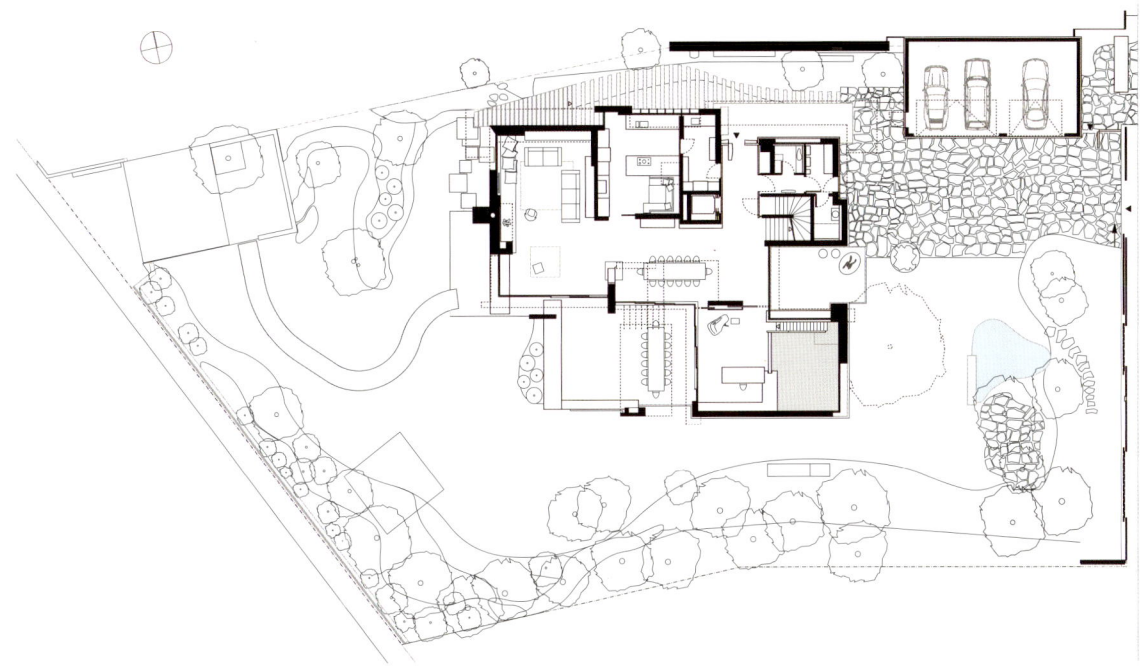

left: Dining area. right: Ground floor plan_Terrace_Bedroom_Living area_Gallery.
links: Essbereich. rechts: Grundriss EG_Terrasse_Schlafzimmer_Wohnbereich_Galerie.
gauche: Salle à manger. droite: Plan RdC_Terrasse_Chambre_Séjour_Galerie.

AALEN, GERMANY **HOUSE AALEN-ZOCHENTAL**

ARCHITECTS: L/A LIEBEL/ARCHITEKTEN BDA
COMPLETION: 2010_**PROPERTY SIZE:** 1,339 M²
GROSS FLOOR AREA: 349 M²_**NUMBER OF ROOMS:** 6
PHOTOS: MICHAEL SCHNELL

A plot in a depression with steep banks on the southern side constituted a special challenge for the design of this villa. The topographic peculiarities were developed into a special form of residence – a split-level house. The existing bank completely conceals the south side of the house, allowing it to fully open up its living spaces and kitchen towards the garden through large glass panels. This way, all rooms can enjoy a wonderful view of the garden's green landscape. Large seating steps playfully connect the different sections, offering relaxation spaces for the many guests of the passionate cook. The result is a home with high living quality – in the midst of greenery, yet in the heart of the city.

Ein Grundstück in einer Senke mit steiler Böschung auf der südlichen Seite stellte eine besondere Herausforderung an die Konzeption dieser Villa. Aus der topographischen Besonderheit wurde eine individuelle Wohnform entwickelt – ein Split-Level-Haus. Die vorhandene Böschung schottet die Südseite des Hauses komplett ab, sodass sich das Gebäude mit seinen Wohnräumen und der Küche zum Garten hin mit großen Verglasungen vollständig öffnen kann. Von allen Räumen aus hat man so einen wunderschönen Blick ins Grüne. Große Sitzstufen verbinden die verschiedenen Bereiche spielerisch und bieten den vielen Gästen der leidenschaftlichen Köchin Platz zum Verweilen. Entstanden ist ein Zuhause mit großer Wohnqualität: Mitten im Grünen und doch mitten in der Stadt.

En concevant cette villa, les architectes ont dû tenir compte des particularités du terrain, notamment un talus en forte pente du côté sud. Ils ont répondu à cette topographie particulière avec un concept original : la « maison à demi-niveaux ». Blotti contre le talus, le bâtiment s'ouvre intégralement sur le jardin grâce aux grandes baies vitrées de la cuisine et des pièces de séjour, ces espaces bénéficiant ainsi de vues agréables sur la verdure. Les gradins se transformant en marches qui établissent une liaison entre la cuisine et le salon permettent à la maîtresse de maison – un fin cordon bleu – de rester en contact visuel avec ses nombreux invités. Cette villa urbaine entourée de verdure offre ainsi une qualité de vie exceptionnelle.

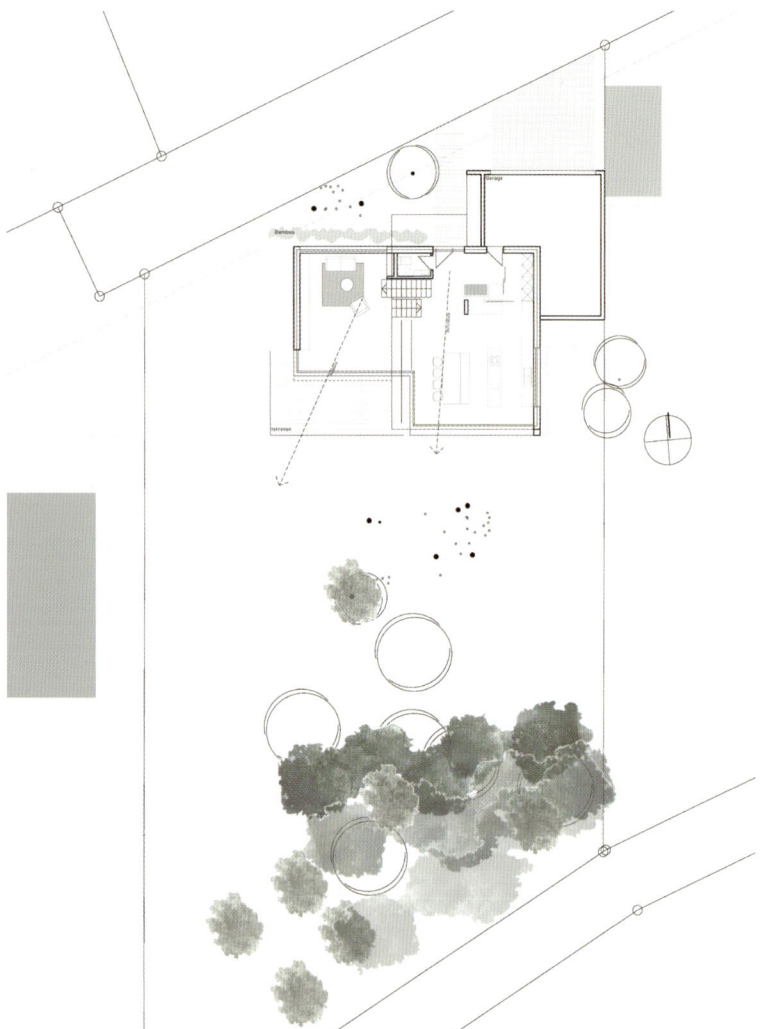

left: Ground floor plan_Street view_Main view. right: Garden view.
links: Grundriss EG_Straßenansicht_Hauptansicht. rechts: Gartenansicht.
gauche: Plan RdC_Vue de la rue_Façade principale. droite: Vue du jardin.

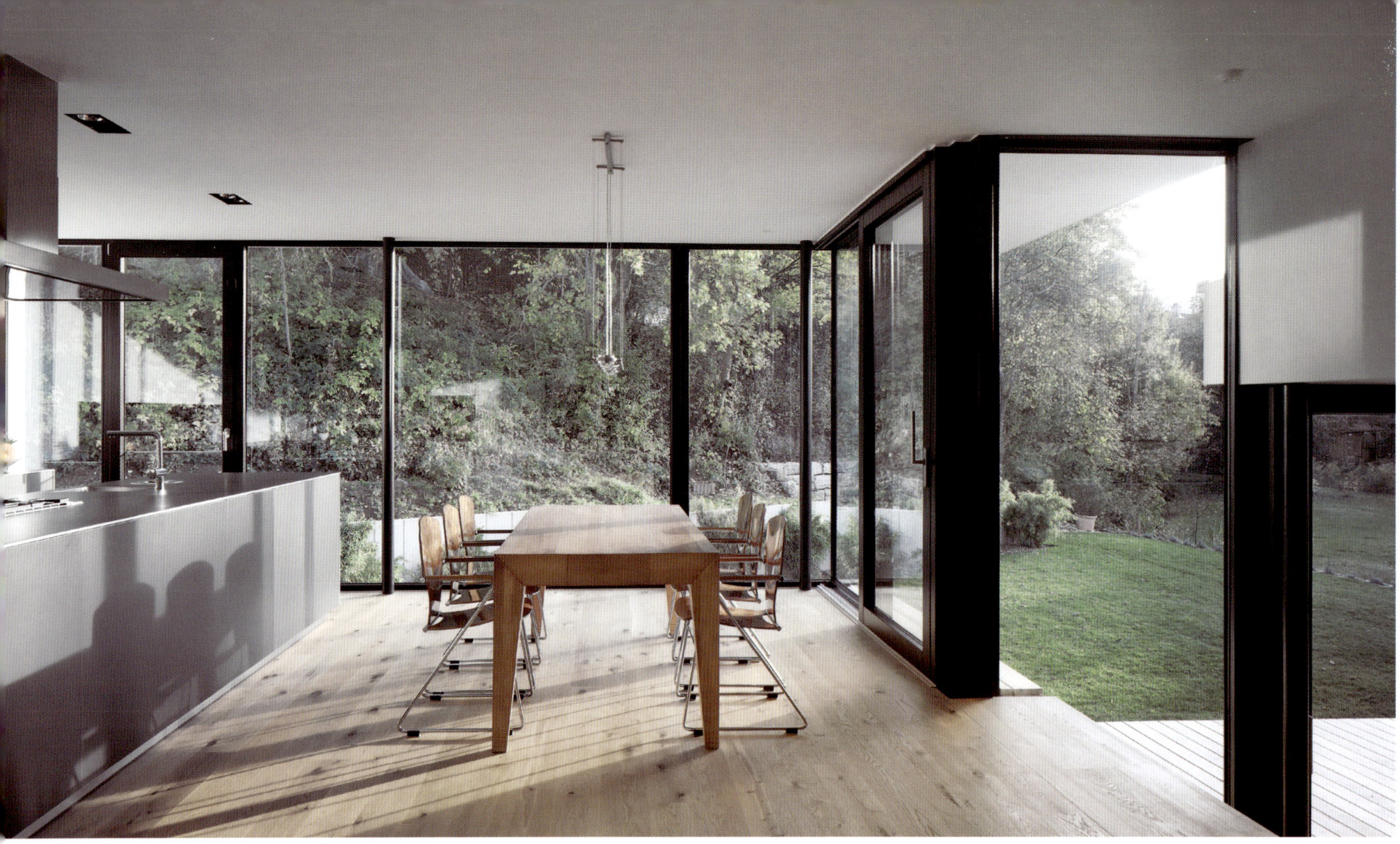

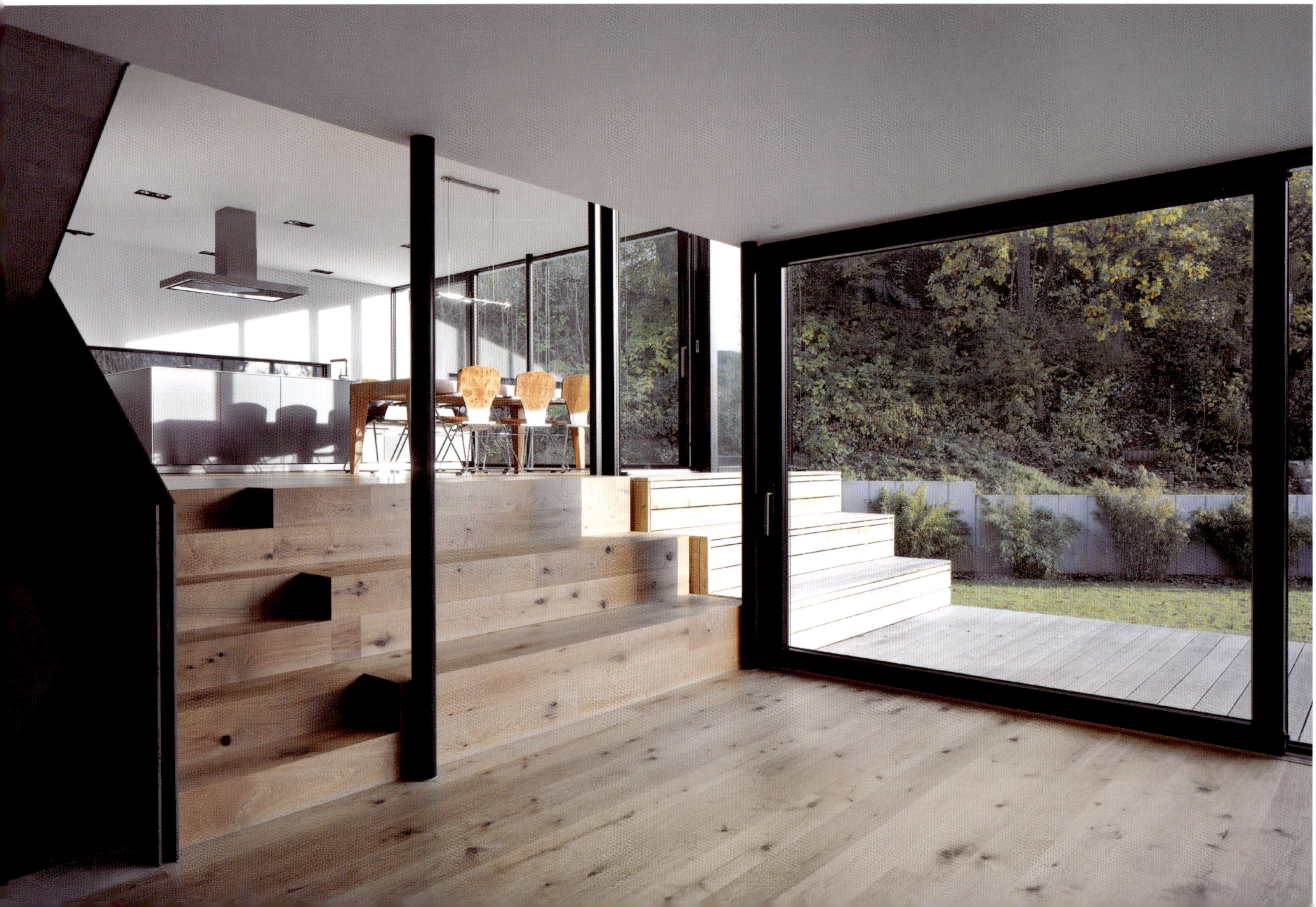

left: Dining area_Living room. right: Section_Stairs_Kitchen_Living area.
links: Essbereich_Wohnraum. rechts: Schnitt_Treppe_Küche_Wohnbereich.
gauche: Salle à manger_Séjour. droite: Vue en coupe_Escalier_Cuisine_Séjour.

DARMSTADT, GERMANY **RESIDENCE MADE OF WOOD**

ARCHITECTS: MENZEL | KOSSOWSKI ARCHITEKTEN
COMPLETION: 2011_**PROPERTY SIZE:** 480 M²
GROSS FLOOR AREA: 190 M²_**NUMBER OF ROOMS:** 5
PHOTOS: THOMAS OTT

The building plot is located at the southern edge of Darmstadt, in the immediate vicinity of the adjacent Odenwald region. The two-floor residence is a wooden post-and-beam structure. The exterior is dominated by the Siberian larch used for the façade and windows. To benefit from the view, the open living area with the kitchen, dining section, bedroom, and home office are located on the second floor. Large sliding windows allow outdoor living in the summer. The ground floor contains the children's bedrooms, bathroom, and utility room. Across the courtyard there is a roofed area containing the carport and the entrance. The garden is dominated by acacias, grasses and boulders.

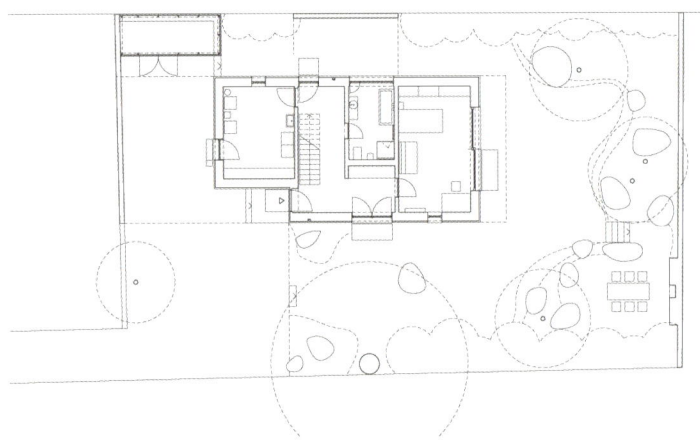

Das Grundstück befindet sich am Südrand Darmstadts, in unmittelbarer Nähe zum angrenzenden Odenwald. Das zweigeschossige Wohnhaus wurde in Holzständerbauweise errichtet. Sibirische Lärche für Fassade und Fenster prägen das äußere Erscheinungsbild. Auf Grund der Aussicht befindet sich der offene Wohnbereich mit Küche, Essplatz, Schlafzimmer und Arbeitsbereich im 1. Obergeschoss. Großzügige Schiebefenster ermöglichen im Sommer ein Wohnen im Freien. Im Erdgeschoss liegen Kinderzimmer, Bad und Hauswirtschaftsraum. Über einen Hof gelangt man zu einem überdachten Bereich mit Carport und Eingang. Der Garten ist geprägt von Akazien, Gräsern und Findlingen.

Ce bâtiment sur deux niveaux à ossature plate-forme se trouve au sud de Darmstadt, à proximité immédiate de la forêt d'Odenwald. Il se caractérise à l'extérieur par le mélèze de Sibérie utilisé pour la façade et les fenêtres. Afin de permettre aux occupants de bénéficier d'une meilleure vue, la chambre des parents ainsi que l'espace cuisine/bureau/salle à manger se trouve au premier étage et s'ouvre sur l'extérieur par de grandes baies vitrées coulissantes. Le rez-de-chaussée accueille pour sa part la salle de bain, la chambre des enfants et la buanderie. Un espace couvert sert de porche et d'abri pour voiture. Le jardin et sa pelouse, où poussent des acacias et où l'on trouve quelques gros rochers, sont très accueillants en été.

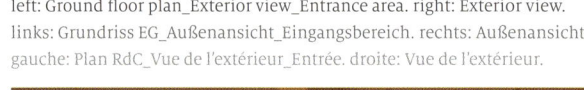

left: Ground floor plan_Exterior view_Entrance area. right: Exterior view.
links: Grundriss EG_Außenansicht_Eingangsbereich. rechts: Außenansicht.
gauche: Plan RdC_Vue de l'extérieur_Entrée. droite: Vue de l'extérieur.

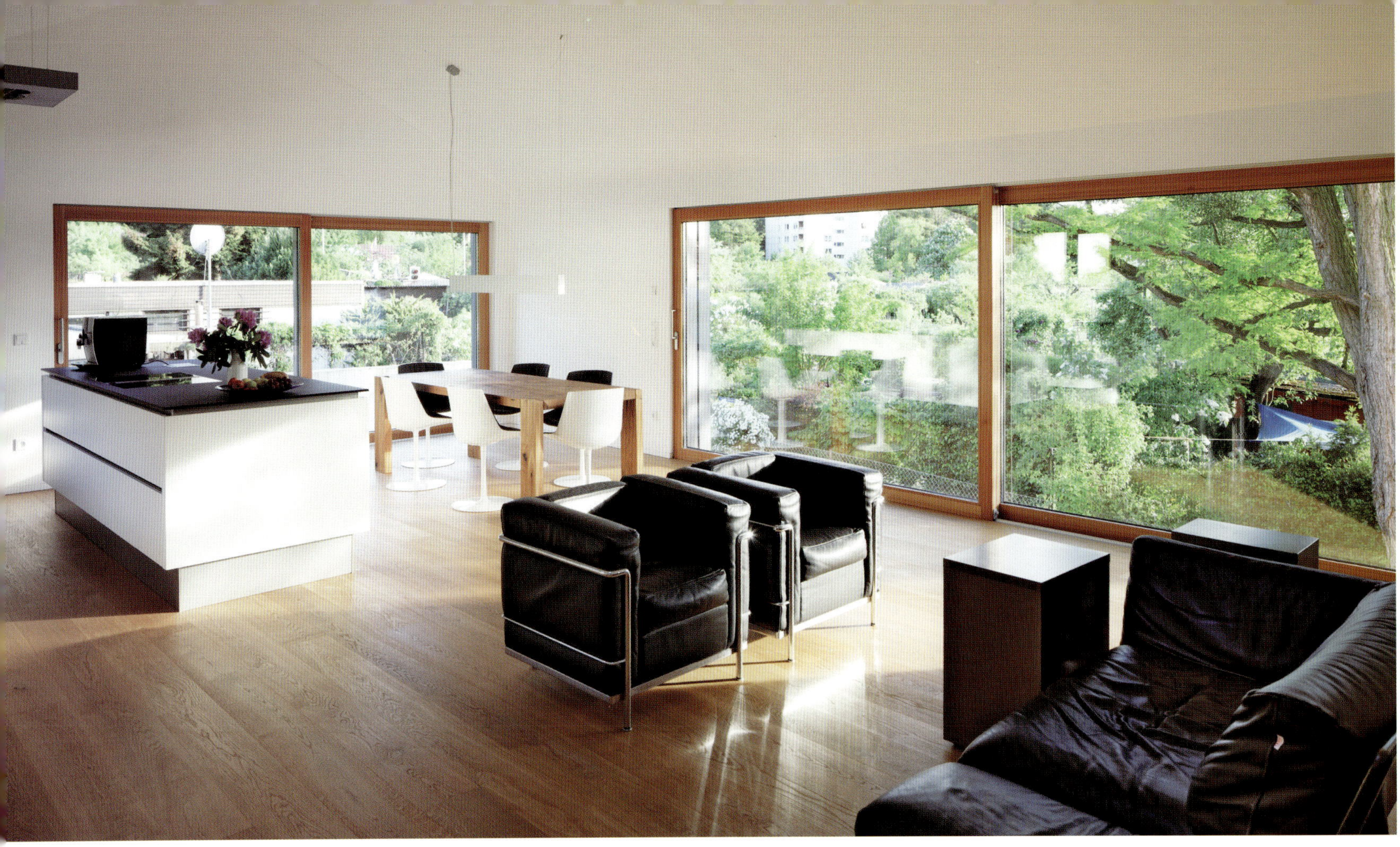
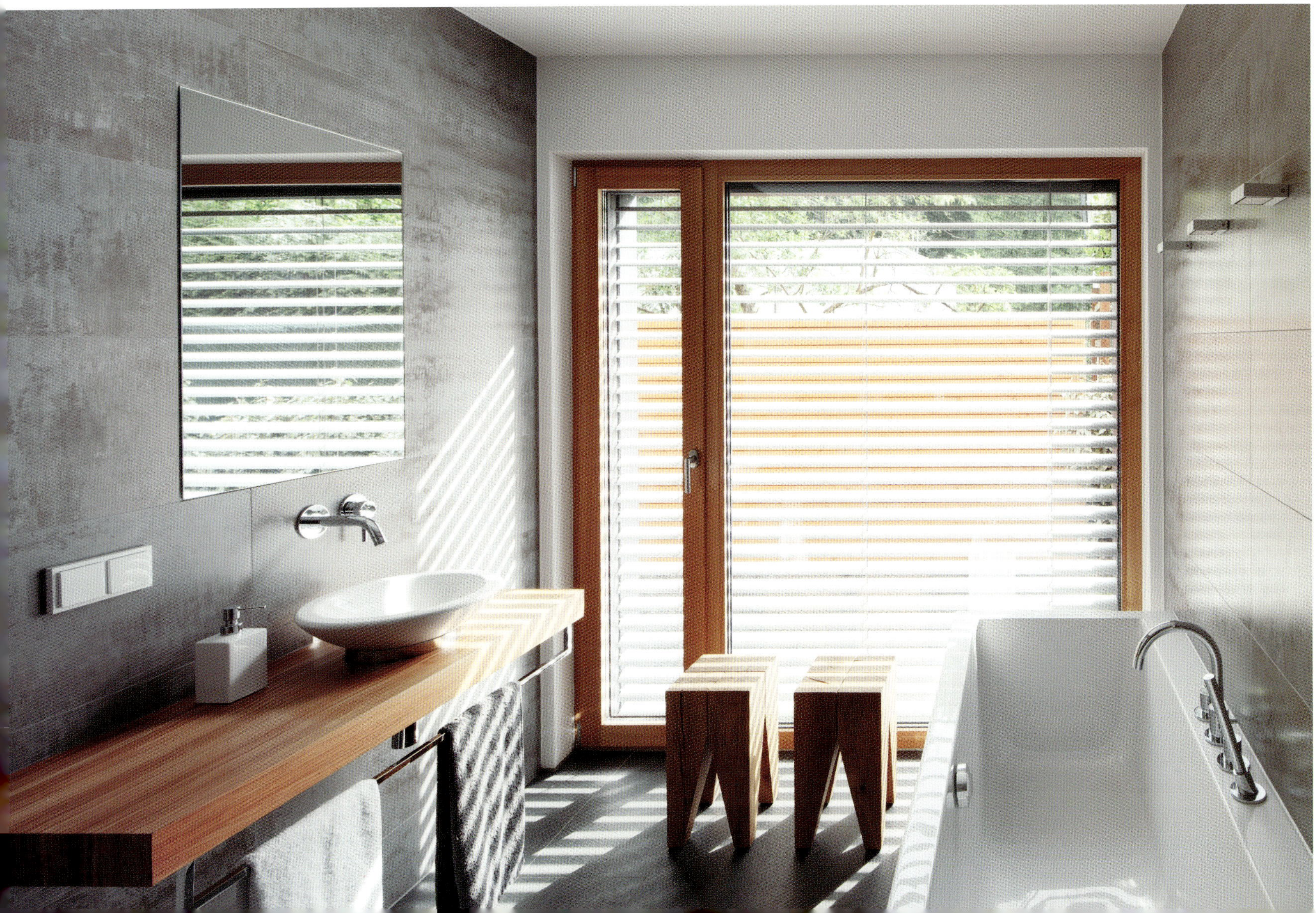

left: Living and dining area_Bathroom. right: Elevation_Stairs_Living room_Kitchen.
links: Wohn- und Essbereich_Bad. rechts: Ansicht_Treppe_Wohnraum_Küche.
gauche: Séjour et salle à manger_Salle de bains. droite: Élévation_Escalier_Cuisine.

LONDRINA, BRAZIL **SN HOUSE**

ARCHITECTS: STUDIO GUILHERME TORRES
COMPLETION: 2010
PROPERTY SIZE: 843 M²_**GROSS FLOOR AREA:** 808 M²
PHOTOS: DENILSON MACHADO

The monumental villa is docked on a slope, which released the space underneath it for the garden, a swimming pool, and living rooms. Suspended without pillars, the construction has straight, pure and simple forms. Contrasting with the white masonry, stone and wood coatings warm the look without breaking the contemporary overall style. The independent functioning of the two floors was another convenient solution. The daily life of the family is focused on the upper floor, which is accessed from the side ramp and garage to the upper hall. On weekends, however, they enjoy to receive their large family in the spacious and comfortable leisure area with a pool, garden, gourmet barbecue, and two generous lounges.

Die monumentale Villa liegt auf abschüssigem Gelände, was unterhalb des freischwebenden Obergeschosses viel Raum für Garten, Pool und Wohnbereiche lässt. Die Formgebung ist klar und geradlinig. Einen Kontrast zum weißen Mauerwerk bilden Naturstein und Holz, die Wärme ausstrahlen, ohne den modernen Gesamteindruck zu brechen. Die beiden Geschosse sind weitgehend unabhängig voneinander. So spielt sich der Alltag der Familie im oberen Stockwerk ab, dessen separater Eingangsbereich über eine seitliche Rampe und die Garage zugänglich ist. Am Wochenende empfängt man die große Verwandtschaft im weitläufigen und komfortablen Freizeitbereich mit Pool, Garten, Grill und zwei großzügigen Lounges.

Cette villa monumentale construite sur un terrain en pente se complète d'un jardin et d'une piscine. Il s'agit d'un bâtiment aux formes pures et austères, composé d'une barre dont le béton contraste avec des matériaux naturels tels que le bois et la pierre dont les teintes chaudes se marient parfaitement au style contemporain de l'ensemble. Les architectes ont conçu deux niveaux indépendants l'un de l'autre : un niveau supérieur qui abrite le garage (auquel on accède par une rampe) ainsi que la cuisine, trois suites et les pièces de séjour ; et un rez-de-chaussée où se trouvent des espaces de loisirs vastes et confortables, lieu convivial où la grande famille apprécie de se rassembler le week-end.

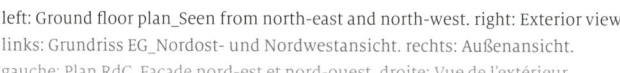

left: Ground floor plan_Seen from north-east and north-west. right: Exterior view.
links: Grundriss EG_Nordost- und Nordwestansicht. rechts: Außenansicht.
gauche: Plan RdC_Façade nord-est et nord-ouest. droite: Vue de l'extérieur.

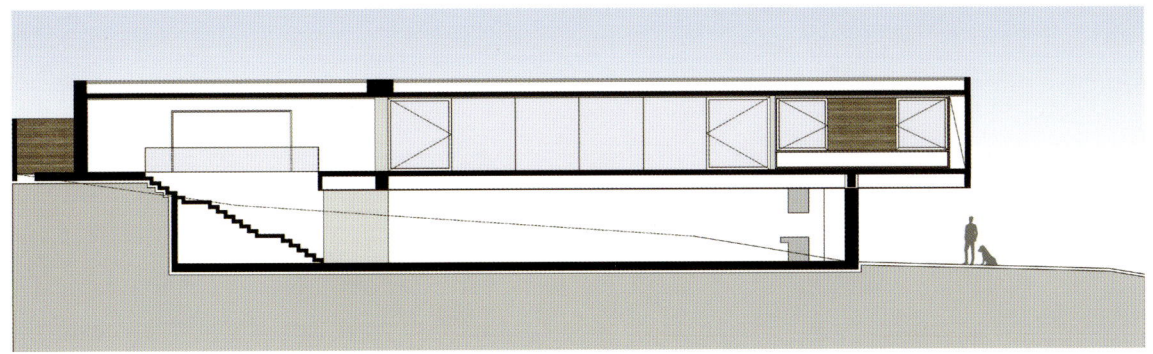

left: Hall. right: Section_Seen from north-east_Covered outdoor area_Street view.
links: Flur. rechts: Schnitt_Nordostansicht_Überdachter Außenbereich_Straßenansicht.
gauche: Couloir. droite: Vue en coupe_Façade nord-est_Extérieur couvert_Vue de la rue.

KASTANIENBAUM, SWITZERLAND **TWIN HOUSES**

ARCHITECTS: LUSSI+HALTER PARTNER AG
COMPLETION: 2011_**PROPERTY SIZE:** 1,550 M²
GROSS FLOOR AREA: 620 M²_**NUMBER OF ROOMS:** 2 X 6
PHOTOS: LEONARDO FINOTTI

The duplex house lies in the immediate vicinity of Lake Lucerne at the edge of a mixed forest. The suspended structure incorporates nature and creates a space with two interpretations. Depending on the use of the wooden shutters, the terrace can be part of the interior or the exterior space. The length of the building is expressed in a ramp, which is the connecting spatial element from the open living room to the introverted rooms on the top floor. The roof landscape is dominated by a pool of black exposed concrete. Black concrete and timber elements made of Brazilian cherry wood are present across the entire residence. The dark atmosphere of the interior contrasts with its surroundings. Mirrored surfaces and large windows bring the outdoors inside.

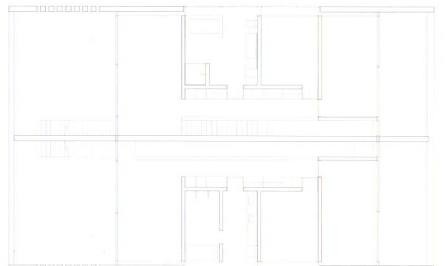

Das Doppelhaus befindet sich in unmittelbarer Nähe des Vierwaldstättersees am Rande eines Mischwaldes. Der schwebende Gebäudekörper nimmt die Natur auf und bildet einen zweifach lesbaren Raum. Je nach Benutzung der Holzroll-läden zählt die Terrasse zum Aussen- oder Innenraum. Die Länge des Gebäudes wird durch eine Rampe erfahrbar. Sie ist das verbindende, räumliche Element vom offenen Wohnraum zu den introvertierten Räumen im Obergeschoss. Die Dachlandschaft wird von einem Pool in schwarzem Sichtbeton geprägt. Schwarzer Beton und Holzelemente aus brasilianischem Kirschbaum sind im ganzen Haus thematisiert. Die dunkle Atmosphäre im Innenraum steht als Kontrast zur Umgebung. Spiegelnde Flächen und große Fenster holen die Natur ins Innere.

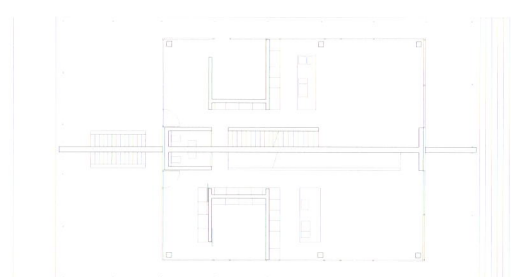

Ces maisons jumelles se trouvent en bordure d'une forêt près du lac des Quatre-Cantons. Semblant flotter dans l'air, l'ensemble construit fait corps avec la nature environnante et constitue un double espace architectural. Des stores en bois permettent de convertir le rez-de-chaussée tantôt en terrasse, tantôt en espace d'intérieur. Des rampes s'étirant sur toute la longueur de l'immeuble desservent les différents étages, allant de l'espace ouvert du rez-de-chaussée aux pièces plus intimes du premier étage. Le toit en terrasse accueille pour sa part une piscine en béton brut de coffrage teinté en noir. Ce matériau dont la teinte sombre contraste avec l'environnement se retrouve dans tout le bâtiment, où il se complète par des revêtements en merisier du Brésil.

left: Top and ground floor plans_Exterior view_Seen from south-west. right: Entrance area_Seen from north-west_Outdoor area. links: Grundrisse OG und EG_Außenansicht_Südwestansicht. rechts: Eingangsbereich_Nordwestansicht_Außenbereich. gauche: Plan niveau 1 et RdC_Vue de l'extérieur_Façade sud-ouest. droite: Entrée_Façade nord-ouest_ Extérieur.

left: Roof terrace_Living area. right: Section_Gallery_Balcony.
links: Dachterrasse_Wohnbereich. rechts: Schnitt_Galerie_Balkon.
gauche: Terrasse au toit_Séjour. droite: Vue en coupe_Galerie_Balcon.

NAXXAR, MALTA **HANGING HOME**

ARCHITECTS: CHRIS BRIFFA ARCHITECTS
COMPLETION: 2011_**PROPERTY SIZE:** 250 M²
GROSS FLOOR AREA: 311 M²_**NUMBER OF ROOMS:** 13
PHOTOS: DAVID PISANI

"Hanging Home" - a residence in Malta built for a family of three, was conceived to work around a demanding brief and strict zoning regulations, while somehow managing to appear pure and weightless. With only 40% site coverage permitted, Briffa cantilevered practically half the house over a large pool area. Upstairs, the bedroom suite "floats" over the whole house, progressively introducing more private areas along the length of it. The core of the three-floor home is the double height living area and piano salon, with the private dining area extending into the garden, hovering above the 12-meter pool surrounded by olive trees facing south. Sharing a wall with the pool is the peculiar, in part underground, home office. In early summer, water reflections from the pool dance on its ceiling.

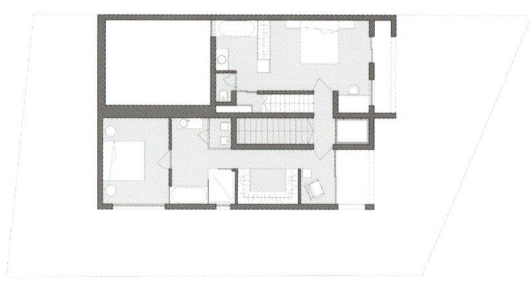

„Hanging Home" auf Malta ist für eine dreiköpfige Familie konzipiert. Die Villa musste strengen Bebauungsvorschriften und einem anspruchsvollen Auftrag gerecht werden, dabei sollte sie pur und schwerelos wirken. Nur 40% des Grundstücks durften bebaut werden, weshalb der Architekt praktisch die Hälfte des Baukörpers über dem großen Pool auskragen ließ. Auch die Suite im Obergeschoss scheint zu schweben, während die Privatheit der Räume der Länge nach zunimmt. Herz des dreigeschossigen Hauses ist der Wohnbereich mit offenem Klavierzimmer, das über doppelte Deckenhöhe verfügt. Der Essbereich öffnet sich zum Garten und schwebt über dem zwölf Meter langen Pool, mit dem sich das teilweise unterirdisch gelegene Büro eine Wand teilt. Im Frühsommer tanzen Wasserspiegelungen des Pools an der Decke.

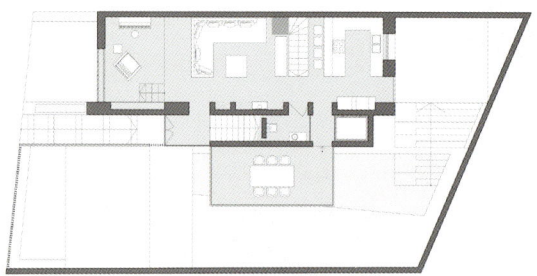

Cette villa a été construite à Malte en tenant compte d'un cahier des charges strict, tant en matière de zonage que de la part du maître d'ouvrage, qui souhaitait un bâtiment puriste et léger. La législation locale n'autorisant de bâtir que quarante pour cent du terrain, l'architecte a placé près de la moitié de la villa en porte-à-faux, de sorte que les chambres du niveau supérieur semblent flotter au-dessus du rez-de-chaussée. Au cœur de ce bâtiment sur trois niveaux se trouve le séjour/salon de piano, espace particulièrement haut de plafond se prolongeant par une salle à manger qui surplombe la piscine de douze mètres et donne sur un jardin orienté au sud et planté d'oliviers. L'un des bords de la piscine est constitué par le mur extérieur du bureau semi-enterré. Au début de l'été, des reflets de l'eau de la piscine dansent sur le plafond.

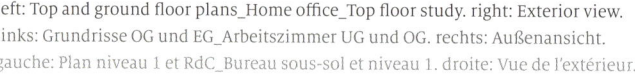

left: Top and ground floor plans_Home office_Top floor study. right: Exterior view.
links: Grundrisse OG und EG_Arbeitszimmer UG und OG. rechts: Außenansicht.
gauche: Plan niveau 1 et RdC_Bureau sous-sol et niveau 1. droite: Vue de l'extérieur.

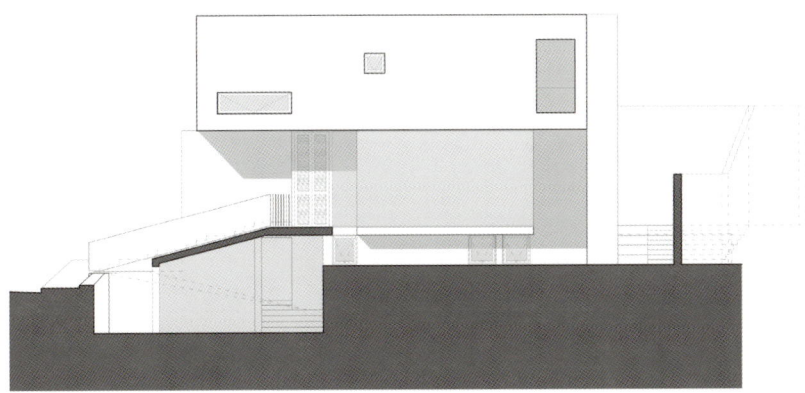

left: Pool. right: Elevation_Living area_Stairs.
links: Pool. rechts: Ansicht_Wohnbereich_Treppe.
gauche: Piscine extérieure. droite: Élévation_Séjour_Escalier.

HEINSBERG, GERMANY **HOUSE IN HEINSBERG**

ARCHITECTS: DÖRING DAHMEN JOERESSEN ARCHITEKTEN
COMPLETION: 2009_**PROPERTY SIZE:** 1,483 M²
GROSS FLOOR AREA: 571 M²_**NUMBER OF ROOMS:** 8
PHOTOS: MANOS MEISEN

The building is incorporated into an evolved row of houses typical of this region where it replaced an old house that was torn down. The newly designed flat-roof house is an angled building that is accessed by an entrance atrium. Located on a slope, the residence features different floors and floor heights in reaction to the terrain. Simple materials were used – the façade is covered with dark felted plaster while the windows are made of aluminum. The house has large windows facing the garden.

Das Gebäude fügt sich in einer für die Region typisch gewachsenen Straßenzeile ein und ersetzt dort ein altes Haus, das abgerissen wurde. Das neu entworfene Flachdachhaus ist als winkelförmiges Gebäude geplant und wird über einen zur Straße vorgeschalteten Eingangs- und Lichthof erschlossen. Das im Hang stehende Wohnhaus reagiert mit unterschiedlichen Geschossigkeiten und Geschosshöhen auf die Geländesituation. Die Materialien sind einfach gehalten: die Fassade ist mit einem dunkelgrauen Filzputz gestaltet und die Fenster sind aus Aluminium. Zur Gartenseite öffnet sich das Haus mit großen Fensteröffnungen.

Venue remplacer un vieux bâtiment aujourd'hui démoli, cette maison angulaire à toit plat s'intègre à une rue de style traditionnel. L'accès se fait par une cour fermée. Le terrain étant légèrement en pente, les architectes ont compensé la dénivellation en jouant sur la hauteur sous plafond dans les différentes pièces du rez-de-chaussée. Ils se sont par ailleurs confinés à une palette de matériaux assez sobre : enduit lisse de couleur gris foncé pour les façades, aluminium pour les fenêtres. De grandes baies vitrées ouvrent le bâtiment sur le jardin.

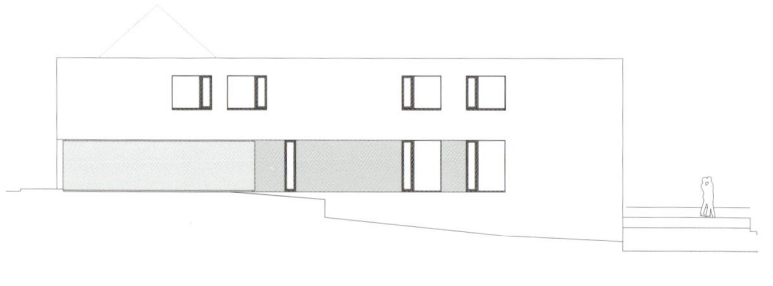

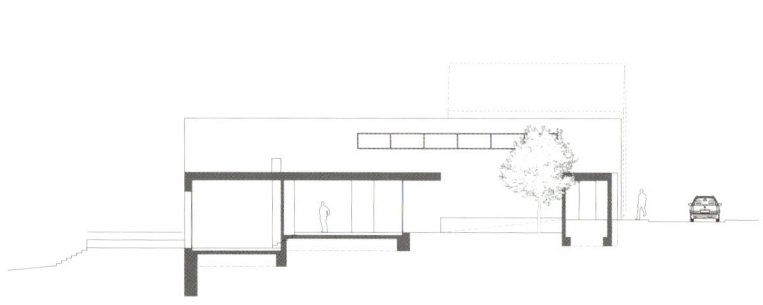
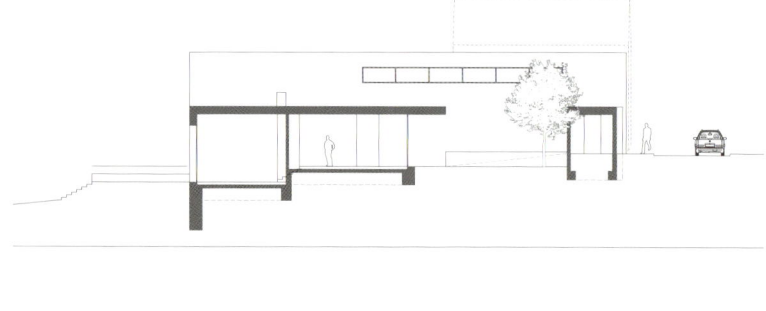

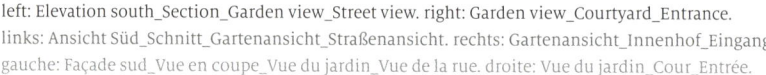

left: Elevation south_Section_Garden view_Street view. right: Garden view_Courtyard_Entrance.
links: Ansicht Süd_Schnitt_Gartenansicht_Straßenansicht. rechts: Gartenansicht_Innenhof_Eingang.
gauche: Façade sud_Vue en coupe_Vue du jardin_Vue de la rue. droite: Vue du jardin_Cour_Entrée.

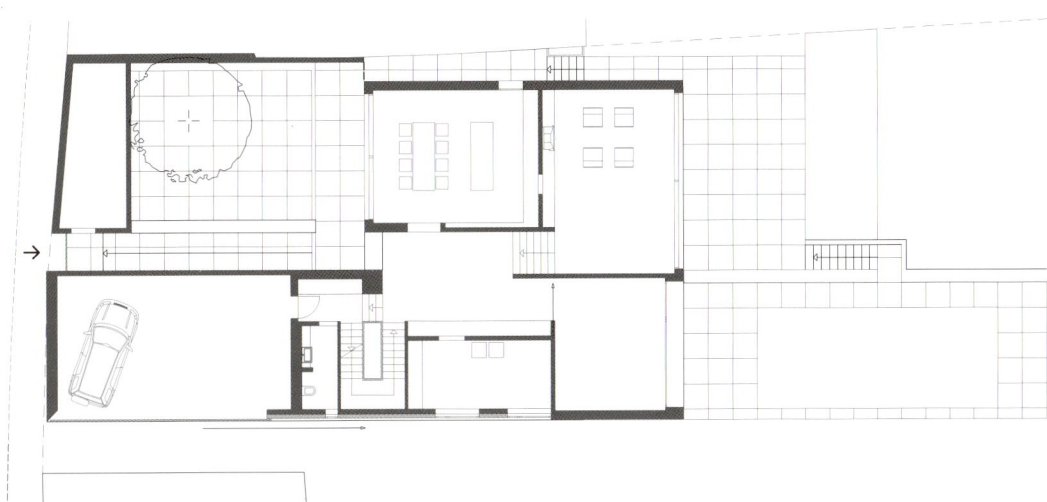

left: Stairs. right: Ground floor plan_Living room 1_Kitchen_Stairs on ground floor_View.
links: Treppe. rechts: Grundriss EG_Wohnraum 1_Küche_Treppe im Erdgeschoss_Ausblick.
gauche: Escalier. droite: Plan RdC_Séjour 1_Cuisine_Escalier au RdC_Vue panoramique.

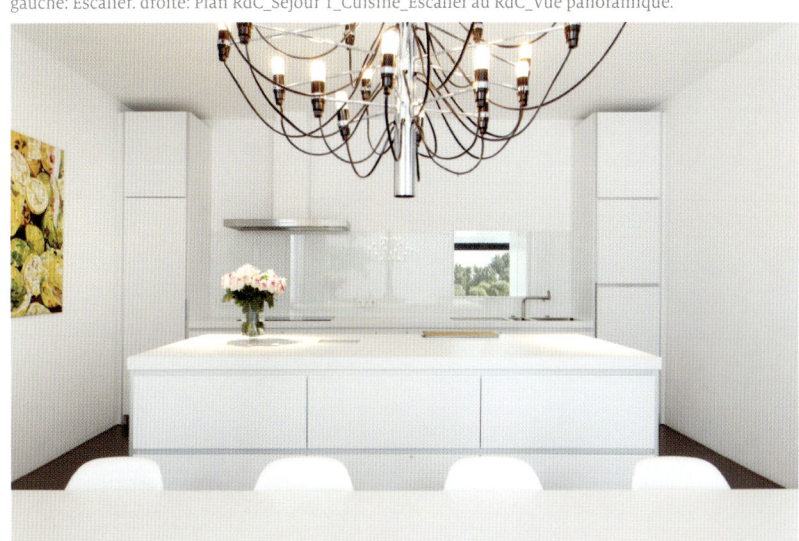

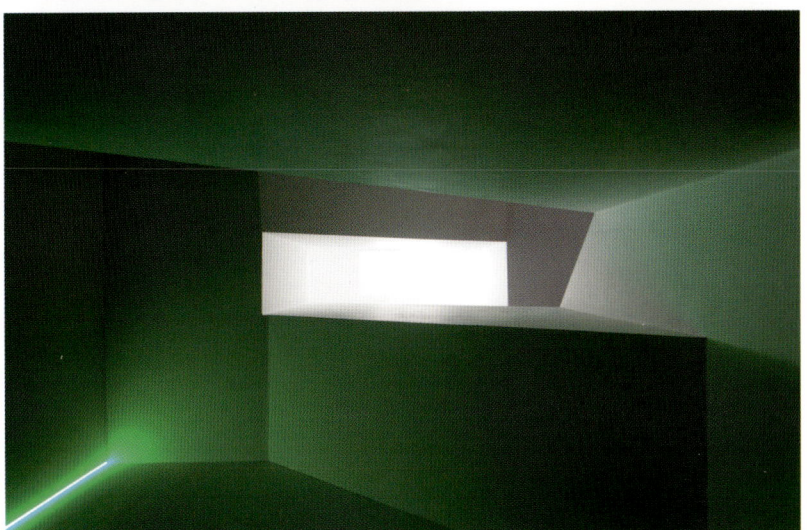

OUDENAARDE, BELGIUM **HOUSE DZ IN MULLEM**

ARCHITECTS: GRAUX & BAEYENS ARCHITECTEN
COMPLETION: 2012_**PROPERTY SIZE:** 810 M²
GROSS FLOOR AREA: 263 M²_**NUMBER OF ROOMS:** 6
PHOTOS: LUC ROYMANS

A narrow plot in combination with a very dense program (a home and a physiotherapist practice) resulted in a building that pushes the limits of the planning regulations. To escape the limitations of open areas on the sides of the house, the traditional dwelling program was switched: the day-light functions are located on top of the night functions. The monolithic volume of the house is chopped up into smaller entities. By shifting these entities, direct sunlight enters the house and different relationships occur within the house and its surroundings. The relationship with the surrounding plot was optimized by the positioning of the windows. The right façade opens up to the neighboring garden and the morning sun floods the living area.

Ein schmales Grundstück und die anspruchsvolle Aufgabe, Wohnen und eine Physiotherapiepraxis zu kombinieren, resultierten in einem Entwurf, der die Baubestimmungen voll ausreizt. Um die Begrenzung offener Flächen an den Seiten der Villa zu umgehen, wurde das traditionelle Design ins Gegenteil verkehrt: Die Tageslichtfunktionen liegen über den Nachtfunktionen. Der monolithische Bau ist in kleinere Einheiten aufgeteilt. Durch deren versetzte Lage zueinander strömt direktes Sonnenlicht ins Haus. Mannigfaltige Bezüge zwischen den Innenräumen und der Umgebung entstehen, auch dank der optimierten Anordnung der Ausblicke. Die rechte Fassade öffnet sich zum Nachbargarten hin und Morgensonne strömt in den Wohnbereich.

Construire une maison d'habitation doublée d'un cabinet de physiothérapie sur un terrain somme toute étroit constituait un défi à relever pour les architectes. Les contraintes liées à l'espace devant rester libre des deux côtés de la maison ont rendu nécessaire d'intervertir la configuration traditionnelle des pièces en plaçant les chambres au rez-de-chaussée et les pièces à vivre au premier étage. Afin d'éviter le monolithisme, les architectes ont divisé le volume en plusieurs unités décalées les unes par rapport aux autres, ce qui présente par ailleurs l'avantage d'optimiser l'éclairage naturel et de dynamiser l'interaction de la villa avec son environnement. Le positionnement des fenêtres a par ailleurs été optimisé : la façade droite s'ouvre sur le jardin voisin et le soleil du matin inonde le séjour de lumière.

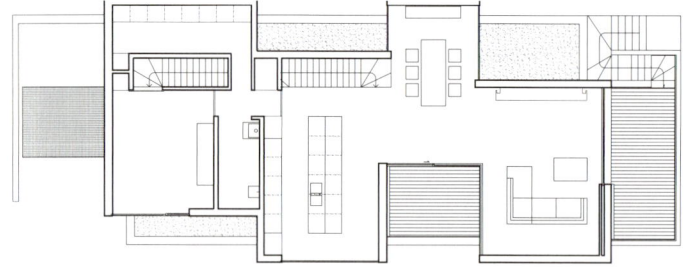

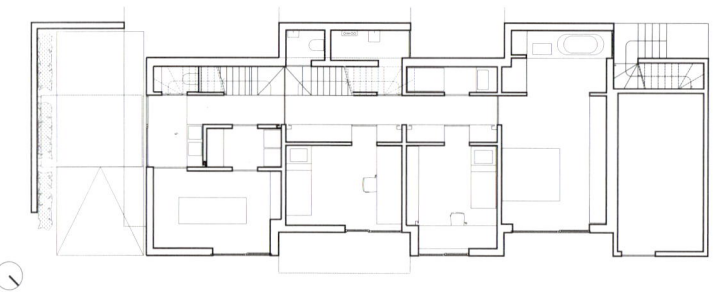

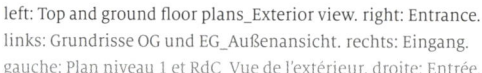
left: Top and ground floor plans_Exterior view. right: Entrance.
links: Grundrisse OG und EG_Außenansicht. rechts: Eingang.
gauche: Plan niveau 1 et RdC_Vue de l'extérieur. droite: Entrée.

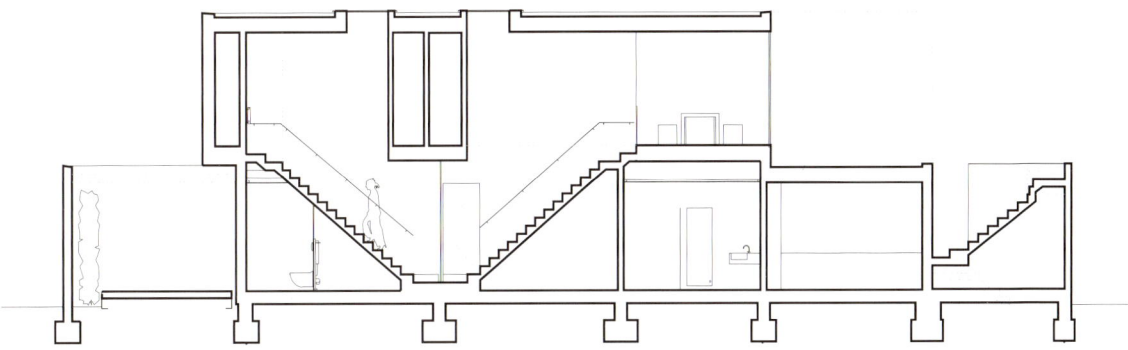

left: Bathroom. right: Section_Kitchen_Living area_Stairs.
links: Bad. rechts: Schnitt_Küche_Wohnbereich_Treppen.
gauche: Salle de bains. droite: Vue en coupe_Cuisine_Séjour_Escaliers.

STUTTGART, GERMANY **HOUSE TAZZELWURM**

ARCHITECTS: ARCHITEKTUR 109
MARK ARNOLD + ARNE FENTZLOFF BDA
COMPLETION: 2011_**PROPERTY SIZE:** 1,000 M²
GROSS FLOOR AREA: 325 M², 525 M²_**NUMBER OF ROOMS:** 5/6
PHOTOS: BRIGIDA GONZALES

The building is located on a narrow plot of land in an elevated location with a magnificent view of downtown Stuttgart. The openings of the sturdy, robust, yet well-balanced structure deliberately interact with the surroundings to stage the beautiful view. The design principle is that of a Black Box - White Space – rough and black on the outside, white and smooth on the inside. The building represents a "monolith of peace" in relation to the erratic architectural styles surrounding it. Made of oil shale, the façade's anthracite-black surface only releases it colors in the sunlight. The interior layout resembles a city – multiple uses, market place, views, arcades, private and public spaces, stairways and plazas, extended views, and constrictions.

Auf einem schmalen Grundstück in Höhenlage steht das Gebäude mit herrlichem Blick über die Stuttgarter Innenstadt. Der kräftige robuste, aber in sich ruhige Baukörper reagiert mit den Öffnungen bewusst auf die Umgebung und inszeniert den Ausblick. Durch das gestalterische Prinzip Black Box - White Space: außen ruppig schwarz, innen weiß und glatt präsentiert sich das Gebäude als ein „Monolith der Ruhe" inmitten umliegender baulicher Aufgeregtheit. Die Fassade aus ölhaltigem Schiefer auf seiner anthrazit-schwarzen Oberfläche gibt erst im Licht der Sonne die Farben frei. Das innenräumliche Gefüge gleicht einer Stadt: Nutzungsvielfalt, Marktplatz, Blickverbindung, Arkaden, Rückzug und Öffentlichkeit, Treppen und Plätze, Weitsicht und Enge.

La villa Tazzelwurm se dresse sur un terrain exigu offrant un magnifique panorama sur la ville de Stuttgart. Ce cube d'allure à la fois robuste et sobre est pourvu d'ouvertures tirant le meilleur parti possible d'une bonne implantation. Conçu selon le principe « Black Box – White Space », le bâtiment joue sur le contraste entre une enveloppe sombre et un intérieur clair, s'affirmant ainsi comme un monolithe de sérénité dans un environnement architectural tourmenté. Le revêtement extérieur en plaques de schiste anthracite scintille de multiples couleurs sous les rayons du soleil. L'organisation intérieure n'est pas sans rappeler une ville : diversité des fonctions, place du marché, perspectives, arcades, zones de repos et zones publiques, escaliers et places, espaces vastes et confinés.

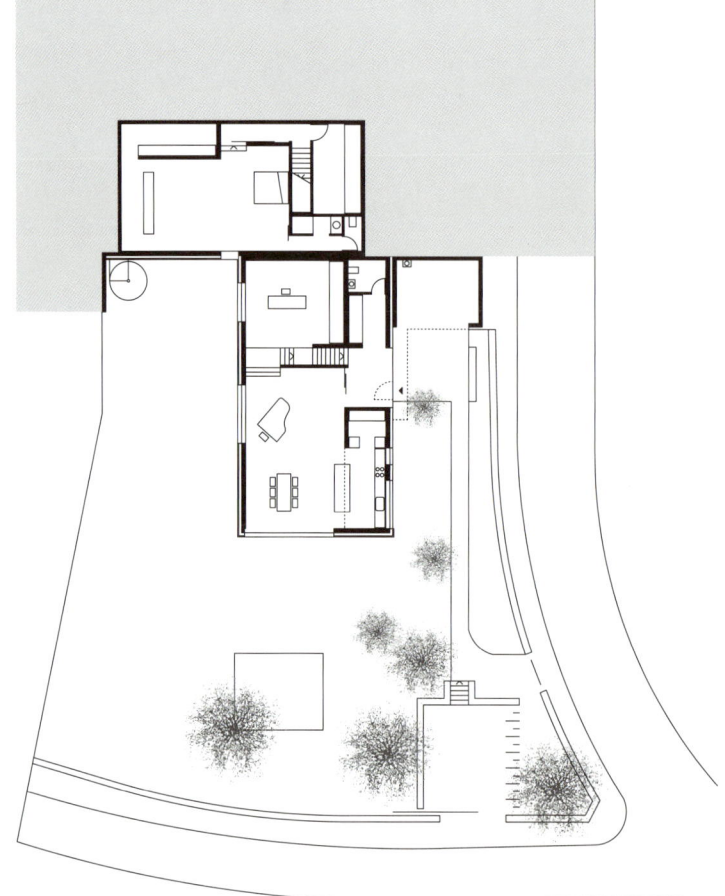

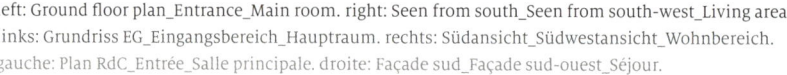

left: Ground floor plan_Entrance_Main room. right: Seen from south_Seen from south-west_Living area.
links: Grundriss EG_Eingangsbereich_Hauptraum. rechts: Südansicht_Südwestansicht_Wohnbereich.
gauche: Plan RdC_Entrée_Salle principale. droite: Façade sud_Façade sud-ouest_Séjour.

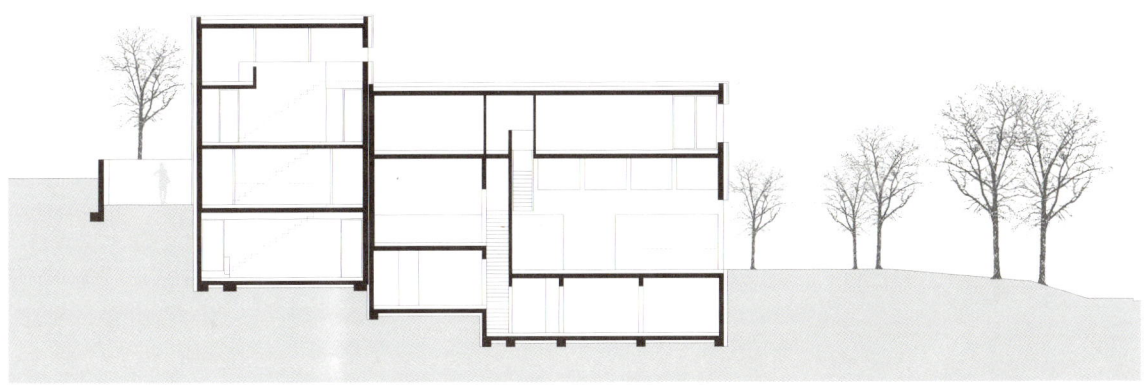

left: Stairs view. right: Section_Gallery_Bedroom with loggia.
links: Blick zur Treppe. rechts: Schnitt_Galerie_Schlafzimmer mit Loggia.
gauche: Escalier. droite: Vue en coupe_Galerie_Chambre avec loggia.

BRUSINO ARSIZIO, SWITZERLAND **LAKE LUGANO HOUSE**

ARCHITECTS: JM ARCHITECTURE
COMPLETION: 2010_**PROPERTY SIZE:** 600 M²
GROSS FLOOR AREA: 320 M²_**NUMBER OF ROOMS:** 3
PHOTOS: JACOPO MASCHERONI

The villa consists of two volumes organized on different levels due to the particular topography of the site. A polygonal shaped glass pavilion with rounded edges stands above a linear underground block. Each level relates itself with independent outdoor spaces, which are closely related with the interiors. The glass pavilion overlooks two very defined areas: the first, toward the mountain, is a very private zone resulted in the area between the property line and the building setback line according to the local building code. The second is a garden overlooking the lake. In the same way, the bedrooms face a garden enclosed by the building and the perimeter wall.

Aufgrund der besonderen Topografie des Grundstücks ist die Villa auf zwei Ebenen angelegt. Ein polygonaler Glaspavillon mit abgerundeten Kanten steht auf einem geradlinigen Sockelgeschoss. Jede Ebene hat unabhängige Außenflächen, die mit der Einrichtung korrespondieren. Vom Glaspavillon fällt der Blick auf zwei markante Bereiche: der erste, zum Berg gewandt, ist eine unbebaute private Zone, die den örtlichen Bauvorschriften entsprechend zwischen der Grundstücksgrenze und der Gebäuderückschlaglinie liegt. Der zweite ist ein Garten mit Blick auf den See. Auch von den Schlafzimmern aus fällt der Blick auf einen vom Gebäude und der Außenmauer umschlossenen Garten.

La topographie particulière du terrain a rendu nécessaire de répartir les pièces de cette villa sur deux niveaux. Le bâtiment se compose d'une structure en verre de plan polygonal arrondi aux angles, posée sur une base linéaire en béton. Chacun des deux niveaux se complète par des espaces extérieurs. Deux perspectives s'offrent au regard à partir de la structure en verre : la première, en direction de la colline, révèle une zone privée qui s'étend entre l'arrière du bâtiment et la limite du terrain et doit rester non bâtie conformément à la législation locale ; la seconde perspective s'ouvre sur le jardin et va jusqu'au lac voisin. Les fenêtres des chambres donnent quant à elles sur un autre jardin délimité par le bâtiment et le mur de clôture.

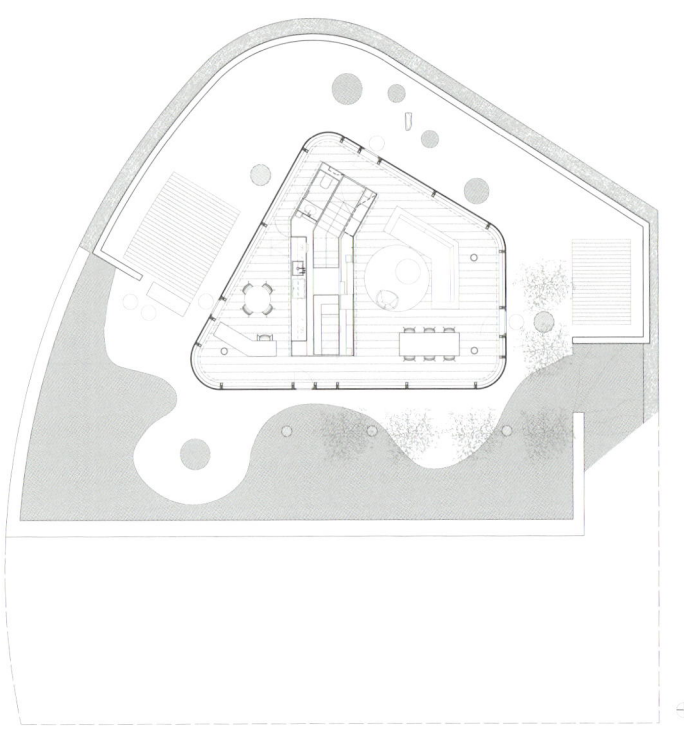

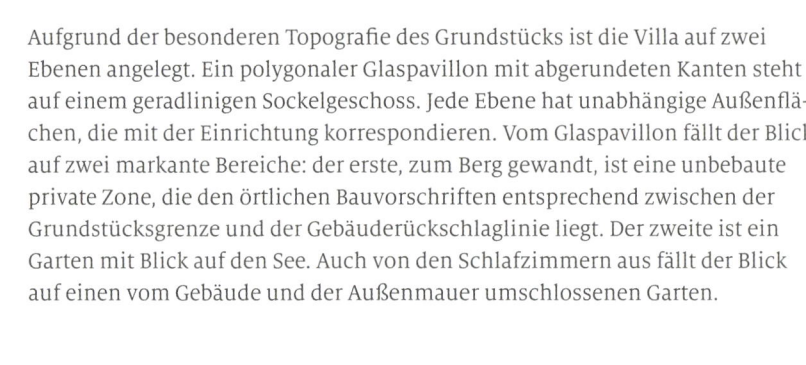

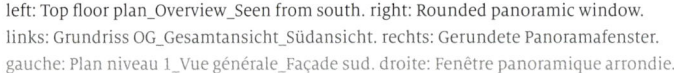

left: Top floor plan_Overview_Seen from south. right: Rounded panoramic window.
links: Grundriss OG_Gesamtansicht_Südansicht. rechts: Gerundete Panoramafenster.
gauche: Plan niveau 1_Vue générale_Façade sud. droite: Fenêtre panoramique arrondie.

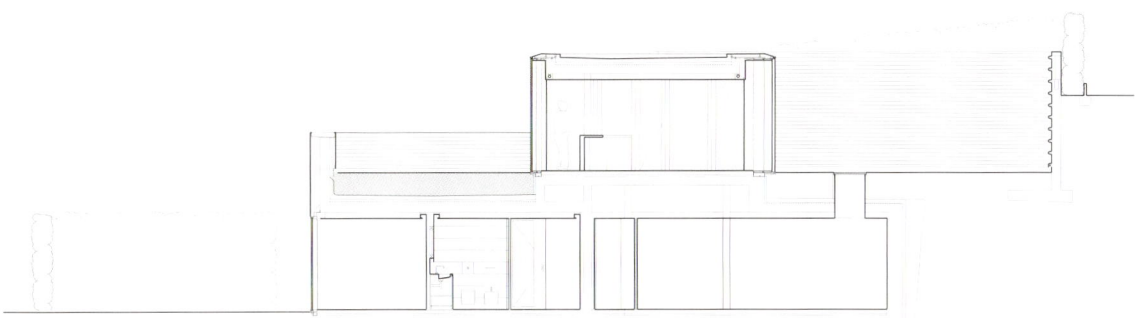

left: Outdoor area. right: Section_Living area_Bedroom_Dining area.
links: Außenbereich. rechts: Schnitt_Wohnbereich_Schlafzimmer_Essbereich.
gauche: Extérieur. droite: Vue en coupe_Séjour_Chambre_Salle à manger.

CÁCERES, SPAIN **HOME IN EXTREMADURA**

ARCHITECTS: ÁBATON ARCHITECTS
COMPLETION: 2010_**PROPERTY SIZE:** 50,000 M²
GROSS FLOOR AREA: 322 M²
PHOTOS: ÁBATON ARCHITECTURE AND BELEN IMAZ

Located in a privileged environment in the province of Cáceres, Spain, an abandoned stable was turned into a family home by completely renovating it in a way that was consistent and respectful of the environment. The position of the architecture was kept intact and the same materials were also used, though given the home's crumbling state the façade was rebuilt with a mix of cement and local stone. Inside, supporting walls were replaced by light metal pillars, the haylofts in the upper area were converted into bedrooms, and the enormous central lounge now serves various purposes. The result is a mix of modern cement and iron beams that coexist with well-worn stone, weather-beaten wood, and local stone.

Ein verlassener Stall, gelegen in der ursprünglichen Landschaft der spanischen Provinz Cáceres, wurde zum Familiendomizil umgestaltet. Die Komplettsanierung erfolgte im Hinblick auf Nachhaltigkeit und einen respektvollen Umgang mit der Natur. Die Ausrichtung wurde ebenso beibehalten wie die ursprünglichen Materialien, wobei die bröckelnde Fassade durch eine Mischung aus Zement und örtlichem Gestein stabilisiert wurde. Im Inneren ersetzen dezente Metallstützen die ehemaligen Stützmauern. Die Heuböden im Obergeschoss wurden zu Schlafzimmern umgebaut, während die großzügige zentrale Lounge verschiedene Funktionen erfüllt. Das Ergebnis ist eine Mischung aus den modernen Materialien Zement und Eisen in Koexistenz mit verwittertem Stein und Holz.

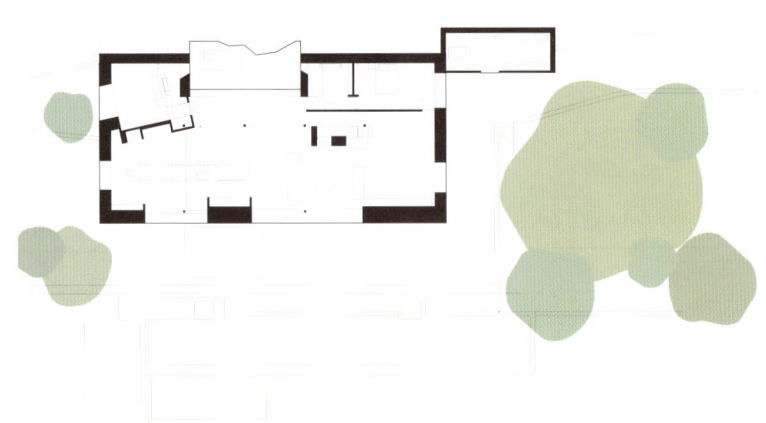

La tâche des architectes consistait à transformer en maison d'habitation une ancienne grange des environs de Cáceres, en Espagne, tout en respectant un site et un environnement de qualité exceptionnelle. Les volumes ont été laissés tels quels mais il a été nécessaire de reconstruire certaines parties en utilisant des matériaux traditionnels : le ciment et les pierres de la région. À l'intérieur, les architectes ont remplacé les murs de soutènement par des piliers métalliques, converti en chambres les anciens greniers à foin et aménagé un vaste espace central multifonctionnel. Avec pour résultat une synthèse harmonieuse entre ciment et acier d'une part, vieux bois et pierre locale d'autre part.

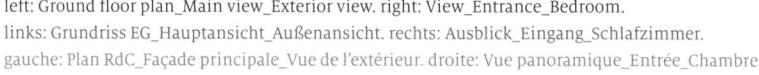

left: Ground floor plan_Main view_Exterior view. right: View_Entrance_Bedroom.
links: Grundriss EG_Hauptansicht_Außenansicht. rechts: Ausblick_Eingang_Schlafzimmer.
gauche: Plan RdC_Façade principale_Vue de l'extérieur. droite: Vue panoramique_Entrée_Chambre.

left: Dining area. right: Section_Stairs_Living area_Interior view.
links: Essbereich. rechts: Schnitt_Treppe_Wohnbereich_Innenansicht.
gauche: Salle à manger. droite: Vue en coupe_Escalier_Séjour_Vue de l'intérieur.

UITIKON, SWITZERLAND **HOUSE UITIKON**

ARCHITECTS: M3 ARCHITEKTEN
COMPLETION: 2012_**PROPERTY SIZE:** 937 M²
GROSS FLOOR AREA: 290 M²_**NUMBER OF ROOMS:** 7.5
PHOTOS: BRUNO HELBLING

This single-family home with a pool enjoys a very unique location with a wonderful view. The existing garage is incorporated into the general concept and the basement floor designed as an accessory apartment. Located at the level of the garden, exterior and interior spaces merge smoothly on the living area level. The top floor contains the bedrooms and bathroom areas. The building has a compact design from which it only deviates in the entrance area and the attic. The volumetric composition is supported by the understated color scheme of shades of grey and white and the use of different types of plastering.

Dieses Einfamilienhaus mit Pool ist an einem einmaligen Ort positioniert und verfügt über eine wunderbare Aussicht. Die bestehende Garage wird mit ins Gesamtkonzept integriert und das Untergeschoss als Einliegerwohnung konzipiert. Im Wohngeschoss, welches auf Gartenniveau liegt, fließen die Aussen- und Innenräume nahtlos zusammen. Das Obergeschoss beherbergt die Zimmer und die Nasszellen. Das Gebäude ist kompakt geplant und wird lediglich im Bereich der Eingänge und der Attika ausgeklinkt. Die volumetrische Komposition wird durch das dezente Farbkonzept in Weiß- und Grautönen sowie durch das Verwenden verschiedener Putzarten unterstützt.

Cette villa avec piscine offre une vue panoramique sur un village pittoresque et les Alpes. Elle intègre un garage et un appartement séparé au sous-sol. Les pièces de séjour de l'appartement principal, situées au niveau jardin, se caractérisent par un passage fluide de l'intérieur aux espaces extérieurs. Le dernier étage abrite les chambres et les salles de bains. L'ensemble du bâtiment forme un cube presque parfait, avec juste quelques décrochements au niveau de l'entrée et de l'attique. Le revêtement des façades, qui utilise plusieurs sortes d'enduits mais une palette limitée au blanc et quelques tons de gris, vient confirmer l'austérité de la composition volumétrique.

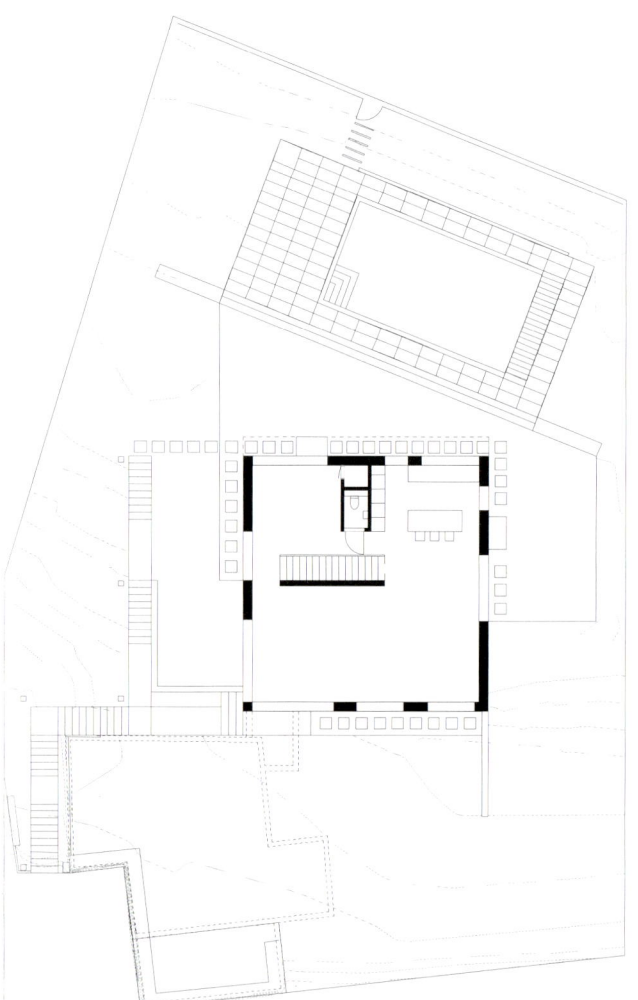

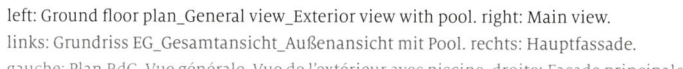

left: Ground floor plan_General view_Exterior view with pool. right: Main view.
links: Grundriss EG_Gesamtansicht_Außenansicht mit Pool. rechts: Hauptfassade.
gauche: Plan RdC_Vue générale_Vue de l'extérieur avec piscine. droite: Façade principale.

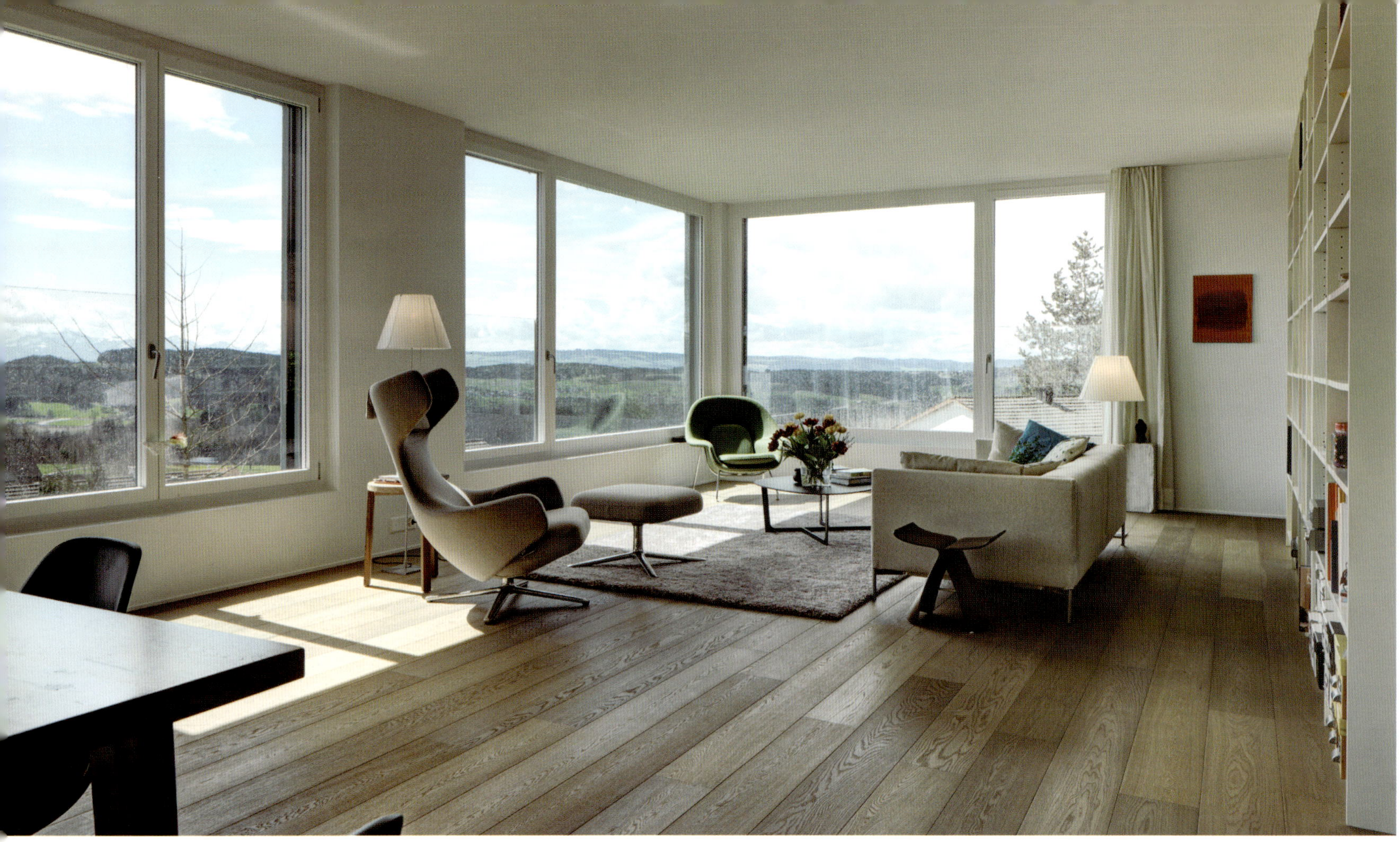

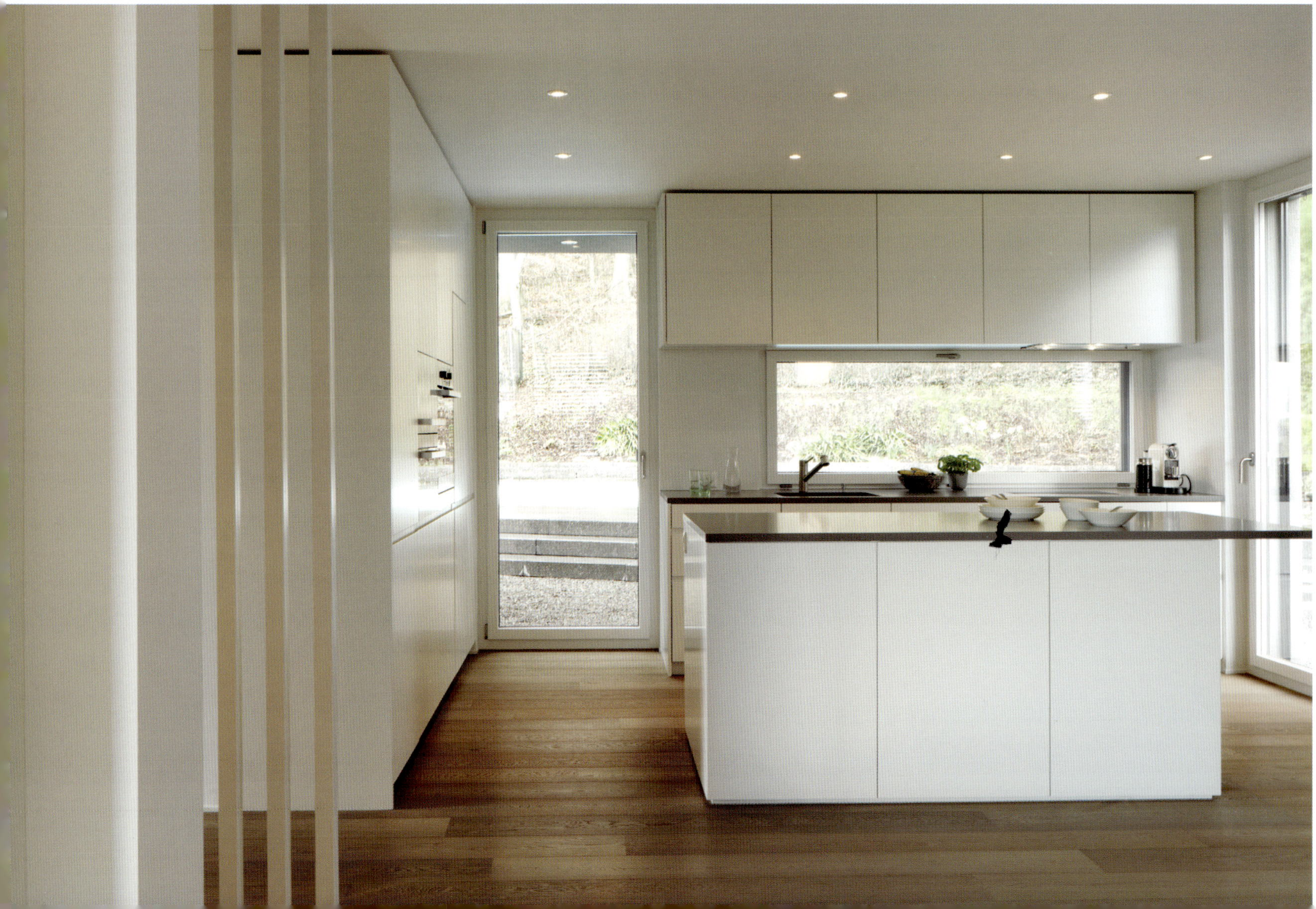

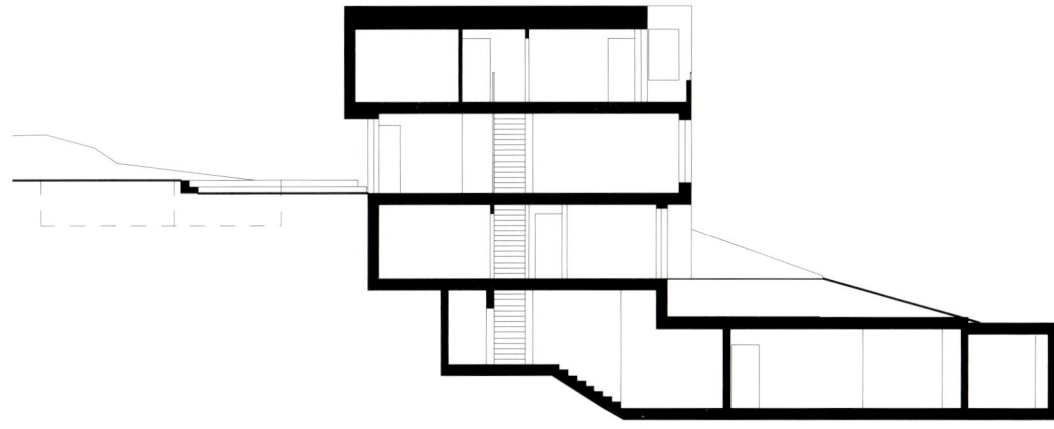

left: Living room_Kitchen. right: Section_Stairs_Bathroom_Room sequence.
links: Wohnzimmer_Küche. rechts: Schnitt_Treppe_Badezimmer_Raumsequenz.
gauche: Séjour_Cuisine. droite: Vue en coupe_Escalier_Salle de bains_Enfilade.

WIESBADEN, GERMANY **HOUSE S**

ARCHITECTS: CHRIST.CHRIST. ASSOCIATED ARCHITECTS
COMPLETION: 2011_**PROPERTY SIZE:** 873 M²
GROSS FLOOR AREA: 452 M²_**PHOTOS:** THOMAS HERRMANN

A bungalow-style home from the 1960s was completely restructured and renovated. The vastly projecting flat roof was complemented by three individual white structures that are only connected by a glass aisle. These new structures define different functional areas. One contains the master bedroom with a dressing room and bathroom. The other two serve as living area and offices for the two owners. Most walls and fitted elements were removed from the ground floor, allowing the living space to extend almost across the entire floor space. The open kitchen was placed in the center of this living area. This level also includes the children's bedrooms with a dressing room and bathroom.

Ein bungalowartiges Wohnhaus aus den 1960er Jahren wurde komplett umgebaut und saniert. Das weit auskragende Flachdach wurde durch drei einzelne weiße Baukörper ergänzt, welche lediglich durch einen Glasgang miteinander verbunden sind. Diese neuen Baukörper definieren unterschiedliche Frei- und Funktionsbereiche. In einem ist das Elternschlafzimmer mit Ankleide und Bad untergebracht. Die beiden anderen dienen als Wohn- und Arbeitszimmer für die Bauherrin und den Bauherrn. Das Erdgeschoss wurde größtenteils von bestehenden Wänden und Einbauten befreit, sodass der Wohnraum nahezu über die gesamte Geschossfläche reicht. Die offene Küche wurde inmitten des Wohnraums gestellt. Auf dieser Ebene befinden sich auch die Kinderzimmer mit Ankleide und Bad.

La tâche des architectes consistait ici à moderniser et remanier totalement un bungalow datant des années 1960. Trois volumes blancs reliés par un couloir vitré ont été construits sur le toit plat d'origine formant un large surplomb. Ces rajouts sont affectés à diverses fonctions : le premier abrite la chambre des parents, un vestiaire et une salle de bain, les deux autres le bureau du père et celui de la mère. Au rez-de-chaussée, les architectes ont supprimé pratiquement toutes les cloisons, de manière à créer une grande pièce de séjour s'organisant autour d'une cuisine ouverte. On trouve également à ce niveau les chambres des enfants, un second vestiaire et une seconde salle de bain.

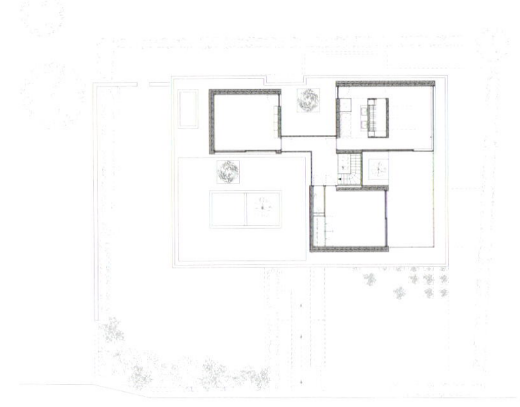

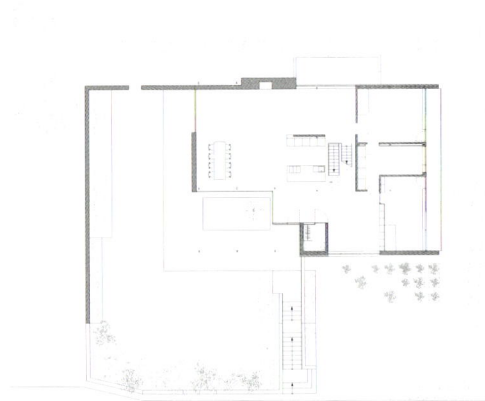

left: Top and ground floor plans_Roof terrace_Exterior view. right: Exterior views_Added floor.
links: Grundrisse OG und EG_Dachterrasse_Außenansicht. rechts: Außenansichten_Aufstockung.
gauche: Plan niveau 1 et RdC_Terrasse au toit_Vue de l'extérieur. droite: Vues de l'extérieurs_Étage supplémentaire.

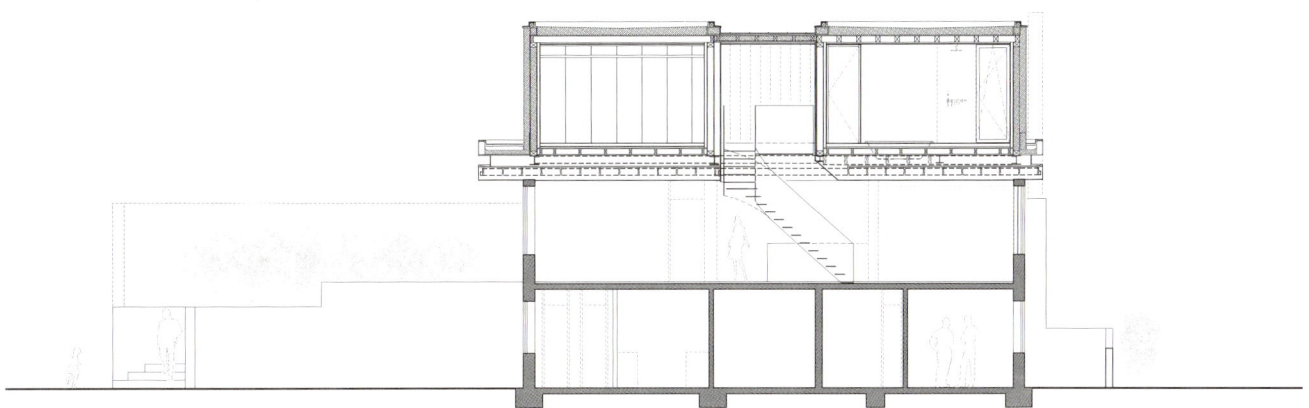

left: Bathroom. right: Section_Bedroom_Terrace_Top floor_Living and dining area.
links: Badezimmer. rechts: Schnitt_Schlafzimmer_Terrasse_Obergeschoss_Wohn- und Essbereich.
gauche: Salle de bains. droite: Vue en coupe_Chambre_Terrasse_Niveau 1_Séjour et salle à manger.

VERMONT, USA **CANTILEVER HOUSE**

ARCHITECTS: BIRDSEYE DESIGN
PRINCIPAL: BRIAN J. MAC, AIA_PROJECT MANAGER: JOE FISHER
COMPLETION: 2012_**PROPERTY SIZE:** 4,047 M²
GROSS FLOOR AREA: 186 M²_**NUMBER OF ROOMS:** 10
PHOTOS: WESTPHALEN PHOTOGRAPHY

The Cantilever House offers a modern interpretation of the traditional camp aesthetic while maintaining contextual sensitivity. Recessed into the existing hillside, the design of the house avoids excessive vertical massing while simultaneously creating a walk-out lower level adjacent to the lake. The private spaces are situated in the buried portion of the residence, allowing the open, communal spaces to flow directly into the shoreline through the large glass façade. Simple, orthogonal forms, shed roofs, and a minimalist material palette contribute to lessening the impact of the house on the waterfront landscape.

Das Cantilever House nimmt als moderne Interpretation traditioneller Camp-Ästhetik besondere Rücksicht auf den Kontext. Die Villa ist in die umgebende Hügellandschaft eingebettet, sodass sie in der Vertikalen weniger massiv wirkt. Gleichzeitig wurde ein direkter Zugang zum See geschaffen. Im unteren Teil befinden sich die Privaträume, während der offene Gemeinschaftsbereich durch eine großzügige Glasfassade zur Uferlinie hin ausläuft. Eine geradlinige Form-sprache, das Flachdach sowie die zurückhaltende Materialwahl minimieren die Wirkung des baulichen Eingriffs auf die Uferlandschaft.

Cette villa est une interprétation moderne du style « maison des bois ». Con-struite au bord d'un lac sur une berge en pente douce, elle évite la verticalité excessive et intègre une vaste terrasse qui fait face à la rive. Les chambres, semi-enterrées, sont à l'arrière, tandis que les espaces communs s'ouvrent largement sur l'extérieur au moyen de grandes baies vitrées offrant une vue panoramique sur le lac. Une forme orthogonale simple au possible, alliée à un toit à une pente et une palette de matériaux minimaliste, contribue à minimiser l'impact du bâtiment sur son environnement.

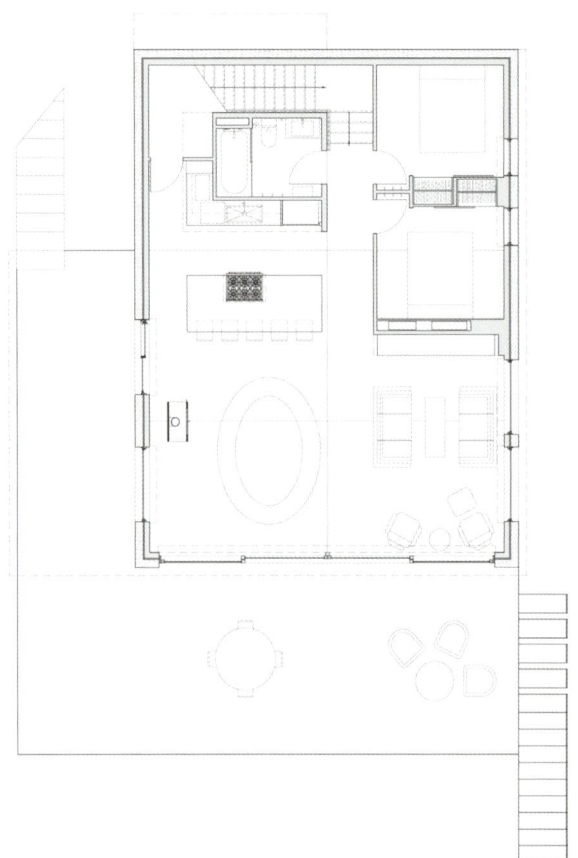

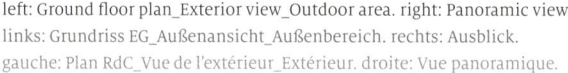

left: Ground floor plan_Exterior view_Outdoor area. right: Panoramic view.
links: Grundriss EG_Außenansicht_Außenbereich. rechts: Ausblick.
gauche: Plan RdC_Vue de l'extérieur_Extérieur. droite: Vue panoramique.

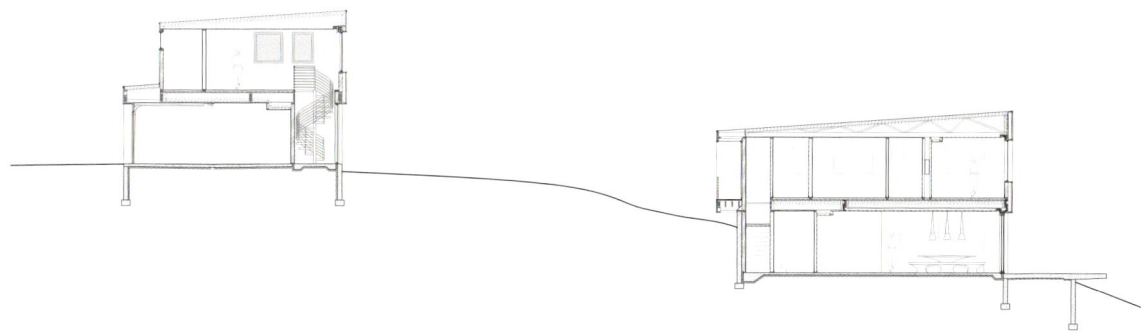

left: Residential level_Loggia. right: Section_General view_Studio_Kitchen.
links: Wohnebene_Loggia. rechts: Schnitt_Gesamtansicht_Studio_Küche.
gauche: Séjour_Loggia. droite: Vue en coupe_Vue générale_Studio_Cuisine.

STUTTGART, GERMANY   SINGLE FAMILY HOUSE AT MEDIAN HEIGHT

ARCHITECTS: BLOCHER BLOCHER PARTNERS
ARCHITECTURE AND DESIGN
COMPLETION: 2010_**PROPERTY SIZE:** 802 M²
GROSS FLOOR AREA: 1,600 M²
PHOTOS: BBP / NIKOLAUS KOLIUSIS

Simple, clearly structured, yet filled with a special atmosphere – natural materials and exposed concrete enter into a special symbiosis in this single family dwelling located at median height in Stuttgart. With its extensive glazing towards the south and the west, the terrace appears pleasantly understated. The same goes for the interior design whose Far Eastern accents exude peacefulness. Innovative, resource-saving building methods, targeted lighting and deliberately chosen design elements ensure highest living comfort. The daily life of the residents takes place on three levels plus the garage level. Created by a skilled gardener, the outdoor areas offer attractive retreats, even beyond the pool.

Schlicht, klar und doch atmosphärisch – natürliche Materialien und Sichtbeton gehen in diesem Einfamilienhaus in Stuttgarts Halbhöhenlage eine besondere Symbiose ein. Die Fassade erscheint mit ihrer großzügigen Verglasung nach Süden und Westen angenehm reduziert; genauso wie die Innenraum-Ausstattung, deren asiatische Akzente fernöstliche Ruhe verströmen. Innovative, ressourcenschonende Gebäudetechnik, gezielte Lichtführung und pointierte Gestaltungselemente sorgen für höchstes Wohnniveau. Das Leben der Bewohner spielt sich auf drei Etagen nebst Garagengeschoss ab, die von Gärtnerhand arrangierten Außenanlagen bieten reizvolle Rückzugsorte, nicht nur am Pool.

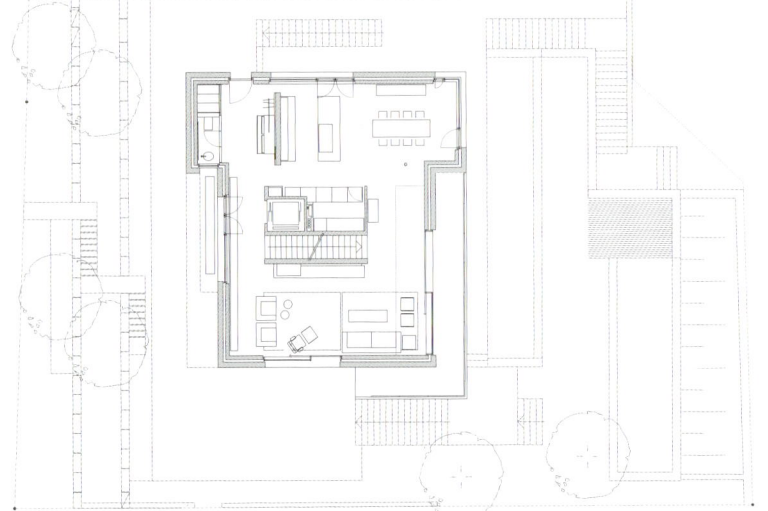

Des matériaux naturels s'allient au béton brut de coffrage pour conférer un charme indéniable à cette villa d'un style clair et sobre. Les façades sud et ouest sont très largement vitrées et l'intérieur se caractérise par un minimalisme dans lequel le mobilier asiatique irradie la sérénité. Un éclairage judicieux, des éléments décoratifs soigneusement choisis et une domotique novatrice conçue pour économiser les ressources contribuent à la haute qualité de vie qu'on trouve dans ce bâtiment sur trois niveaux, dont un réservé au garage. La piscine et les espaces extérieurs entretenus par un jardinier offrent par ailleurs de multiples possibilités de relaxation.

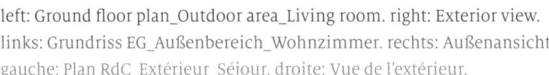

left: Ground floor plan_Outdoor area_Living room. right: Exterior view.
links: Grundriss EG_Außenbereich_Wohnzimmer. rechts: Außenansicht.
gauche: Plan RdC_Extérieur_Séjour. droite: Vue de l'extérieur.

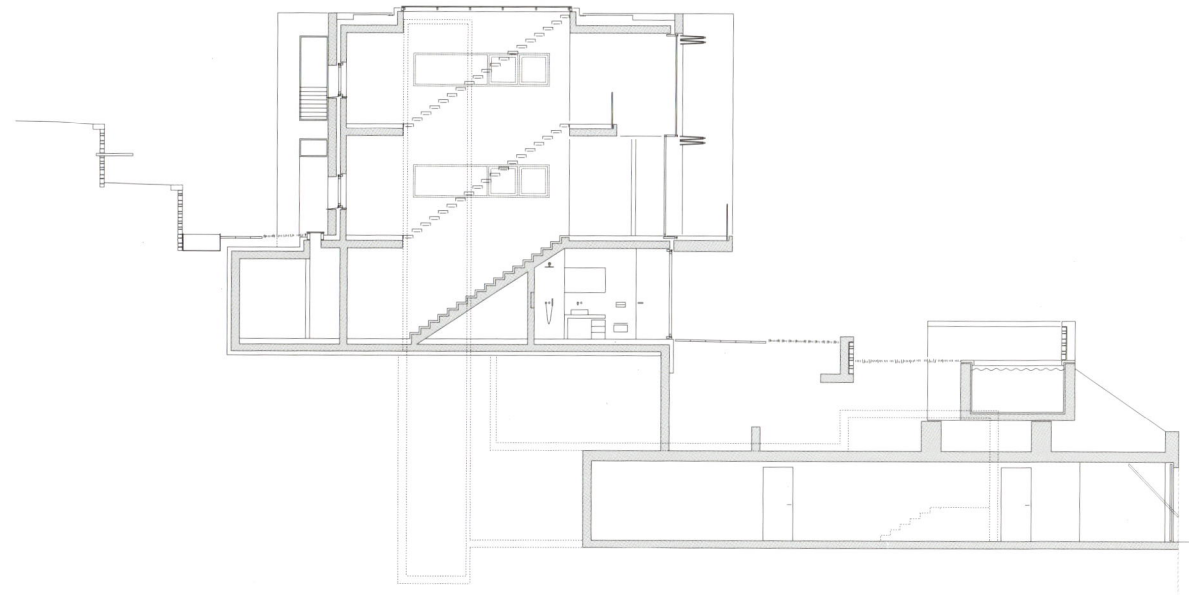

left: Living room. right: Section AA_Terrace_Kitchen_Living room.
links: Wohnzimmer. rechts: Schnitt AA_Terrasse_Küche_Wohnzimmer.
gauche: Salle de séjour. droite: Vue en coupe AA_Terrasse_Cuisine_Séjour.

TOKYO, JAPAN **LIK HOUSE**

ARCHITECTS: SATORU HIROTA ARCHITECTS
COMPLETION: 2010_**PROPERTY SIZE:** 295 M²
GROSS FLOOR AREA: 129 M²_**NUMBER OF ROOMS:** 5
PHOTOS: SATORU HIROTA ARCHITECTS

A single family dwelling within a quiet residential area of a business district in Tokyo, Japan. It is designed as three tunnel-like volumes wrapped around an outdoor courtyard, with each room linked to the next within the continuous volume of this single floor house. The building is surrounded by stores and medium-rise buildings, therefore its low profile structure is concealed by the built environment, adding a sense of privacy and creating a resort-like atmosphere. Thin exterior walls infuse each space with a soft light, creating a link between the interior and exterior. Floor-to-ceiling ribbon windows delineate the internal spaces, providing the rooms with views of the bamboo garden and outdoor greenery.

Das Einfamilienhaus liegt in ruhiger Wohnlage in einem Tokioter Geschäftsviertel. Es setzt sich aus drei tunnelartigen Baukörpern zusammen, die den Innenhof einrahmen. Die Räume des einstöckigen Baus reihen sich in kontinuierlicher Abfolge aneinander. Umgeben von Geschäften und mittelhohen Gebäuden taucht die niedrige Villa geradezu im baulichen Umfeld ab, was ein Gefühl von Privatheit vermittelt und eine erholsame Atmosphäre schafft. Transparente Außenwände lassen weiches Licht in alle Räume und stellen so eine Verbindung zwischen Innen und Außen her. Die bodentiefen Fensterbänder definieren die Innenräume und öffnen Ausblicke in den Bambusgarten sowie über die Grünflächen.

Cette maison construite dans une zone tranquille d'un quartier d'affaires de Tokyo se compose de trois « tunnels » disposés de manière à former une cour intérieure. Toutes les pièces s'y trouvent en enfilade sur un même niveau. Entouré de boutiques et d'immeubles relativement hauts, ce bâtiment se fait discret, ce qui lui confère une atmosphère intime et reposante. Des murs entièrement transparents assurent un bon éclairage naturel de toutes les pièces et ouvrent des perspectives sur une pelouse et des bambous, réalisant ainsi une interconnexion entre l'intérieur et l'extérieur.

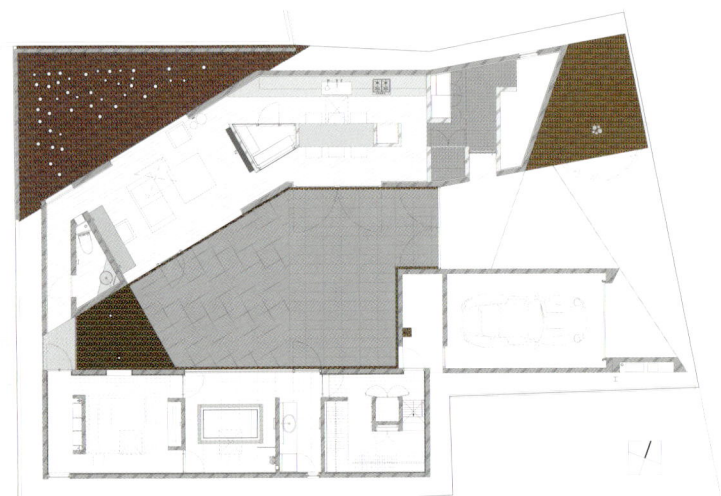

left: Ground floor plan_Front courtyard_Street view. right: Outdoor area_Living area_Bathroom.
links: Grundriss EG_Vorhof_Straßenansicht. rechts: Außenbereich_Wohnbereich_Bad.
gauche: Plan RdC_Cour_Vue de la rue. droite: Extérieur_Séjour_Salle de bains.

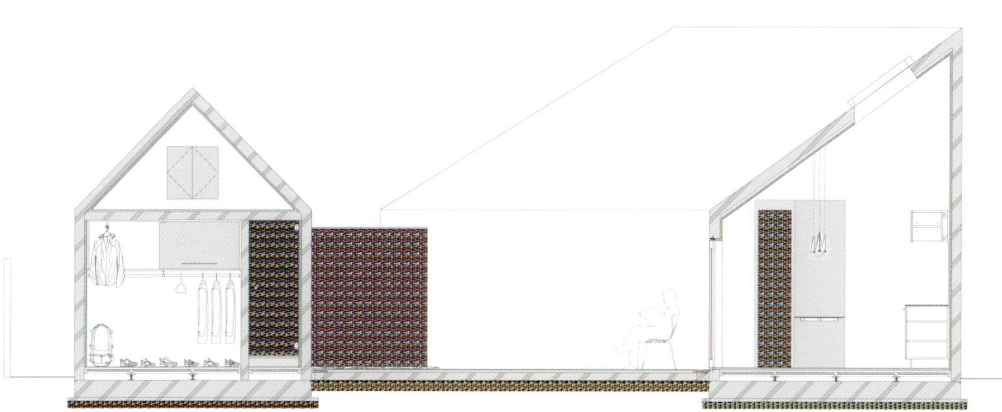

left: Room sequence. right: Section_Dining area_Front courtyard_Living room.
links: Raumsequenz. rechts: Schnitt_Essbereich_Vorhof_Wohnraum.
gauche: Enfilade. droite: Vue en coupe_Salle à manger_Cour_Séjour.

WÜRMTAL, GERMANY **ROCK ON A SLOPE**

ARCHITECTS: UNTERLANDSTÄTTNER ARCHITEKTEN
COMPLETION: 2010
GROSS FLOOR AREA: 470 M²_**NUMBER OF ROOMS:** 14
PHOTOS: MICHAEL HEINRICH (136–138, 139 L.),
CHRISTINE DEMPF (139 R.)

The landmarked villa of the year 1890 was comprehensively renovated. The extensive interventions of recent years that were contrary to the preservation of monuments were removed and the former room structure restored. The new front section made of exposed concrete was implemented with a cast surface finish resembling the rock and thus acting as a link between the landscape and the plinth of the historic building. The modern architecture of the new building is interlinked with the historic building substance and the natural landscape. Cavernous incisions in the volume of the constructed rock define the new building and the illumination scheme.

Die denkmalgeschützte Villa aus dem Jahre 1890 wurde von Grund auf saniert. Die umfangreichen, nicht denkmalgerechten Eingriffe der letzten Jahrzehnte wurden zurückgebaut und die überlieferte Raumstruktur wiederhergestellt. Der vorgelagerte Neubau aus Sichtbeton wurde mit gespitzter Oberfläche ausgeführt und so als gebaute Felswand zum Vermittler zwischen Landschaftsraum und Sockel des historischen Gebäudes. Die moderne Architektur des Neubaus verzahnt sich mit der historischen Bausubstanz und der natürlichen Landschaft. Höhlenartige Einschnitte im Volumen der gebauten Felswand prägen den Neubau und die Belichtung.

Les architectes étaient chargés de la rénovation totale de cette villa construite en 1890 et classée monument historique. Ils ont tout d'abord supprimé les éléments rajoutés ces dernières décennies de manière à restituer au bâtiment son aspect d'origine. Ils ont ensuite rajouté un sous-sol dont la façade en béton traitée de manière à évoquer la roche sert d'intermédiaire entre le bâtiment et le parc, créant ainsi un ensemble harmonieux. Les ouvertures de ce rajout moderne, qui assurent un bon éclairage naturel du sous-sol, ne sont pas sans évoquer des grottes.

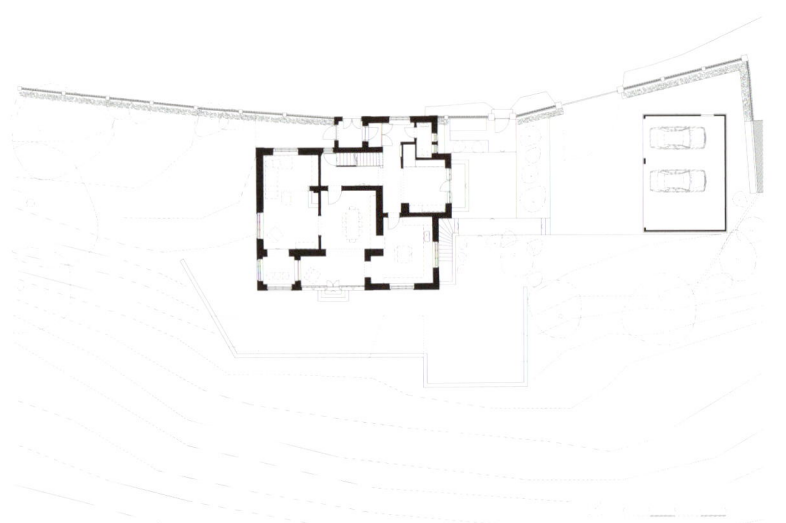

left: Ground floor plan_Seen from south_Garage. right: Hall_Entrance area_Loggia.
links: Grundriss EG_Südansicht_Garage. rechts: Blick aus dem Neubau_Blick aus der Sauna_Höhlenartiger Einschnitt. gauche: Plan RdC_Façade sud_Garage. droite: Nef_Entrée_Loggia.

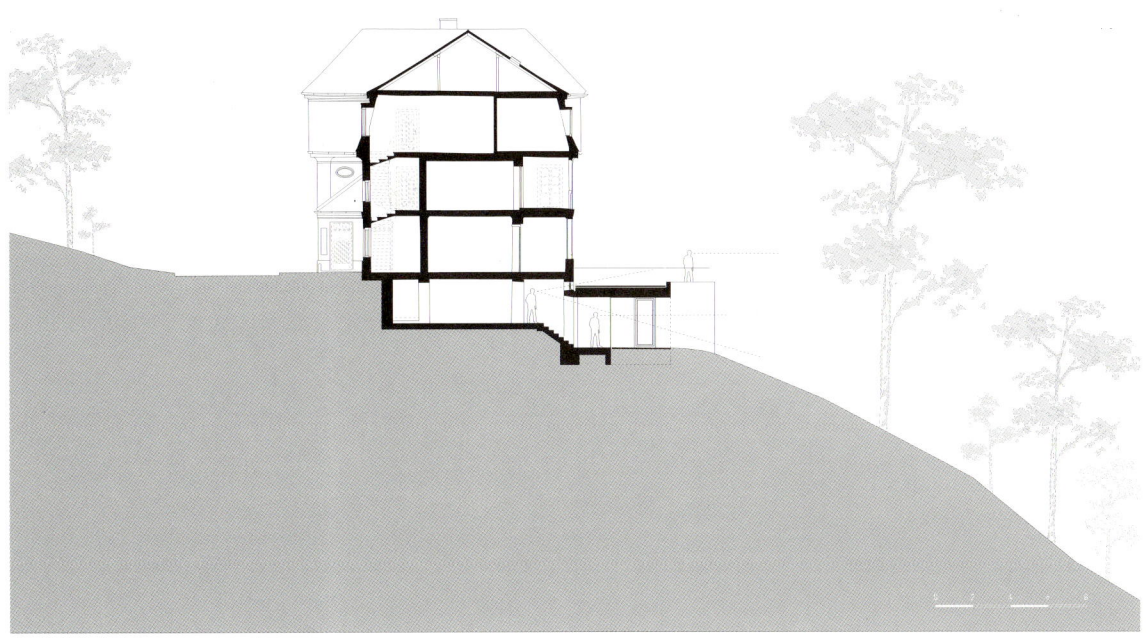

left: Detail of the façade. right: Section_Loggia_Dining area_Kitchen.
links: Fassadendetail. rechts: Schnitt_Höhlenartiger Einschnitt_Eingangsbereich_Essbereich.
gauche: Détail de la façade. droite: Vue en coupe_Loggia_Salle à manger_Cuisine.

IBIZA, SPAIN **DUPLI DOS**

ARCHITECTS: JUMA ARCHITECTS
COMPLETION: 2010_**PROPERTY SIZE:** 258 M²
GROSS FLOOR AREA: 258 M²_**NUMBER OF ROOMS:** 4
PHOTOS: VERNE

Two separate houses were merged to create this new villa, which directly faces south, giving it plenty of sun all day. The architects searched for a uniform design that would give the impression that it had always been a single building, merging the two buildings by a wooden construction and steel porches. The two former duplexes were located on different levels. This was used as a positive element to add momentum to the design by creating different zones on the terrace and inside, for example for the kitchen and living room. The two external staircases were demolished and replaced by an internal staircase. This created a large outdoor space with a vastly expanded view. The steel canopies and wooden sundecks overlap both houses to add to the visual fusion of the entire structure.

Zwei separate Apartments wurden zu dieser neuen Villa zusammengelegt, die dank Südlage reichlich Sonne genießt. Das Design sollte den Eindruck erwecken, es habe sich schon immer um ein einziges Gebäude gehandelt. So verbanden die Architekten die Baukörper über Holz- und Stahlkonstruktionen. Dass die Haushälften auf unterschiedlicher Höhe liegen, ging als positives Element in den Entwurf ein: Die Dynamik wurde in unterschiedliche Zonen übersetzt, auf der Terrasse wie auch im Innern, beispielsweise zwischen Küche und Wohnzimmer. Die beiden Außentreppen ersetzt nun ein innen liegendes Treppenhaus. So entstand ein großzügiger Außenbereich mit Panoramablick. Die Vordächer aus Holz und Stahl erstrecken sich über beide Haushälften und tragen zur Verschmelzung bei.

Le projet consistait ici à réunir deux villas en duplex orientées au sud et baignées de lumière tout au long de la journée. Afin de donner l'impression que ces deux unités distinctes n'en avaient jamais formé qu'une seule, les architectes les ont unifiées à l'aide d'une pergola en bois et de structures métalliques. Les différences de niveaux entre les constructions d'origine ont été utilisées pour dynamiser l'espace : on les retrouve sur la terrasse comme à l'intérieur, notamment entre la cuisine et le séjour. Les architectes ont également remplacé les deux escaliers extérieurs par un seul escalier intérieur, augmentant ainsi la surface de la terrasse d'où l'on bénéficie d'une vue panoramique sur la mer.

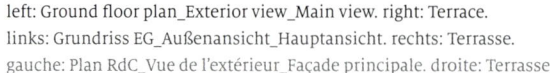

left: Ground floor plan_Exterior view_Main view. right: Terrace.
links: Grundriss EG_Außenansicht_Hauptansicht. rechts: Terrasse.
gauche: Plan RdC_Vue de l'extérieur_Façade principale. droite: Terrasse.

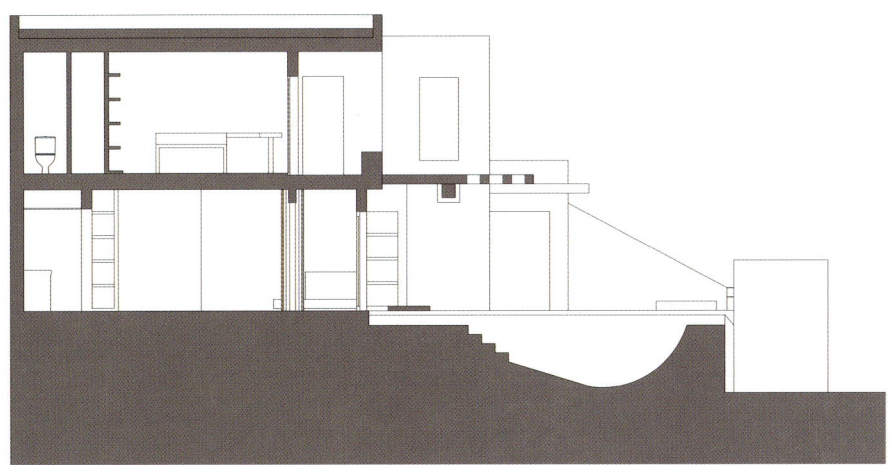

left: Pool. right: Section_Panorama_Bedroom_Living area.
links: Pool. rechts: Schnitt_Panorama_Schlafzimmer_Wohnbereich.
gauche: Piscine extérieure. droite: Vue en coupe_Panorama_Chambre_Séjour.

WAIBLINGEN, GERMANY **GOLDEN GATE**

ARCHITECTS: ARCHITEKTEN LEE + MIR
COMPLETION: 2010_**PROPERTY SIZE:** 505 M²
GROSS FLOOR AREA: 530 M²_**NUMBER OF ROOMS:** 9
PHOTOS: CHRISTINA KRATZENBERG

Located on a slope on the edge of a former stone quarry, the typical gabled roof typology of this villa was altered by chamfered window incisions. The "gold" cladding that includes functional elements such as garage and entrance doors is a key design element on the entrance side. The garden level contains the wellness area, the terrace, as well as children's and guest bedrooms. The entrance level houses the open cooking, dining, and living area with associated terraces. A one-way mirror creates a special connection between the classic car garage and the living area. The attic floor, where the parent's area is located, is connected to the living room via an air space.

In Hanglage, am Rande eines ehemaligen Steinbruchs, liegt diese Villa bei der die klassische Satteldach-Typologie durch schräge Fenstereinschnitte verfremdet wurde. Gestalterisches Element auf der Zugangsseite ist die Verkleidung aus „goldenem" Plattenmaterial, in der Funktionen wie Garagentore und Türen zusammengefasst sind. Auf der Gartenebene befinden sich der Wellnessbereich, die Terrasse sowie die Kinder- und das Gästezimmer. Im Eingangsgeschoss erschließt sich der offene Koch-, Ess-, und Wohnbereich mit angeschlossener Terrasse und die Garagen. Eine Spionglasscheibe schafft eine besondere Verbindung zwischen Oldtimergarage und dem Wohnbereich. Das Dachgeschoss, in dem sich der Elternbereich befindet, ist über einen Luftraum mit dem Wohnzimmer verbunden.

Bien que couverte par un toit à deux pentes conventionnel, cette villa construite sur un terrain incliné se singularise par la forme inhabituelle de ses fenêtres. Du côté de la rue, l'élément décoratif principal est le revêtement « doré » de la porte d'entrée et de la porte du garage. Derrière l'entrée s'ouvre un grand espace qui sert de cuisine/séjour/salle à manger et donne sur une terrasse côté jardin. On trouve également ici un grand miroir sans tain offrant une vue sur le garage des voitures anciennes. Toujours du même côté, mais au niveau inférieur, l'espace bien-être ainsi que la chambre d'amis et la chambre des enfants se prolongent par une seconde terrasse. Un espace sur deux niveaux relie la grande pièce du rez-de-chaussée aux combles aménagées, où se trouve la chambre et la salle de bain des parents.

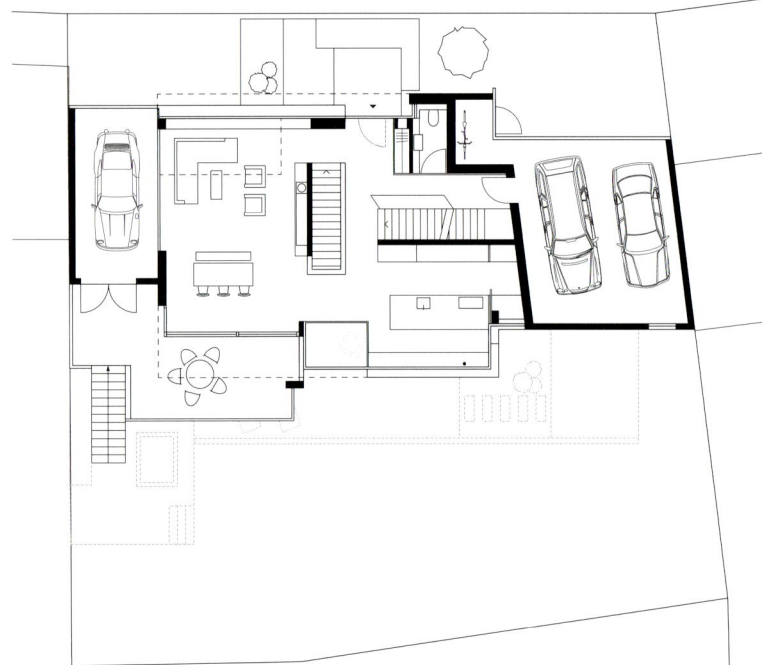

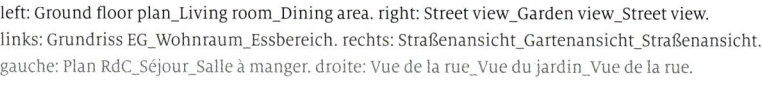
left: Ground floor plan_Living room_Dining area. right: Street view_Garden view_Street view.
links: Grundriss EG_Wohnraum_Essbereich. rechts: Straßenansicht_Gartenansicht_Straßenansicht.
gauche: Plan RdC_Séjour_Salle à manger. droite: Vue de la rue_Vue du jardin_Vue de la rue.

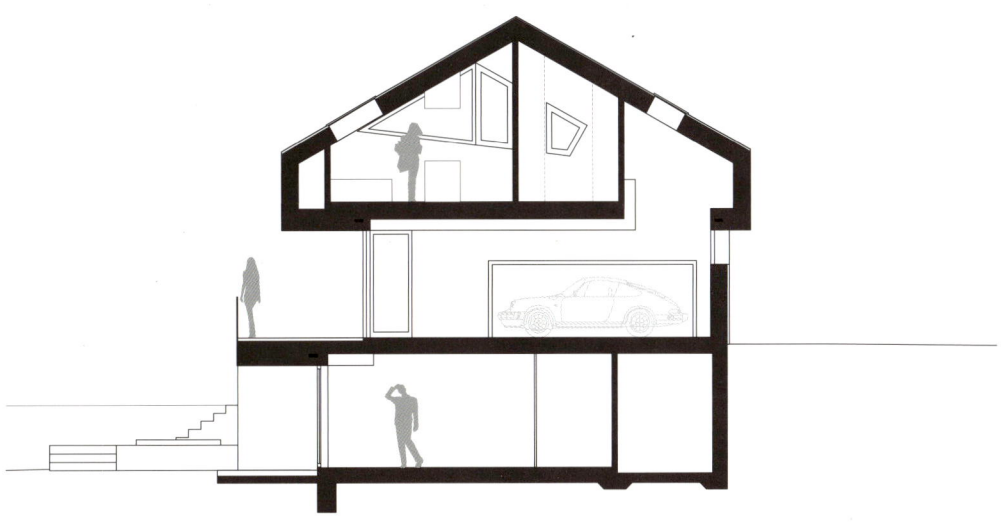

left: Kitchen_Vintage car one-way mirror on and off. right: Section_Bathroom_Stairs.
links: Küche_Spionspiegel Oldtimer aus_an. rechts: Schnitt_Bad_Treppe.
gauche: Cuisine_Vitre sans tain. droite: Vue en coupe_Salle de bains_Escalier.

WOLFURT, AUSTRIA **HOUSE A**

ARCHITECTS: HAMMER PFEIFFER ARCHITEKTEN
COMPLETION: 2011_**PROPERTY SIZE:** 950 M²
GROSS FLOOR AREA: 395 M²_**PHOTOS:** ADOLF BEREUTER

The house is a compact, two-floor structure with a distinctive tented roof. Large windows coupled with a building skin made of large fiber cement slabs for walls and ceiling, as well as building-integrated Photovoltaic dominate its appearance. Inside, on the ground floor an open living room, which is divided into cooking, dining and living space around the large centralized clay oven, opens up towards the swimming pond. The top floor is reserved for the bedrooms. Intersecting air spaces from the ground floor to the attic create fascinating views across all levels of the building that combine with the noble surface materials to create a unique room atmosphere.

Das Haus präsentiert sich als kompakter, zweigeschossiger Baukörper mit markantem Zeltdach. Großformatige Fenster, eine Gebäudehülle aus großflächigen Faserzementplatten für Wand und Dach, sowie eine gebäudeintegrierte Photovoltaikanlage prägen das äußere Erscheinungsbild. Im Innenraum befindet sich ebenerdig ein offener Wohnraum, der sich um den zentralen Lehmofen in Koch, Ess- und Wohnbereich gliedert. Das Obergeschoss ist den Schlafräumen vorbehalten. Sich verschränkende Lufträume vom Erdgeschoss bis in den Dachraum ermöglichen spannungsvolle Sichtbeziehungen über alle Ebenen des Gebäudes, die – zusammen mit den edlen Oberflächen – den Raumeindruck prägen.

Cette maison sur deux niveaux se présente sous la forme d'un bâtiment compact couvert par un toit à quatre pentes. Elle se caractérise à l'extérieur par de grandes fenêtres, l'utilisation de panneaux de fibrociment pour le revêtement des murs et la couverture du toit et le photovoltaïque intégré. Au rez-de-chaussée se trouve un grand espace cuisine/séjour/salle à manger pourvu d'une cheminée en terre glaise et donnant sur la piscine. Le premier étage est quant à lui réservé aux chambres. Des revêtements muraux de haute qualité et divers puits de lumière établissant un lien visuel entre les différents niveaux confèrent à la décoration intérieure un charme particulier.

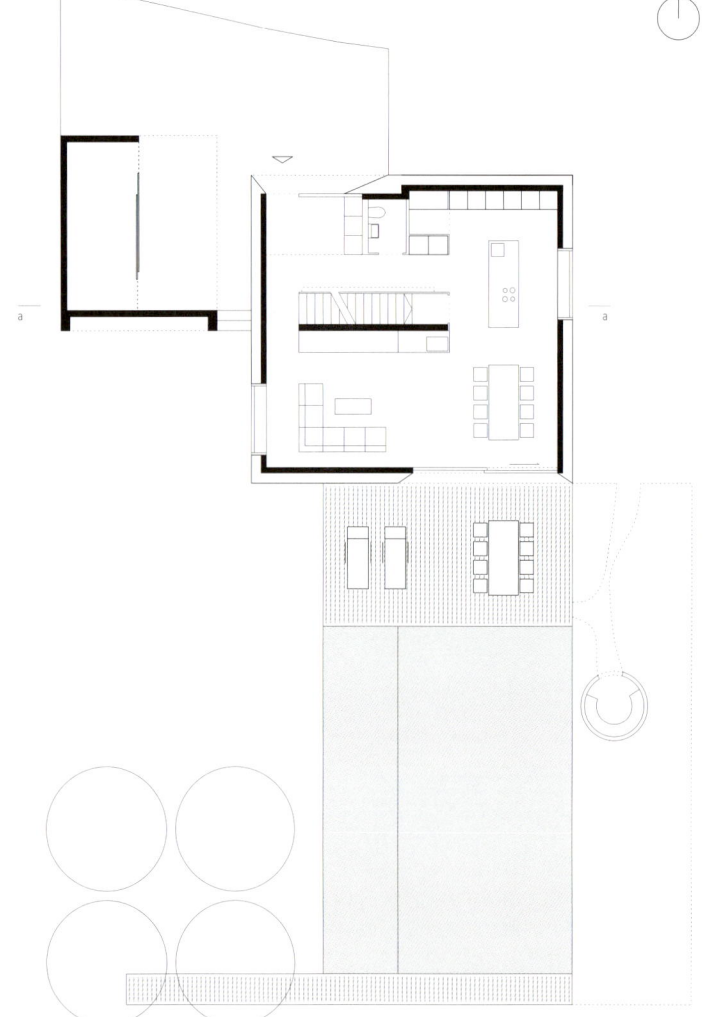

left: Ground floor plan_Seen from west and north. right: Seen from south_Living room_Seen from south-west. links: Grundriss EG_West- und Nordansicht. rechts: Südansicht_Wohnraum_Südwestansicht. gauche: Plan RdC_Façade ouest et nord. droite: Façade sud_Séjour_Façade sud-ouest.

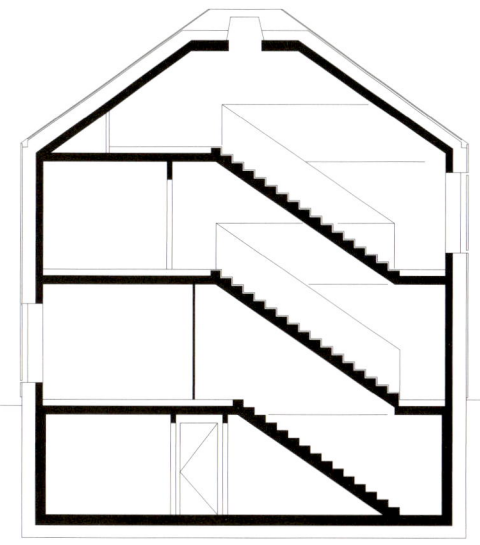

left: Stairs. right: Section_Living area_Dining area_Skylight.
links: Treppe. rechts: Schnitt_Wohnbereich_Essbereich_Oberlicht.
gauche: Escalier. droite: Vue en coupe_Séjour_Salle à manger_Éclairage zénithal.

TORRELODONES, MADRID, SPAIN **CASA PITCH**

ARCHITECTS: IÑAQUI CARNICERO ARCHITECTURE OFFICE
COMPLETION: 2009_**PROPERTY SIZE:** 610 M²
GROSS FLOOR AREA: 240 M²_**NUMBER OF ROOMS:** 4
PHOTOS: IÑAQUI CARNICERO (152,153,155), EUGENI PONS (154)

The design of these two semi detached houses is very unconventional. Although the program for both houses is identical, the layout is not symmetrical. It meets the client's needs, but can also be transformed into a single house for future use. The house denies its surroundings and the abrupt topography of the site by delicately leaning on the rocks with a large horizontal plane that defines the footprint of the building. The floor of this noble plane is covered by white calcareous stone. The house is organized in two independent sections. The bottom level includes the service area and the car park, while the top level includes the living area of the house. The entrance to the house is between these two different worlds via an almost hidden stair positioned around a huge rock.

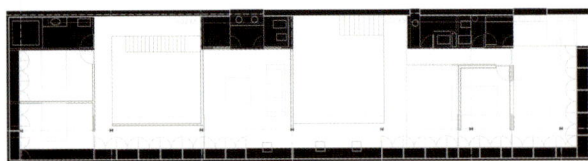

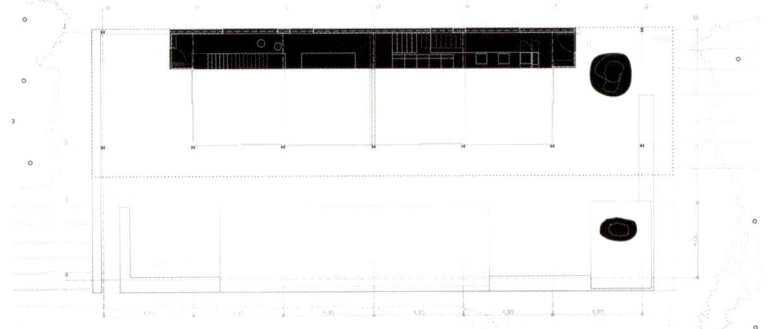
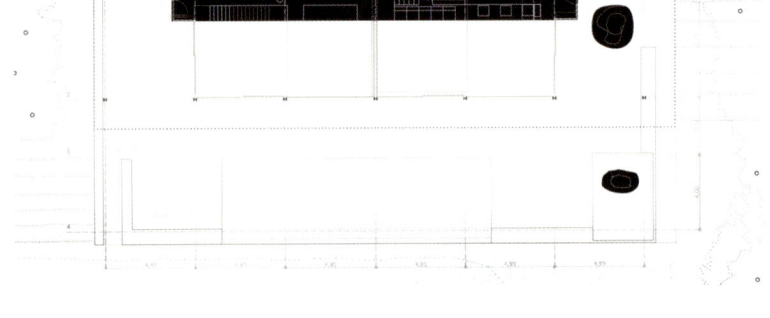

Der Entwurf dieser Doppelhaushälften ist recht unkonventionell. Obwohl die Funktionen beider Hälften identisch sind, ist der Grundriss nicht symmetrisch. Er wird den Bedürfnissen des Bauherrn gerecht und kann bei Bedarf in ein Einfamilienhaus transformiert werden. Die Villa hebt sich deutlich von der Umgebung und der schroffen Topografie des Grundstücks ab. Ein langer Riegel schmiegt sich an die Felsen und definiert die Grundfläche. Das großzügige Stockwerk ist mit weißem Kalkstein verkleidet. Die Villa ist in zwei unabhängige Sektionen unterteilt. Unten befinden sich Haustechnik und Großgarage, während der Wohnbereich im Obergeschoss liegt. Der Zugang erfolgt zwischen den beiden Ebenen über eine nahezu verborgene Treppe, die sich um einen großen Felsen windet.

Cette villa rassemblant deux logements est d'un style parfaitement inhabituel du fait de son asymétrie. L'ensemble répond toutefois aux instructions du maître d'ouvrage, qui souhaite pouvoir regrouper les deux unités s'il l'estime un jour nécessaire. Faisant fi de son environnement et de la topographie du terrain, le bâtiment repose délicatement sur des rochers avec un volume horizontal qui détermine l'empreinte de la construction sur le terrain. Cet « étage noble » est pourvu d'un revêtement en plaques de calcaire blanches. Les pièces s'agencent sur deux niveaux indépendants l'un de l'autre : garage et locaux techniques en bas, pièces de séjour au-dessus. L'accès à ces deux univers radicalement différents se fait par un escalier presque invisible positionné près d'un gros rocher.

left: Top and ground floor plans_Exterior view_Living area. right: Pool_Exterior view.
links: Grundrisse OG und EG_Wohnbereich. rechts: Pool_Außenansicht.
gauche: Plan niveau 1 et RdC_Vue de l'extérieur_Séjour. droite: Piscine extérieure_Vue de l'extérieur.

left: Living area. right: Section_Living area_Terrace.
links: Wohnbereich. rechts: Schnitt_Wohnbereich_Terrasse.
gauche: Séjour. droite: Vue en coupe_Séjour_Terrasse.

BERLIN, GERMANY **VILLA AT FICHTENBERG**

ARCHITECTS: OLFEARCHITEKTUR
H.-H. OLFE & R. OLFE-SCHLOTHAUER
COMPLETION: 2011_**PROPERTY SIZE:** 1,100 M²
GROSS FLOOR AREA: 585 M²_**NUMBER OF ROOMS:** 6
PHOTOS: OLFEARCHITEKTUR

The close association of vivid urbanity and quiet suburb with Berlin's Fichtenberg district was the basis for merging the interior and exterior spaces. The opening of the L-shaped structure towards the slope with expansive views, the large window panes and strict horizontality, which are all characteristics of Classical Modernity, all aimed at this single purpose. Light permeates all. All paths meet at the apex of the axes. This is where the staircase is located whose skylight illuminates the building deep into the areas that are away from the sun. Sun-flooded rooms alternate with well-dosed light accents. Curved softly shaped fitted elements break up the peaceful orthogonal room concept.

Die enge Verbindung von lebhafter Urbanität und ruhiger Vorstadtatmosphäre des Berliner Fichtenbergs erzeugte die Verschmelzung von Innen- und Außenraum. Die Öffnung des L-förmigen Baukörpers zum Hang mit weiten Ausblicken, große Fensterflächen und strikte Horizontalität, alles charakteristische Elemente der Klassischen Moderne, sind auf diesen einen Zweck hin ausgerichtet. Überall ist Licht. Im Scheitelpunkt der Achsen treffen sich die Wege. Hier befindet sich das Treppenhaus, dessen Oberlicht den Baukörper bis tief in die der Sonne abgewandten Bereiche beleuchtet. Sonnendurchflutete Räume wechseln sich mit Räumen mit wohldosierten Lichtakzenten ab. Geschwungene, weich geformte Einbauten durchbrechen das Ruhe und Gelassenheit spendende orthogonale Raumkonzept.

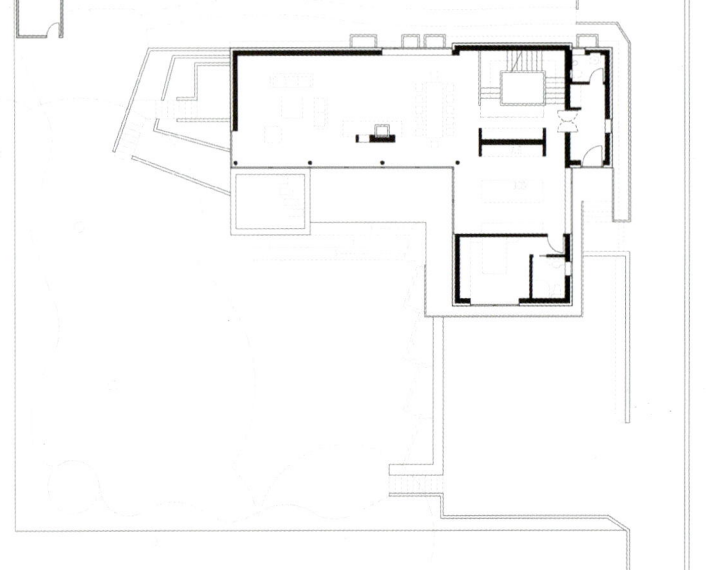

Construite sur la colline de Fichtenberg, un quartier de Berlin qui allie la tranquillité des zones périphériques aux avantages de la proximité d'un grand centre urbain, cette villa réalise également une synthèse entre intimité et ouverture sur l'extérieur. Elle reprend à cette fin plusieurs caractéristiques de l'architecture moderne : plan en « L », stricte horizontalité et bandes de fenêtres qui offrent des vues panoramiques sur le jardin et inondent l'intérieur de lumière. À l'intersection des deux barres du « L » se trouve un escalier pourvu d'un éclairage zénithal, de sorte que la lumière naturelle parvient jusque dans les pièces orientées au nord. Divers éléments aux formes douces et arrondies forment contraste dans ces intérieurs caractérisés par une ambiance sereine et décontractée.

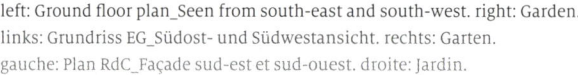

left: Ground floor plan_Seen from south-east and south-west. right: Garden.
links: Grundriss EG_Südost- und Südwestansicht. rechts: Garten.
gauche: Plan RdC_Façade sud-est et sud-ouest. droite: Jardin.

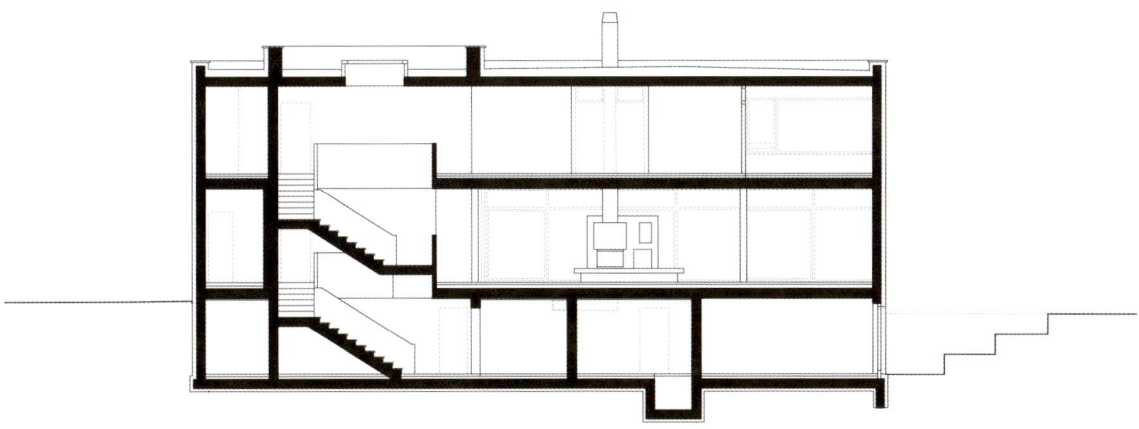

left: Stairs. right: Section_Wellness area_ Bedroom_Guest bathroom.
links: Treppe. rechts: Schnitt_Wellnessbereich_Schlafzimmer_Gästebad.
gauche: Escalier. droite: Vue en coupe_Espace bien-être_Chambre_Seconde salle de bains.

HITZENDORF, AUSTRIA **HOUSE AT STEINBERG**

ARCHITECTS: HOPE OF GLORY - HOG ARCHITEKTUR
COMPLETION: 2012_**PROPERTY SIZE:** 2,741 M²
GROSS FLOOR AREA: 306 M²_**NUMBER OF ROOMS:** 5
PHOTOS: WOLFGANG SILVERI

House Oberberg is the transformation of a traditional wine cellar used for agricultural purposes in this fruit and wine-growing area into contemporary architecture. The historical wooden building was preserved and transformed into the ideal arrangement of a so-called Paarhof with separate residential and farm buildings. For this purpose, a self-contained structure was built opposite the wine cellar on the west side. The arrangement thus created consists of two two-storey buildings with parallel roof ridges which are related in terms of form and materials. Both buildings become one functional unit via a cubic glass living room situated between them. This connecting element also serves as the main entrance to the building. The traditional basement level of the old building was demolished in the new building.

Das Projekt Haus Oberberg ist die Transformation eines im Obst- und Weinbaugebiet traditionellen, landwirtschaftlich genutzten Kellerstöckls in eine zeitgenössische Architektur. Das historische Blockhaus wurde bewahrt und in die idealtypische Anordnung eines Paarhofes überführt. Dazu wurde dem Kellerstöckl ein eigenständiger Baukörper an der Westseite hinzugefügt. Die so geschaffene Anordnung besteht aus zwei in Form und Materialität verwandten, firstparallelen Bauten. Über einen gläsernen, kubisch dazwischenliegenden Wohnraum werden die beiden Gebäude zu einer funktionalen Einheit. Dieses Verbindungselement dient zugleich als Haupteingang des Gebäudes. Das traditionelle Sockelgeschoss des alten Gebäudes wird beim Neubau aufgelöst.

Le maître d'ouvrage souhait transformer en villa contemporaine une maison-cave traditionnelle jadis utilisée par un viticulteur autrichien. L'architecte a conservé le bâtiment d'origine en rondins délignés et l'a complété, à l'ouest, par un bâtiment indépendant, construit dans le même axe que le premier en utilisant une forme et des matériaux similaires. La structure en verre qui relie l'ancienne maison-cave à l'extension moderne unifie l'ensemble et lui sert d'entrée principale. Le niveau inférieur du bâtiment moderne, semi-souterrain comme sur les constructions traditionnelles, est largement dégagé et couvert d'une terrasse en porte-à-faux.

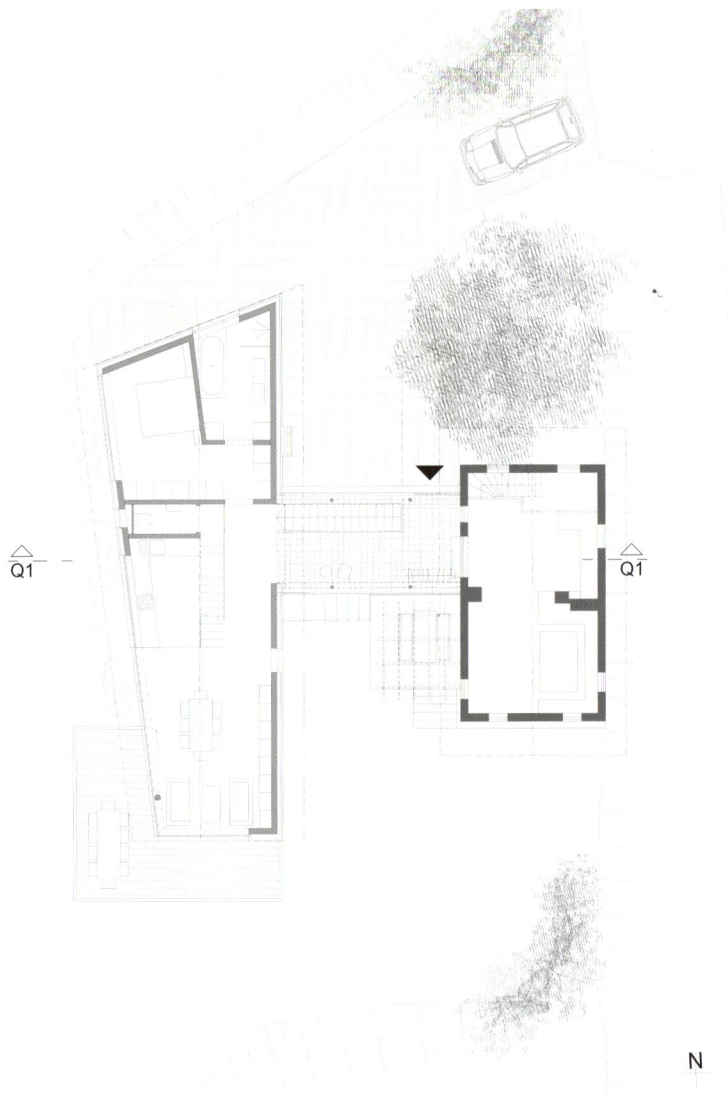

N

left: Ground floor plan_Detail of the façade_Exterior view. right: Exterior view.
links: Grundriss EG_Fassadendetail_Außenansicht. rechts: Außenansicht.
gauche: Plan RdC_Détail de la façade_Vue de l'extérieur. droite: Vue de l'extérieur.

left: Gallery. right: Section_Living area_View.
links: Galerie. rechts: Schnitt_Wohnbereich_Ausblick.
gauche: Galerie. droite: Vue en coupe_Séjour_Vue panoramique.

STUTTGART, GERMANY **HOUSE IN THE VINEYARD**

ARCHITECTS: UNSTUDIO
COMPLETION: 2011_**PROPERTY SIZE:** 1,280 M²
GROSS FLOOR AREA: 920 M²_**NUMBER OF ROOMS:** 16
PHOTOS: IWAN BAAN (164, 165, 166 A., 167),
CHRISTIAN RICHTERS (166 B.)

The volume and roofline of the house respond directly to the sloping landscape of the site, with the inclinations of the vineyard slopes reflected in the volumetric appearance of the house. The inner circulation, organization of the views, and the spatial layout are based on a single concept, 'the twist'. This central element supports the main staircase as it guides and organizes the main flows through the house. As the spatial layout follows the path of the sun, each evolution of the twist leads to situations in which views of the outside become an integral experience of the interior. The interior is arranged into spaces with varying atmospheres and spatial qualities, while the four glazed and open corners allow daylight to enter deep into the house.

Volumen und Dachlinie dieser Villa korrespondieren unmittelbar mit der hügeligen Lage des Grundstücks, indem sie die Schichten der umgebenden Weinberge abbilden. Die innere Wegführung sowie die Organisation der Ausblicke und Räume folgen dem Konzept der „Drehung". Dieses zentrale Thema findet sich in der Haupttreppe wieder und gibt die Abfolge der Räume im Gebäude vor. Deren Anordnung folgt dem Lauf der Sonne und jede Entwicklung der „Drehung" führt zu neuen Situationen, in denen Außen und Innen verschmelzen. Atmosphäre und Eigenschaften der unterschiedlichen Bereiche variieren, während durch die vier verglasten Ecken Tageslicht bis weit ins Haus dringen kann.

Différentes lignes de cette villa, notamment la forme du toit, répondent directement au profil de la colline sur laquelle le bâtiment est implanté. Ce concept baptisé « Twist » structure en fait tous les espaces : on le retrouve à l'intérieur, par exemple dans l'escalier principal et divers endroits où il détermine le flux de circulation. Conçu pour suivre la course du soleil à travers le ciel, ce concept contribue également à intégrer à la décoration intérieure diverses vues sur l'extérieur, en particulier le vignoble voisin. Chacune des pièces a une atmosphère et des qualités spatiales qui lui sont propres, les grandes baies vitrées positionnées aux quatre coins de la villa assurant d'autre part un bon éclairage naturel de l'ensemble du bâtiment.

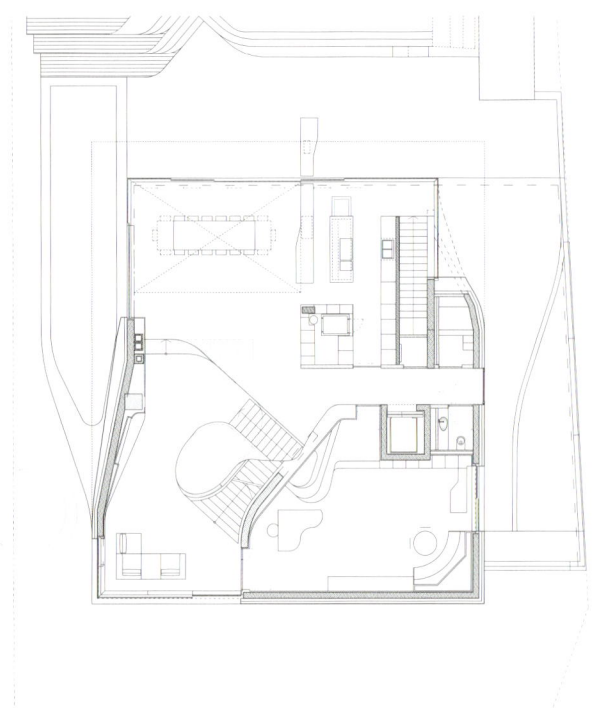

left: First floor plan_General view_Garden view. right: Pool_Exterior view_Interior view.
links: Grundriss 1. OG_Gesamtansicht_Gartenansicht. rechts: Pool_Außenansicht_Innenansicht.
gauche: Plan niveau 1_Vue générale_Vue du jardin. droite: Piscine_Vue de l'extérieur_Vue de l'intérieur.

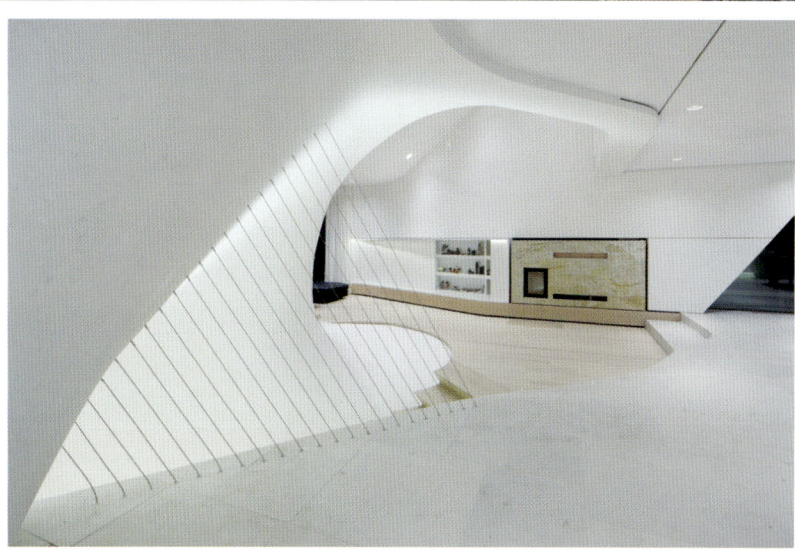

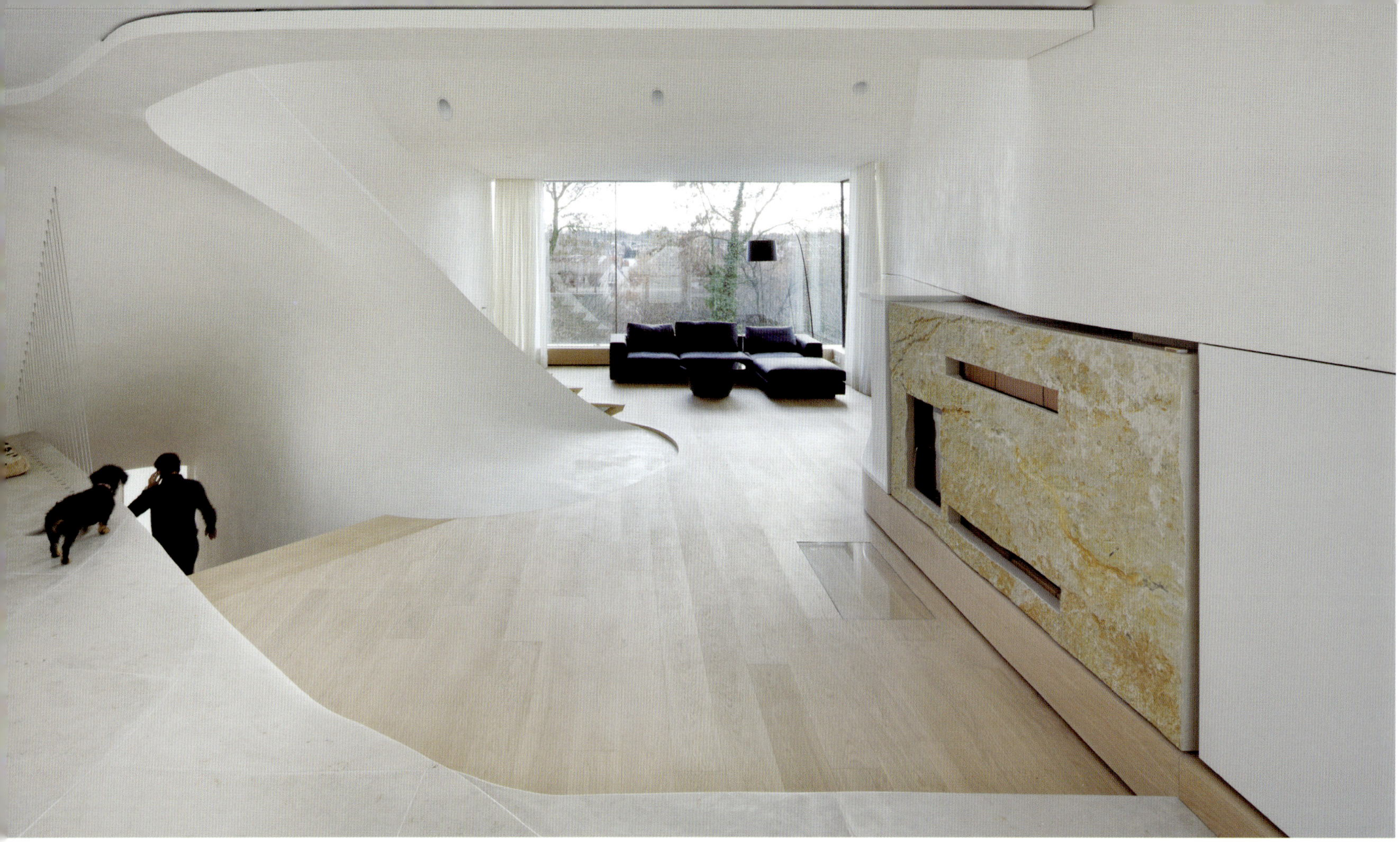

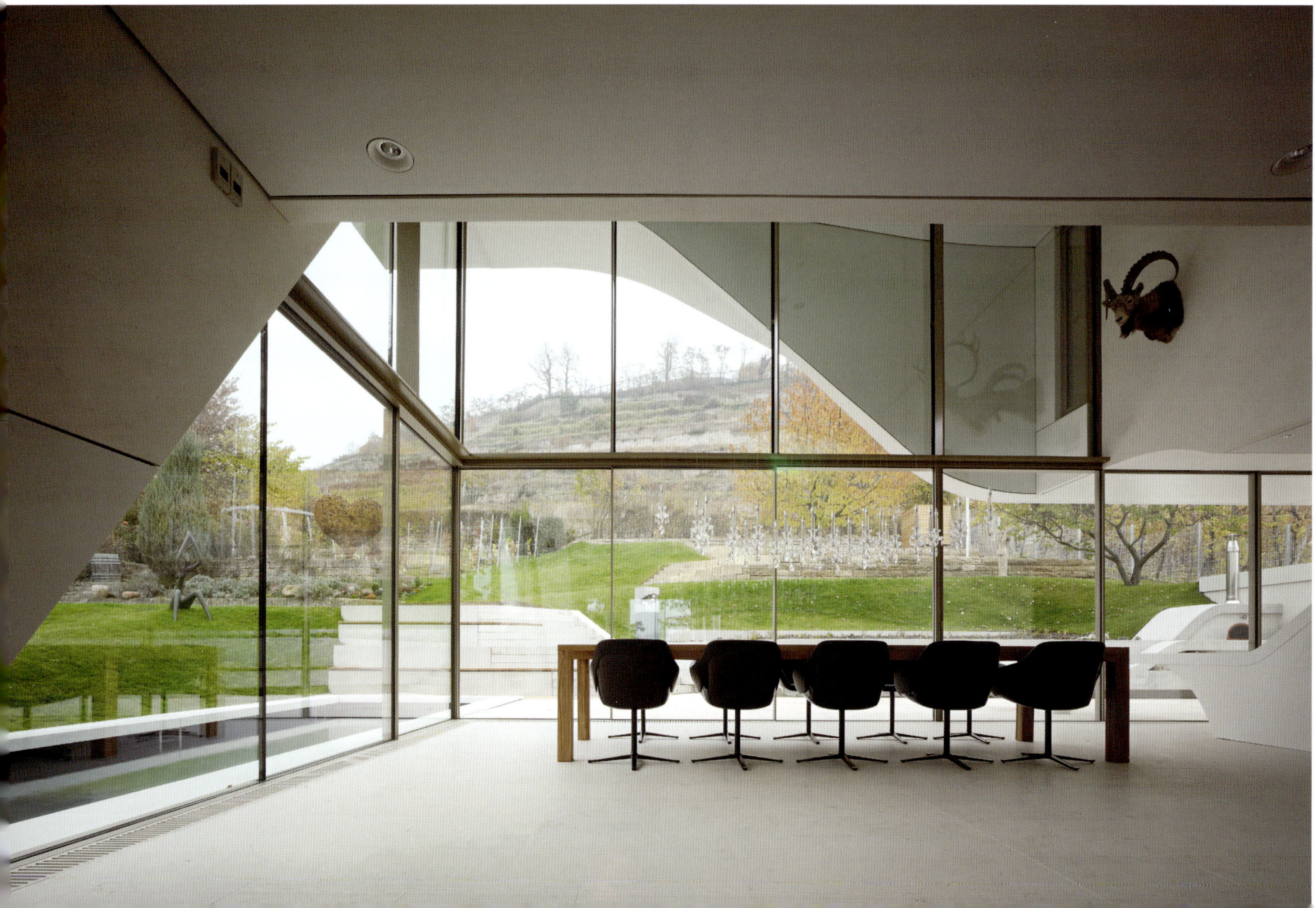

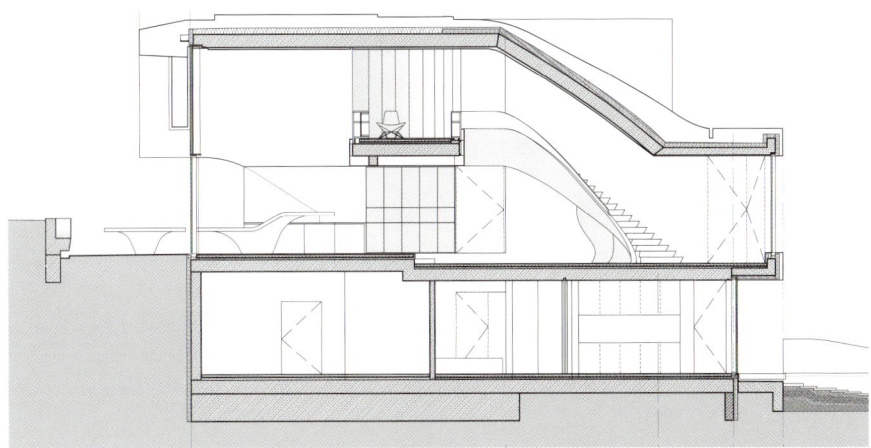

left: Living area_Dining area. right: Section_Bathroom_Stairs_Kitchen.
links: Wohnbereich_Essbereich. rechts: Schnitt_Bad_Treppe_Küche.
gauche: Séjour_Salle à manger. droite: Vue en coupe_Salle de bains_Escalier_Cuisine.

POTSDAM, GERMANY **URBAN VILLA**

ARCHITECTS: ECKERT NEGWER SUSELBEEK ARCHITEKTEN
COMPLETION: 2012_**PROPERTY SIZE:** 1,150 M²
GROSS FLOOR AREA: 507 M²_**NUMBER OF ROOMS:** 9
PHOTOS: STEFAN MÜLLER

The late Neoclassicism house was constructed in the year 1872 during the establishment era of the German Reich, by the Prussian court master mason Carl Partik. Today it is a listed monument of the city of Potsdam. During the 140-year history of the house, there were small additions that always intended to maintain the entirety and morphology of the house without architectural violations. The aim of not immediately identifying constructional interventions as new or old became the basis and aim of the renovation and modernization that was implemented in direct cooperation with the Potsdam authority for the preservation of monuments and small "young" handicraft establishments.

Das spätklassizistische Haus wurde 1872 zu Zeiten der deutschen Reichsgründung von preußischem Hofmaurermeister Carl Partik erbaut. Heute ist es ein eingetragenes Baudenkmal der Stadt Potsdam. In der 140jährigen Geschichte des Hauses, erfolgten kleinere Anbauten, immer in der Absicht das Haus in seiner Gesamtheit und Morphologie zu wahren ohne Aufzeigen baulicher Brüche. Die Haltung, bauliche Eingriffe nicht unmittelbar als neu oder alt ablesbar zu machen, wurde zum Ausgangspunkt und Ziel der Restaurierung und Modernisierung, welche in direkter Abstimmung mit der Potsdamer Denkmalpflege und kleinen „jungen" Handwerksbetrieben erfolgte.

Ce bâtiment néoclassique aujourd'hui classé monument historique a été construit en 1872, peu après la fondation de l'Empire allemand, par Carl Partik, « maître maçon à la Cour de Prusse ». Au cours de son siècle et demi d'existence, il a été agrandi à plusieurs reprises, mais toujours en veillant à ne pas rompre l'unité de la morphologie ni trahir le style d'origine. Cette attitude respectueuse de l'ancien a servi de base au concept de restauration et modernisation développé par les architectes, qui ont travaillé en étroite collaboration avec le service des monuments historiques de Potsdam et plusieurs jeunes artisans.

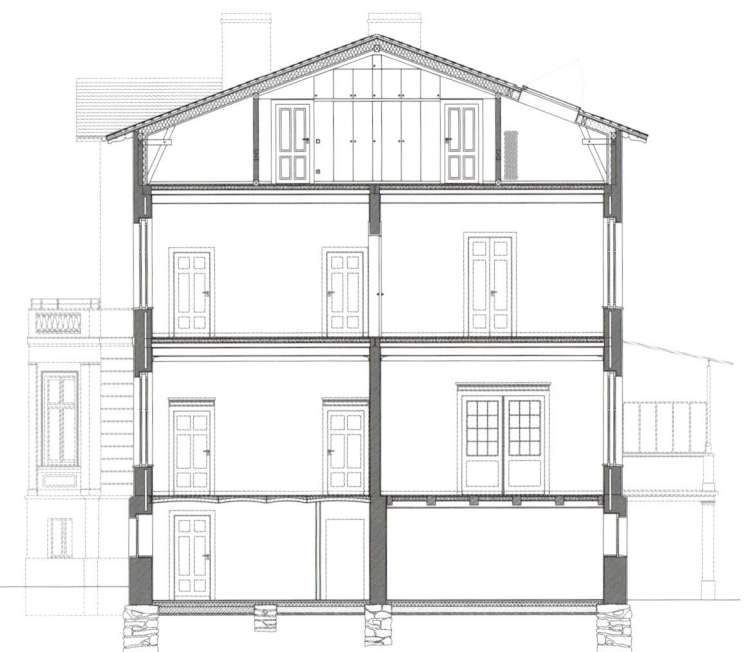

left: Section_Garden view_Street view. right: Living room on ground floor.
links: Schnitt_Gartenansicht_Straßenansicht. rechts: Wohnraum Erdgeschoss.
gauche: Vue en coupe_Vue du jardin_Vue de la rue. droite: Séjour au RdC.

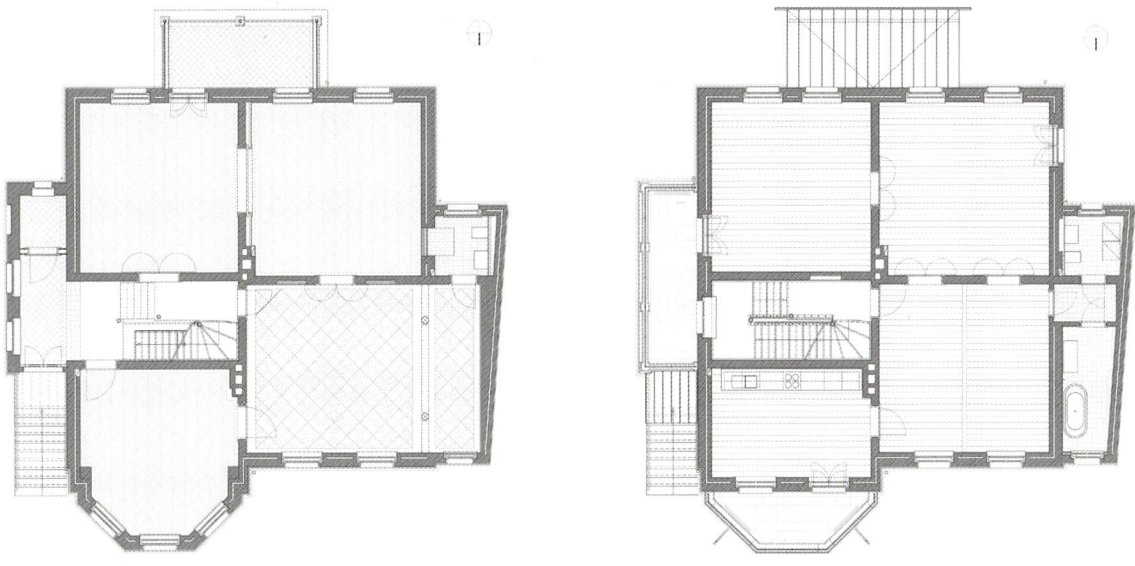

left: Living area on ground floor. right: Ground and top floor plans_Attic floor.
links: Wohnbereich Erdgeschoss. rechts: Grundrisse EG und OG_Dachgeschoss.
gauche: Séjour au RdC. droite: Plan RdC et niveau 1_Mansarde.

SHIGA, JAPAN **HOUSE OF SILENCE**

ARCHITECTS: FORM / KOUICHI KIMURA ARCHITECTS
COMPLETION: 2012_**PROPERTY SIZE:** 395 M²
GROSS FLOOR AREA: 322 M²_**NUMBER OF ROOMS:** 6
PHOTOS: TAKUMI OTA, KEI NAKAJIMA

The client requested a house that is independent of the environment of its location. This architecture, which is composed of a concrete volume, has few windows and is closed by walls, offering a variety of spaces inside that can never be imagined from the outside. Constituting a landmark in the town, its rough concrete finish, shiny tiles and opening resembling a belfry give a hint of the nature of spaces inside. These vary in terms of ceiling height, the different levels of floors and type of lights, but are all connected by the circular line of flow. The inner court is cut off from the outside environment and shows a variety of expressions as the light changes.

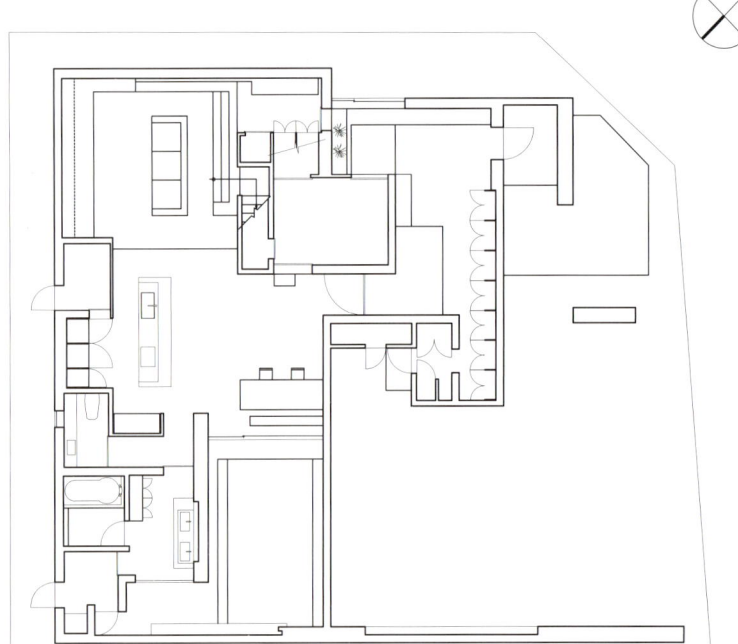

Der Bauherr wünschte einen von der Umgebung unabhängigen Entwurf. Die hermetische Architektur des Betonkörpers, der nur wenige Fenster hat, lässt von außen kaum die Vielfalt der Innenräume erahnen. So grenzt sich der außergewöhnliche Solitär zwar von der umgebenden Architektur ab, jedoch erlauben seine raue Betonoberfläche, die blanken Kacheln und der glockenturmartige Aufbau Rückschlüsse auf den besonderen Charakter der Innenräume. Diese variieren in der Deckenhöhe, der Anzahl der Stockwerke und Art der Beleuchtung, sind aber alle über die spiralförmige Wegführung verbunden. Der Innenhof ist abgeschlossen und bietet im Tagesverlauf eine Vielfalt an Stimmungen.

Le propriétaire de cette maison avait demandé aux architectes de concevoir un bâtiment indépendant de son environnement. Le résultat est un édifice qui ne passe pas inaperçu dans la ville : le béton brut de coffrage se complète par deux panneaux en briques, tandis que de rares ouvertures confèrent à l'ensemble l'aspect d'une forteresse. L'intérieur offre néanmoins des espaces d'une variété difficilement imaginable de l'extérieur, tant en ce qui concerne la hauteur de plafond que le type d'éclairage. Au cœur de ce bâtiment dont toutes les pièces sont reliées entre elles par un concept de circulation en boucle se trouve une cour dont l'éclairage change constamment l'expression.

left: Ground floor plan_Exterior view_Street view. right: Front courtyard_Kitchen_Bedroom.
links: Grundriss EG_Außenansicht_Straßenansicht. rechts: Vorhof_Küche_Schlafzimmer.
gauche: Plan RdC_Vue de l'extérieur_Vue de la rue. droite: Cour_Cuisine_Chambre.

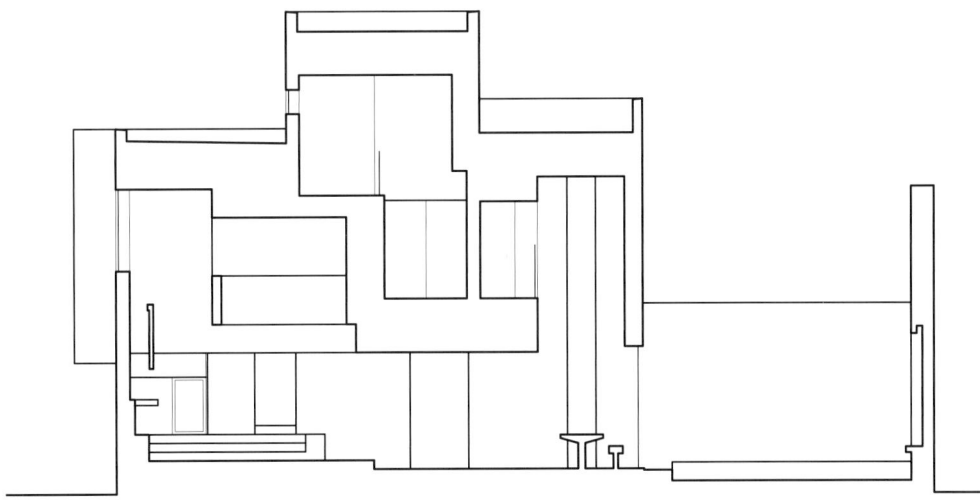

left: Front courtyard. right: Section_Air space_Living room_Dining room.
links: Vorhof. rechts: Schnitt_Luftraum_Wohnraum_Essbereich.
gauche: Cour. droite: Vue en coupe_Nef_Séjour_Salle à manger.

CAPUTH, GERMANY **HOUSE W**

ARCHITECTS: THOMAS BEYER ARCHITEKTEN
COMPLETION: 2010_**PROPERTY SIZE:** 1,640 M²
GROSS FLOOR AREA: 301 M²_**NUMBER OF ROOMS:** 6
PHOTOS: THOMAS BEYER

House W was erected on a hillside plot in Caputh with a view of Lake Schwilow. With a rectangular layout the building follows the longitudinal stretch of the plot. It consists of three levels of offset cubes, each with its own terrace. The living area of the house extends across the entire ground floor and is closed off on the north-east side by two concrete walls set at an angle. The staircase leads directly from the living room to the studio on the top floor from where other rooms can be reached. Floor-to-ceiling glazing smoothly expands the interior via the terraces to incorporate the garden outside. The garden's changing atmospheres throughout the day thus become part of the overall design concept.

Das Haus W ist auf einem Hanggrundstück in Caputh mit Blick auf den Schwilowsee errichtet. Das Gebäude folgt mit rechteckigem Grundriss der Längsausdehnung des Grundstückes und entwickelt sich über drei Ebenen aus zu einander versetzten Kuben, denen jeweils eigene Terrassen vorgelagert sind. Der Wohnbereich des Hauses nimmt das gesamte Erdgeschoß ein und ist durch zwei, einen Winkel bildende Betonwände an der Nord-Ostseite geschlossen. Die Treppe führt direkt aus dem Wohnraum in das Studio im Obergeschoß über das man sich in die weiteren Räume verteilt. Raumhohe Verglasungen erweitern den Innenraum fließend nach aussen über die Terrassen in den Garten und beziehen diesen, mit seinen über den Tagesverlauf veränderten Stimmungen als Bestandteil des Wohnens insgesamt mit ein.

La villa W a été construite à Caputh, près de Potsdam, sur un terrain longiforme avec vue sur un lac. Elle se compose de trois parallélépipèdes superposés se complétant par des terrasses. Le rez-de-chaussée, réservé aux pièces de séjour, est entièrement vitré sur deux côtés et délimité par des murs en béton sur les deux autres. Un escalier conduit aux différentes pièces du niveau supérieur. De grandes baies vitrées coulissantes donnent accès aux terrasses et agrandissent ainsi la surface habitable dans la mesure où elles établissent un contact avec le jardin et son atmosphère qui change constamment en fonction de l'heure et des saisons.

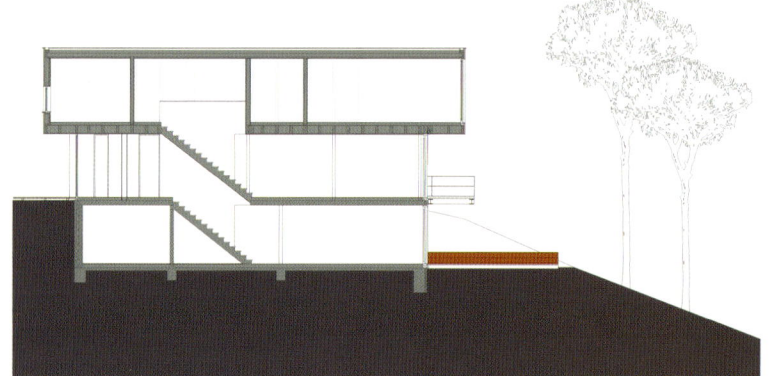

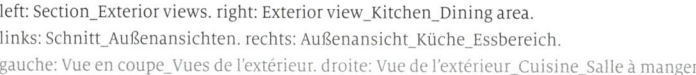

left: Section_Exterior views. right: Exterior view_Kitchen_Dining area.
links: Schnitt_Außenansichten. rechts: Außenansicht_Küche_Essbereich.
gauche: Vue en coupe_Vues de l'extérieur. droite: Vue de l'extérieur_Cuisine_Salle à manger.

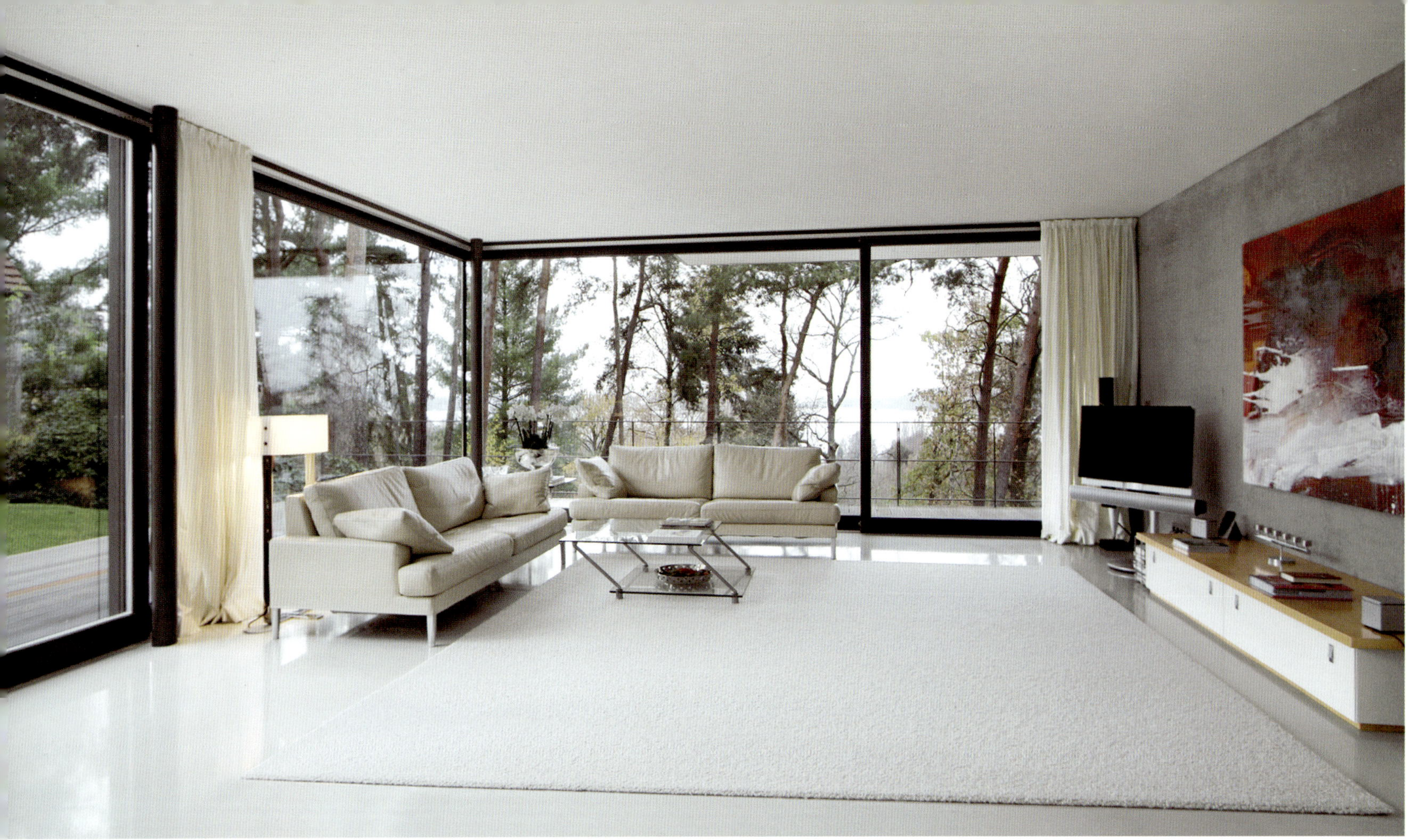

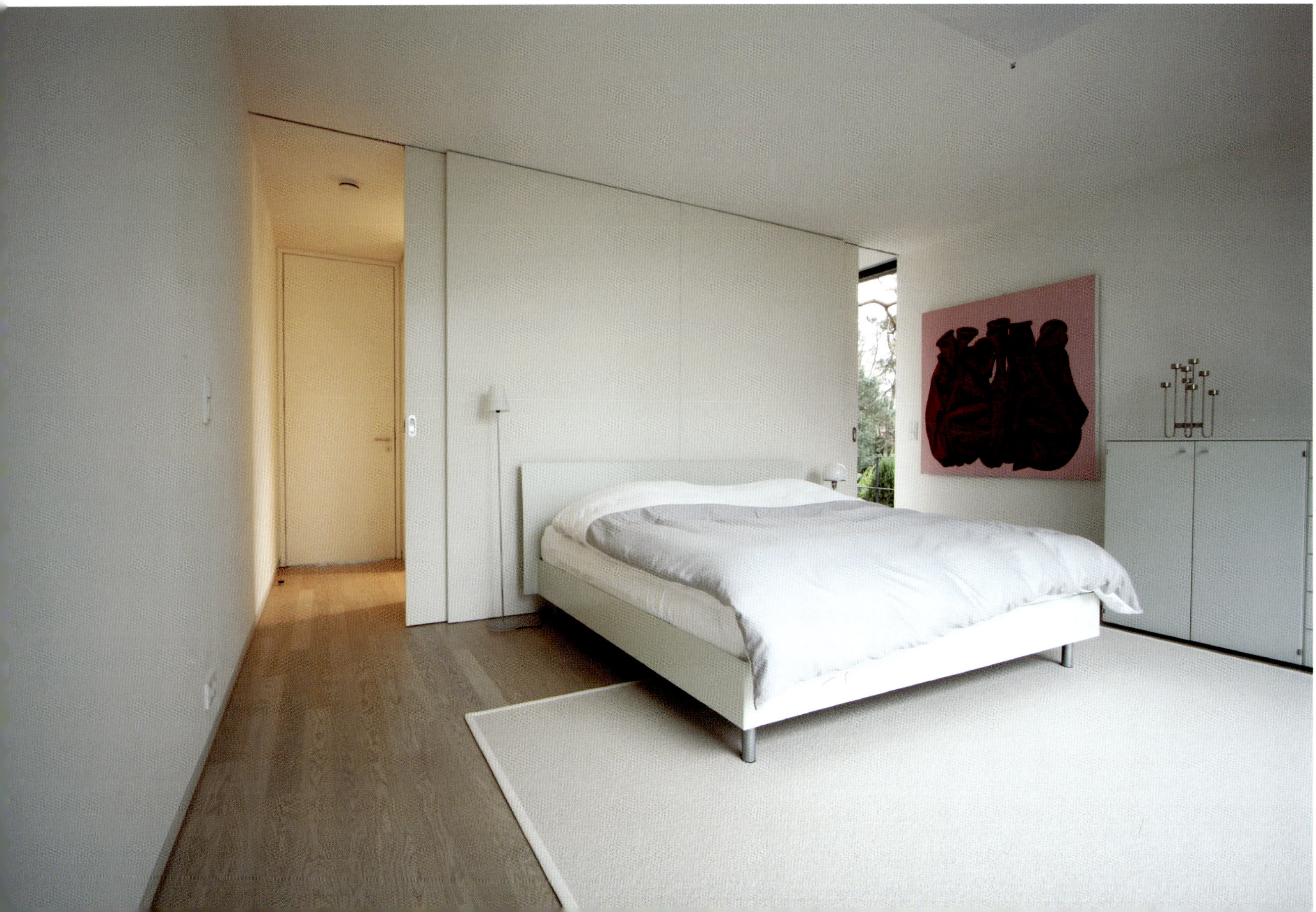

left: Living area_Bedroom. right: Top and ground floor plans_Stairs_Studio_Bathroom.
links: Wohnbereich_Schlafzimmer. rechts: Grundrisse OG und EG_Treppe_Studio_Bad.
gauche: Séjour_Chambre. droite: Plan niveau 1 et Plan RdC_Escalier_Atelier_Salle de bains.

AMSTERDAM, THE NETHERLANDS **VILLA RIETEILAND-OOST**

ARCHITECTS: EGEON ARCHITECTEN
COMPLETION: 2012_**GROSS FLOOR AREA:** 225 M²
NUMBER OF ROOMS: 6_**PHOTOS:** CHIEL DE NOOYER

The client's brief was to design an urban family house in a responsible way, using fair and sustainable materials with a comfortable tactile touch, and to combine living and working, with the possibility of separate use. The architectural response was a private house made of wood and glass. To the traditional arrangement of living on the ground floor and sleeping on the upper floors an additional floor was added for working from home. The ground floor has a glass façade with large sliding doors on the garden side, allowing the residents to benefit most from the view. The bedroom floor is open towards the inside and closed to the outside. The office floor has all-around views.

Der Bauherr wünschte eine familienfreundliche und energieeffiziente Stadt-villa. Bei den Materialien legte er Wert auf faire und nachhaltige Produktion sowie angenehme Haptik. Die Kombination aus Wohnen und Arbeiten sollte ebenso möglich sein wie eine gesonderte Nutzung. Die architektonische Ant-wort ist eine private Villa aus Holz und Glas, deren traditionelle Raumaufteilung mit Wohnen im Erdgeschoss und Schlafen im Obergeschoss um ein Stockwerk für die Büroräume ergänzt wurde. Die Glasfassade des Erdgeschosses öffnet sich über Schiebetüren zum Garten hin, sodass die Bewohner den Ausblick genießen können. Der Schlafbereich ist im Innern offen gestaltet, verschließt sich aber nach außen. Das Bürogeschoss bietet Ausblicke nach allen Seiten.

Les exigences du maître d'ouvrage étaient les suivantes pour cette villa urbaine : utilisation de matériaux répondant aux critères du développement durable, apparence « tactile et confortable », association d'espaces de travail et de pièces à vivre. Les architectes y ont répondu en utilisant le bois et le verre, et en rajoutant un étage de bureaux au rez-de-chaussée (traditionnellement réservé aux pièces de séjour) et au premier étage (abritant les chambres). Le niveau inférieur communique avec le jardin par de grandes baies vitrées coulissantes. Le premier étage s'ouvre sur l'extérieur par des fenêtres pourvues de volets. L'étage de bureaux, enfin, est pourvu de fenêtres panoramiques.

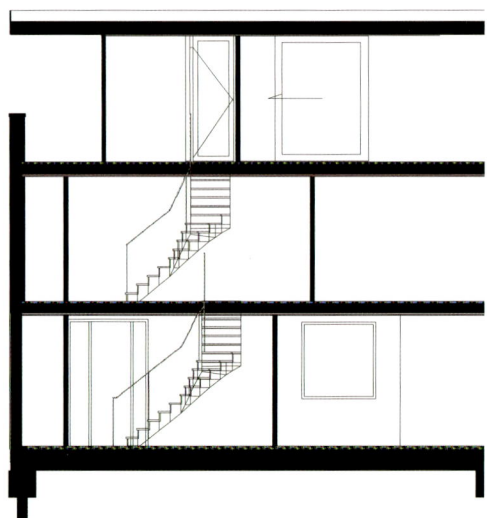

left: Section_Living room_Entrance. right: Exterior view_Garden view_Roof terrace.
links: Schnitt_Wohnraum_Eingang. rechts: Außenansicht_Gartenansicht_Dachterrasse.
gauche: Vue en coupe_Séjour_Entrée. droite: Vue de l'extérieur_Vue du jardin_Terrasse au toit.

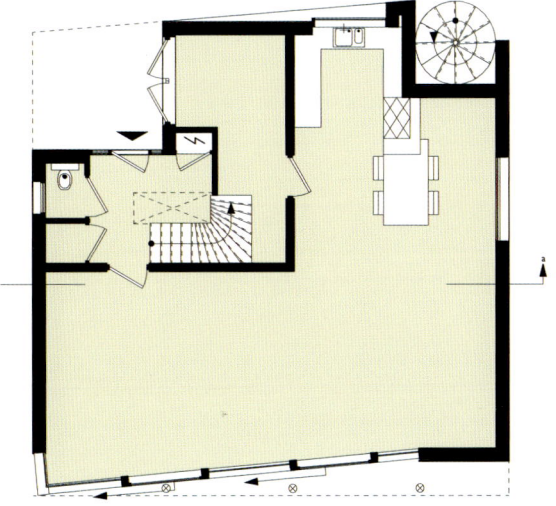

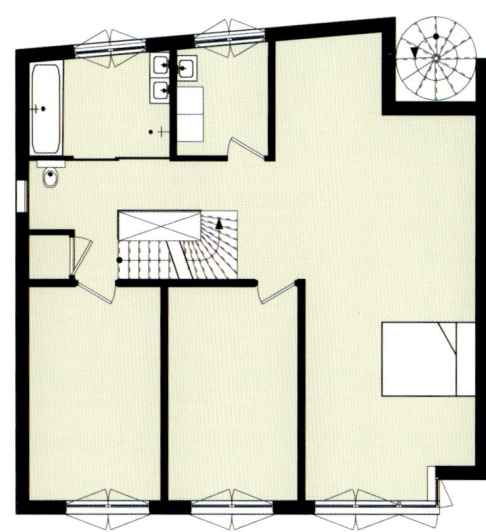

left: Stairs. right: Ground and first floor plans_Kitchen_Bathroom_Studio.
links: Treppe. rechts: Grundrisse EG und 1. OG_Küche_Bad_Studio.
gauche: Escalier. droite: Plan RdC et niveau 1_Cuisine_Salle de bains_Studio.

STUTTGART, GERMANY **HOUSE ARB**

ARCHITECTS: FUCHS, WACKER ARCHITEKTEN BDA
COMPLETION: 2012_**PROPERTY SIZE:** 1,024 M²
GROSS FLOOR AREA: 450 M²_**NUMBER OF ROOMS:** 6
PHOTOS: BRIGIDA GONZALES

The residence is situated in one of Stuttgart's prime elevated locations. From the street, the building appears understated. Upon entering through the main gate with a specially structured timber surface, however, visitors are grandly received in a two-floor entrance hall. A room-high door covered in noble leather leads to the living spaces. In coordination with the owners, the interior features an individual comprehensive system of illumination, furniture and surfaces, also incorporating objects of art. Room-high glazing in the living room provides a view of the garden, the swimming pool and two terrace levels. The architect's consistent design concept from the interior to the exterior results in a harmonious entity up to the minutest detail.

Das Wohnhaus steht in einer der bevorzugten Hanglagen in Stuttgart. Von der Straße aus betrachtet, erscheint das Gebäude zurückhaltend. Bei Eintritt durch das Hausportal mit speziell strukturierter Holzoberfläche wird der Besucher von einer zweigeschossigen Eingangshalle stattlich empfangen. Eine raumhohe, mit feinstem Leder belegte Türe führt zu den Wohnräumen. In Gesprächen mit den Eigentümern entstand hier ein individuelles Gesamtkonzept aus Beleuchtung, Möblierung und Oberflächen bis hin zu Kunstgegenständen. Vom Wohnraum aus blickt man durch die raumhohe Verglasung in den Garten, auf den Pool und die zwei Terrassenebenen. Das durchgängige Gestaltungskonzept der Architekten vom Innen- zum Außenraum führt zu einem stimmigen Ganzen durch alle Details hindurch.

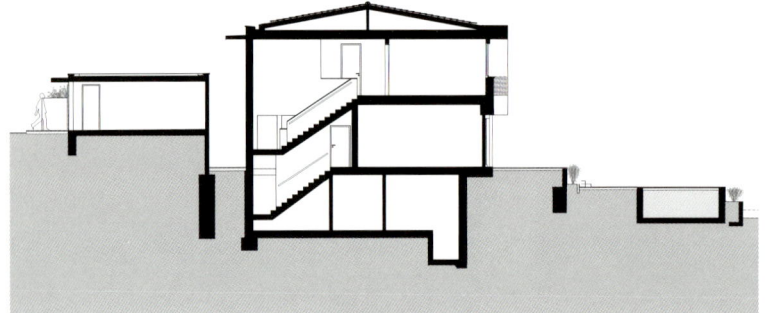

Construite sur un terrain en pente dans une banlieue résidentielle de Stuttgart, cette villa présente une façade sobre du côté de la rue. L'entrée se fait par un portail dont le revêtement en bois se caractérise par une structure spéciale. On accède alors à un vestibule majestueux dont la hauteur sous plafond correspond à deux étages. Une porte gigantesque recouverte de cuir s'ouvre sur le séjour. Des murs entièrement vitrés permettent d'apprécier le jardin, la piscine et les deux terrasses. En concertation avec le maître d'ouvrage, l'architecte a élaboré pour cette villa un concept global intégrant l'éclairage, le mobilier, les revêtements et diverses œuvres d'art, de sorte que l'intérieur et l'extérieur y constituent un ensemble harmonieux.

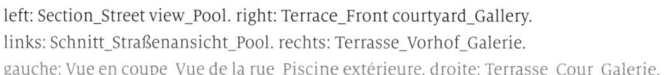

left: Section_Street view_Pool. right: Terrace_Front courtyard_Gallery.
links: Schnitt_Straßenansicht_Pool. rechts: Terrasse_Vorhof_Galerie.
gauche: Vue en coupe_Vue de la rue_Piscine extérieure. droite: Terrasse_Cour_Galerie.

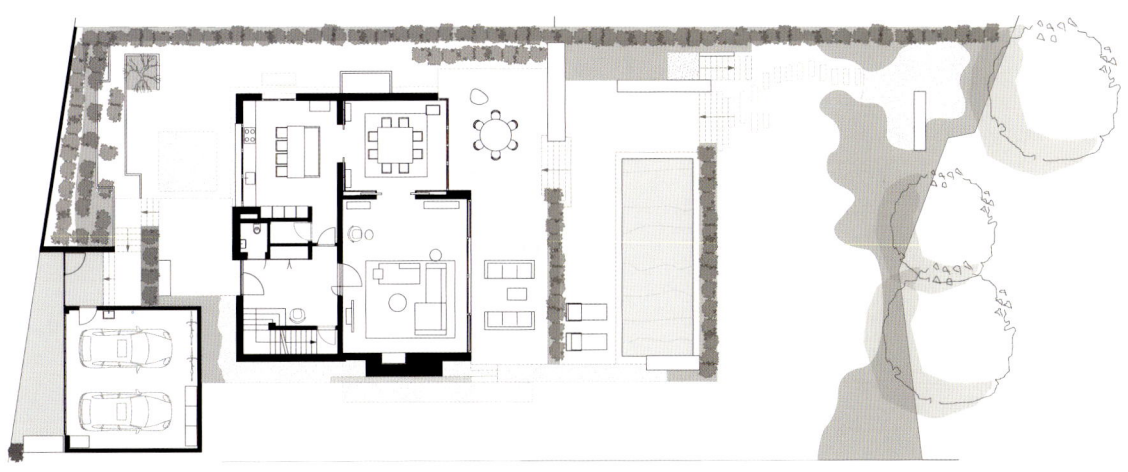

left: Front courtyard. right: Ground floor plan_Entrance_Hall.
links: Vorhof. rechts: Grundriss EG_Eingang_Halle.
gauche: Cour. droite: Plan RdC_Entrée_Nef.

NORTHCOTE, VICTORIA, AUSTRALIA **HILL HOUSE**

ARCHITECTS: ANDREW MAYNARD ARCHITECTS
COMPLETION: 2011_**PROPERTY SIZE:** 410 M²
GROSS FLOOR AREA: 192 M²
PHOTOS: NICK GRANLEESE (188, 190, 191 R.),
ANDREW MAYNARD ARCHITECTS (189, 191 L.)

Rather than repeating past mistakes and extending from the rear in a new configuration, the proposal was to build a new structure on the rear boundary, the southern edge of the block, upon the footprint of what had been, until now, the backyard. The new structure faces the sun, with the pure cantilevered box above acting as a passive solar eave, cutting out the summer sun, while letting winter sun flood in. Following the decision to build at the rear of the block, a ubiquitous modern box was first imagined. Soon it seemed necessary to pursue the opportunity to activate the new, once shaded, now sunny façade. The new structure faces the original house. The backyard is now the center of the house activated by the constructed form around it.

Vergangene Fehler sollten sich nicht wiederholen, darum schlugen die Architekten anstelle eines weiteren rückwärtigen Anbaus an das Haupthaus einen Neubau im Garten vor. An der südlichen Grundstücksgrenze gelegen ist der Neubau der Sonne zugewandt. Der auskragende Riegel dient als Sonnendach, das im Sommer Schatten spendet und im Winter Licht einlässt. Infolge der Entscheidung, den hinteren Teil des Grundstücks zu bebauen, war zunächst ein moderner Kubus angedacht, wie er heute allgegenwärtig ist. Die Fassade hätte im Schatten gelegen. Doch die Architekten fanden eine Möglichkeit, sie durch Sonnenlicht zu aktivieren. Der Neubau liegt dem Bestand direkt gegenüber, sodass der Garten zum neu belebten Zentrum wurde.

Plutôt que de répéter les erreurs du passé en construisant une extension adossée à un bâtiment préexistant, avec les conséquences que cela n'aurait pas manqué d'avoir sur l'ensoleillement, les architectes ont choisi de construire tout au fond du jardin le nouveau bâtiment souhaité par les propriétaires. Omniprésente quel que soit l'endroit où l'on se trouve sur le terrain, la boîte moderne ainsi imaginée fait face au soleil, la partie en porte-à-faux n'empêchant aucunement les rayons d'éclairer le rez-de-chaussée en hiver, tout en apportant une ombre bienfaisante en été. La cour située entre l'ancien bâtiment et la nouvelle extension est maintenant le véritable centre de cet ensemble original.

left: Ground and top floor plans_Roof terrace_Garden view. right: Exterior view.
links: Grundrisse EG und OG_Dachterrasse_Gartenansicht. rechts: Außenansicht.
gauche: Plan RdC et niveau 1_Terrasse au toit_Vue du jardin. droite: Vue de l'extérieur.

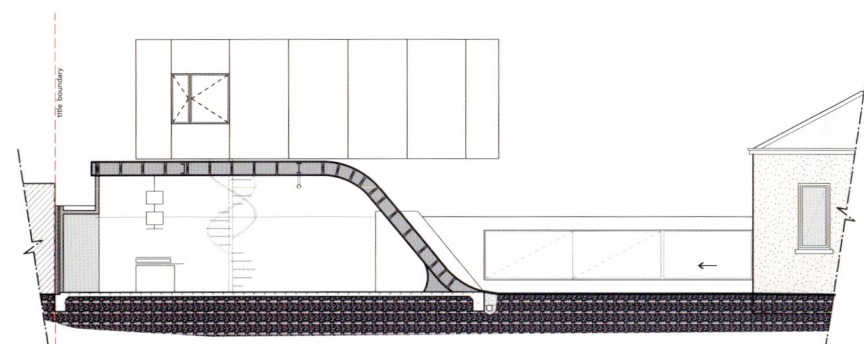

left: Kitchen. right: Section_Bedroom_Studio_Interior view.
links: Küche. rechts: Schnitt_Schlafzimmer_Studio_Innenansicht.
gauche: Cuisine. droite: Vue en coupe_Chambre_Studio_Vue de l'intérieur.

URSWIL, SWITZERLAND **HOUSE NEAR THE BROOK**

ARCHITECTS: DOLMUS ARCHITEKTEN
COMPLETION: 2012_**PROPERTY SIZE:** 763 M²
GROSS FLOOR AREA: 240 M²_**NUMBER OF ROOMS:** 4.5
PHOTOS: AYTAC PEKTEMIR (192 L., 193, 194, 195 R.),
MARTIN GUGGISBERG (192 R., 195 L.)

The trapezoid plot in the Seetal valley near Lucerne is bordered to the south by a brook and to the north by a street. The plinth was designed as a flood protection measure towards the brook and mirrors the basic shape of the plot. The plinth constitutes an ensemble together with the residence and the garage. In combination with the gabled roof, this results in an exciting interplay of dimensions. The layout is zoned by two enclosed spatial structures that are connected by a two-level space at the center of the house. The facades have different openings on every side in reaction to their environment. The vertical structure of the plastering gives them a vivacity that contrasts with the strict geometry of the building.

Die trapezförmige Parzelle im Luzerner Seetal wird im Süden durch einen Bach mit hohen Bäumen und im Norden durch eine Straße begrenzt. Der Sockel wurde als Hochwasserschutz zum Bach ausgebildet und spiegelt die Grundform der Parzelle wieder. Mit dem Wohnhaus und der Garage bildet der Sockel ein Ensemble, welches mit dem Satteldach eine spannende Volumetrie entstehen lässt. Der Grundriss wird durch zwei geschlossene Raumkörper zoniert und gleichzeitig durch einen zweigeschossigen Bereich, das Zentrum des Hauses, verbunden. Die Fassaden unterscheiden sich im Öffnungsverhalten auf allen Seiten und reagieren so auf ihre Umgebung. Durch die vertikale Struktur des Verputzes erhalten sie eine Lebendigkeit, die mit der strengen Geometrie des Gebäudes bricht.

Cette villa a été construite près de Lucerne, sur un terrain trapézoïdal délimité au nord par une route et au sud par un ruisseau bordé d'arbres. Le rez-de-chaussée, d'une forme identique à celle du terrain, a été conçu pour résister aux crues du ruisseau. Le toit à deux pentes de la maison, dont la prolongation correspond à la pente unique du toit du garage, génère une volumétrie particulièrement dynamique. Le volume principal présente en son centre une nef sur deux niveaux. Le percement des ouvertures sur chacune des façades a été conçu en fonction de l'environnement immédiat de la villa. Les stries verticales du revêtement extérieur confèrent à l'ensemble un dynamisme qui vient atténuer l'austérité de la géométrie.

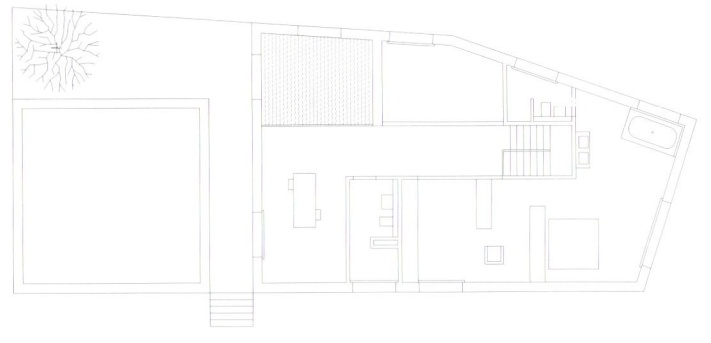

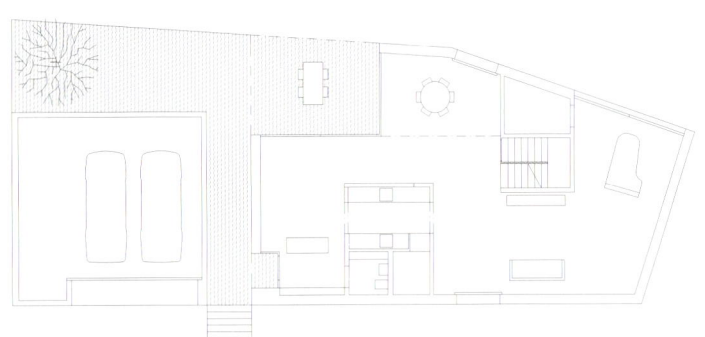

left: Top and ground floor plans_Seen from south and south-west. right: Gallery.
links: Grundrisse OG und EG_Süd- und Südwestansicht. rechts: Galerie.
gauche: Plan niveau 1 et RdC_ Façade sud et sud-ouest. droite: Galerie.

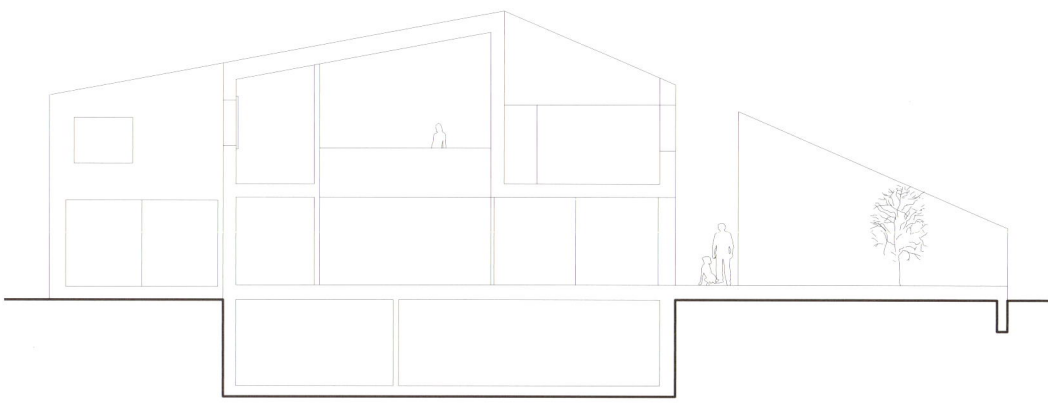

left: Roof terrace_Living room_Bedroom. right: Section_Kitchen_Dining area.
links: Dachterrasse_Wohnraum_Schlafzimmer. rechts: Schnitt_Küche_Essraum.
gauche: Toit en terrasse_Séjour_Chambre. droite: Vue en coupe_Cuisine_Salle à manger.

THE NETHERLANDS **VILLA VETH**

ARCHITECTS: 123 DV MODERN VILLAS
COMPLETION: 2011_**PROPERTY SIZE:** 6,000 M²
GROSS FLOOR AREA: 480 M²_**NUMBER OF ROOMS:** 11
PHOTOS: CHRISTIAAN DE BRUIJNE

Villa Veth is a modern, customized, private two-storey residence. It is situated on a large parcel of land by a forest in the eastern part of the Netherlands. The house looks sleek and abstract on the outside, but has a warm and cozy interior. The principal living area on the ground floor is divided into two sections. On one side are the bedrooms and two small studios. The other half of the floor plan is taken up by an open-concept living area that includes the kitchen, dining and living spaces. This part faces south. The curved glass wall is designed to visually minimize the boundaries between the inside and outside. Supported by a single column clad in reflective metal, the low-profile roof extends to cover an outdoor patio.

Die zweistöckige Villa Veth ist ein moderner und maßgeschneiderter Wohnsitz. Sie liegt im Osten der Niederlande auf einer großen Parzelle am Waldrand. Hinter der eher kühlen und abstrakten Fassade verbergen sich warme und gemütliche Innenräume. Das Erdgeschoss ist in zwei Sektionen aufgeteilt. Gen Norden liegen die Schlafzimmer und zwei kleinere Ateliers. Die südliche Hälfte des Grundrisses wird von einem offenen Konzept eingenommen, bestehend aus Küche, Ess- und Wohnbereich. Eine geschwungene Glaswand schwächt die visuelle Grenze zwischen Innen und Außen ab. Gestützt von einer einzigen verspiegelten Säule kragt das Flachdach über der Veranda aus.

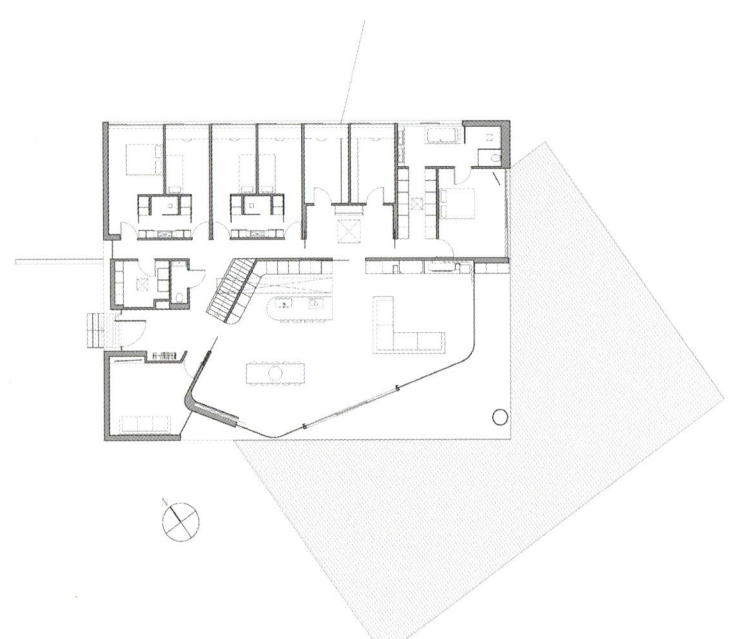

La villa Veth est une réalisation moderne sur deux niveaux située sur un grand terrain en bordure d'une forêt à l'est des Pays-Bas. À un extérieur lisse et abstrait répondent des intérieurs chaleureux et confortables. Le rez-de-chaussée se divise en deux parties : la première abrite les chambres et deux petits studios ; la seconde, sur la façade sud, accueille un grand espace ouvert où se trouvent la cuisine, le séjour et la salle à manger. Les formes arrondies du grand mur vitré contribuent à minimiser la distinction entre intérieur et extérieur. Sur la façade principale, le toit plat, qui couvre un patio, repose sur une unique colonne pourvue d'un revêtement en métal chromé.

left: Ground floor plan_Exterior views. right: Terrace_Driveway.
links: Grundriss EG_Außenansichten. rechts: Terrasse_Einfahrt.
gauche: Plan RdC_Vues de l'extérieur. droite: Terrasse_Entrée.

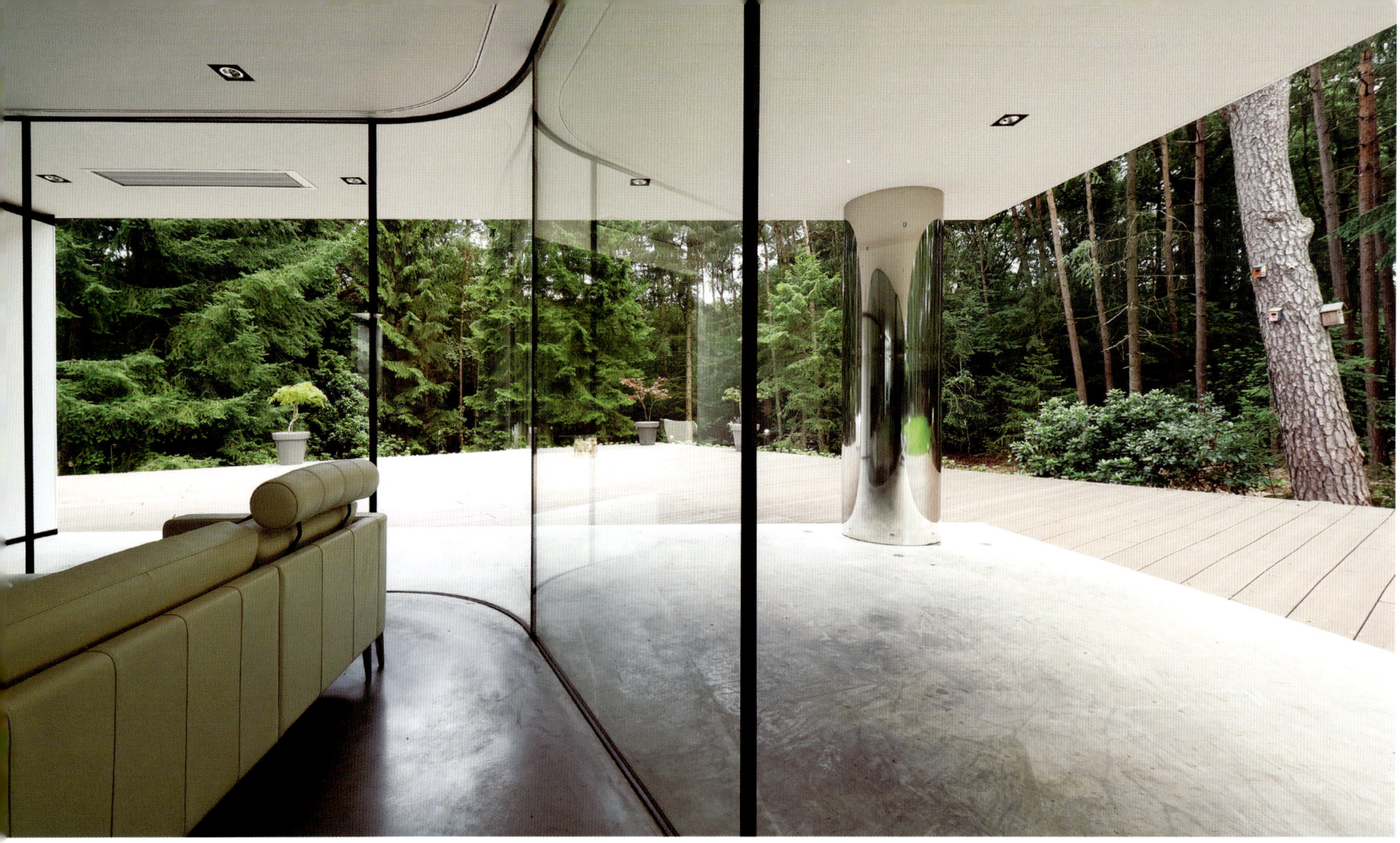

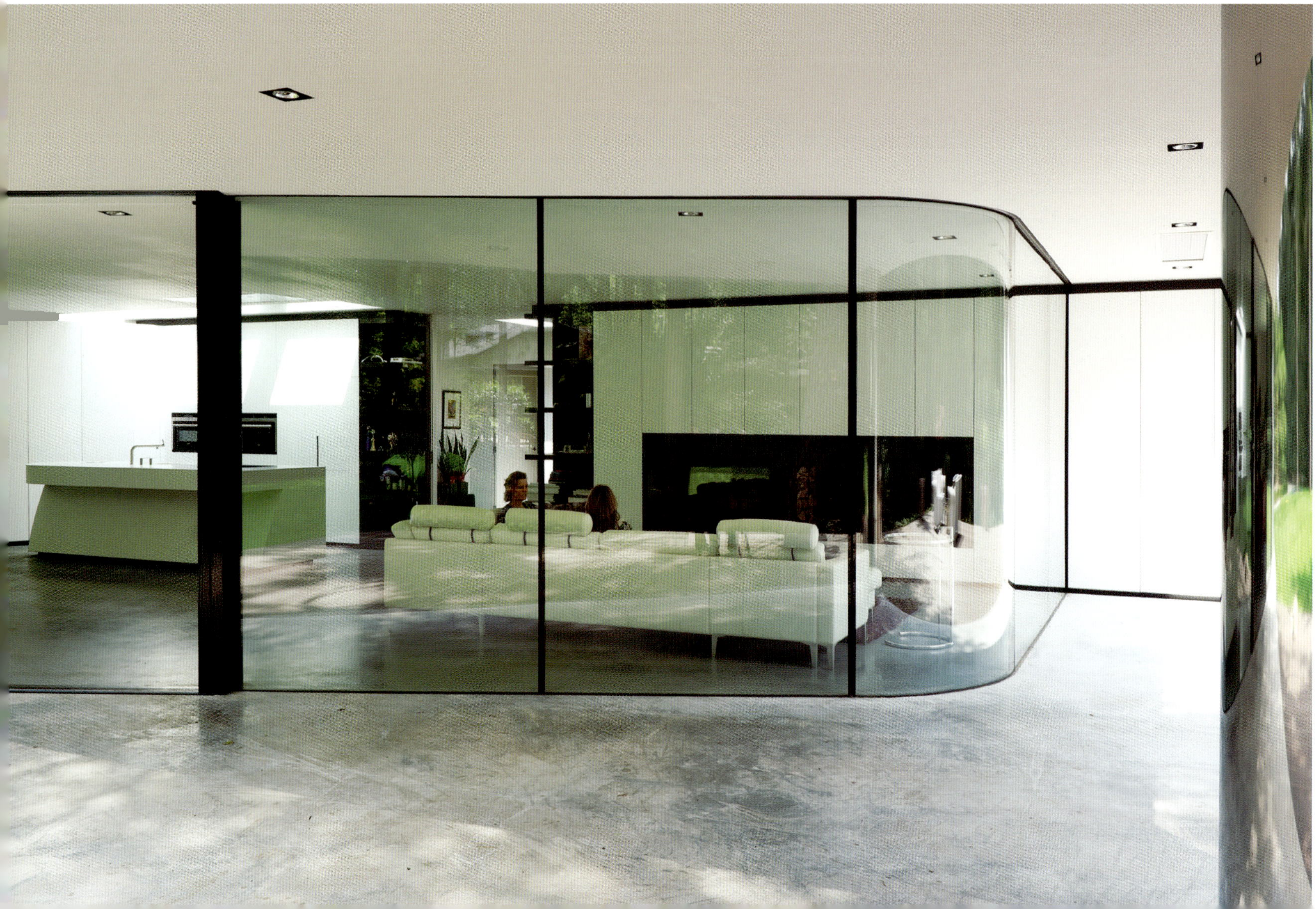

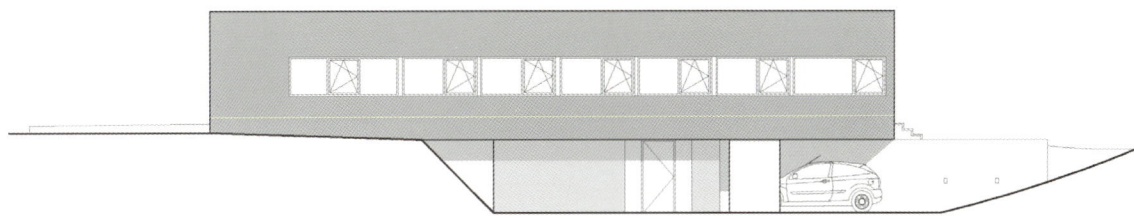

left: Living area_Outdoor area. right: Elevation_Bathroom_Living area_Kitchen.
links: Wohnbereich_Außenbereich. rechts: Ansicht_Bad_Wohnbereich_Küche.
gauche: Séjour_Extérieur. droite: Élévation_Salle de bains_Séjour_Cuisine.

MUNICH, GERMANY **VILLA IN SOLLN**

ARCHITECTS: UNTERLANDSTÄTTNER ARCHITEKTEN
COMPLETION: 2011
GROSS FLOOR AREA: 380 M²_**NUMBER OF ROOMS:** 10
PHOTOS: MICHAEL HEINRICH (200, 203 L., 203 B. R.),
FLORIAN HOLZHERR (201, 202, 203 A. R.)

Built 1902 in Munich, the landmarked villa was altered several times in the previous decades and the historic room structures changed. Within the scope of its rehabilitation, the original appearance and character of the monument were restored, unsuitable additions removed, and the façade renovated in keeping with monumental restoration regulations. New building sections and fitted furniture were inserted as clearly discernible independent elements in an understated and reversible manner. This preserved the historic character of the building, while bringing the internal room structure to life.

Die 1902 in München errichtete, denkmalgeschützte Villa wurde in den vorangegangenen Jahrzehnten mehrfach umgebaut und die historischen Raumstrukturen verändert. Im Zuge der Sanierung wurde das Denkmal in seinem ursprünglichen Erscheinungsbild und Charakter wiederhergestellt, nicht denkmalgerechte Einbauten aus früheren Baumaßnahmen zurückgebaut und die Fassade denkmalgerecht restauriert. Neue Bauteile und Möbeleinbauten wurden als erkennbare, eigenständige Bauteile klar, zurückhaltend und reversibel eingefügt. Hierdurch wird der historische Charakter des Gebäudes bewahrt und zugleich die Raumstruktur im Inneren erlebbar gemacht.

Cette villa de Munich datant de 1902, aujourd'hui classée monument historique, avait subi de multiples transformations avant d'être entièrement rénovée et reconstruite à l'original. Les ajouts de décennies passées ont alors été supprimés, tandis que la façade retrouvait son aspect d'antan. Pour l'intérieur, les architectes ont conçu des éléments nouveaux et des meubles intégrés d'un style sobre qu'il sera éventuellement possible de supprimer sans problème. Ce double concept de rénovation a permis de redonner à la villa son caractère d'origine, tout en optimisant la répartition des espaces intérieurs.

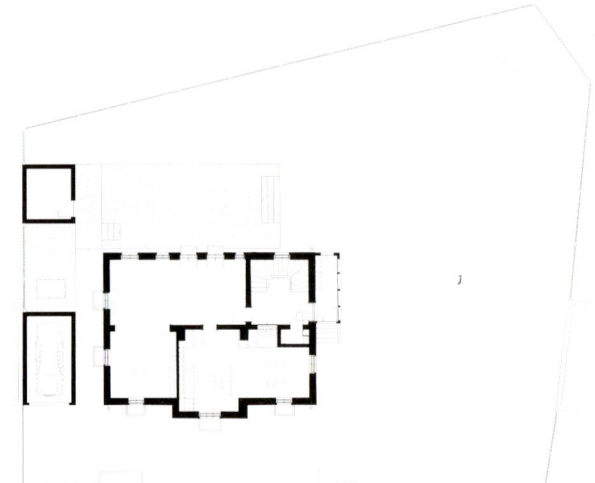

left: Ground floor plan_Garden view_Street view. right: Children's bedroom and stairs.
links: Grundriss EG_Gartenansicht_Straßenansicht. rechts: Kinderzimmer und Möbeltreppe.
gauche: Plan RdC_Vue du jardin_Vue de la rue. droite: Chambre d'enfant et escalier.

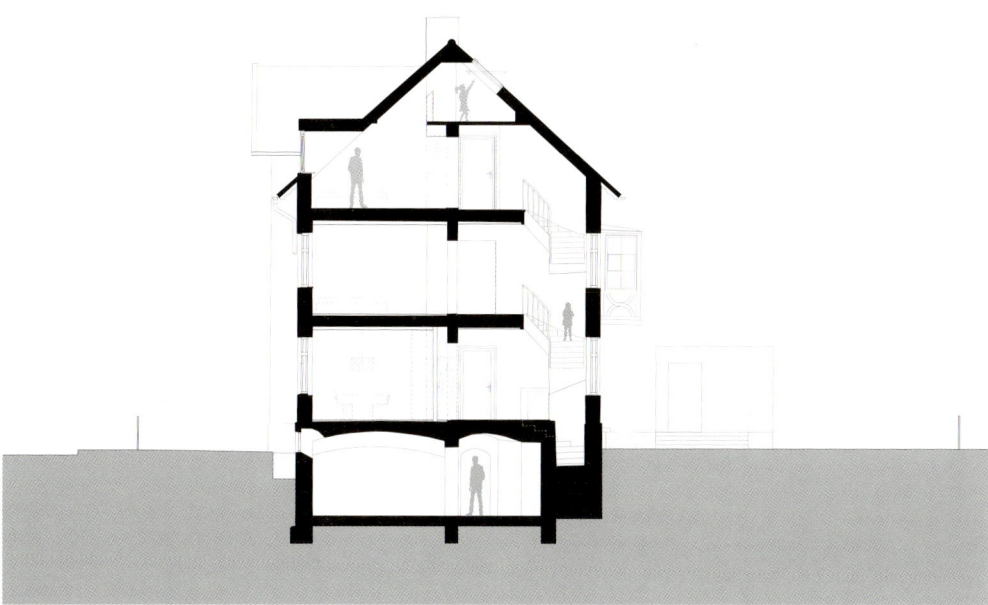

left: Children's bedroom and stairs. right: Section_Terrace and garage_Kitchen_Terrace detail.
links: Kinderzimmer und Möbeltreppe. rechts: Schnitt_Terrasse und Garage_Küche_Terrassendetail.
gauche: Chambre d'enfant et escalier. droite: Vue en coupe_Terrasse et garage_Cuisine_Detail de la terrasse.

HJELLESTAD, NORWAY **VILLA G**

ARCHITECTS: SAUNDERS ARCHITECTURE
COMPLETION: 2009_**PROPERTY SIZE:** 3,600 M²
GROSS FLOOR AREA: 368 M²
PHOTOS: BENT RENÉ SYNNEVÅG (204, 206, 207),
JAN LILLEBØ (205)

Villa G lies like a white landmark in the soft landscape of Hjellestad, near Bergen, Norway. The house is large yet not dominating, modern but not pretentious. Despite its futuristic form, it is built with traditional Nordic materials and architectural elements firmly based on Norwegian building methods. The timber cladding of the house consists of three different sizes mounted in a random pattern. The house has an overbuilt outside space, while the second floor covers the entrance below, helping the house to accommodate to the rough climate of the west coast of Norway.

Wie ein weißer Markstein ragt die Villa G aus der sanften Landschaft von Hjellestad, nahe der norwegischen Stadt Bergen. Der Bau ist großzügig und doch unaufdringlich, modern und doch unprätentiös. Trotz der futuristischen Formgebung besteht er aus traditionellen nordischen Materialien und architektonischen Elementen, die sich eng an die norwegische Bautradition anlehnen. Die Verkleidung setzt sich aus Hölzern in drei verschiedenen Größen zusammen, sodass ein zufälliges Muster entsteht. Die Villa verfügt über eine überdachte Terrasse. Zudem überragt das zweite Geschoss den Eingang – ein Zugeständnis an das raue Klima der norwegischen Westküste.

On ne peut pas véritablement dire que cette villa blanche passe inaperçue dans le paysage des environs de Hjellestad, petite ville située près de Bergen, en Norvège. Le bâtiment, raisonnablement vaste, est moderne sans ostentation. En dépit de son allure futuriste, il intègre des matériaux et des techniques de construction fortement enracinés dans la tradition architecturale scandinave. Le bardage des façades, par exemple, se compose de lattes de bois de trois tailles différentes assemblées au hasard. Afin de tenir compte du climat de la côte toute proche, l'architecte a prévu plusieurs espaces extérieurs couverts.

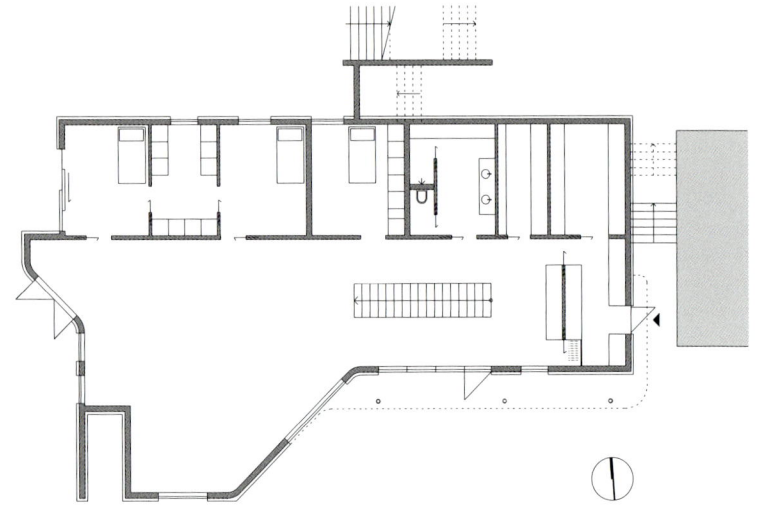

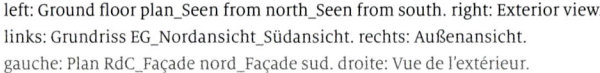

left: Ground floor plan_Seen from north_Seen from south. right: Exterior view.
links: Grundriss EG_Nordansicht_Südansicht. rechts: Außenansicht.
gauche: Plan RdC_Façade nord_Façade sud. droite: Vue de l'extérieur.

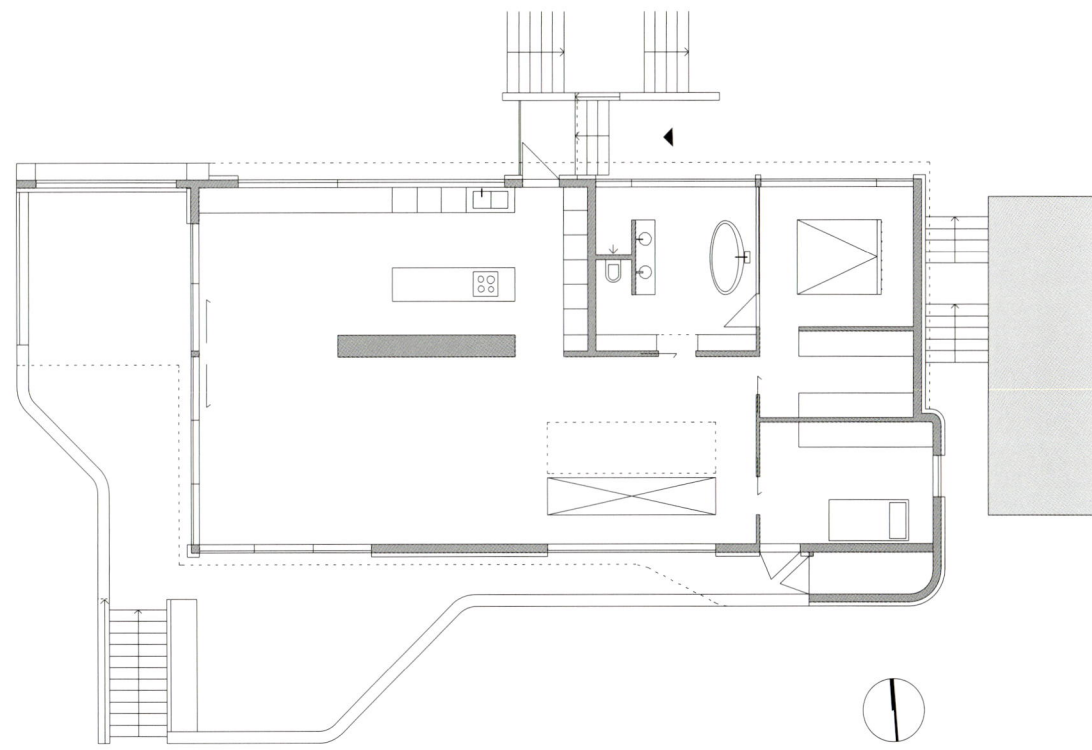

left: Dining area. right: Top floor plan_Living room_Dining area_Children's room.
links: Essbereich. rechts: Grundriss OG_Wohnraum_Essbereich_Kinderzimmer.
gauche: Salle à manger. droite: Plan niveau 1_Séjour_Salle à manger_Chambre d'enfant.

HAMBURG, GERMANY **VILLA LINARI**

ARCHITECTS: DIBELIUS ARCHITEKTEN
COMPLETION: 2011_**PROPERTY SIZE:** 955 M²
GROSS FLOOR AREA: 975 M²_**NUMBER OF ROOMS:** 6
PHOTOS: HEINER LEISKA / ARTUR IMAGES (208, 211),
ANDERS SUNE BERG (209, 210)

The 2-floor cubic new building is integrated into a homogenous row of listed single-family dwellings from the 1920s with hip roofs, small projections and clinker façades in a quiet residential street of Hamburg. The basic shape of the structure is a simple cube. It is situated on a narrow east-west site where it complements the orderly pattern of urban development that is typical of this area. Structurally designed with large expanses of glass, it nevertheless mirrors the scale and character of the neighboring buildings with its sculptural structure and anthracite-colored clinker bricks. On the street side towards the east, the house appears solid and rather closed off, whereas towards the garden in the west it appears as a three-dimensional opened up structure.

Der 2-geschossige kubische Neubau integriert sich in eine homogene Reihung ensemblegeschützter Einfamilienhäuser aus den 1920ger Jahren mit Walmdächern, kleinen Vorbauten und Klinkerfassaden in einer ruhigen Hamburger Wohnstraße. Die Grundform des Gebäudes ist ein einfacher Quader. Er liegt auf einem schmalen tiefen Ost-West- Grundstück und ergänzt das hier typische städtebauliche Ordnungs- und Erschließungsprinzip. Er ist plastisch durchformt mit großen Glasflächen, nimmt jedoch durch den anthrazitfarbenen Klinker und durch seine skulpturale Gliederung Bezug zum Maßstab und Charakter der Nachbarbebauung. Zur Straße im Osten zeigt sich das Wohnhaus körperhaft und eher geschlossen, zum Garten im Westen zeigt sich ein dreidimensional aufgelöster Baukörper.

Ce cube moderne sur trois niveaux s'intègre dans une rue tranquille de Hambourg dont les pavillons, construits dans les années 1920, font l'objet d'un classement pour la qualité architecturale de leurs façades en briques. La villa, construite sur un terrain de forme allongée orienté est/ouest, répond aux prescriptions locales en matière d'urbanisme. Bien que pourvue de grandes baies vitrées, elle s'inspire du caractère des immeubles voisins, notamment par son revêtement en briques de couleur anthracite structuré de manière plastique et sculpturale. La façade côté rue est relativement fermée et la façade ouest, qui donne sur le jardin, est fortement déstructurée dans les trois dimensions.

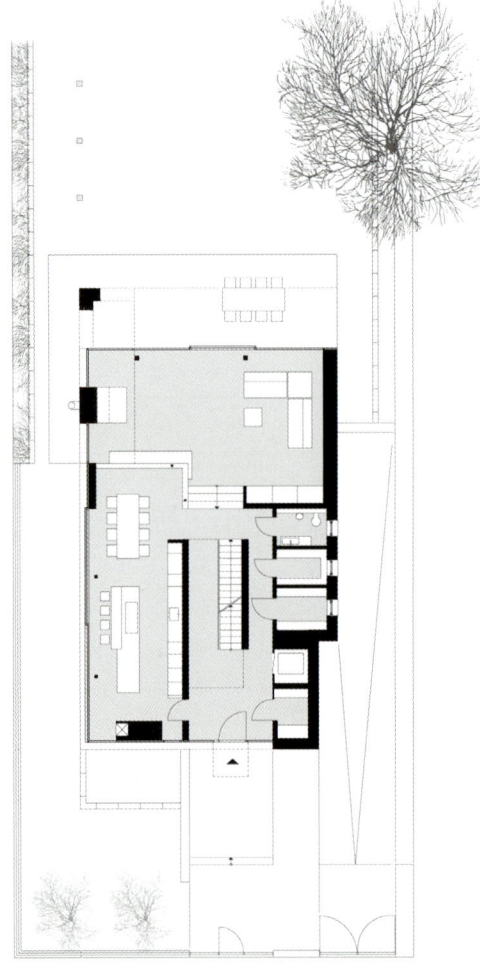

left: Ground floor plan_Detailed view of the passage to the garden_Garden view. right: Street view.
links: Grundriss EG_Detail Übergang Garten_Gartenansicht. rechts: Straßenansicht.
gauche: Plan RdC_Accès au jardin_Vue du jardin. droite: Vue de la rue.

left: Entrance area, artwork: Andrea Anatas, Hamburg. right: Section_Living room.
links: Eingangsbereich, Kunstwerk: Andrea Anatas, Hamburg. rechts: Schnitt_Wohnbereich.
gauche: Entrée, œuvre d'art: Andrea Anatas, Hamburg. droite: Vue en coupe_Séjour.

LAKE LUCERNE, SWITZERLAND **LAKESIDE VILLA**

ARCHITECTS: UNGER & TREINA AG
COMPLETION: 2009_**PROPERTY SIZE:** 970 M²
GROSS FLOOR AREA: 745 M²_**NUMBER OF ROOMS:** 6
PHOTOS: UNGER & TREINA AG

This stately villa sits on a steep slope where it enjoys a breathtaking view across the lake basin and the alps. The building consists of five levels. All walls and ceilings have oblique angles and are covered in light etched exposed concrete. The three top floors have different layouts. Each floor has an angled structure and is stacked box-like on the one below it. The clever arrangement creates insertions, angles and protrusions that give the entire building a vivid and three-dimensional appearance. Floor-to-ceiling windows were inserted at the angled ends of every floor. Each one focuses on a different section of the surrounding landscape.

Hoch oben an einem steilen Hang thront diese herrschaftliche Villa mit einer atemberaubenden Aussicht über das Seebecken und den Alpen. Das Bauwerk gliedert sich in fünf Ebenen. Alle Wände und Decken weisen schiefe Winkel auf und sind in einem hellen, abgesäuerten Sichtbeton gehalten. Die drei oberen Wohngeschosse haben unterschiedliche Grundrisse. Jedes Geschoss hat eine gewinkelte Anordnung und ist schachtelartig auf das darunterliegende gestapelt. Durch eine geschickte Differenzierung entstehen Einschübe, Winkel und Auskragungen, die dem ganzen Bauwerk eine lebendige, plastische Erscheinung geben. An den Enden der Verwinkelungen eines jeden Geschosses sind raumgrosse Fenster eingelassen. Sie fokussieren jeweils einen Ausschnitt der Landschaft.

On découvre un panorama impressionnant sur les Alpes et le lac des Quatre-Cantons à partir de cette magnifique villa construite à flanc de montagne. Le bâtiment se structure sur cinq niveaux. Les murs et plafonds, en béton brut de coffrage de couleur claire, se coupent en formant des angles irréguliers. Les cinq étages se superposent avec un certain décalage, les trois niveaux supérieurs ayant des plans dissemblables. Une différentiation subtile des volumes a pour résultat toute une série d'emboîtements et de porte-à-faux qui confèrent à l'ensemble un dynamisme plastique indéniable. À chacun des trois niveaux supérieurs, des côtés entièrement vitrés offrent des vues panoramiques sur le paysage environnant.

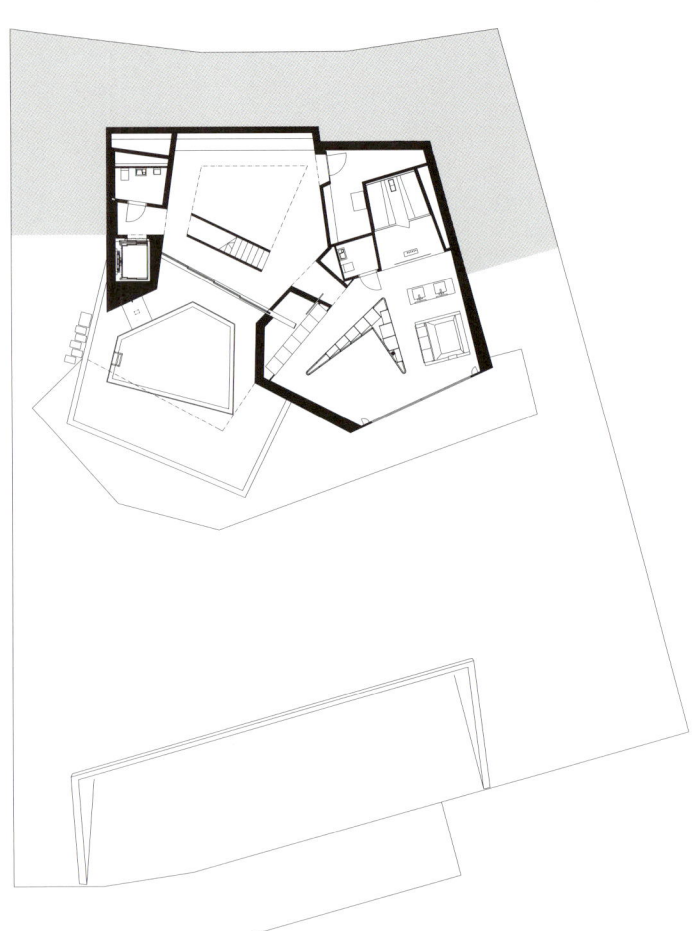

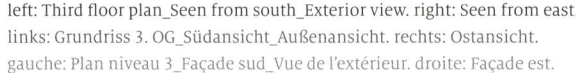

left: Third floor plan_Seen from south_Exterior view. right: Seen from east.
links: Grundriss 3. OG_Südansicht_Außenansicht. rechts: Ostansicht.
gauche: Plan niveau 3_Façade sud_Vue de l'extérieur. droite: Façade est.

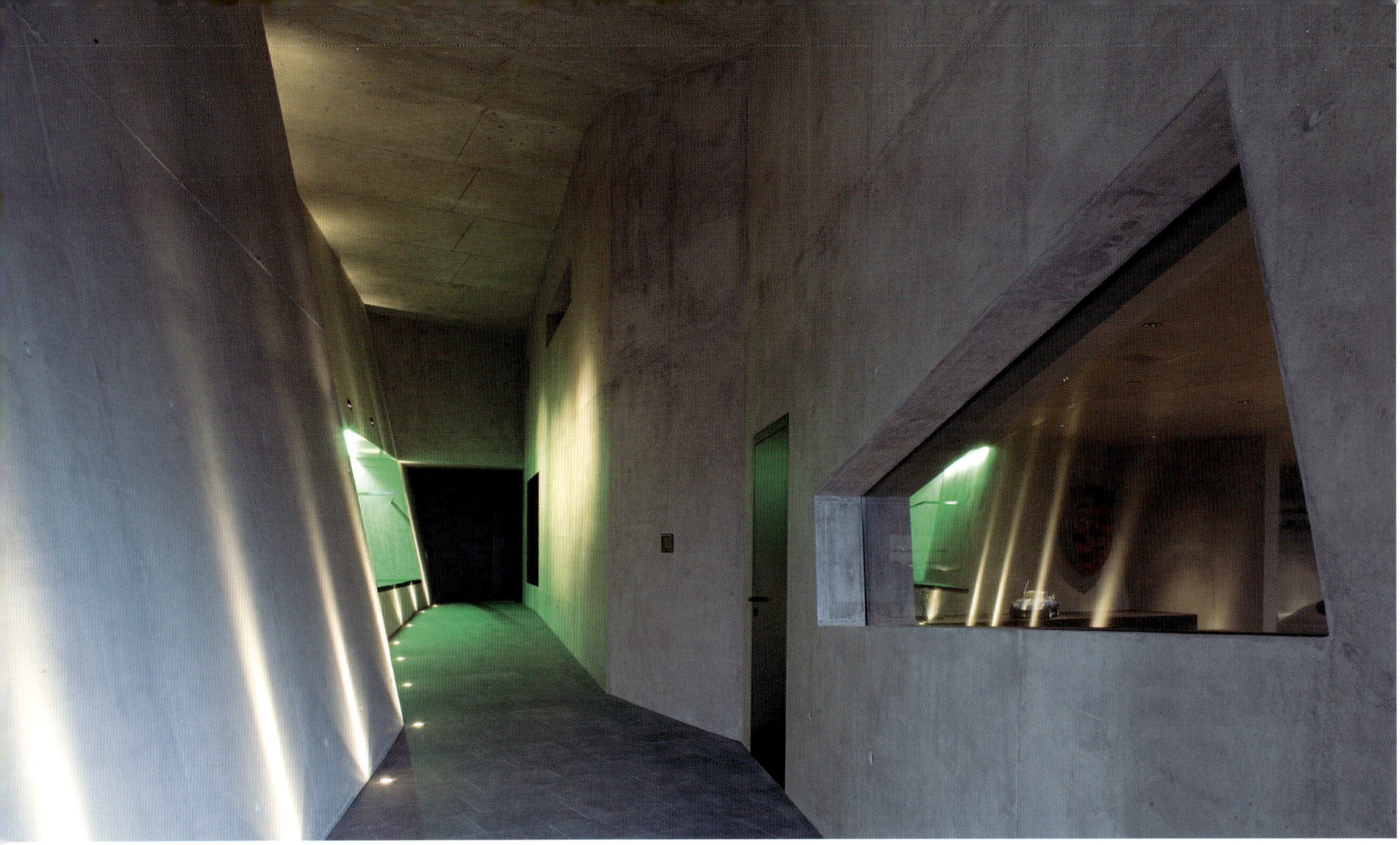
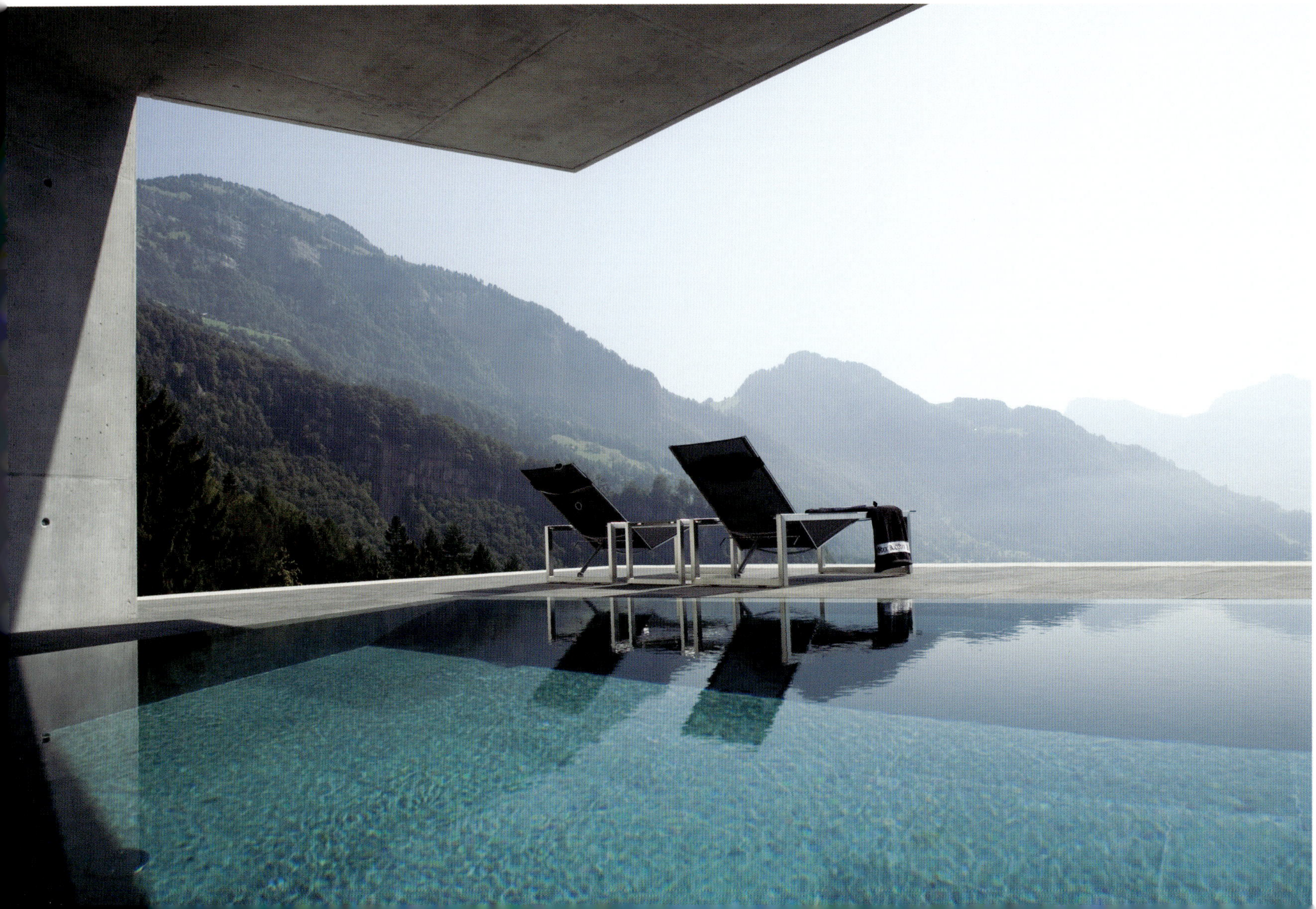

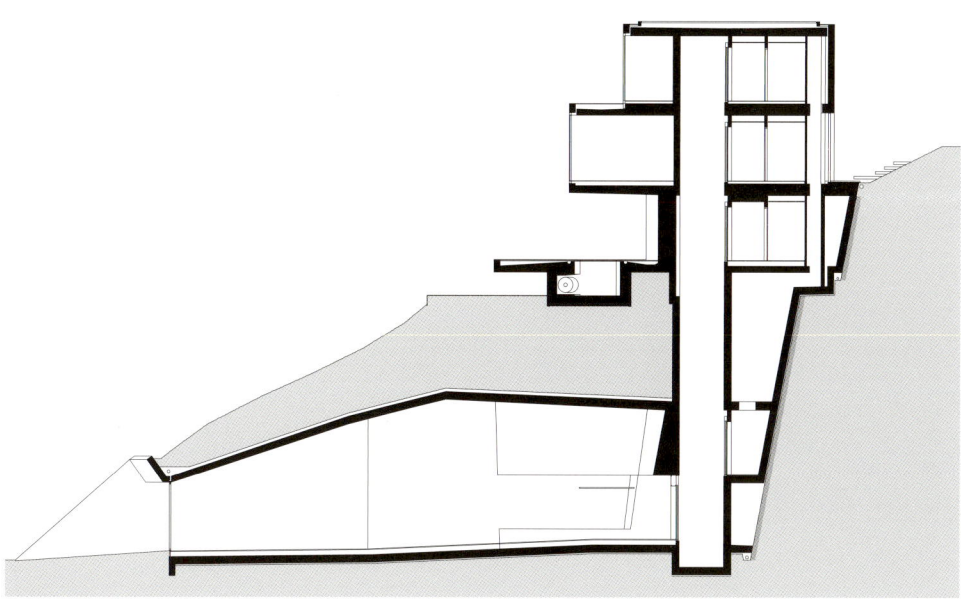

left: Access corridor_Pool. right: Section_Exterior view_Kitchen_Office.
links: Erschliessungskorridor_Pool. rechts: Schnitt_Außenansicht_Küche_Büro.
gauche: Corridor_Piscine extérieure .droite: Vue en coupe_Vue de l'extérieur_Cuisine_Bureau.

BAVARIA, GERMANY **PAVILION VILLA**

ARCHITECTS: WEBER + HUMMEL ARCHITEKTEN BDA
COMPLETION: 2010_**PROPERTY SIZE:** 1,977 M²
GROSS FLOOR AREA: 780 M²_**NUMBER OF ROOMS:** 30
PHOTOS: ROLAND HALBE / ARTUR IMAGES

To maintain the proportions of this detached single family home, the living space was divided into individual pavilions connected by yards. These yards are not only an integral part but also constitute the "heart" of the entire complex whose room-high glass panels creates flowing transitions between the interior and exterior. The pavilions themselves are understated with a uniform reduced material concept, which nevertheless generates a specific room atmosphere by its positioning and the individual furniture designs. Depending on whether one looks from the guest pavilion at the "quiet yard" or from the bedroom at the landscape of Franconian Switzerland, there is a balanced alternation between extroversion and introversion.

Um die Maßstäblichkeit dieses freistehenden Einfamilienhauses nicht zu sprengen, wurden die Wohnflächen in einzelne Pavillons aufgeteilt, die durch Höfe miteinander verbunden sind. Diese Höfe sind nicht nur integraler Bestandteil sondern auch „Herz" der Gesamtanlage, das durch raumhohe Verglasungen fließende Übergänge zwischen Innen und Außen herstellt. Die Pavillons selbst halten sich zurück und folgen einem einheitlichen reduzierten Materialkonzept, das jedoch durch Lage sowie individuelle Möbelentwürfe eine spezifische Raumstimmung generiert. Und je nachdem, ob man vom Gästepavillon in den „Stillen Hof" oder vom Schlafzimmer in die Fränkische Schweiz blickt, wechseln sich Introvertiertheit und Extrovertiertheit ausgewogen ab.

Afin d'éviter de créer un bâtiment aux proportions inadéquates, les architectes ont conçu pour cette villa divers volumes reliés par des cours qui non seulement font partie intégrante de l'ensemble, mais en constituent même le véritable cœur. L'usage intensif de murs entièrement vitrés contribue à dissoudre la distinction traditionnelle entre intérieur et extérieur. Conçus comme des pavillons, les différents volumes se caractérisent par leur retenue et l'usage des mêmes matériaux. Des meubles faits sur mesure viennent toutefois adoucir l'austérité de l'ensemble et générer une atmosphère spécifique. Que le regard aille du « pavillon des amis » à la « cour sereine » ou de la chambre principale au panorama qu'elle offre sur les collines de Haute-Franconie, on apprécie toujours ici un parfait équilibre entre intériorité et extériorisation.

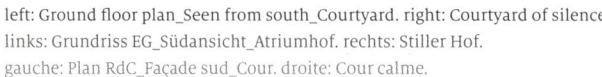

left: Ground floor plan_Seen from south_Courtyard. right: Courtyard of silence.
links: Grundriss EG_Südansicht_Atriumhof. rechts: Stiller Hof.
gauche: Plan RdC_Façade sud_Cour. droite: Cour calme.

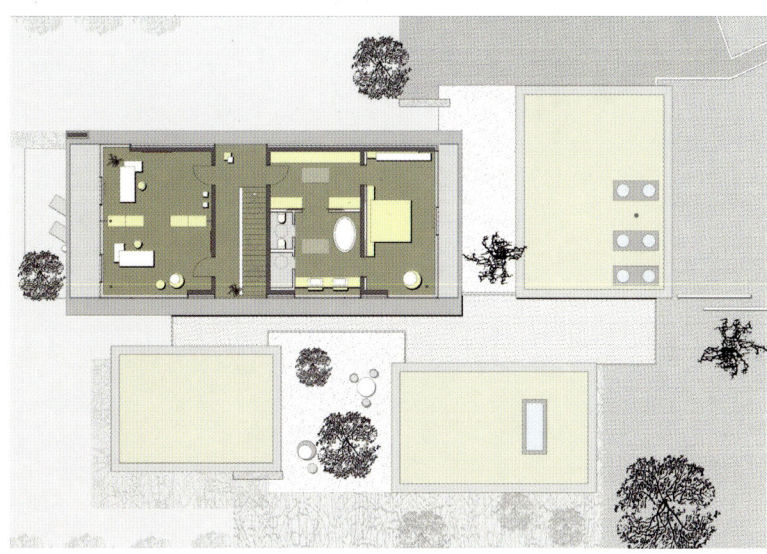

left: Foyer of the parlor. right: Top floor plan_Master bathroom on top floor.
links: Salonfoyer. rechts: Grundriss OG_Masterbad OG.
gauche: Foyer du salon. droite: Plan niveau 1_Salle de bains générale au niveau 1.

SESMA, NAVARRA, SPAIN **CASA MP**

ARCHITECTS: ALCOLEA+TÁRRAGO ARQUITECTOS
COMPLETION: 2012_**PROPERTY SIZE:** 507 M²
GROSS FLOOR AREA: 314 M²_**NUMBER OF ROOMS:** 4
PHOTOS: IÑAKI BERGERA

Casa MP is a monolithic, archetypal geometry in concrete and stained pine-wood. The aim was to improve the orientation and views, and to clear the plot for a small garden and orchard. The house was therefore placed on the upper level of the site and based on restrictive alignment and height regulations, which optimized the southern view of the surrounding grain fields. A garage is separated from the main volume closing the north side, with large pine board sliding doors to the garden. There is a three-meter-wide patio access between the house and garage. The living room area and kitchen consist of a single space. Four bedrooms, two bathrooms and a laundry room are on the upper floor. The basement features a multipurpose space, facilities and storage rooms.

Die monolithische Casa MP ist ein in seiner Geometrie archetypischer Bau aus Sichtbeton und gebeiztem Kiefernholz. Um optimale Ausblicke und Raum für einen kleinen Garten zu schaffen, wurde die Villa auf dem oberen Teil des Grundstücks errichtet. Dabei waren strenge Bauvorschriften betreffend Ausrichtung und Höhe zu beachten. Im Süden öffnet sich der Blick über die umliegenden Getreidefelder. Im Norden schließt eine freistehende Garage mit großen Schiebetüren den Komplex ab. Den Eingangsbereich bildet eine drei Meter breite Veranda. Im Erdgeschoss liegt der Wohnbereich mit offener Küche. Vier Schlafzimmer, zwei Bäder und die Waschküche befinden sich im Obergeschoss. Der Keller enthält einen multifunktionalen Raum, die Haustechnik sowie Lagermöglichkeiten.

La villa MP est un archétype monolithique en béton qui entend optimiser l'orientation et les vues sur les environs, tout en ménageant de la place pour un jardin. Afin de répondre à ces exigences, les architectes l'ont construite sur la partie haute du terrain, en tenant compte de la législation locale en matière d'alignement et de hauteur du toit. La façade principale, orientée au sud, s'ouvre par de grandes portes-fenêtres sur un champ de blé voisin. Sur le côté nord, le volume principal se complète d'un garage et d'un patio de trois mètres de large. Le rez-de-chaussée est occupé par un séjour avec cuisine ouverte, tandis que le premier étage abrite quatre chambres, deux salles de bains et une buanderie. Un espace multifonctionnel, un débarras et un local technique se trouvent par ailleurs à la cave.

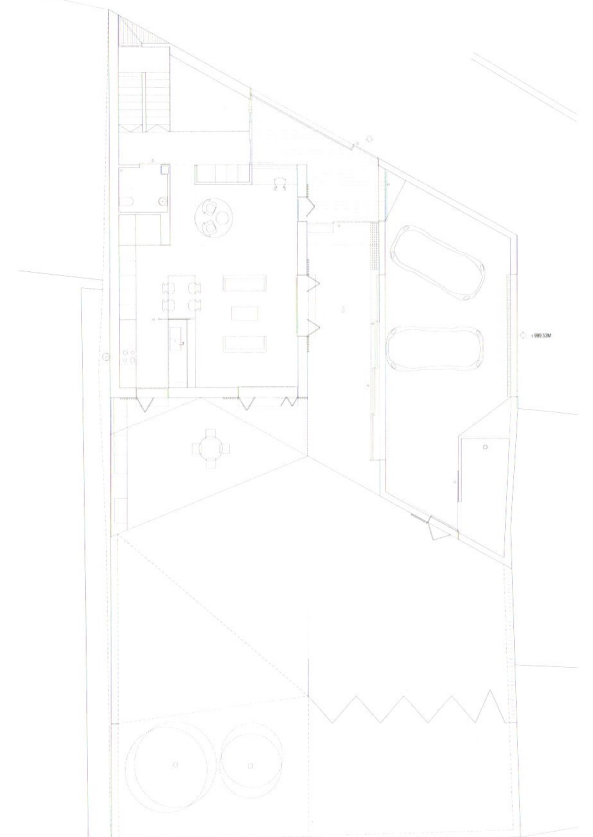

left: Ground floor plan_Exterior view_Detail of the façade. right: Main view.
links: Grundriss EG_Außenansicht_Fassadendetail. rechts: Hauptansicht.
gauche: Plan RdC_Vue de l'extérieur_Détail de la façade. droite: Façade principale.

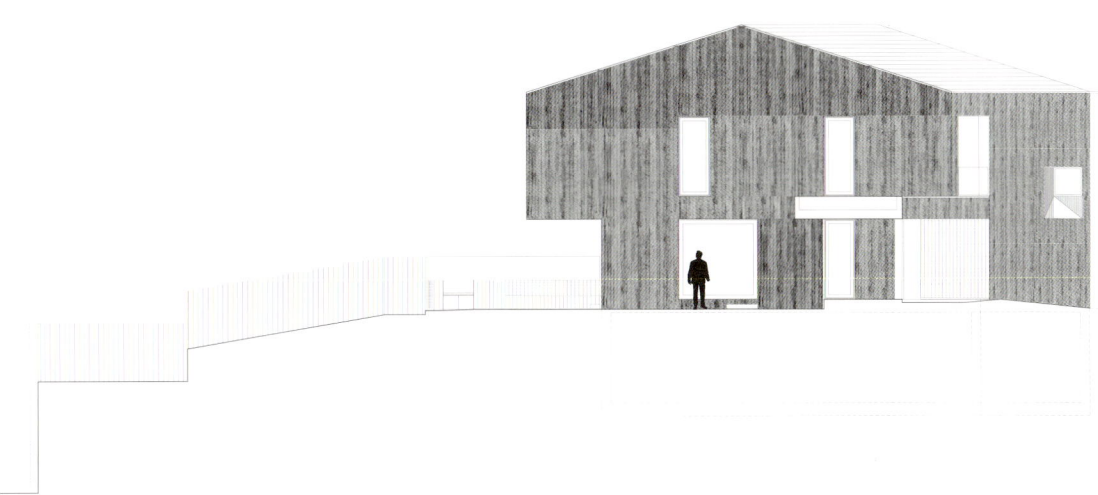

left: Exterior view with garage. right: Elevation_Entrance_Living room_Garage.
links: Außenansicht mit Garage. rechts: Ansicht_Eingang_Wohnbereich_Garage.
gauche: Vue de l'extérieur avec garage. droite: Élévation_Entrée_Séjour_Garage.

ST. NIKLAUSEN, SWITZERLAND **CASA STUTZ**

ARCHITECTS: RO.MA. ROEOESLI & MAEDER
COMPLETION: 2011_**PROPERTY SIZE:** 1,150 M²
GROSS FLOOR AREA: 310 M²_**NUMBER OF ROOMS:** 6
PHOTOS: FRANZ RINDLISBACHER

The Casa Stutz has a clearly defined volume as an analog reaction to the villas surrounding it. Along the access road, the new building consists of a single volume, which develops into a two-floor volume towards the south-east, opening up towards the garden and the lake with large glass panels and a generously proportioned terrace. The building sections that are closed off towards the street are illuminated by courtyards and guarantee visual and acoustic insulation. Designed as a single space, the ground floor is zoned by the central staircase structure. This is in contrast to the arrangement of the rooms on the top floor, which include the bedrooms and bathroom areas, for which it provides the required intimacy and retreat options.

Die Casa Stutz versteht sich als klar definiertes Volumen und reagiert damit analog auf die das Grundstück umgebenden Villenbauten. Der entlang der Zufahrtsstraße eingeschossige Neubau tritt in südöstlicher Richtung als zweigeschossiges Volumen in Erscheinung, welches sich zum Garten und zum See mit grossformatigen Verglasungen und einem grosszügigen Loggiabereich öffnet. Die straßenseitig geschlossenen Gebäudeteile werden über Höfe belichtet und garantieren den Sicht- und Schallschutz. Das als ein Raum konzipierte Erdgeschoss wird einzig durch den zentralen Treppenkörper zoniert. Demgegenüber kontrastiert die Zimmeranordnung im Obergeschoss, welches die Schlaf- und Sanitärbereiche beherbergt und die nötige Intimität und Rückzugsmöglichkeit bieten.

Le volume clairement défini de la « Casa Stutz » établit une analogie avec les villas voisines. De plain-pied côté rue, le bâtiment s'élève sur deux niveaux côté jardin. Sur cette façade orientée au sud-est, une loggia spacieuse et de grandes baies vitrées donnent sur la verdure et le lac qu'on aperçoit à proximité. La façade côté rue est dépourvue d'ouvertures afin d'assurer une bonne isolation phonique et visuelle des occupants, mais bénéficie tout de même d'un bon éclairage naturel grâce à des cours intérieures. Le rez-de-chaussée est une seule et même grande pièce dans laquelle seul l'escalier vient établir un zonage. Le niveau supérieur, par contre, se subdivise en plusieurs chambres et salles de bains offrant l'intimité nécessaire.

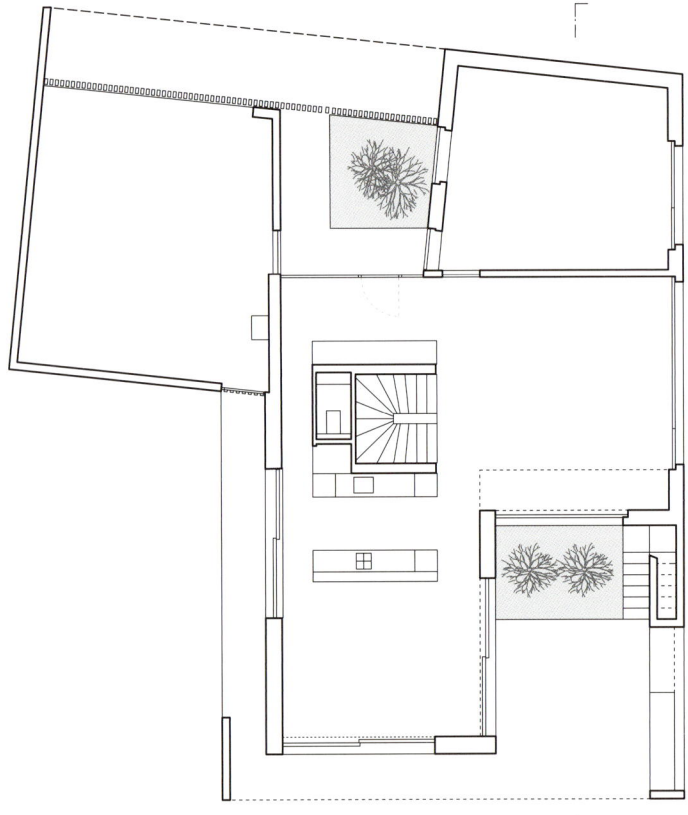

left: Ground floor plan_Seen from south-east and north-east. right: Seen from south-west_Kitchen_Anteroom top floor. links: Grundriss EG_Südost- und Nordostansicht. rechts: Südwestansicht_Küche_Vorzone OG. gauche: Plan RdC_ Façade sud-est et nord-est. droite: Façade sud-ouest_Cuisine_Couloir niveau 1.

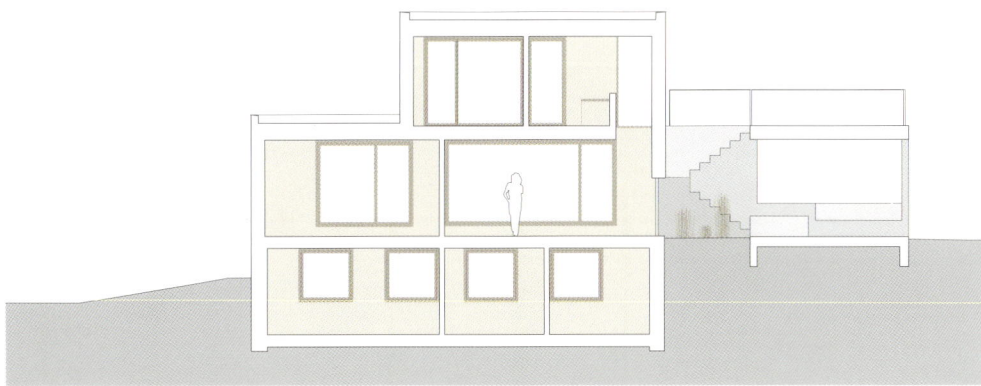

left: Living area. right: Section_Patio_Dining area with loggia_Bathroom.
links: Wohnen. rechts: Schnitt_Patio_Essbereich mit Loggia_Badezimmer.
gauche: Séjour. droite: Vue en coupe_Patio_Salle à manger avec loggia_Salle de bains.

MUNAVALI, ALIBAUG, INDIA **THE BRICK KILN HOUSE**

ARCHITECTS: SPASM DESIGN ARCHITECTS
COMPLETION: 2012_**PROPERTY SIZE:** 9,800 M²
GROSS FLOOR AREA: 830 M²_**NUMBER OF ROOMS:** 7
PHOTOS: SEBASTIAN ZACHARIAH

Around the Raigad district, one often sees local brick stacks being baked on the green lots that surround them. Using this image the red earth brick house forms just another ambiguous STACK. The two main wings of the house, sit at right-angles to each other holding a curious mango tree, with aspects like orientation, wind and rain direction duly considered. The living space has a curious shed-like volume, where the materials of the house come together rather loosely. Insinuating incompleteness and creating a sense of being immersed in the vegetation around. The sequencing of the rooms is frugal, and in series as a farm building.

Im indischen Distrikt Raigad ist Backstein allgegenwärtig. Stapelweise ist er zwischen Hütten aufgeschichtet, wo er auch gebrannt wird. Dies inspirierte zum Entwurf der Villa, die wie ein weiterer vielschichtiger Stapel aus roten Ziegeln wirkt. Die Hauptflügel stehen im rechten Winkel zueinander und rahmen einen vorwitzigen Mangobaum ein. Die Ausrichtung berücksichtigt Regen und Windrichtung. Der Wohnbereich liegt in einem Volumen, das an einen Schuppen erinnert. Zwischen den unterschiedlichen Materialien scheint nur ein loser Zusammenhang zu bestehen. So spielt die Villa mit dem Anschein von Unvollständigkeit, was den Eindruck erweckt, der Bau gehe in die Vegetation über. Die Räume folgen in schlichter Reihung aufeinander wie auf einer Farm.

Cette villa s'inscrit dans la tradition des maisons en briques rouges entourées d'un jardin qui sont fréquentes dans la région de Raigad, en Inde. Elle se compose de deux ailes disposées à angle droit autour d'un vieux manguier en tenant compte de facteurs tels que l'orientation, les vents dominants et la pluie. Les pièces de séjour occupent un volume évoquant une grange dans lequel divers matériaux s'associent de manière assez aléatoire. Une façade entièrement vitrée ouvre largement cet espace sur la végétation environnante. Les autres pièces, à la décoration sobre, se succèdent comme dans les fermes indiennes traditionnelles.

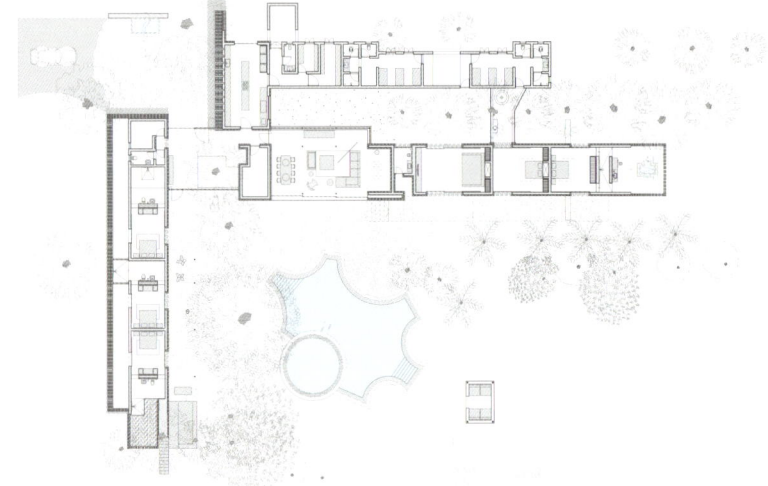

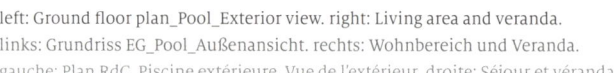

left: Ground floor plan_Pool_Exterior view. right: Living area and veranda.
links: Grundriss EG_Pool_Außenansicht. rechts: Wohnbereich und Veranda.
gauche: Plan RdC_Piscine extérieure_Vue de l'extérieur. droite: Séjour et véranda.

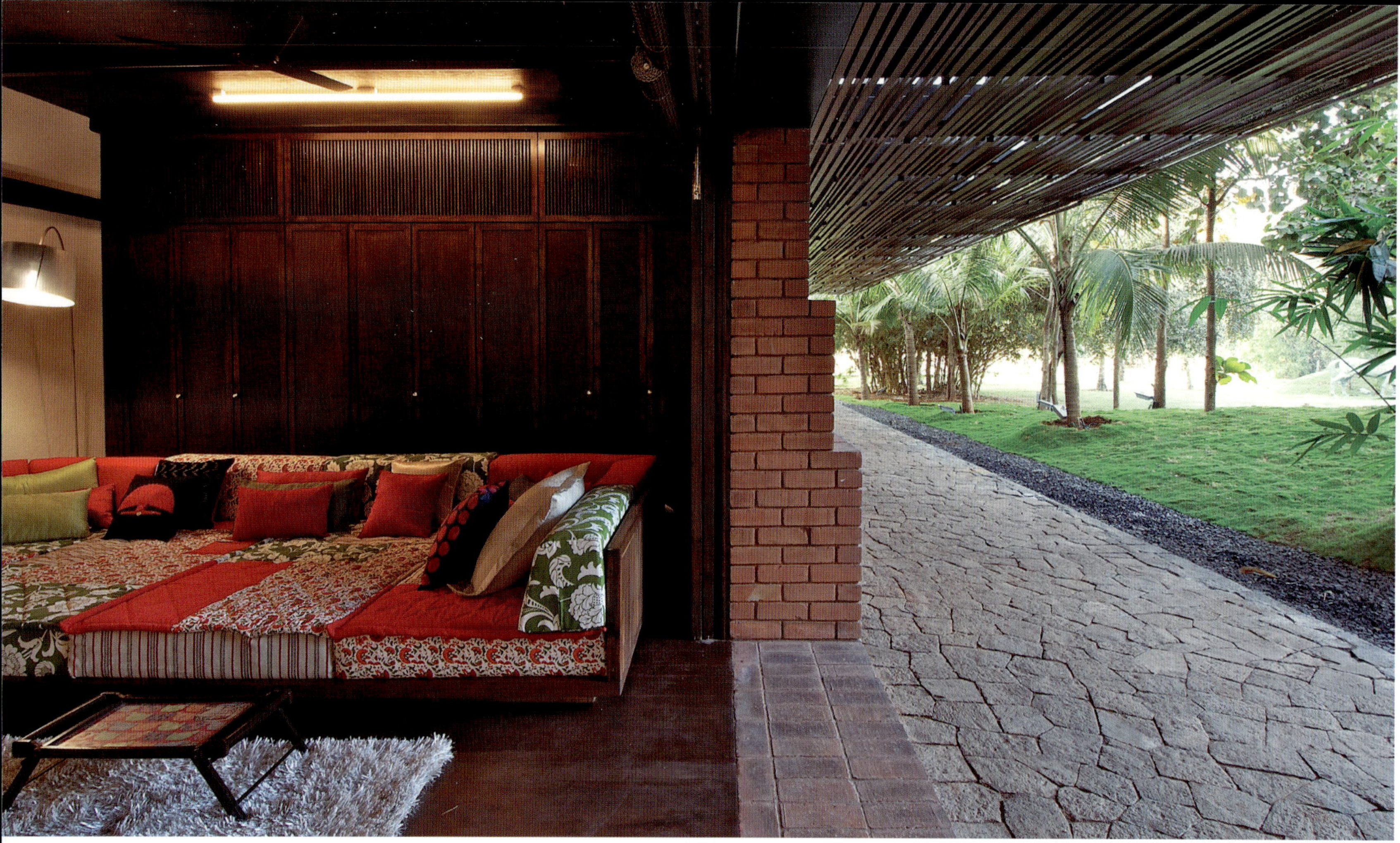

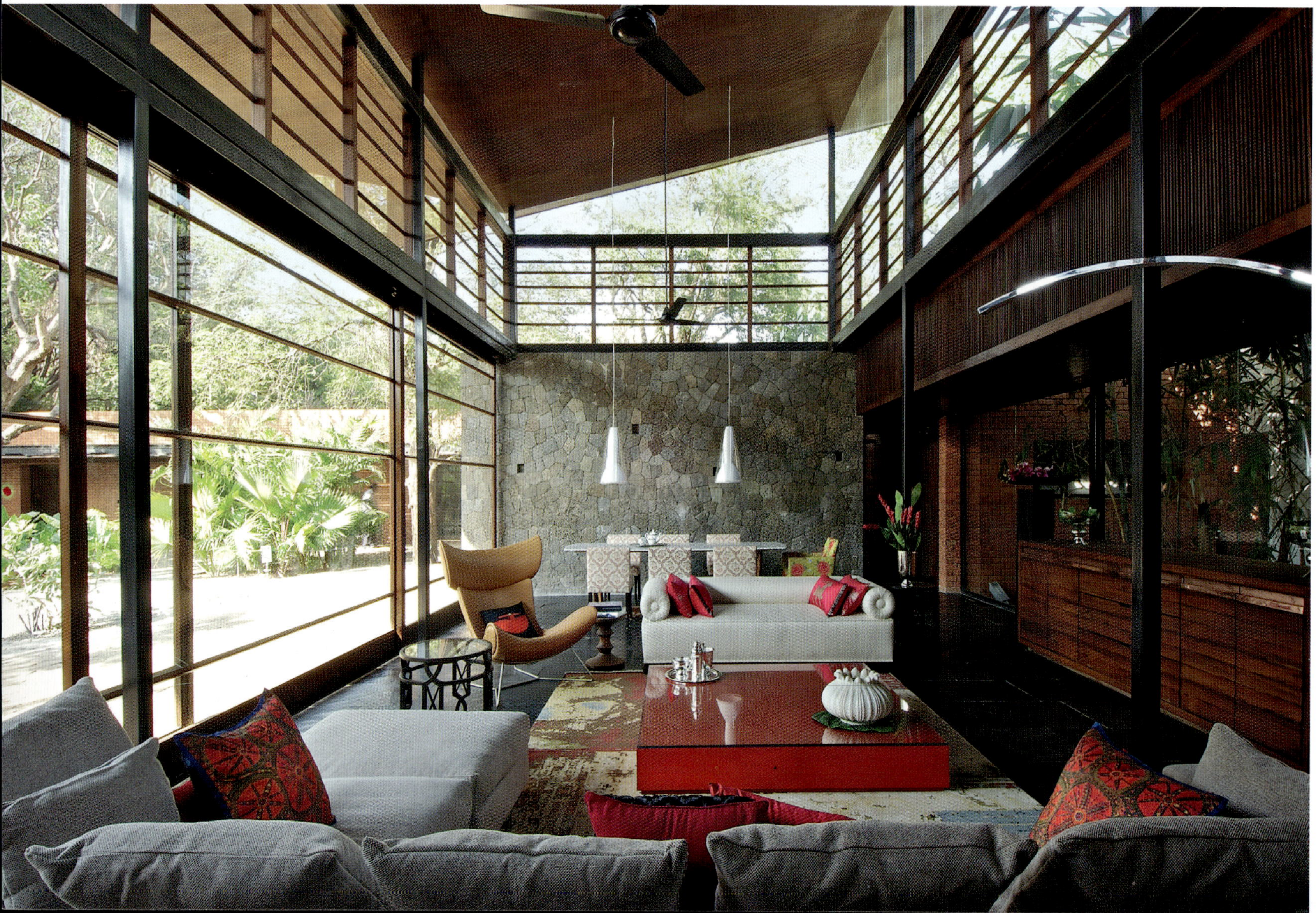

left: Media room_Living area. right: Section_Stairs_Bathroom_Terrace.
links: Medienzimmer_Wohnbereich. rechts: Schnitt_Treppe_Bad_Terrasse.
gauche: Salle des médias_Séjour. droite: Vue en coupe_Escalier_Salle de bains_Terrasse.

RAGUSA IBLA, ITALY **CASA LR**

ARCHITECTS: ARCHITREND ARCHITECTURE
GAETANO MANGANELLO, CARMELO TUMINO
COMPLETION: 2012_**PROPERTY SIZE:** 19,620 M²
GROSS FLOOR AREA: 310 M²_**NUMBER OF ROOMS:** 6
PHOTOS: CRISTINA FIORENTINI

The house is located on a hillside in front of the historical center of Ragusa Ibla, Italy. Due to its strategic position, it enjoys a scenic view. The project focused on the existing building, which was renovated carefully. The house is divided into two levels. The first level is on the altitude of the street-side entrance and includes the living area and a large entrance room with a central staircase that descends to the lower level where the sleeping area is located. Across from the entrance there is a large space covered in laminated timber beams painted white. It includes the kitchen, living, and dining room areas. The sleeping area consists of three bedrooms with services and a study. All rooms overlook the scenic landscape.

Die Villa liegt an einem Hang über dem historischen Zentrum der italienischen Stadt Ragusa - eine strategisch günstige Lage für einen atemberaubenden Ausblick. Im Zentrum des Projekts stand die sorgfältige Renovierung des Bestands. Der Wohnraum erstreckt sich über zwei Ebenen: Das Erdgeschoss auf Höhe der Zufahrtsstraße beherbergt den Wohnbereich sowie einen großen Eingangsbereich mit der Haupttreppe, die zu den Schlafzimmern im unteren Geschoss führt. Der großzügige Bereich gegenüber des Eingangs ist mit weiß laminierten Holzbalken verkleidet. Hier befinden sich Küche, Wohn- und Essbereich. Der Schlafbereich besteht aus drei Zimmern, daneben liegen Haustechnik und Büro. Der malerische Ausblick lässt sich aus allen Räumen genießen.

Cette villa est située sur une colline offrant une vue panoramique sur la vieille ville de Raguse, en Sicile. Il s'agit d'une maison ancienne entièrement rénovée, construite sur deux niveaux : le premier, auquel on accède en venant de la rue, abrite un grand vestibule où se trouve un escalier central menant aux chambres du niveau inférieur. Derrière le vestibule s'ouvre un vaste espace couvert en lamellé posé sur des poutres peintes en blanc, qui rassemble la cuisine, le séjour et la salle à manger. Aux chambres du niveau inférieur viennent s'ajouter les sanitaires et un bureau. Toutes les pièces bénéficient de vues magnifiques sur les environs.

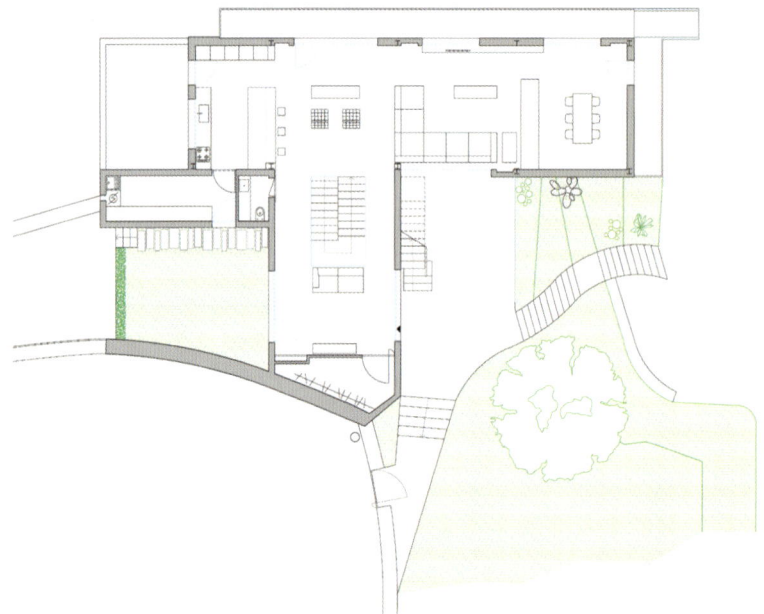

left: Ground floor plan_Pool_Stairs outside. right: Exterior view_Panorama_Outdoor area.
links: Grundriss EG_Pool_Außentreppe. rechts: Außenansicht_Panorama_Außenbereich.
gauche: Plan RdC_Piscine extérieure_Escalier extérieur. droite: Vue de l'extérieur_Panorama_Extérieur.

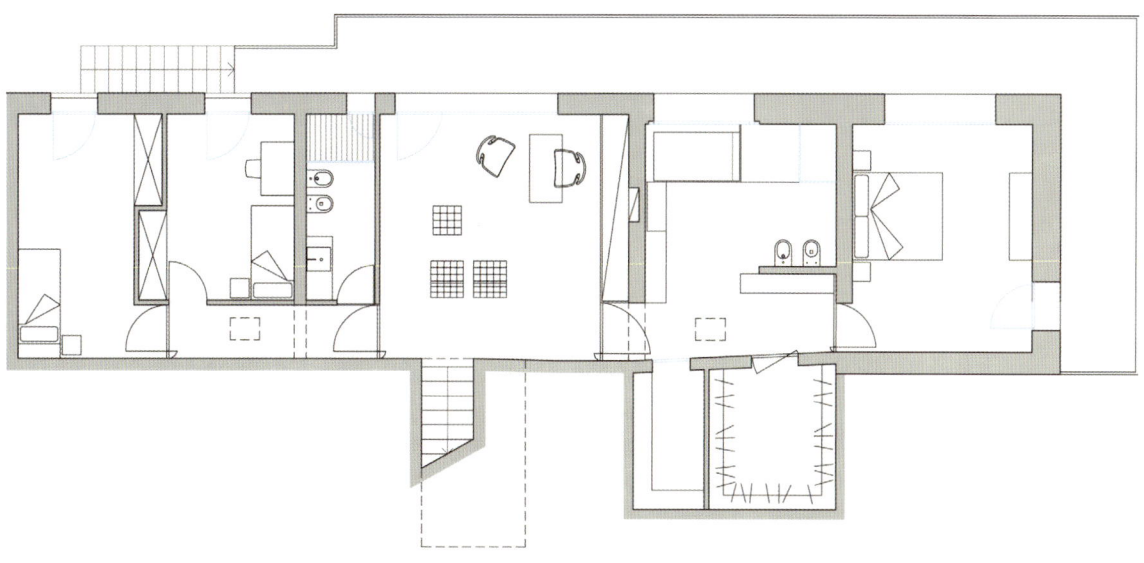

left: Dining area. right: Top floor plan_Living room_Kitchen_Bathroom_Balcony.
links: Essbereich. rechts: Grundriss OG_Wohnraum_Küche_Bad_Balkon.
gauche: Salle à manger. droite: Plan niveau 1_Séjour_Cuisine_Salle de bains_Balcon.

WINDISCH, SWITZERLAND **HOUSE BACHMANN**

ARCHITECTS: MISCHA BADERTSCHER ARCHITEKTEN AG
COMPLETION: 2010_**PROPERTY SIZE:** 670 M²
GROSS FLOOR AREA: 280 M²_**NUMBER OF ROOMS:** 6
PHOTOS: ROGER FREI (236–238, 239 L.), ATILLA KARATAY (239 R.)

The shape of the building is a reaction to the geometry of the borders and the edge of the slope that runs diagonally across the plot with the house located immediately on the edge. The exposed concrete skin combines the complex geometry of the building into a single entity. The large sliding windows of the living/dining area create a unit with the garden and the terrace located in front. Interior and exterior spaces are smoothly merged. The private rooms are arranged on the top floor. Each room has an open connection to a private bathroom.

Das Gebäude reagiert in seiner Form auf die Geometrie der Grenzverläufe sowie der diagonal über das Grundstück verlaufende Böschung und positioniert sich direkt an der Hauskante. Die Sichtbetonhülle fasst die komplexe Geometrie des Gebäudes zu einer Einheit zusammen. Die großzügigen Schiebefenster im Wohn-Essbereich lassen gemeinsam mit dem Garten und der gegenüber in Richtung Grünraum vorgelagerten Terrasse, ein Zusammen entstehen. Die Innen- und Aussenräume gehen hier nahtlos ineinander über. Im Obergeschoss sind die privaten Räume angeordnet. Hier erhält jedes Zimmer ein eigenes Bad mit offener Verbindung zum Schlafraum.

La forme de ce bâtiment est due à la configuration d'un terrain dont la pente est encore visible à une pointe végétalisée. L'enveloppe en béton brut de coffrage confère son unité à l'ensemble. Les grandes baies vitrées coulissantes du salon/salle à manger établissent une connexion entre l'intérieur, la terrasse et le jardin qui la prolonge, de sorte que le passage d'un espace à l'autre se fait tout en douceur. Chacune des chambres disposées au niveau supérieur communique directement avec sa propre salle de bain.

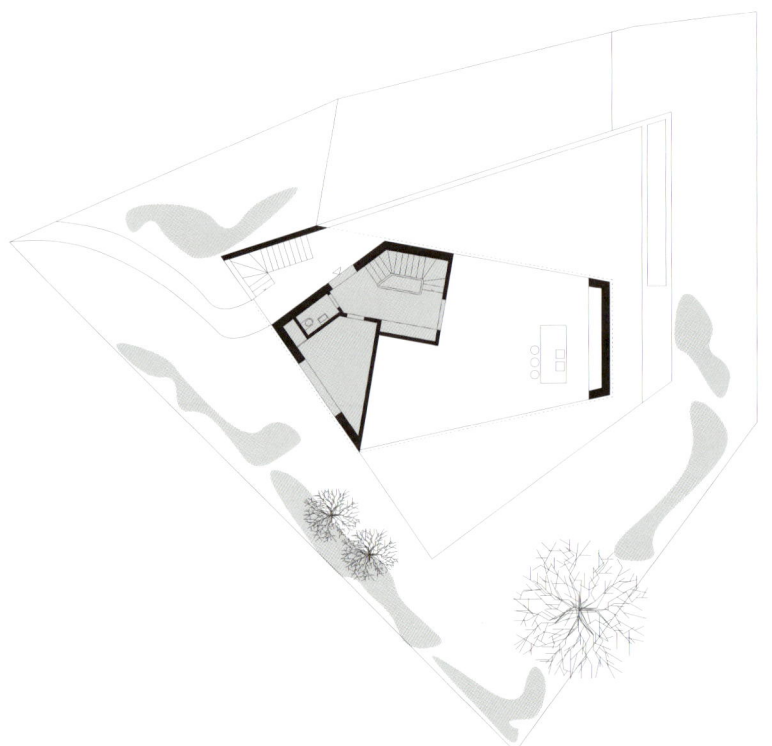

left: Ground floor plan_Seen from south_Seen from north. right: Seen from north-east.
links: Grundriss EG_Südansicht_Nordansicht. rechts: Nordostansicht.
gauche: Plan RdC_Façade sud_Façade nord. droite: Façade nord-est.

left: Stairs. right: Cross section_Seen from south-west_Stairs.
links: Treppe. rechts: Längsschnitt_Südwestansicht_Treppe.
gauche: Escalier. droite: Coupe longitudinale_Façade sud-ouest_Escalier.

KARUIZAWA, JAPAN **SHELL**

ARCHITECTS: KOTARO IDE / ARTECHNIC ARCHITECTS
COMPLETION: 2008_**PROPERTY SIZE:** 1,711 M²
GROSS FLOOR AREA: 330 M²_**NUMBER OF ROOMS:** 6
PHOTOS: NACASA & PARTNERS INC.

A large shell shaped structure finds itself in the middle of the woods. It is hard to determine what exactly the structure is, and unlike the surrounding caves and rocks, it clearly is not a part of nature – nor is it a ruin. A frame, a shape, made at a completely different place for a completely different purpose. Within this shell shaped structure one will find floors constructed, wall separating spaces, and rooms furnished. The scenery conjures a science ficton film-like image, in which locals inhabit over an abandoned spacecraft. With time, trees start to grow encircling the spacecraft, harmonizing it into the landscape.

Inmitten eines Waldes stößt man auf ein großes schalenartiges Gehäuse. Die eigenartige Form lässt sich kaum definieren, doch anders als die Höhlen und Felsen in der Umgebung handelt es sich eindeutig nicht um ein natürliches Gebilde – noch um eine Ruine. Es scheint aus einer völlig anderen Welt zu stammen, geschaffen für einen fremdartigen Zweck. Im Innern der Struktur findet man eingezogene Ebenen vor, Wände, die Räume abgrenzen, und möblierte Zimmer. Es wirkt wie die Kulisse eines Science-Fiction-Films, in dem Einheimische ein verlassenes Raumschiff in Besitz nehmen. Mit der Zeit wachsen Bäume, die die Konturen des Raumschiffs verwischen, sodass es eins wird mit der Natur.

S'il est clair que ce n'est ni une ruine ni un élément naturel, il reste bien difficile de définir exactement ce qu'évoque cette coquille entourée d'arbres, posée sur un terrain où abondent grottes et rochers. Serait-ce un cadre, une forme provenant d'ailleurs et remplissant une fonction mystérieuse ? On trouve à l'intérieur des espaces meublés, séparés par des cloisons et structurés sur différents niveaux. Et si c'était plutôt un vaisseau spatial abandonné, occupé par quelques autochtones ? Avec le temps, des arbres semblent avoir poussé autour de ce véhicule de science-fiction pour mieux l'intégrer à son environnement terrien.

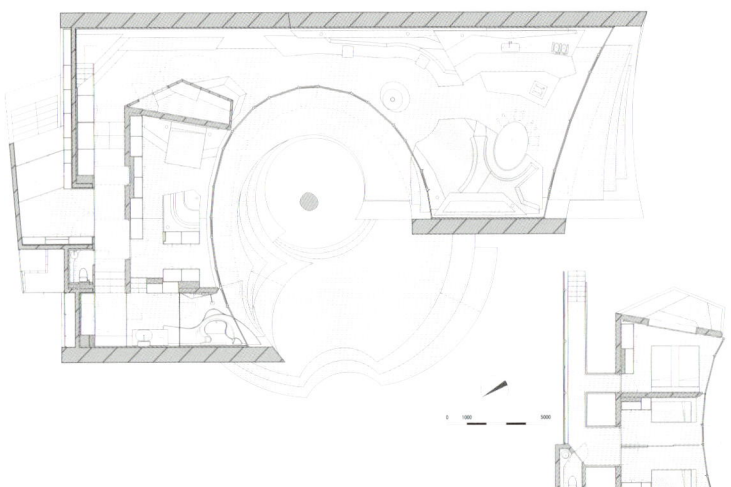

left: Floor plans_Exterior view_Garden view. right: Outdoor area.
links: Grundrisse_Außenansicht_Gartenansicht. rechts: Außenbereich.
gauche: Plans_Vue de l'extérieur_Vue du jardin. droite: Extérieur.

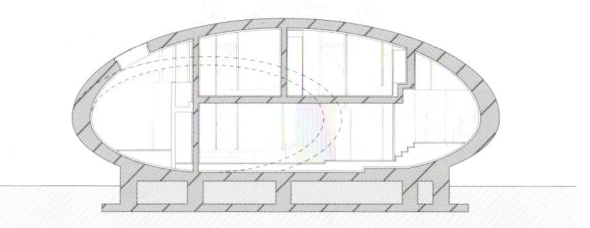

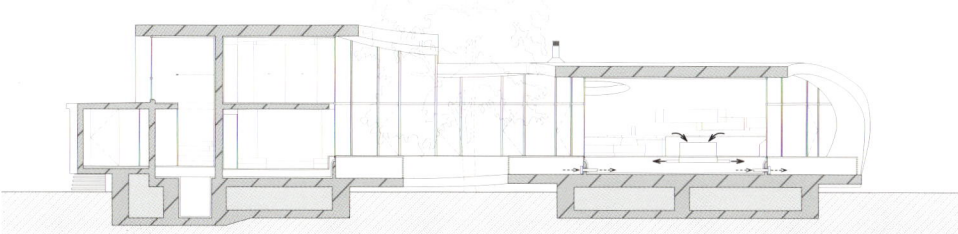

left: Living area. right: Sections_Skylight_Study area_Bathroom.
links: Wohnbereich. rechts: Schnitte_Oberlicht_Arbeitszimmer_Bad.
gauche: Séjour. droite: Vues en coupe_Éclairage zénithal_Bureau_Salle de bains.

HALDENSTEIN, SWITZERLAND **HOUSE WITH STUDIO**

ARCHITECTS: ROBERT ALBERTIN
COMPLETION: 2009_**PROPERTY SIZE:** 630 M²
GROSS FLOOR AREA: 245 M²_**NUMBER OF ROOMS:** 7
PHOTOS: RALF FEINER

The plot is located right in the center of the village on the communal road that leads to the Haldenstein Alps and the SAC cottage on the Calanda. The plot offers along its east to west axis a fantastic panorama of the entire Chur Rhine valley in direct relation to the village located in the front. The location oscillates between the seamless village expansion and the reclusiveness of the slope. The surrounding buildings are primarily residential, occasionally complemented by commercial establishments. The room concept consists of a 4.5 room apartment and a studio, which can also function as a 2.5 room apartment. Each room has a specific view – the original design concept of the house.

Das Grundstück liegt direkt am Dorfkern an der Gemeindestrasse, die zu den Haldensteiner Alpen und zur SAC Hütte am Calanda führt. Auf der Parzelle hat man von Osten nach Westen ein fantastisches Panorama über das gesamte Churer Rheintal, mit einem direkten Bezug zum im Vordergrund liegenden Dorf. Die Lage oszilliert zwischen der nahtlosen Dorferweiterung und der Abgeschiedenheit der Hanglage. Das Raumprogramm besteht aus einer viereinhalb Zimmerwohnung und einem Atelier, welches auch als Zweieinhalbzimmerwohnung funktionieren könnte. Jeder Raum besitzt eine spezifische Aussicht – dem eigentliche Entwurfsthema des Hauses.

Cette maison se dresse à la sortie du village de Haldenstein dans le canton des Grisons, au bord d'une petite route menant au refuge de Calanda. On y bénéficie d'une vue panoramique d'est en ouest sur la haute vallée du Rhin et le village tout proche. L'implantation associe les avantages de la pente (isolement) et ceux liés à la proximité du village (commodité). Les bâtiments les plus proches sont des maisons d'habitation, certaines se complétant par de petits commerces. La maison qui nous intéresse se compose d'un appartement de quatre pièces et d'un atelier pouvant être converti en appartement de deux pièces et demi. Elle se caractérise par le fait que chaque pièce bénéficie d'une vue dans une direction différente.

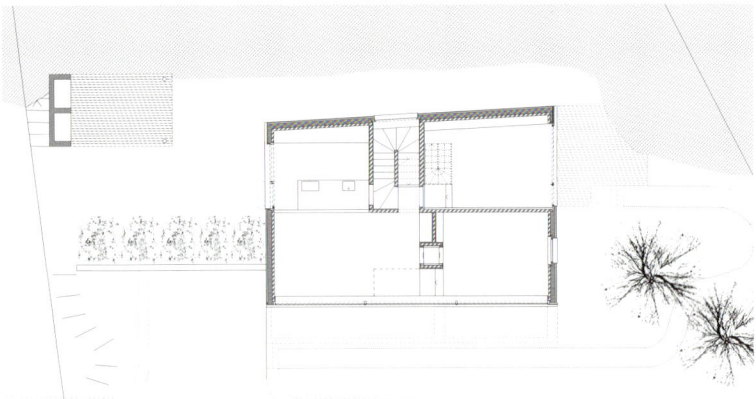

left: Top and ground floor plans_Outdoor area_Living area. right: Street view_Garden view_Exterior view. links: Grundrisse OG und EG_Außenbereich_Wohnbereich. rechts: Straßen-_ Garten-_Außenansicht. gauche: Plan niveau 1 et RdC_Extérieur_Séjour. droite: Vue de la rue_Vue du jardin_Vue de l'extérieur.

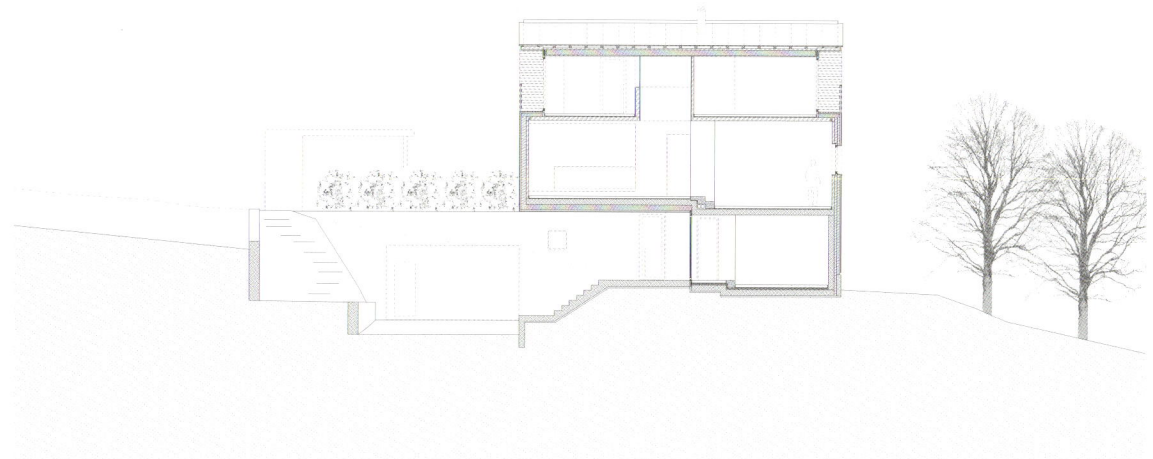

left: Terrace. right: Section_Kitchen_Bedroom_Dining room_Children's bedroom.
links: Terrasse. rechts: Schnitt_Küche_Schlafzimmer_Essbereich_Kinderzimmer.
gauche: Terrasse. droite: Vue en coupe_Cuisine_Chambre_Salle à manger_Chambre d'enfant.

HEESCH, THE NETHERLANDS HOUSE AT THE EDGE OF A FOREST

ARCHITECTS: HILBERINKBOSCH ARCHITECTEN
COMPLETION: 2009_**PROPERTY SIZE:** 1,600 M²
GROSS FLOOR AREA: 300 M²_**NUMBER OF ROOMS:** 7
PHOTOS: RENE DE WIT

The house, situated on a beautiful lot at the edge of the forest, consists of two different volumes: an L-shaped base on which an oblong volume is balanced. Together they form a sculpture which resembles a fallen tree on a pile of earth. The public functions of the house are situated in the L-shaped base. The outside walls of the L-shape, which face the public road, look unapproachable and secretive. The interior of the house is open and light. The living space is connected to the terrace, the garden, and the forest while the house is flooded in light. A timber volume is placed on this basement in which the more private rooms such as bed- and bathrooms are situated.

Die Villa liegt auf einem schönen Grundstück am Waldrand und besteht aus zwei gegensätzlichen Baukörpern: über der L-förmigen Basis kragt ein längliches Volumen aus. Zusammen ergeben die beiden Elemente einen skulpturales Bild, das an einen umgestürzten Baum erinnert, der auf einem Erdhügel aufliegt. Die L-förmige Basis beherbergt die öffentlichen Bereiche. Ihre Außenwände wirken von der Zufahrtsstraße aus gesehen unnahbar und verschlossen. Das Innere der Villa präsentiert sich hingegen freundlich und offen. Der lichtdurchflutete Wohnbereich öffnet sich zu Terrasse, Garten und Wald. Die privaten Räume, die Bäder und Schlafbereiche, liegen im oberen hölzernen Volumen.

Cette villa construite en bordure d'une forêt se compose de deux volumes distincts : un rez-de-chaussée en forme de L sur lequel une barre est posée en équilibre. L'ensemble constitue une sculpture évoquant un arbre tombé sur un monticule de terre. Les espaces publics sont situés dans la partie en L, dont la façade tournée vers la route est secrète et dépourvue de fenêtres, tandis que l'autre s'ouvre largement sur l'extérieur. Le séjour, prolongé par une terrasse et baigné de lumière, est ainsi connecté visuellement au jardin et à la forêt toute proche. La barre, pourvue d'un toit et d'un revêtement en bois, abrite les chambres et les salles de bain. Le matériau choisi s'ajoute ainsi à la forme pour évoquer l'arbre tombé mentionné ci-dessus.

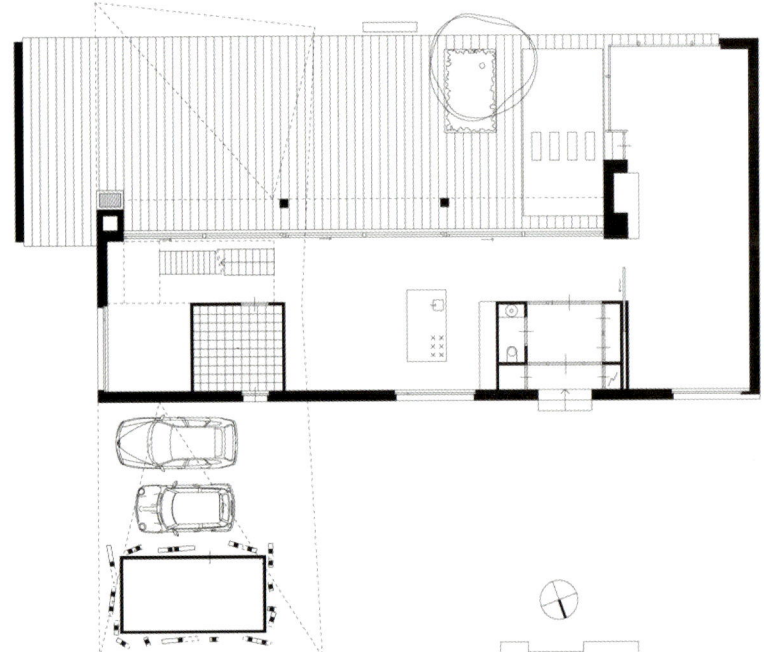

left: Ground floor plan_Outdoor area_Main view. right: Exterior view.
links: Grundriss EG_Außenbereich_Hauptansicht. rechts: Außenansicht.
gauche: Plan RdC_Extérieur_Façade principale. droite: Vue de l'extérieur.

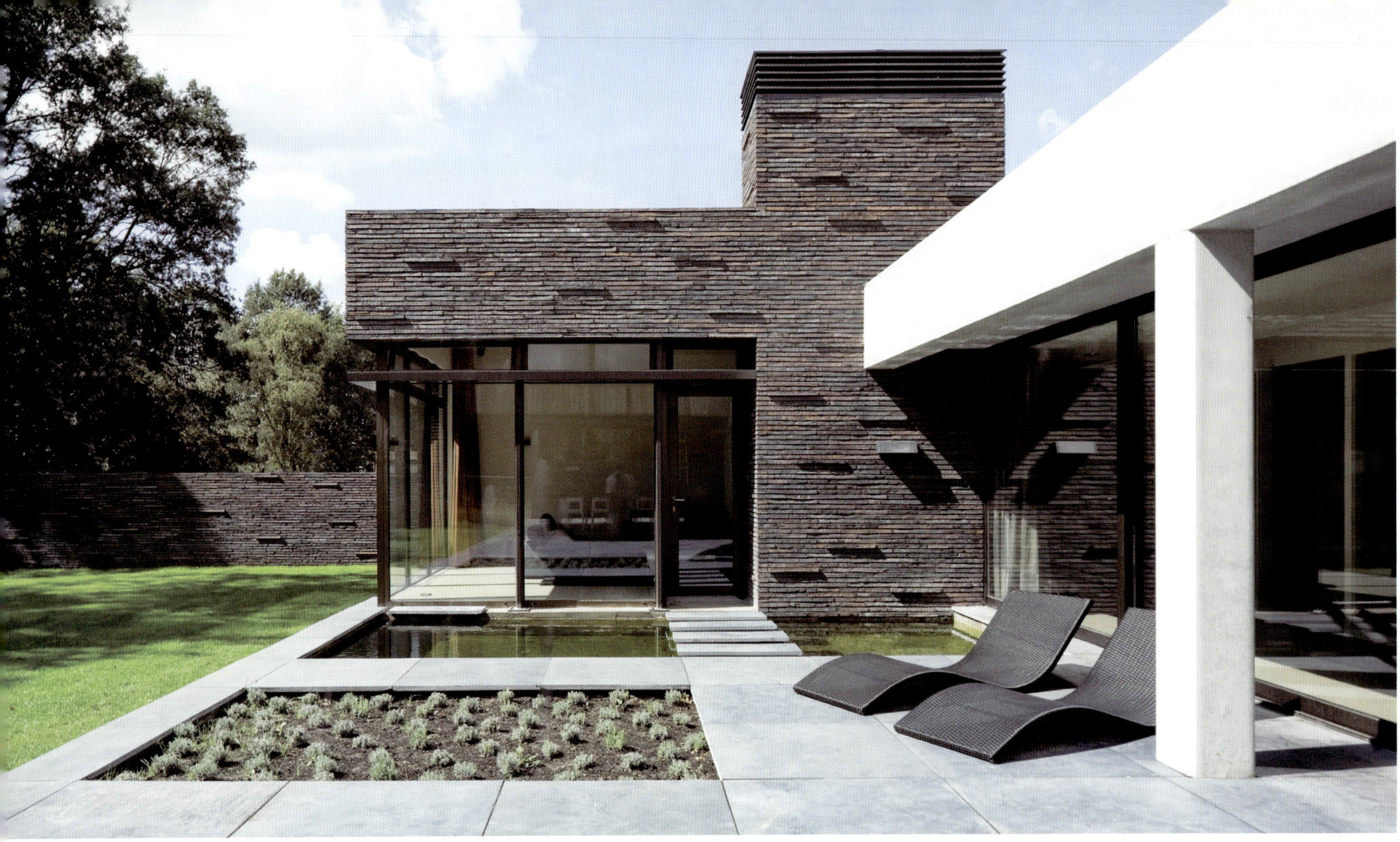
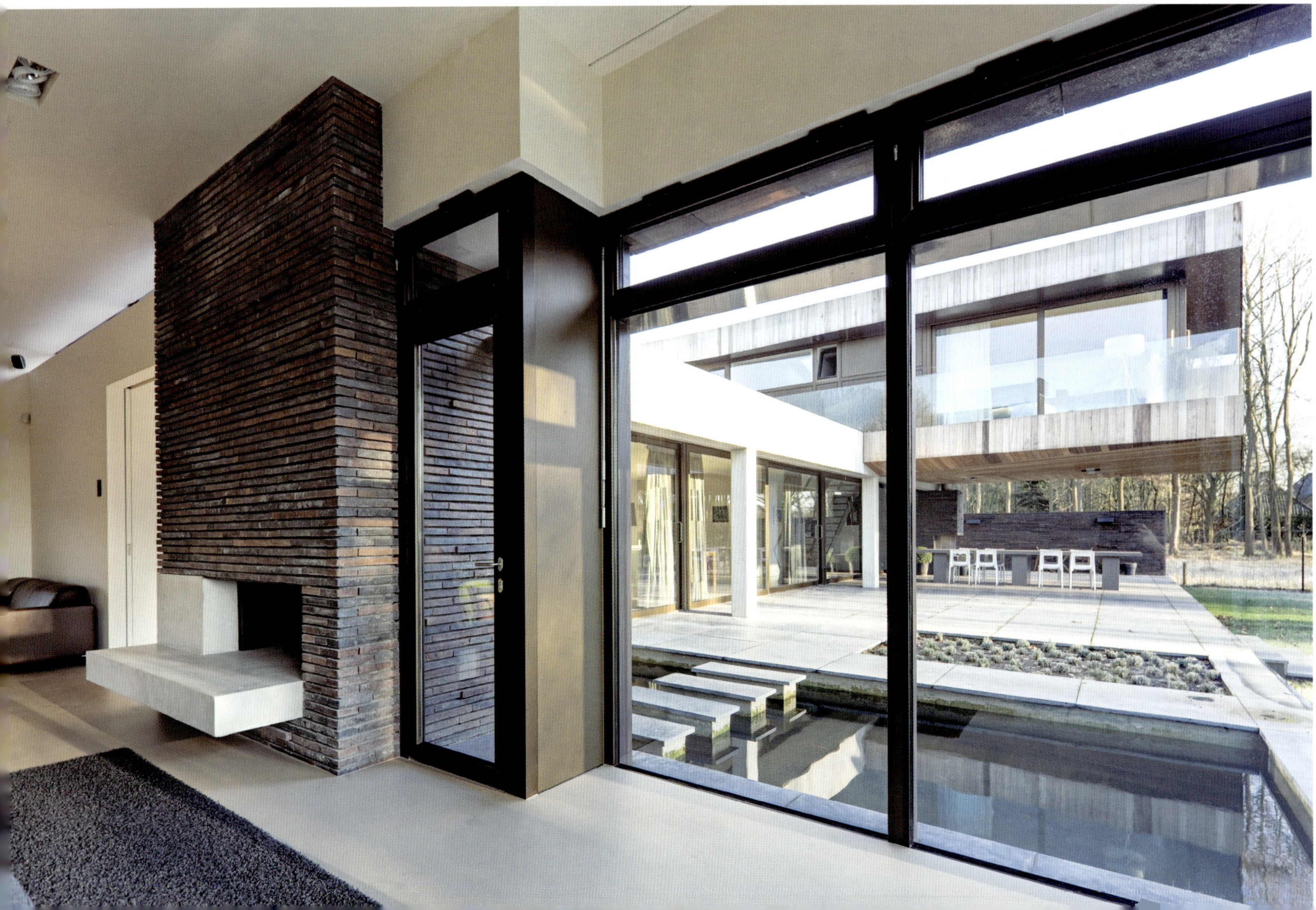

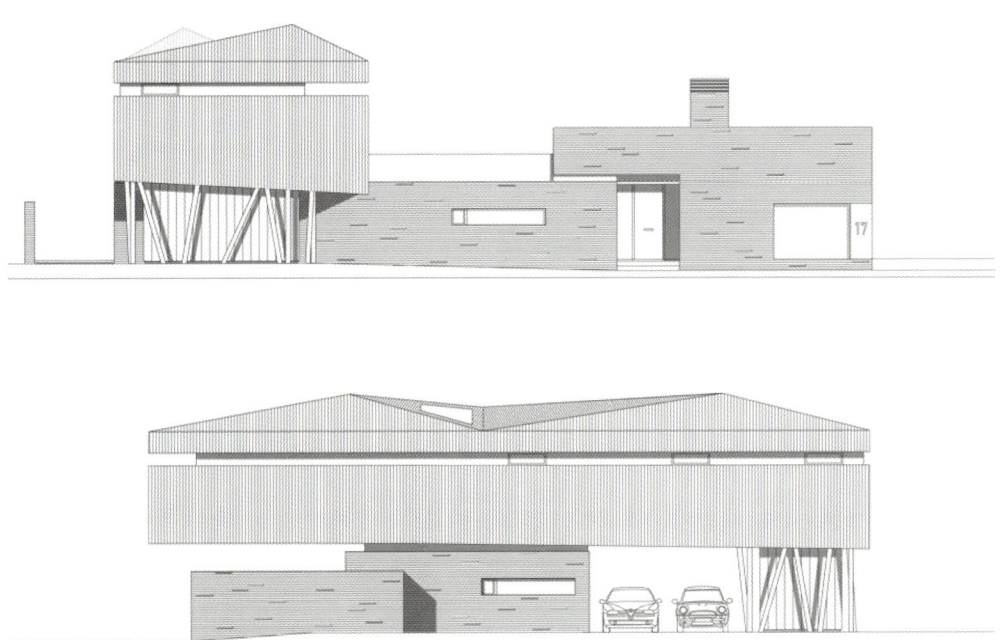

left: Terrace_Living area. right: Elevations_Stairs_Garden view.
links: Terrasse_Wohnbereich. rechts: Ansichten_Treppe_Gartenansicht.
gauche: Terrasse_Séjour. droite: Élévations_Escalier_Vue du jardin.

BERLIN, GERMANY **VILLAS IN BERLIN-GRUNEWALD**

ARCHITECTS: WIEGAND/HOFFMANN
GESELLSCHAFT VON ARCHITEKTEN MBH
COMPLETION: 2012_**PROPERTY SIZE:** 6,500 M²
GROSS FLOOR AREA: 875 M²_**NUMBER OF ROOMS:** 16
PHOTOS: REINHARD GÖRNER

The project is situated in Berlin's Grunewald Park. The generous site presents a spacious impressive ensemble of four villas with terraces and generous gardens. The architecture revives the wealthy Grunewald villas and interprets their classical style in a modern, elegant, and timeless architecture. Grouped around a central court and framed by green hedges, the ensemble invites visitors to walk through the villas' entrance halls. The interior is distinguished by a cosmopolitan tailor-made design including English, Italian, and French furniture, wallpaper, and mosaics. The villas are an impressive statement of living at a very elevated level – the architecture, interior design and landscape form a complete unity and present a fascinating view of New Berlin.

Das eindrucksvolle Ensemble aus vier Villen mit Terrassen und großzügigen Gärten liegt auf einem weitläufigen Grundstück im Berliner Grunewald. Der klassische Stil herrschaftlicher Grunewald-Villen wurde modern, elegant und zeitlos interpretiert. Die Villen gruppieren sich um den zentralen Platz, der von grünen Hecken umgeben ist und den Besucher in die Eingangshallen hineinzieht. Kennzeichnend für das Interieur ist ein maßgeschneidertes Design, dessen kosmopolitische Komposition sich aus englischen, italienischen und französisches Möbeln, Tapeten und Mosaiken zusammensetzt. Die vollendete Einheit aus Architektur, Interieur und Landschaft steht für Wohnen auf höchstem Niveau und repräsentiert das faszinierende neue Berlin.

Le projet consistait ici à revitaliser quatre villas néoclassiques entourées d'un vaste parc et situées dans le quartier huppé de Grunewald, à Berlin. L'architecte a opté pour un style élégant et intemporel. Les villas sont disposées autour d'une cour centrale sur un terrain bordé de haies. Les intérieurs se distinguent par leur caractère cosmopolite intégrant des meubles, mosaïques et papiers peints de style anglais, italien et français fabriqués à la demande. Il s'en dégage une impression générale d'excellence. Cette réalisation dans laquelle l'architecture, la décoration intérieure et le cadre naturel se complètent offre un bel exemple de ce qu'il est convenu d'appeler le « nouveau Berlin ».

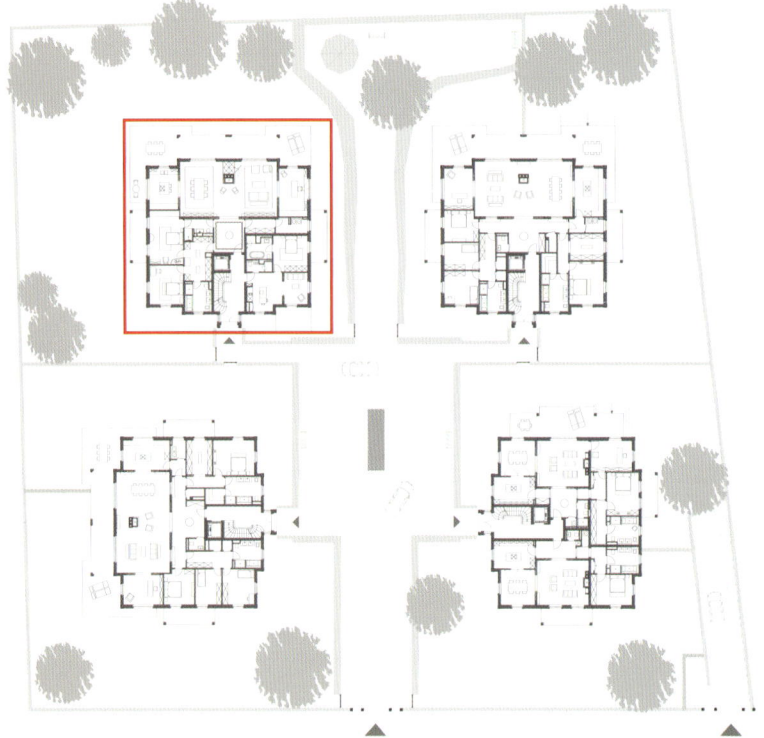

left: Site plan_General view _Living area. right: Exterior view.
links: Lageplan_Gesamtansicht_Wohnbereich. rechts: Außenansicht.
gauche: Plan de situation_Vue générale_Séjour. droite: Vue de l'extérieur.

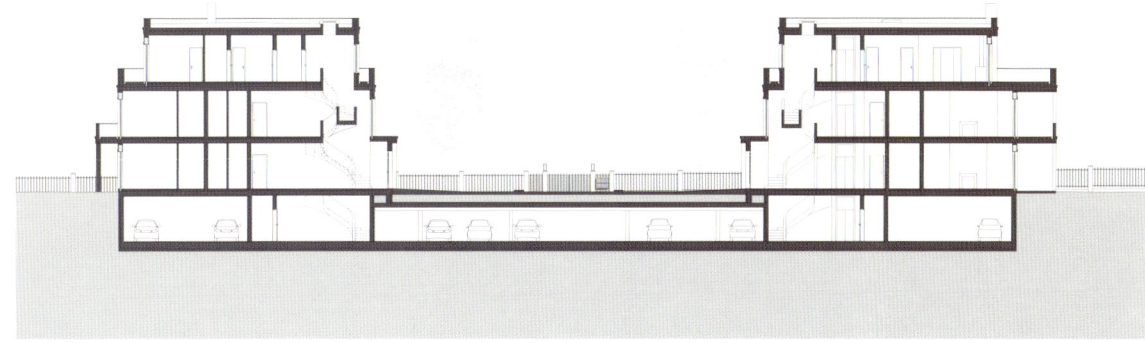

left: Bathroom. right: Section_Room sequence_Living area_Study.
links: Bad. rechts: Schnitt_Raumsequenz_Wohnbereich_Arbeitszimmer.
gauche: Salle de bains. droite: Vue en coupe_Enfilade_Séjour_Bureau.

GLOUCESTERSHIRE, UK **THE ROUND TOWER**

ARCHITECTS: DE MATOS RYAN
COMPLETION: 2009_**PROPERTY SIZE:** 15,575 M²
GROSS FLOOR AREA: 335 M²_**NUMBER OF ROOMS:** 6
PHOTOS: EDMUND SUMNER

The Round Tower, located on the crest of a hill, is a listed building, which had been reduced to ruin by years of neglect and a fire. The design maintains the open relationship with the surrounding agricultural landscape by developing a discreet and substantial underground extension to the tower. It contains the main open plan living space, a central open sunken courtyard, a swimming pool and associated sun terraces, which are all concealed from the public view. The tower remains the dominant structure, providing the front door to the 4-bedroom family house and the means of vertical circulation. It is also the visual focus of the sunken courtyard garden. The restored tower provides additional accommodations and a roof terrace for enjoyment of the panoramic views of the surrounding landscape.

Der denkmalgeschützte Round Tower liegt auf einem Hügelkamm. Durch jahrelange Vernachlässigung und einen Brand war er zur Ruine zerfallen. Der Entwurf erweitert den Turm um einen ebenso unaufdringlichen wie großzügigen unterirdischen Anbau. Dieser birgt den geräumigen und offenen Wohnbereich sowie einen zentralen Hof mit Pool und Sonnenterrassen, die von außen uneinsehbar sind. Die Dominanz des Turms und sein Bezug zur umgebenden Agrarlandschaft bleiben gewahrt. Der Turm ist auch visueller Bezugspunkt des tiefliegenden Hofgartens. Er dient der vertikalen Wegführung und bildet den Haupteingang zur Familienvilla mit vier Schlafzimmern. Zudem bietet er zusätzliche Wohngelegenheiten und eine Dachterrasse, von der aus sich das landschaftliche Panorama genießen lässt.

La tour ronde classée monument historique autour de laquelle les architectes ont construit cette villa était tombée en ruines avec le temps suite à un incendie. Afin de conserver intactes les relations entre le bâtiment et son environnement agricole, les architectes ont conçu une vaste extension souterraine composée d'un espace de séjour à plan ouvert, d'une cour et d'une terrasse où se trouve une piscine à l'abri des regards indiscrets. La tour reste évidemment la caractéristique principale de l'ensemble. Elle abrite le hall d'entrée et assure la circulation verticale à l'intérieur du bâtiment, desservant les quatre chambres ainsi que la cour intérieure, les espaces additionnels et le toit en terrasse d'où l'on découvre un panorama sur la campagne environnante.

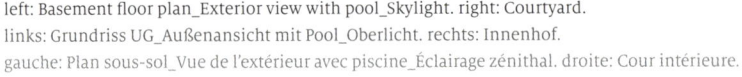

left: Basement floor plan_Exterior view with pool_Skylight. right: Courtyard.
links: Grundriss UG_Außenansicht mit Pool_Oberlicht. rechts: Innenhof.
gauche: Plan sous-sol_Vue de l'extérieur avec piscine_Éclairage zénithal. droite: Cour intérieure.

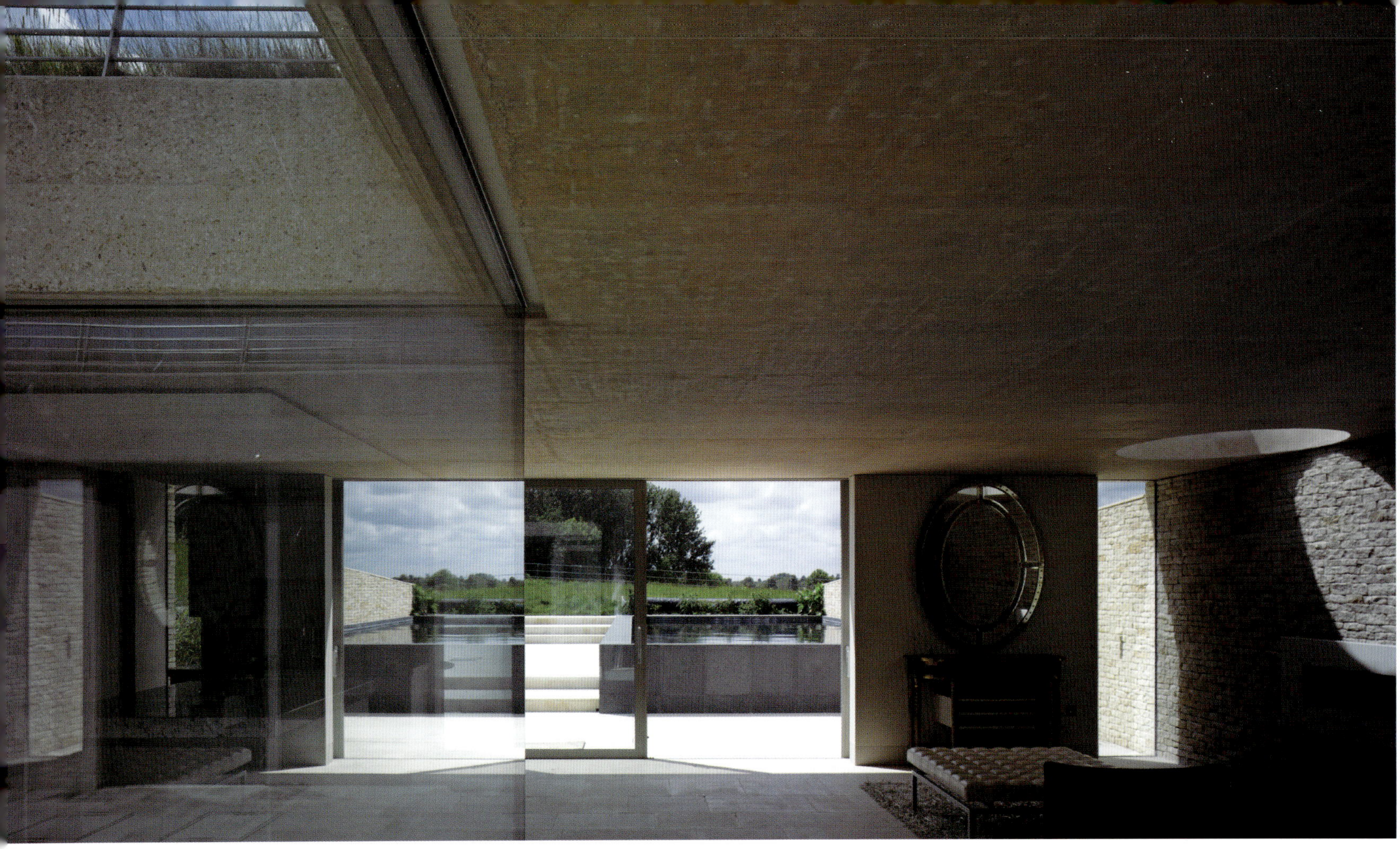

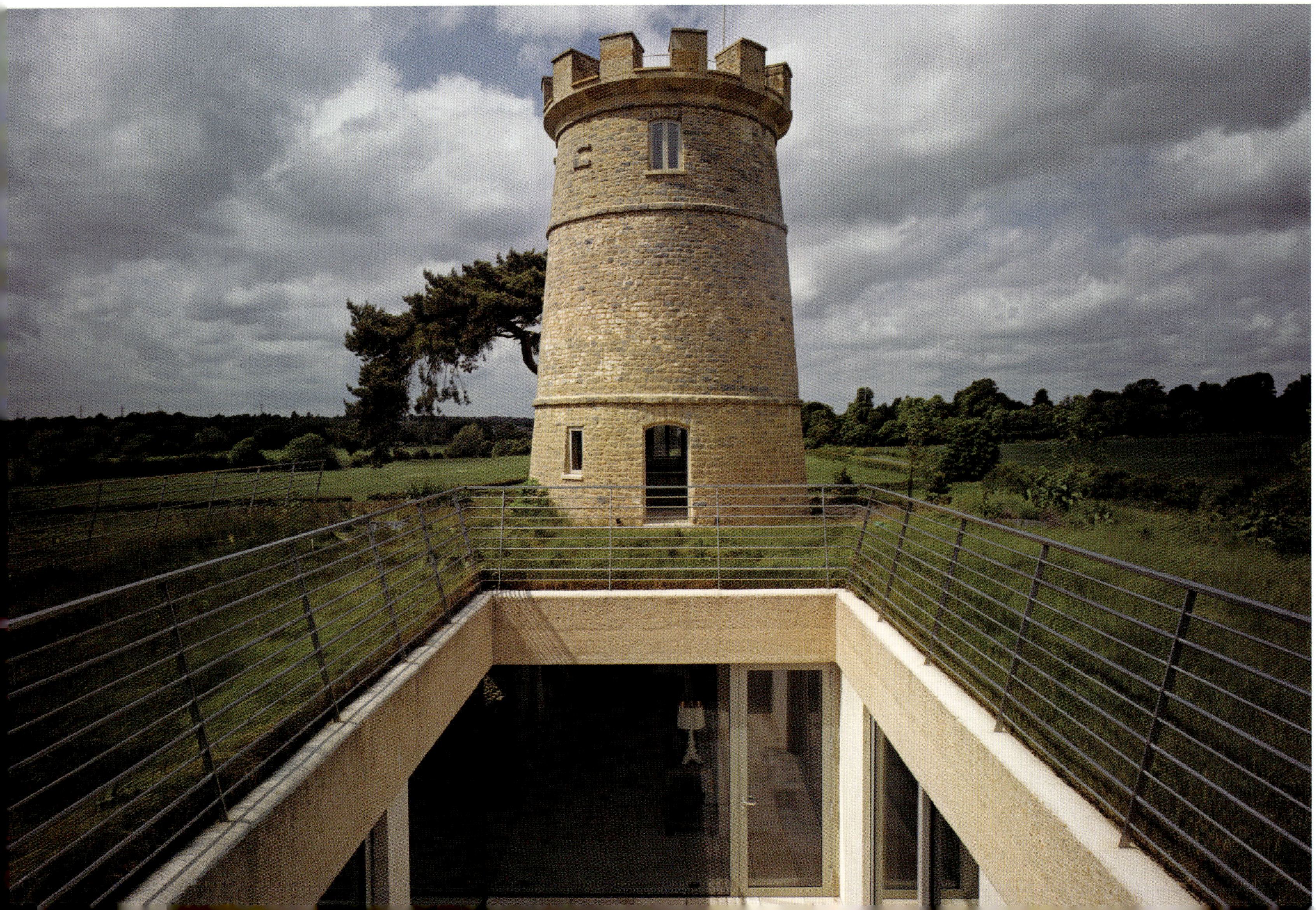

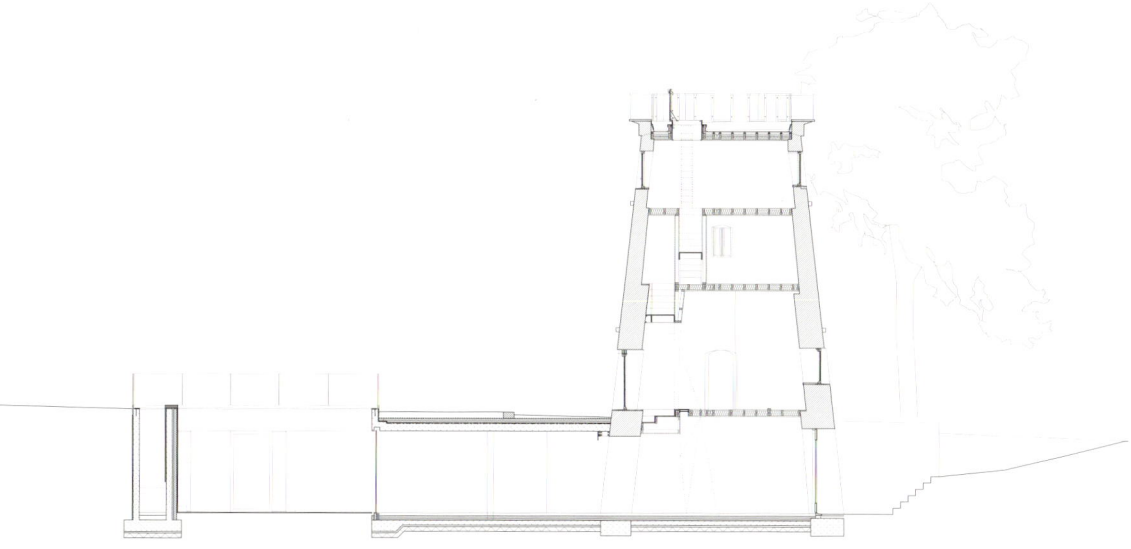

left: Living area_Tower and courtyard. right: Section_Courtyard and living area.
links: Wohnbereich_Turm und Innenhof. rechts: Schnitt_Innenhof und Wohnbereich.
gauche: Séjour_Tour et cour intérieure. droite: Vue en coupe_Cour intérieure et séjour.

KARLSRUHE, GERMANY **HOUSE R**

ARCHITECTS: CHRIST.CHRIST. ASSOCIATED ARCHITECTS
COMPLETION: 2010_**PROPERTY SIZE:** 805 M²
GROSS FLOOR AREA: 455 M²_**PHOTOS:** THOMAS HERRMANN

The plot is imbedded in the greenery of a park, enclosed by walls at the heart of Karlsruhe. On the ground floor, the entrance area leads to the two-floor living hall with the kitchen and dining area at the center of the house where daily life takes place. Towards the east-west, the villa is transparent and light permeable. The floors are connected by an open staircase and an elevator that is glazed on the outside. The upper floor contains a gallery that serves as an intimate retreat area for the family. The open-plan attic floor with a roof terrace is reserved for the parents.

Das Grundstück liegt eingebettet in das Grün eines Parks und umschlossen von Mauern im Zentrum von Karlsruhe. Im Erdgeschoss gelangt man über den Eingangsbereich zu der über zwei Geschosse reichenden Wohnhalle mit Küche und Eßplatz, dem Zentrum des Hauses, in dem sich das tägliche Leben abspielt. Die Villa ist in Ost-West-Richtung transparent und lichtdurchlässig. Die Geschosse untereinander werden durch ein offenes Treppenhaus und eine nach außen verglaste Aufzugsanlage miteinander verbunden. Im Obergeschoss befindet sich eine Galerie als intimer Rückzugsbereich für die Familie. Das offengestaltete Dachgeschoss mit vorgelagerter Dachterrasse ist den Eltern vorbehalten.

Cette villa est construite dans le centre de Karlsruhe sur un terrain verdoyant entouré d'un mur de clôture. Une nef dont le volume s'étire sur deux niveaux s'ouvre immédiatement derrière l'entrée. C'est dans cet espace formant le cœur de la villa que se trouvent le séjour et la cuisine/salle à manger. Les façades est et ouest sont entièrement vitrées, de sorte que l'intérieur est baigné de lumière. Les étages sont desservis par un escalier ouvert et un ascenseur dont la cage est également vitrée vers l'extérieur. Le premier étage, complété par une galerie, abrite les espaces de repos des enfants, tandis que le niveau supérieur, qui donne accès au toit en terrasse, est réservé aux parents.

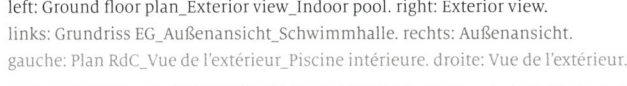

left: Ground floor plan_Exterior view_Indoor pool. right: Exterior view.
links: Grundriss EG_Außenansicht_Schwimmhalle. rechts: Außenansicht.
gauche: Plan RdC_Vue de l'extérieur_Piscine intérieure. droite: Vue de l'extérieur.

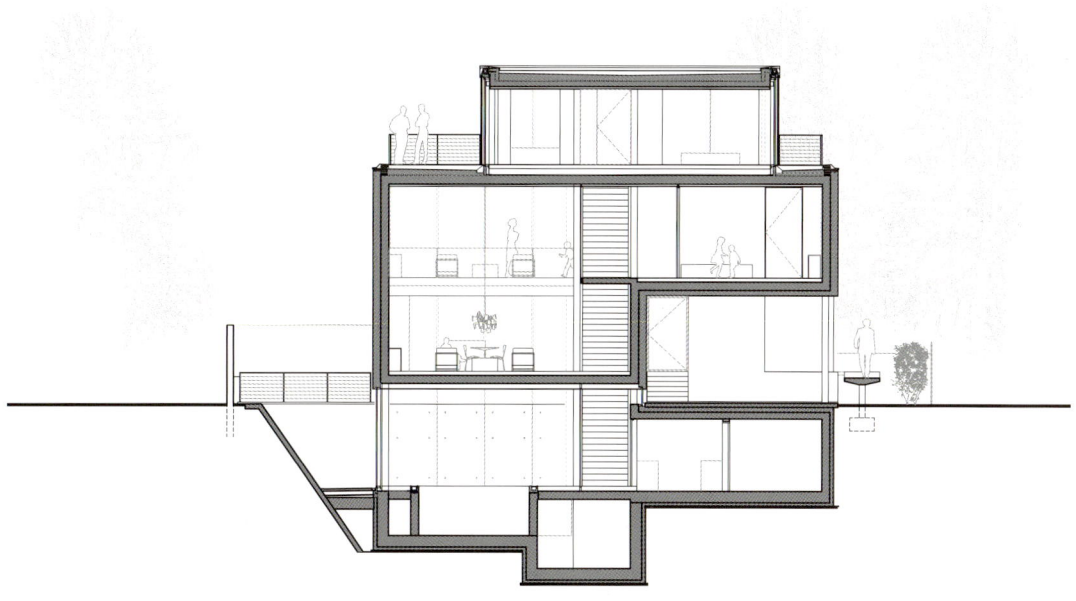

left: Ground floor. right: Section_Staircase_Top floor.
links: Erdgeschoss. rechts: Schnitt_Treppenraum_Obergeschoss.
gauche: Rez-de-chaussée. droite: Vue en coupe_Cage d'escalier_Niveau 1.

TOKYO, JAPAN **TAKANAWA**

ARCHITECTS: HIROYUK ITO ARCHITECTS
COMPLETION: 2011_**PROPERTY SIZE:** 162 M²
GROSS FLOOR AREA: 229 M²_**NUMBER OF ROOMS:** 8
PHOTOS: DAICI ANO

This three-story house is located in an elevated residential area of Tokyo. The house consists of two boxes, each containing several white painted spaces of various proportions including exterior courtyards. A glazed staircase is situated between the two boxes. In contrast to the plain white walls inside the boxes, the outside walls have rough-hewn textures of exposed timber-shuttered concrete. The staircase landings that connect the boxes are bridged by concrete cantilevering floors, which almost touch. This same gap in the roof forms a thin skylight permitting a sliver of sunlight to help illuminate the circulation space below. This simply shaped building provides complex experiences through the relativization of the interior and exterior.

Das dreigeschossige Haus befindet sich in erhöhter Tokioter Wohnlage. Es besteht aus zwei Kuben, die neben unterschiedlich proportionierten Innenräumen auch Atrien enthalten. Die Außenwände kennzeichnet rauer Sichtbeton, dessen Textur eine Holzmaserung nachempfindet. So kontrastiert die Fassade das klare Weiß der Wände im Innern. Zwischen den Kuben liegt das verglaste Treppenhaus. Die Treppenabsätze sind durch schwebende Betonböden verbunden, die sich nur scheinbar berühren. Die schmale Lücke zwischen den Absätzen wiederholt sich im Dach als Oberlicht, durch das Sonnenstrahlen eindringen, die zur Beleuchtung des Treppenhauses beitragen. Die zurückgenommene Gebäudeform relativiert Innen und Außen und erzeugt so ein komplexes Raumerlebnis.

Cette maison sur trois niveaux est située dans une banlieue résidentielle de Tokyo. Elle se compose de deux boîtes séparées par une petite cour vitrée dans laquelle se trouve un escalier. Les intérieurs peints en blanc forment un contraste saisissant avec les façades en bois brut de couleur sombre. Les paliers de l'escalier sont formés par deux moitiés en porte-à-faux séparées par un interstice. Le même interstice se retrouve au niveau du toit, de sorte qu'un rai de lumière assure l'éclairage naturel de l'escalier. D'une manière générale, il s'agit là d'un bâtiment qui, en dépit de sa simplicité apparente, établit des relations complexes entre l'intérieur et l'extérieur.

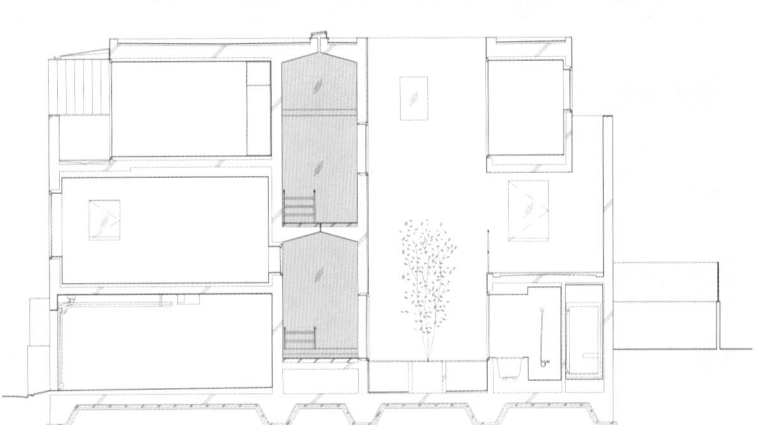

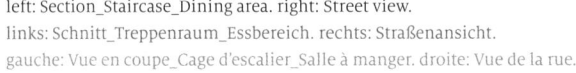

left: Section_Staircase_Dining area. right: Street view.
links: Schnitt_Treppenraum_Essbereich. rechts: Straßenansicht.
gauche: Vue en coupe_Cage d'escalier_Salle à manger. droite: Vue de la rue.

267

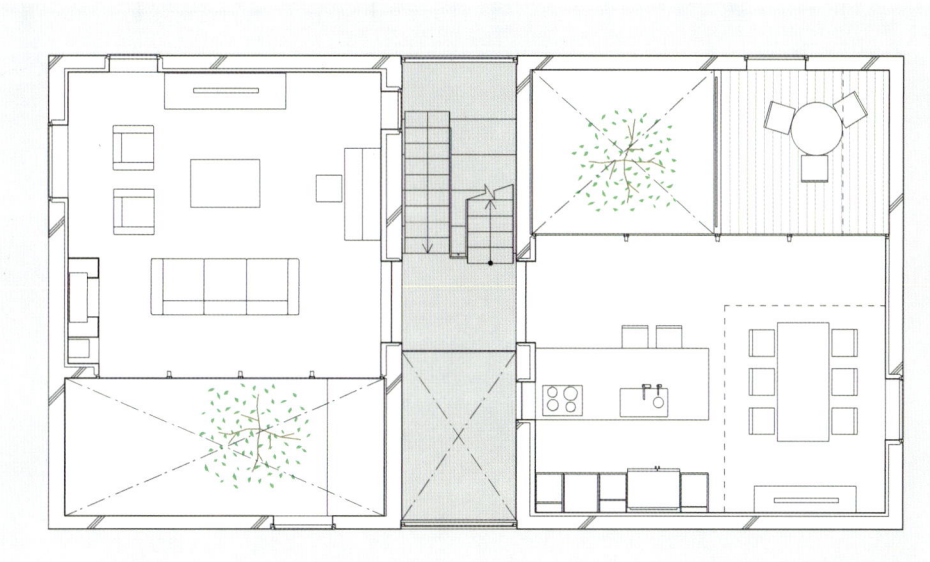

left: Patio. right: First floor plan_Stairs and dining room_Front courtyard.
links: Patio. rechts: Grundriss 1. OG_Treppe und Essbereich_Vorhof.
gauche: Patio. droite: Plan niveau 1_Escalier et salle à manger_Cour.

MUNICH, GERMANY **VILLA OD 15**

DEVELOPER: H-I-M VILLENBAU
ARCHITECTS: GASTEIGER ARCHITEKTEN
COMPLETION: 2011_**PROPERTY SIZE:** 894 M²
GROSS FLOOR AREA: 320 M²_**NUMBER OF ROOMS:** 6
PHOTOS: ANGELO KAUNAT

This large villa with a 2-car garage is located in the garden city of Bogenhausen-Denning in a park-like setting. The layout is structured and the floors are adjusted to the needs of a family with children. The glazed ground floor opens up towards the garden and serves as a living, dining and leisure area. The second floor contains the children's area with its own bathroom and play hallway. A special status is held by the attic floor that is designed as a penthouse. This is the parent's area with a bedroom, wellness bathroom and roof terraces. The basement contains guest rooms plus a sauna and hobby room.

Inmitten der gewachsenen Gartenstadt Bogenhausen-Denning in parkartiger Umgebung liegt diese großzügige Villa mit Doppelgarage. Der Grundriss ist strukturiert aufgebaut und geschossweise den Nutzungen einer Familie mit Kindern angepasst. Das verglaste Erdgeschoß öffnet sich großzügig zum Garten und ist dem Wohnen, Essen und Aufenthalt vorbehalten. Im ersten Obergeschoß befindet sich der Kinderbereich mit eigenem Bad und Spielflur. Einen besonderen Stellenwert hat das als Penthouse ausgebildete Dachgeschoß. Hier befindet sich der Elternbereich mit Schlafzimmer, Wellnessbad und zugeordneten Dachterrassen. Im Souterrain sind ergänzende Gästebereiche mit Sauna und Hobbyraum angeordnet.

Cette villa pourvue d'un garage pour deux voitures se trouve à Bogenhausen-Denning, une banlieue résidentielle de Munich. Elle présente un plan clairement structuré et une répartition des pièces visant à répondre aux besoins d'une famille avec plusieurs enfants. Le rez-de-chaussée, entièrement vitré côté jardin, abrite le séjour et la salle à manger. Au premier étage se trouvent les chambres des enfants, ainsi qu'une salle de bain et un « couloir de jeu ». Le second étage, réservé aux parents, abrite une chambre et une salle de bain avec spa et se complète d'un toit en terrasse. Un sauna, une chambre d'amis et un atelier de bricolage ont de plus été aménagés au sous-sol.

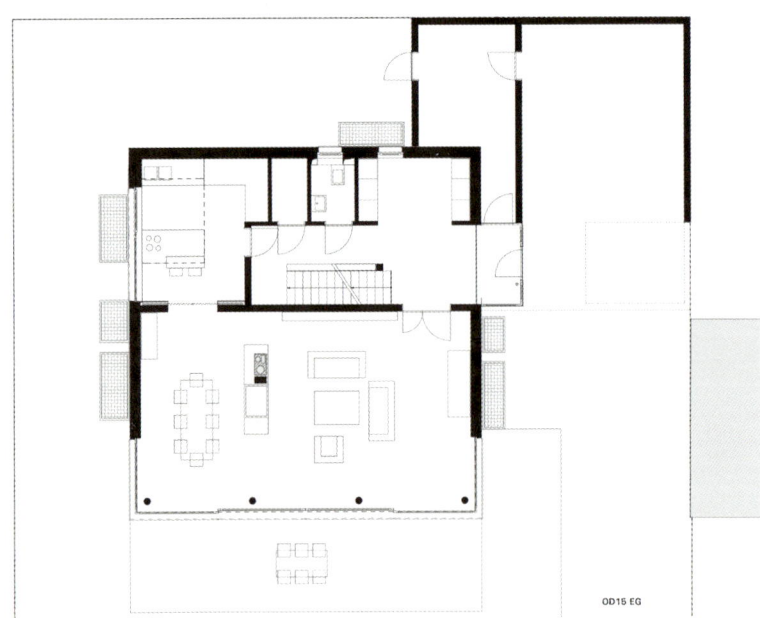

OD15 EG

left: Ground floor plan_Main view_Living area. right: Building corner.
links: Grundriss EG_Hauptansicht_Wohnbereich. rechts: Gebäudeecke.
gauche: Plan RdC_Façade principale_Séjour. droite: Un angle du bâtiment.

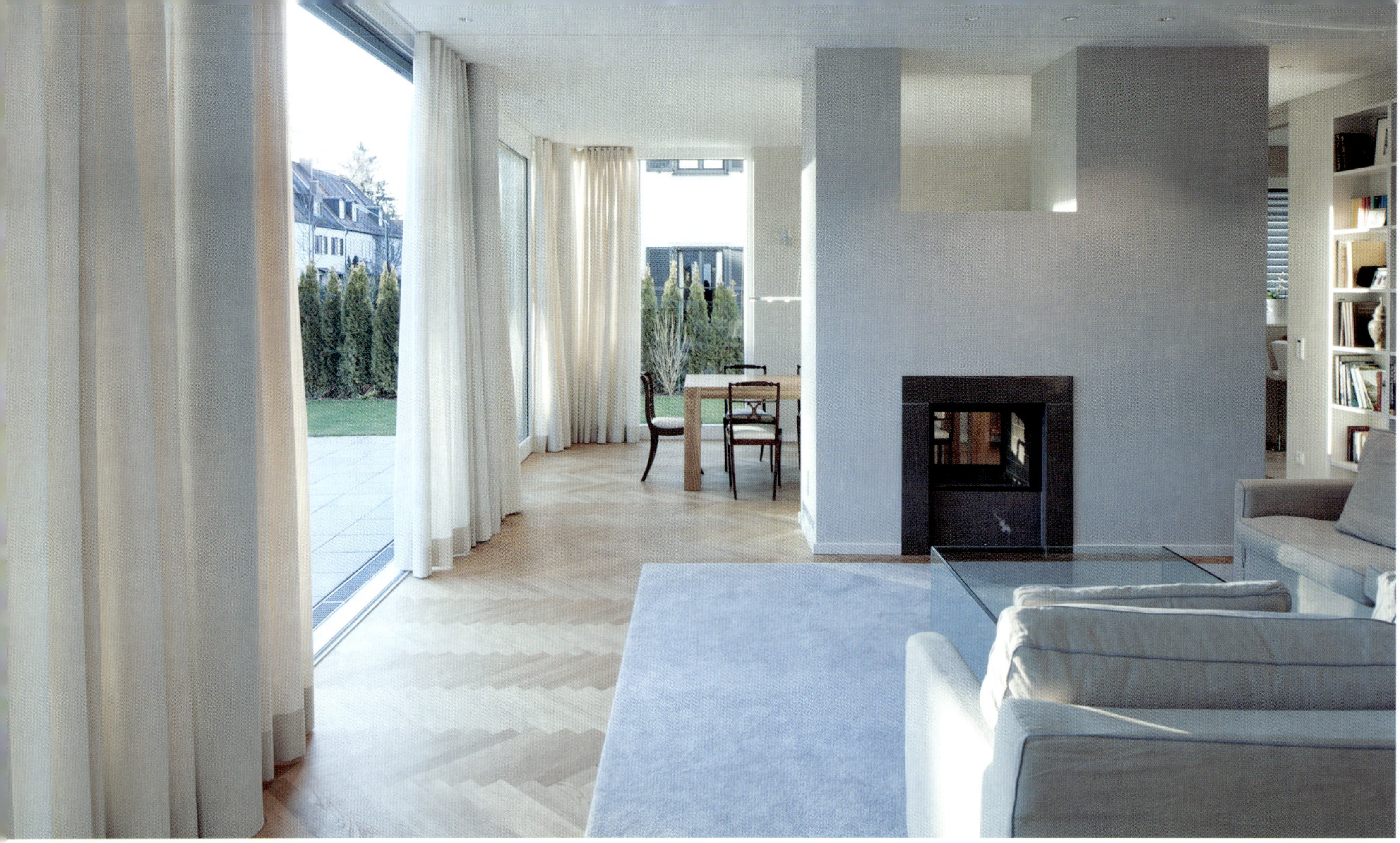

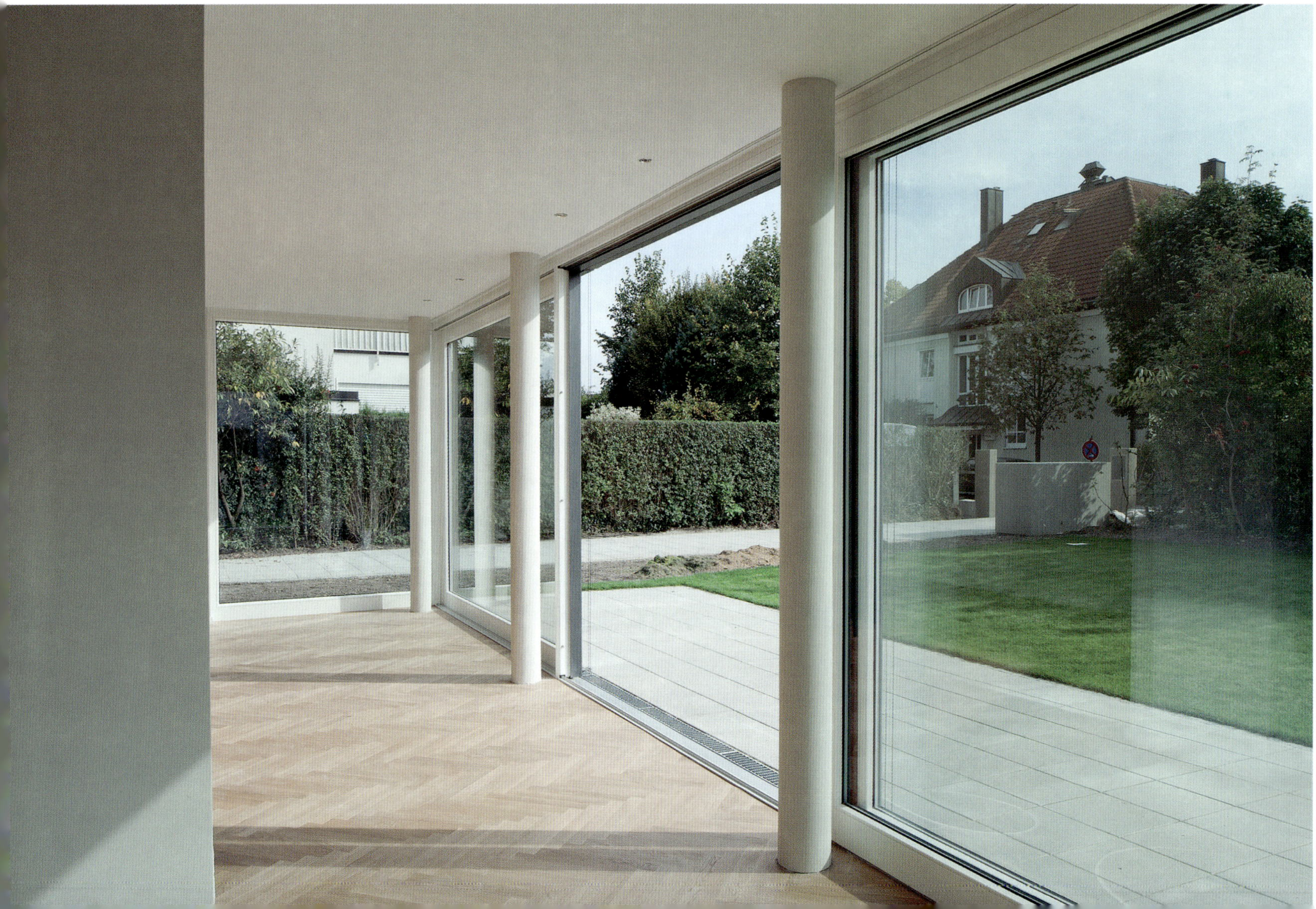

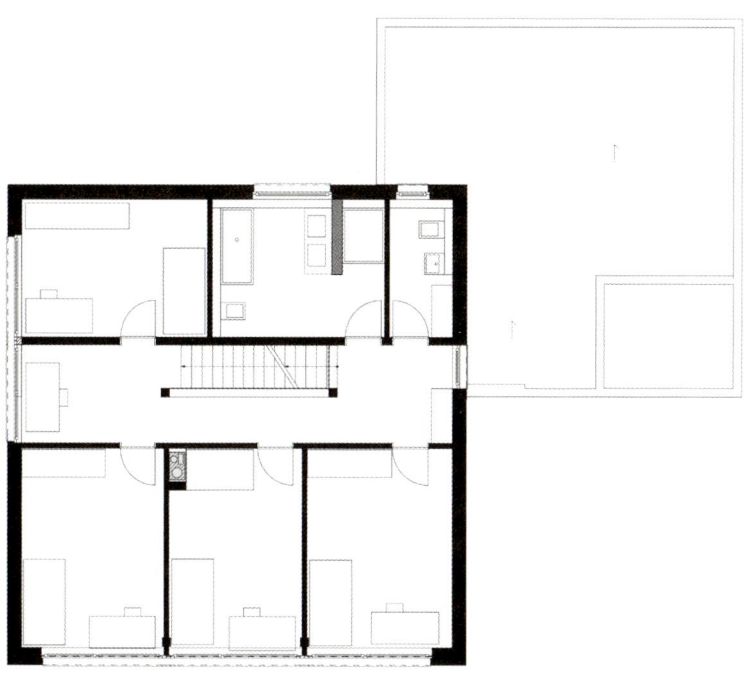

left: Dining area_Living room. right: Top floor plan_Garden view_Living area_Stairs.
links: Essbereich_Wohnraum. rechts: Grundriss OG_Gartenansicht_Wohnbereich_Treppe.
gauche: Salle à manger_Séjour. droite: Plan niveau 1_Vue du jardin_Séjour_Escalier.

CHIBA, JAPAN **FLOW**

ARCHITECTS: APOLLO ARCHITECTS & ASSOCIATES
COMPLETION: 2009_**PROPERTY SIZE:** 149 M²
GROSS FLOOR AREA: 117 M²_**NUMBER OF ROOMS:** 5
PHOTOS: MASAO NISHIKAWA

The owner of a "two-generation" house located near the sea requested a two-car garage and a house that allows light and air to pour in while also securing privacy. The inclined exterior with its stark contrast of concrete and wood represents the owner's minimalist outlook on design. On the ground floor, private rooms are connected with a terrace that penetrates the external wall in a straight line. The main feature of the layout is the misalignment of the ground and first floors. On the first floor, the living room, dining room, kitchen, lounge, terrace and roof-top garden are connected in succession at a congenial distance. The diagonal terrace makes the interiors appear more spacious and brings in light while securing privacy and also allowing for a view of the sky.

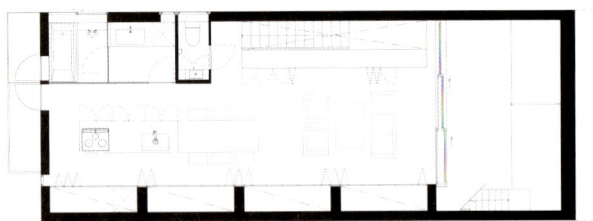

Der Bauherr dieses Zwei-Generationen-Hauses in Meeresnähe wünschte neben einer Doppelgarage lichtdurchflutete Räume und die Sicherstellung der Privatsphäre. Die äußeren Linien zeigen seine Vorliebe für minimalistisches Design, wobei die aufragende Holzfront einen krassen Kontrast zum Beton bildet. Die Privaträume im Erdgeschoss führen auf die Terrasse hinaus, eine Bewegung, die bis zu den Außenmauern vorstößt. Hauptmerkmal ist die versetzte Ausrichtung von Erd- und Obergeschoss. Wohn- und Essbereich, Küche, Lounge, Terrasse und Dachgarten folgen im Obergeschoss sukzessive aufeinander. Durch ihre starke Neigung verhindert die Terrasse unerwünschte Einblicke. Jedoch öffnet sie den Innenraum gen Himmel und lässt ihn so heller und größer erscheinen.

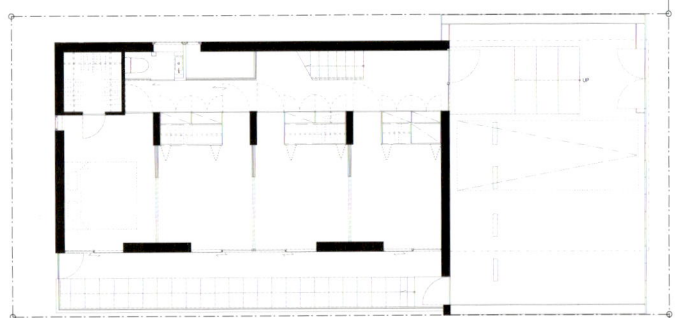

Le maître d'ouvrage avait chargé les architectes de réaliser une maison pour couple avec enfants complétée par un garage pour deux voitures. Le cahier des charges stipulait également que le bâtiment devait avoir un bon éclairage naturel et une bonne ventilation, tout en garantissant l'intimité des occupants. La partie en pointe de l'édifice, qui figure un fort contraste entre bois et béton, illustre les goûts minimalistes du client. Une terrasse prolonge les pièces du rez-de-chaussée, ce niveau se caractérisant par le fait qu'il n'est pas aligné avec le premier étage, où se trouvent le séjour, la salle à manger, la cuisine et une autre terrasse donnant accès au jardin aménagé sur le toit. Cette seconde terrasse est en fait un plan incliné qui optimise l'éclairage intérieur tout en préservant les occupants des regards indiscrets.

left: First and ground floor plans_Street view_Gallery. right: Stairs.
links: Grundrisse OG und EG_Straßenansicht_Galerie. rechts: Treppe.
gauche: Plan niveau 1 et RdC_Vue de la rue_Galerie. droite: Escalier.

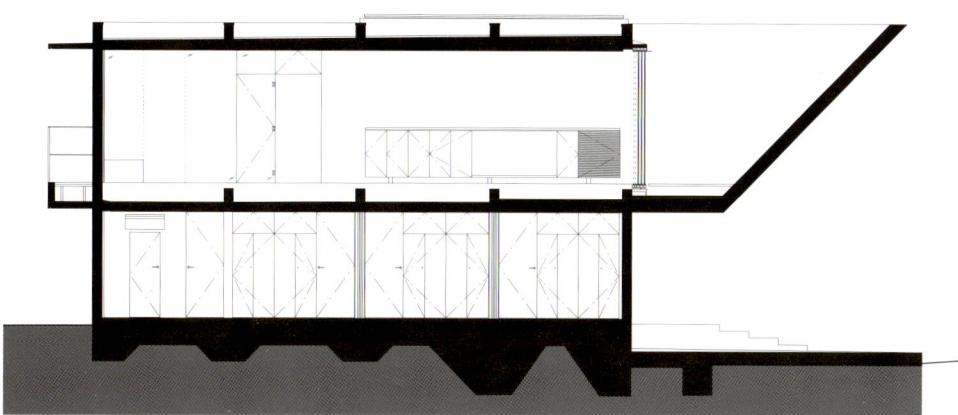

left: Dining area. right: Section_Kitchen_Living room_Room sequence.
links: Essbereich. rechts: Schnitt_Küche_Wohnraum_Raumsequenz.
gauche: Salle à manger. droite: Vue en coupe_Cuisine_Séjour_Enfilade.

STUTTGART, GERMANY **VISTA HOUSE**

ARCHITECTS: ALEXANDER BRENNER ARCHITEKTEN
COMPLETION: 2012_**PROPERTY SIZE:** 1,550 M²
GROSS FLOOR AREA: 636 M²_**PHOTOS:** ZOOEY BRAUN

Located on a hillside plot in the northern part of Stuttgart, the building enjoys a generously proportioned open room concept with a spectacular view of the city. The angled shape of the structure creates a snug, almost courtyard –like outdoor space with a pool and a garden section. The expansively protruding roof windows act as a sun protection for the south-aligned building, while also highlighting and framing the view of the valley. The lower pool level near the garden contains a rather introverted, warmer and intensely colored library and living area with a home office, piano and fireplace. A single-flight stairway in an air space leads to the bright, light-flooded upper living level.

Auf einem Hanggrundstück im Stuttgarter Norden gebaut, entsteht ein großzügiges, offenes Raumkontinuum mit einer spektakulären Aussicht über die Stadt. Durch die Winkelform des Baukörpers entsteht ein geschützter, fast hofartiger Außenraum mit Pool- und Gartenbereich. Die weit auskragenden Dachscheiben dienen dem nach Süden ausgerichteten Haus als Sonnenschutz und leiten und rahmen den Blick in den Talkessel. In der unteren gartennahen Pool-Ebene wurde ein eher introvertierter, wärmerer und farbintensiverer Bibliotheks- und Wohnbereich mit Arbeitsplatz, Klavier und Kamin geschaffen. Über eine einläufige Treppe in einem Luftraum gelangt man auf die helle, lichtdurchflutete obere Wohnebene.

Cet ensemble vaste et largement ouvert sur l'extérieur se dresse sur une colline du nord de Stuttgart offrant un magnifique panorama sur la ville. Les formes anguleuses du bâtiment délimitent un espace de plein air composé d'une piscine et d'un jardin. Sur la façade sud, des toits en surplomb protègent du soleil et encadrent la vue panoramique qui s'offre sur la ville en contrebas. Un espace intime aux couleurs chaleureuses, où se trouvent un bureau, le piano et la cheminée, a été aménagé au niveau inférieur donnant sur la piscine. Un escalier à une volée mène au niveau supérieur baigné de lumière.

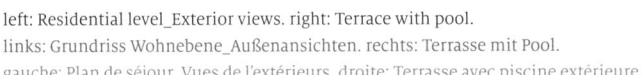

left: Residential level_Exterior views. right: Terrace with pool.
links: Grundriss Wohnebene_Außenansichten. rechts: Terrasse mit Pool.
gauche: Plan de séjour_Vues de l'extérieurs. droite: Terrasse avec piscine extérieure.

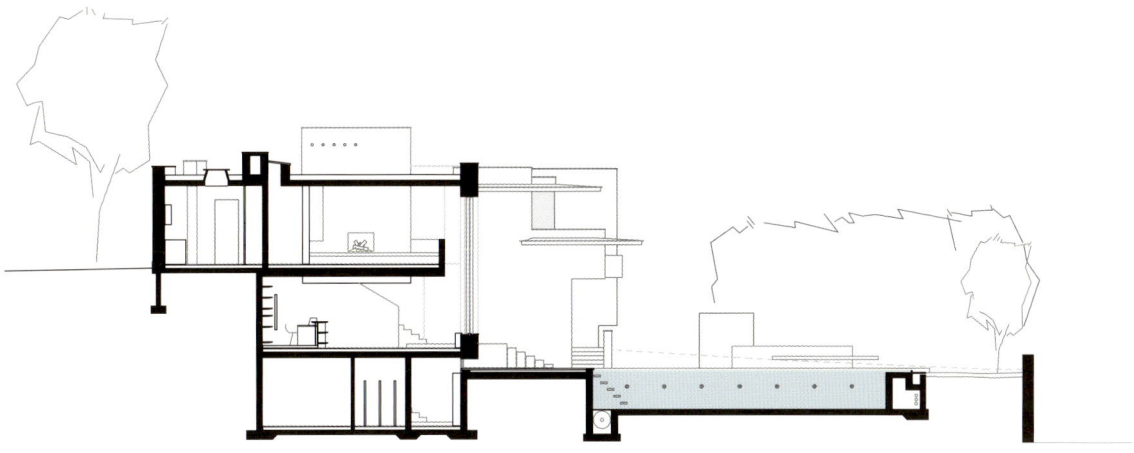

left: Pool level. right: Section_Garage_Residential level_Bathroom.
links: Poolebene. rechts: Schnitt_Garage_Wohnebene_Bad.
gauche: Niveau de la piscine. droite: Vue en coupe_Garage_Salle de séjour_Salle de bains.

PILAR, BUENOS AIRES, ARGENTINA **CARRARA HOUSE**

ARCHITECTS: REMY ARQUITECTOS
COMPLETION: 2010_**PROPERTY SIZE:** 1,200 M²
GROSS FLOOR AREA: 550 M²
PHOTOS: ALEJANDRO PERAL

Located on an irregular plot, the house sits at the back of the property and is parallel to one of the streets to optimize its orientation and capture the best views. A hidden and evocative entrance strongly distinguishes the house. The white of Carrara marble dominates the interior architecture. With its white walls and ceilings, the house appears to rise from the water. Touches of color are used for small details and decorative objects, contrasting with the predominant white and the turquoise of the water. The water that surrounds the house penetrates it as mirrored pools culminating in a unique interior cascade that falls from the top floor creating reflections through a pane of glass.

Die Villa liegt auf dem rückwärtigen Teil eines unregelmäßigen Grundstücks. Sie orientiert sich parallel zu einer der Zufahrtsstraßen, um so die schönsten Ausblicke einzufangen. Der verborgene und überraschende Eingang ist eines der Hauptmerkmale. Im Innern dominiert weißer Carrara-Marmor. So scheint der Bau mit seinen weißen Wänden und Decken förmlich aus dem Wasser aufzusteigen. Details und dekorative Objekte setzen Farbakzente, die einen Kontrast zum vorherrschenden Weiß und dem Türkis des Pools bilden. Das Wasser umgibt das Haus nicht nur, es dringt auch ins Innere vor: Vom Obergeschoss fällt es in Kaskaden entlang einer Glasplatte hinab in ein Bassin im Wohnbereich. Dabei entstehen einzigartige Reflexionen.

Cette villa construite sur un terrain trapézoïdal est disposée de manière à optimiser l'orientation et les vues sur les environs. Elle se caractérise par un porche savamment mis en valeur et l'utilisation intensive du marbre de Carrare. Du côté de la piscine et du bassin, le blanc des murs et des plafonds donne l'impression que le bâtiment émerge de l'eau. Quelques rehauts de couleur viennent mettre en valeur le blanc prédominant et le bleu turquoise. L'élément aquatique, fortement présent à l'extérieur, se retrouve à l'intérieur non seulement lorsque les bassins se reflètent dans les baies vitrées, mais aussi dans une cascade artificielle constituée d'une plaque de verre le long de laquelle de l'eau s'écoule depuis le premier étage.

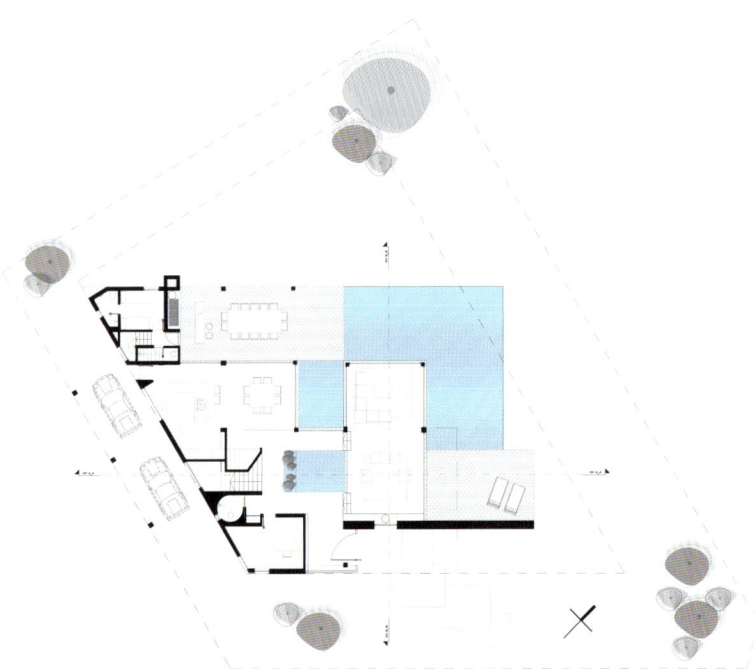

left: Ground floor plan_Garden view_Entrance. right: Exterior view.
links: Grundriss EG_Gartenansicht_Eingang. rechts: Außenansicht.
gauche: Plan RdC_Vue du jardin_Entrée. droite: Vue de l'extérieur.

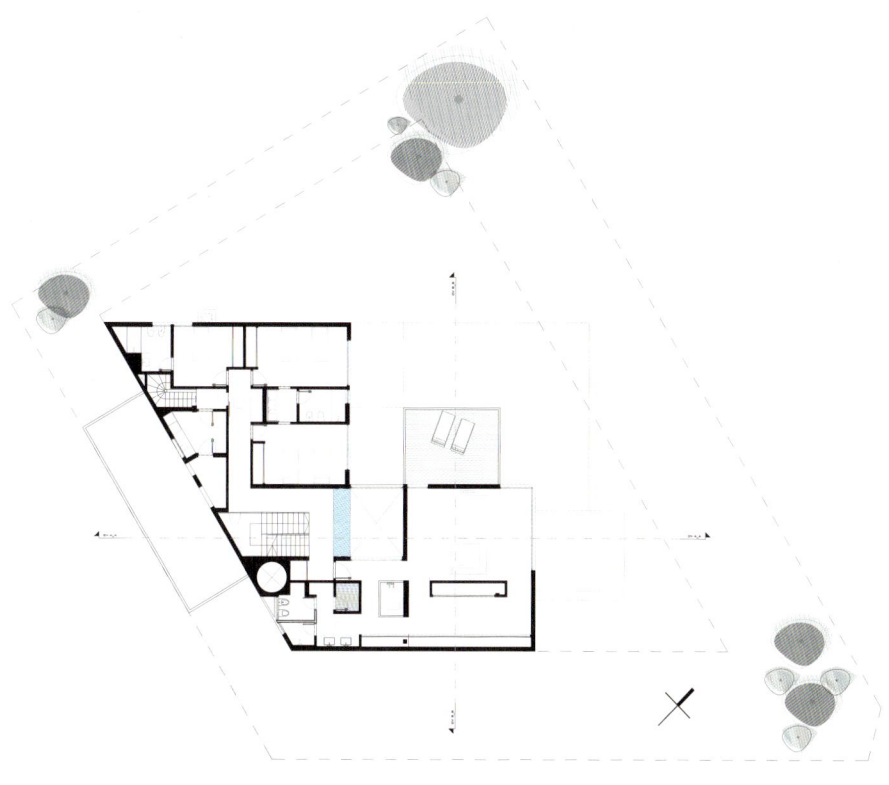

left: Pool. right: Top floor plan_Entrance area_Living area_Living and dining area.
links: Pool. rechts: Grundriss OG_Eingangsbereich_Wohnbereich_Wohn- und Essbereich.
gauche: Piscine extérieure. droite: Plan niveau 1_Entrée_Séjour_Séjour et salle à manger.

SEEHEIM-JUGENHEIM, GERMANY **HOUSE IN SEEHEIM**

ARCHITECTS: FRITSCH + SCHLÜTER ARCHITEKTEN
COMPLETION: 2010_**PROPERTY SIZE:** 835 M²
GROSS FLOOR AREA: 366 M²_**NUMBER OF ROOMS:** 6
PHOTOS: CHRISTOPH KRANEBURG (284–286),
HENNER ROSENKRANZ (287)

The location on a slope with an extended view across the Rhine valley as well as the planning regulation prescribing the archetype of a gable-fronted house were the themes of this design that presents itself as a monolith structure balancing over the edge of the slope. Only four large-scale "incisions" in the corners were used to create very different views. This resulted in a tension between the large-scale, extroverted and introverted spaces. Vertical air spaces with full-scale skylights above the dining area and stairs link the ground and top floor. The roof and façade are enclosed in a skin of pre-oxidized large copper rhombuses.

Die Lage am Hang mit Fernblick über die Rheinebene sowie der planungsrecht-lich vorgegebene Archetypus des Giebelhauses wurden thematisch aufgegriffen und als monolithisch gestalteter Baukörper, der sich balancierend über die Hangkante hinausschiebt, ausgebildet. Mittels nur vier großformatiger „Ein-schnitte" über Eck wurden die sehr unterschiedlichen Ausblicke inszeniert. Es entsteht eine Spannung zwischen großflächigen, extrovertierten und introver-tierten Räumen. Vertikale Lufträume mit vollflächigen Dachverglasungen über Essbereich und Treppe verbinden Erd- und Obergeschoß. Dach und Fassade sind umspannt von einer Haut aus voroxidierten Kupfer-Großrauten.

Tenant compte des particularités du site (un terrain en pente avec vue sur la plaine du Rhin) et des exigences du maître d'ouvrage (habiter une maison cou-verte par un toit à deux pentes), les architectes ont réalisé un bâtiment monoli-thique partiellement en porte-à-faux dans le vide. Grâce à de grandes échancru-res aménagées aux quatre coins, les occupants bénéficient de vues dans toutes les directions. L'intérieur se caractérise par l'alternance de grandes pièces tantôt ouvertes, tantôt intimistes. Des puits de lumière percés au-dessus de l'escalier et de la salle à manger relient visuellement le rez-de-chaussée au premier étage. À l'extérieur, les murs et le toit sont pourvus d'un revêtement en plaques de cuivre préoxydées.

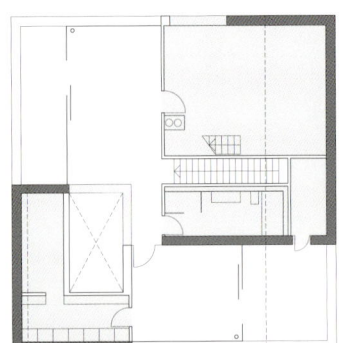

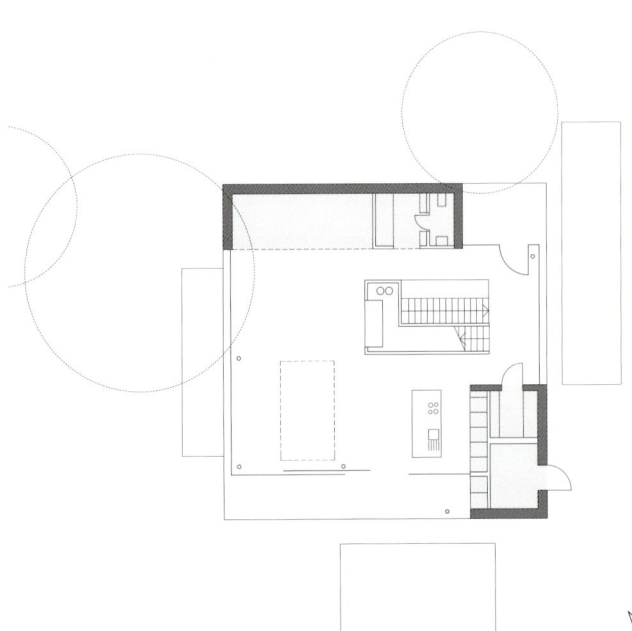

left: Top and ground floor plans_Seen from east_Seen from south. right: Exterior view.
links: Grundrisse OG und EG_Ostansicht_Südansicht. rechts: Außenansicht.
gauche: Plan niveau 1 et RdC_Façade est_Façade sud. droite: Vue de l'extérieur.

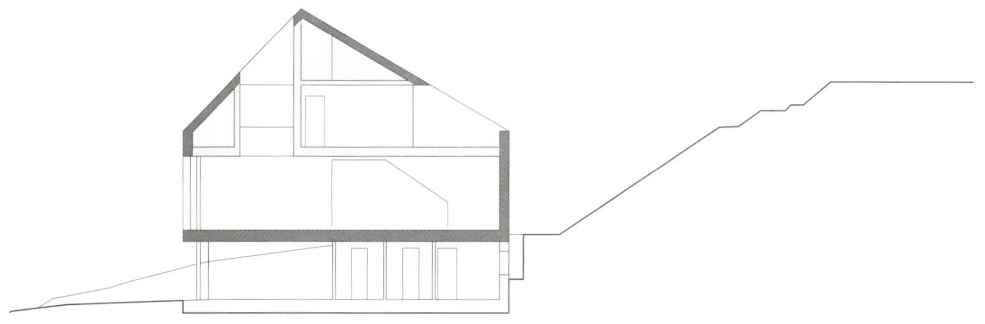

left: Air space. right: Section_Living area.
links: Luftraum. rechts: Schnitt_Wohnbereich.
gauche: Nef. droite: Vue en coupe_Séjour.

EIFEL, GERMANY **LAKE HOUSE**

ARCHITECTS: LHVH ARCHITEKTEN
COMPLETION: 2010_**PROPERTY SIZE:** 3,000 M²
GROSS FLOOR AREA: 100 M²_**NUMBER OF ROOMS:** 3
PHOTOS: LUKAS ROTH

With its enviable location overlooking the Rur reservoir in the Eifel region, the house resembles famous icons on the Californian Pacific coast, despite its moderate size. The functional areas of living, eating and cooking are generously opened towards the lake through the fully glazed corner façade. Sleeping, dressing and bathroom areas are located in the intimate rear section. Angular greywacke, glass, soft exposed concrete, anodized aluminum, galvanized steel, waxed fair-faced screed floors, smooth walls, and manually fitted cherry wood are elegantly combined in the limited, material-focused natural artifact style. Well known elements of modernity are adapted almost timelessly, underscoring the wish for a reduced range of shapes.

Das Haus in beneidenswerter Hanglage über dem Rur-Stausee in der Eifel, erinnert trotz seiner moderaten Größe an berühmte Ikonen der kalifornischen Pazifikküste. Die Funktionen Wohnen, Essen und Kochen öffnen sich großzügig durch die Ganzglas-Übereck-Fassade über die Terrasse zum See. Schlafen, Ankleide und Bad ziehen sich in den hinteren, intimen Teil zurück. Kantige Grauwacke, Glas, weicher Sichtbeton, eloxiertes Aluminium, verzinkter Stahl, gewachster Sichtestrich, glatte Wände und handbelegter Kirschbaum werden elegant kombiniert und bilden das reduzierte, materialbetonte Artefakt in der Natur. Fast zeitlos werden bekannte Motive der Moderne adaptiert und unterstreichen so den Wunsch nach Reduzierung der Formensprache.

En dépit de ses dimensions modestes, cette villa construite dans un site magnifique qui domine le lac de Rur, dans l'Eifel, n'est pas sans rappeler certaines icônes de l'architecture moderne de la côte californienne. De grandes baies vitrées ouvrent l'espace cuisine/séjour/salle à manger sur la terrasse qui fait face au lac, tandis que les chambres et salles de bains sont positionnées à l'arrière du bâtiment. À la nature environnante répond un élégant mélange de matériaux associant le verre, l'aluminium anodisé, l'acier galvanisé, le béton délavé, les blocs de grauwacke et le merisier traité à la main. D'une manière générale, cette villa réinterprète des éléments de l'architecture moderne en exprimant un penchant pour un style minimaliste intemporel.

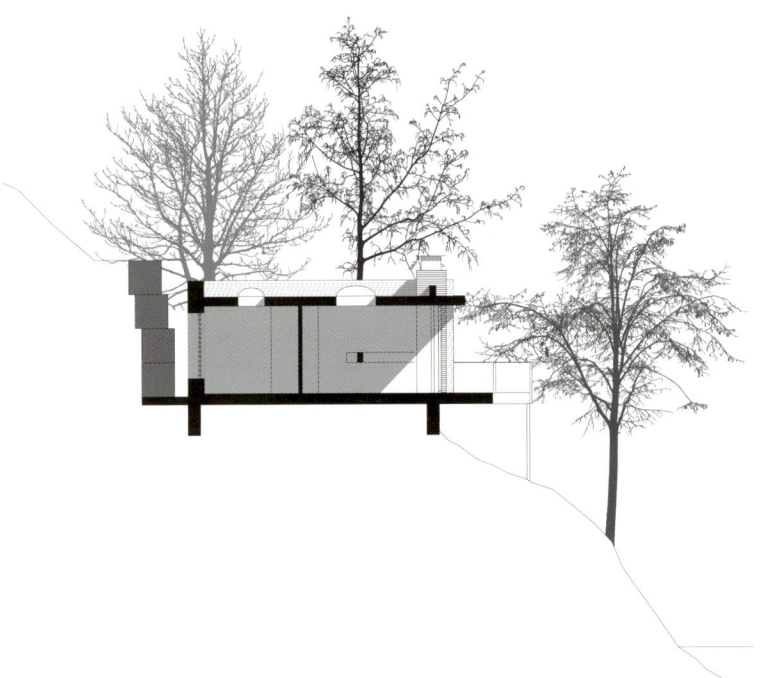

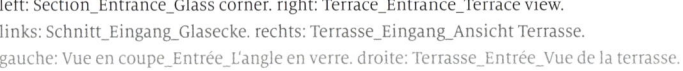

left: Section_Entrance_Glass corner. right: Terrace_Entrance_Terrace view.
links: Schnitt_Eingang_Glasecke. rechts: Terrasse_Eingang_Ansicht Terrasse.
gauche: Vue en coupe_Entrée_L'angle en verre. droite: Terrasse_Entrée_Vue de la terrasse.

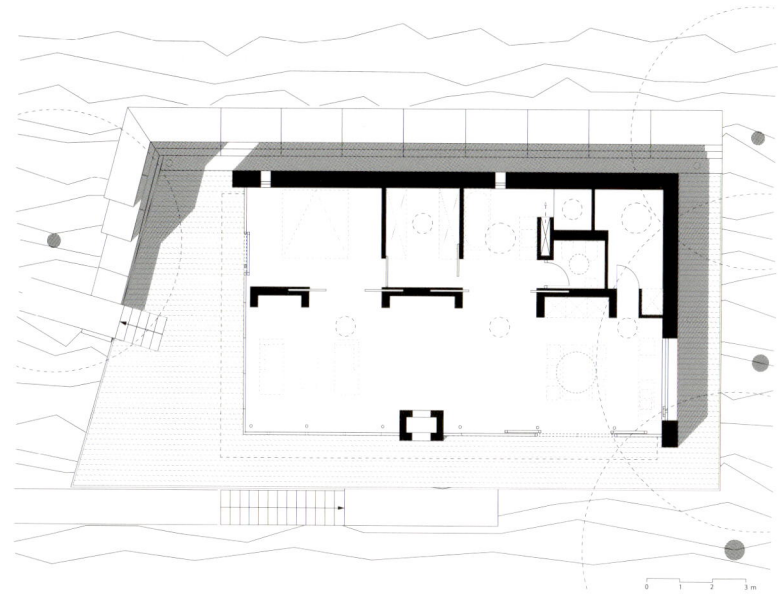

left: Dressing room. right: Floor plan_Bedroom_Living room_Living and dining area_Bathroom.
links: Ankleide. rechts: Grundriss_Schlafraum_Wohnzimmer_Wohn- und Esszimmer_Badezimmer.
gauche: Dressing. droite: Plan_Chambre_Séjour_Séjour et salle à manger_Salle de bains.

NACKA, SWEDEN **VILLA BLÅBÄR**

ARCHITECTS: PS ARKITEKTUR AB
COMPLETION: 2012_**PROPERTY SIZE:** 1,350 M²
GROSS FLOOR AREA: 170 M²_**NUMBER OF ROOMS:** 5
PHOTOS: JASON STRONG

Delightful views of the lush forest, spaciousness, and a daring, uncompromising design were the starting points for the development of this house in Nacka, outside Stockholm, Sweden. The house, which is fully covered in roofing felt, was created during a number of workshops with the client, where different volumes were tested in model. The challenge was to place all rooms on the same level, while also fitting the geometry of the house with the sloping ground. The house is hovering on concrete blocks over the beautiful natural building site, which is covered in heather, blueberries, and slender pines. The slate black surface of the exterior contrasts with the white interior. Wardrobes, lighting and sockets are inset in walls and ceiling to give an even and clean look.

Reizvolle Ausblicke in den Wald, Geräumigkeit und ein ebenso kühnes wie kompromissloses Design bilden die Grundpfeiler dieser Villa in Nacka, nahe Stockholm. Der Bau, der komplett mit Teerpappe verkleidet ist, wurde in enger Zusammenarbeit mit dem Auftraggeber entwickelt. Die Herausforderung bestand darin, alle Räume auf einer Ebene anzuordnen und gleichzeitig die Geometrie an die Hanglage anzupassen. Die Villa schwebt auf Betonpfählen über dem naturbelassenen Grundstück, das mit Heidekraut, Blaubeeren und schlanken Kiefern bewachsen ist. Die schwarze Außenhaut kontrastiert das Weiß der Innenräume. Schränke, Beleuchtung und Steckdosen sind in Wände und Decken eingelassen, sodass ein ebener und klarer Eindruck entsteht.

La conception de cette villa des environs de Stockholm a pris pour points de départ la magnifique forêt environnante et la volonté du maître d'ouvrage de vivre dans un bâtiment à l'architecture osée. Entièrement couverte en carton bituminé, la villa a été conçue en étroite collaboration avec le client, auquel l'architecte a soumis plusieurs maquettes. Le défi à relever consistait à placer toutes les pièces sur le même niveau, tout en adaptant les volumes à la topographie. Le bâtiment repose sur des piliers en béton prenant appui sur la roche d'un terrain couvert de bruyère, de genévriers et de pins. Le revêtement en ardoise des façades contraste avec la blancheur uniforme de l'intérieur. Les armoires intégrées et l'éclairage encastré viennent renforcer l'impression de purisme qui se dégage de l'ensemble.

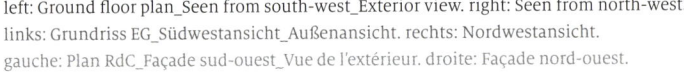

left: Ground floor plan_Seen from south-west_Exterior view. right: Seen from north-west.
links: Grundriss EG_Südwestansicht_Außenansicht. rechts: Nordwestansicht.
gauche: Plan RdC_Façade sud-ouest_Vue de l'extérieur. droite: Façade nord-ouest.

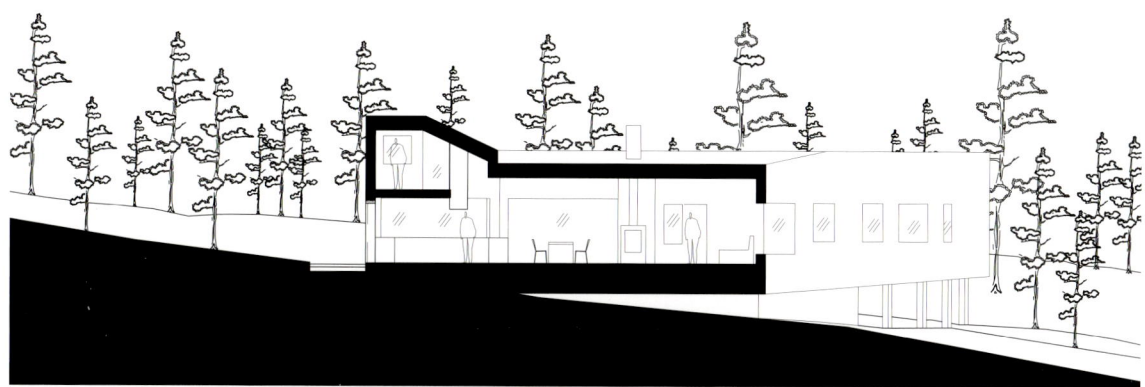

left: Stairs. right: Section_Kitchen_Bedroom_Interior view.
links: Treppe. rechts: Schnitt_Küche_Schlafzimmer_Innenansicht.
gauche: Escalier. droite: Vue en coupe_Cuisine_Chambre_Vue de l'intérieur.

STARNBERG-SÖCKING, GERMANY **HOUSE K**

ARCHITECTS: TITUS BERNHARD ARCHITEKTEN BDA
COMPLETION: 2012_**PROPERTY SIZE:** 2,000 M²
GROSS FLOOR AREA: 375 M²
PHOTOS: JENS WEBER & ORLA CONOLLY

The underlying theme of this single family home is the transition of the interior and exterior spaces and the deliberate placement of "photo mounts" that stage the attractive views inside the plot and block off unwanted looks from the neighborhood. The complex cubature of the house with intersected and interlaced elements, skylights, and light wells, in combination with the expansive terrace landscape, create a smooth transition between the house and the garden. The interior room layout is dominated by contrasting elements of density and expansiveness, light and dark, as well as architecture and nature. It incorporates Classical Modernity style elements in combination with natural elements. The materials are limited to white finely structured marble plaster, warm light-colored sandstone, and glass.

Dieses Einfamilienhaus thematisiert den Übergang von Innen- und Außenraum und die gezielte Setzung von „passepartouts", um die schönen Blickbeziehungen des Grundstücks zu inszenieren und die ungewünschte Nachbarschaft auszublenden. Die komplexe Kubatur des Hauses mit Durchdringungen, Verschachtelungen, Oberlichtern und Lichthöfen sowie die weitläufige Terrassenlandschaft lassen Haus und Garten fließend ineinander übergehen. Die innere Raumbildung ist geprägt von Spannungspaaren aus Weite und Dichte, hell und dunkel sowie Architektur und Natur. Hier finden Stilmittel der Klassischen Moderne jedoch auch von Garten und Natur ihre Anwendung. Die Materialität beschränkt sich auf weißen feinkörnigen Marmorputz, warmen hellen Sandstein und Glas.

Cette villa accorde une importance particulière aux relations intérieur/extérieur et s'efforce de mettre en valeur les vues qui s'offrent sur le terrain, tout en protégeant les occupants des regards indiscrets. Des volumes complexes, alliés à divers enchevêtrements et complétés par des puits de lumière et plusieurs grandes terrasses, contribuent au passage en douceur de la maison au jardin. La décoration intérieure se caractérise par les contrastes entre espace et densité, lumière et ombre, design et nature. L'ensemble fait appel aussi bien à l'art moderne qu'à l'art des jardins. Quant aux matériaux utilisés, ils se limitent au verre, à la pierre calcaire et à l'enduit blanc à base de marbre.

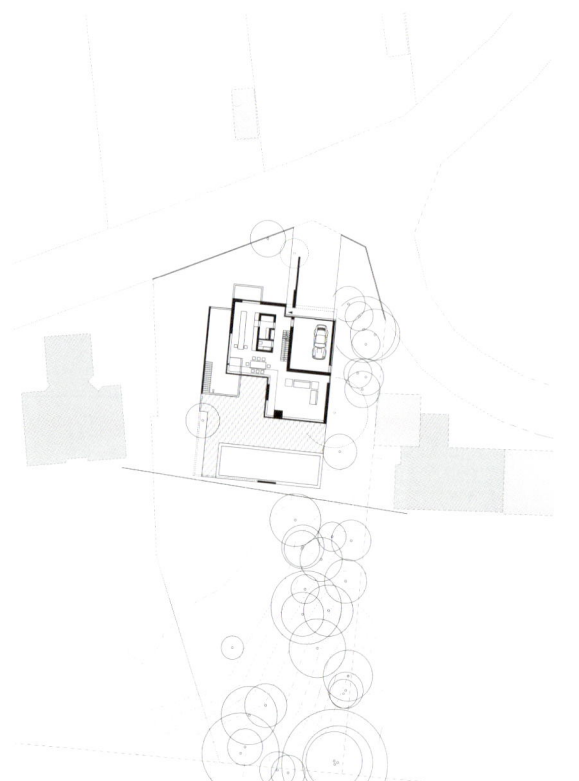

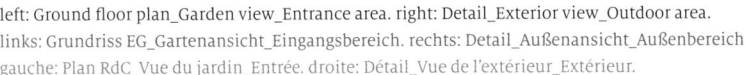

left: Ground floor plan_Garden view_Entrance area. right: Detail_Exterior view_Outdoor area.
links: Grundriss EG_Gartenansicht_Eingangsbereich. rechts: Detail_Außenansicht_Außenbereich.
gauche: Plan RdC_Vue du jardin_Entrée. droite: Détail_Vue de l'extérieur_Extérieur.

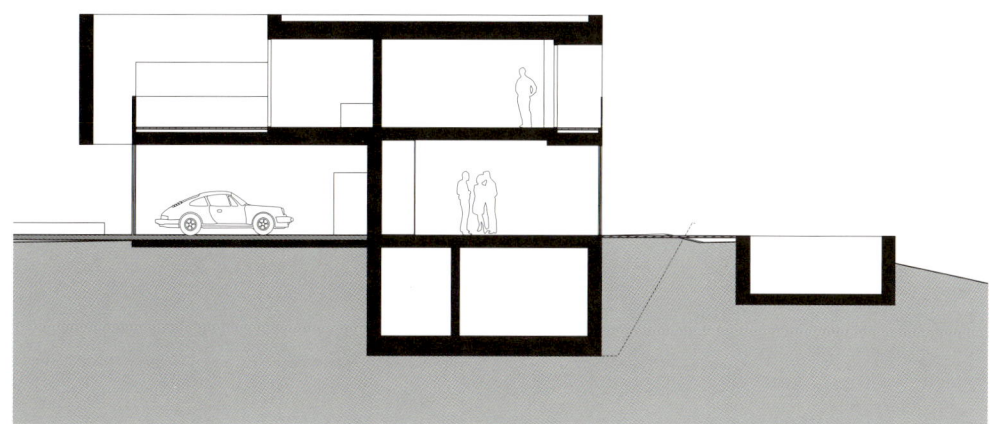

left: Kitchen. right: Section_Stairs_Kitchen.
links: Küche. rechts: Schnitt_Treppe_Küche.
gauche: Cuisine. droite: Vue en coupe_Escalier_Cuisine.

KALTENE, LATVIA **VACATION HOME EASTER ISLAND**

ARCHITECTS: ZAIGAS GAILES BIROJS
COMPLETION: 2010_**PROPERTY SIZE:** 10,067 M²
GROSS FLOOR AREA: 798 M²_**NUMBER OF ROOMS:** 12
PHOTOS: ANSIS STARKS (300–302, 303 R.), AINARS MEIERS (303 L.)

On a fine Easter morning, the architect's family set out on a daytrip along the Baltic sea shore and found an artificial stone island with ruins of a former fish factory pumping station, built in the 1980s and abandoned soon after its completion. The industrial architecture monument of the Soviet era was converted into a vacation home for the architect's family. The project preserves the island's landscape and architectural features. The original red brick facade is covered with rusty Corten steel plates and sliding shutters with perforated images of stone Moai. The interior of the house features 20th century design icons. The shining image of the new Nautilus bathhouse, resembling the turret of a submarine, is added to the background of the rusty main house.

An einem Ostermorgen unternahm der Architekt einen Ausflug entlang der baltischen Küste. Auf einer künstlichen Steininsel fand er ein Pumpwerk aus den 1980er-Jahren vor, das kurz nach der Fertigstellung aufgegeben worden war. Dieses industrielle Baudenkmal aus Sowjetzeiten gestaltete der Architekt zum Feriendomizil um. Dabei konservierte er die Gestalt der Insel und die architektonischen Besonderheiten. Die Originalfassade aus rotem Backstein ist mit korrodiertem Corten-Stahl verkleidet. Die Schiebetüren sind mit den Umrissen von Moai-Skulpturen perforiert. Das Interior wird von Designikonen aus dem 20. Jahrhundert bestimmt. Hinter dem Haupthaus befindet sich das glänzende neue Badehaus „Nautilus", das an den Geschützturm eines U-Boots erinnert.

Par un beau matin de Pâques, l'architecte est sa famille partis en excursion sur la côte de la mer Baltique ont découvert, sur une presqu'île artificielle, les ruines d'un bâtiment industriel construit dans les années 1980 et abandonné peu après. Ce vestige de l'ère soviétique est aujourd'hui la maison de vacances de l'architecte. Les travaux de restauration ont été menés en respectant la configuration de la presqu'île et la structure d'ensemble du bâtiment. La façade en briques a été pourvue d'un revêtement en acier Corten et de volets coulissants agrémentés de silhouettes perforées figurant les statues de l'île de Pâques. On trouve à l'intérieur des objets typiques du design du XXe siècle, et du côté faisant face à la mer une salle de bain en forme de tourelle de sous-marin.

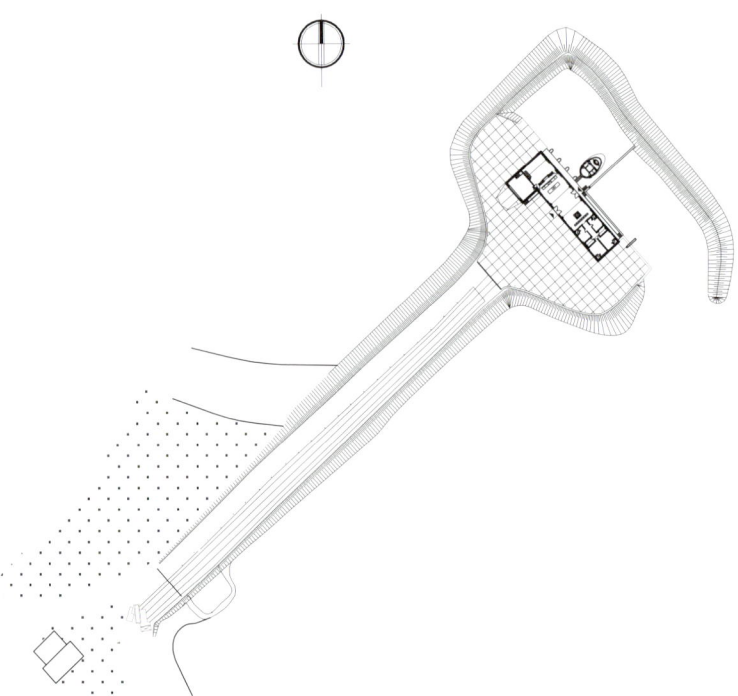

left: Site plan_General view_Exterior view with bathhouse. right: Bathhouse_Tub_Guest appartment.
links: Lageplan_Gesamtansicht_Außenansicht mit Badehaus. rechts: Badehaus_Badewanne_Gästehaus.
gauche: Plan de situation_Vue générale_Vue de l'extérieur avec maison balnéaire. droite: Maison balnéaire_Baignoire_Maison d'amis.

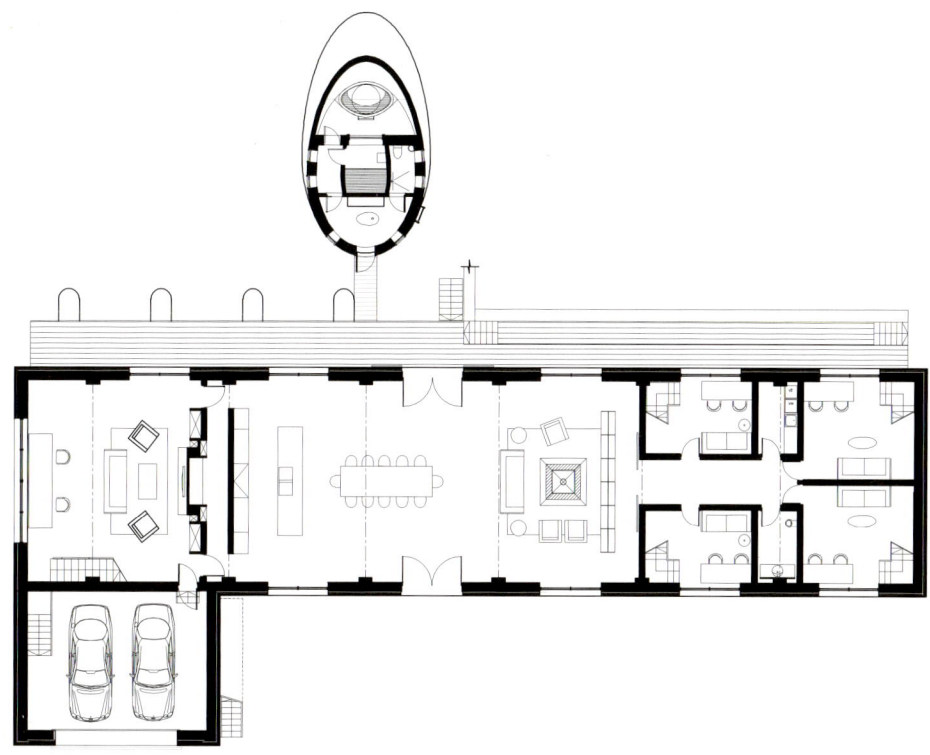

left: Dining area. right: Ground floor plan_Exterior view_Lounge area_Bathhouse interior.
links: Essbereich. rechts: Grundriss EG_Außenansicht_Lounge_Badehaus Innenansicht.
gauche: Salle à manger. droite: Plan RdC_Vue de l'extérieur_Séjour_L'intérieur de la maison balnéaire.

AALEN, GERMANY **HOUSE AFFALTERWANG**

ARCHITECTS: L/A LIEBEL/ARCHITEKTEN BDA
COMPLETION: 2010_**PROPERTY SIZE:** 1,015 M²
GROSS FLOOR AREA: 226 M²_**NUMBER OF ROOMS:** 6
PHOTOS: MICHAEL SCHNELL (304 R., 305),
BERND LIEBEL (304 L., 306,307)

A scraggy area with a rock-covered ground and a crowded plot situation that allows illumination only from the southern side constitute a special challenge for this house. The different levels are offset to each other at half height. The garden is directly accessible via a small banked up slope leading immediately from the terrace to the greenery. The split level concept provides all individual rooms on the upper floor, which face north, with sufficient sun from the south. This is also true for the home office in the basement, which gains additional space and light from a small courtyard in front of it.

Eine karge Gegend mit einem Boden voller Steine und eine beengte Grundstückssituation, die eine gute Belichtung ausschließlich von der Südseite her möglich macht bilden eine besondere Herausforderung für dieses Hauses. Die unterschiedlichen Ebenen sind halbgeschossig zueinander versetzt. Eine direkte Anbindung an den Garten erfolgt über einen kleinen aufgeschütteten Hang direkt vor der Terrasse hinunter ins Grüne. Alle Individualräume im OG, die nach Norden hin orientiert sind, erhalten durch das Split-Level-Konzept ausreichend Sonne von Süden. Ebenso das Arbeitszimmer im Souterrain, welches durch einen vorliegenden Hof zusätzlich an Raum und Licht gewinnt.

Les architectes avaient ici à résoudre plusieurs problèmes liés au site, notamment un sol rocailleux et un terrain si exigu que le bâtiment à construire ne pourrait être suffisamment éclairé que par la façade sud. La solution consistait à créer des demi-niveaux. Un talus artificiel se trouvant devant la terrasse métallique permet aux occupants d'accéder directement au jardin. Grâce au concept « demi-niveaux », toutes les pièces du dernier étage, situées au nord du bâtiment, bénéficient d'un bon ensoleillement par le sud. Il en va de même du bureau demi-souterrain qui se prolonge par une petite terrasse.

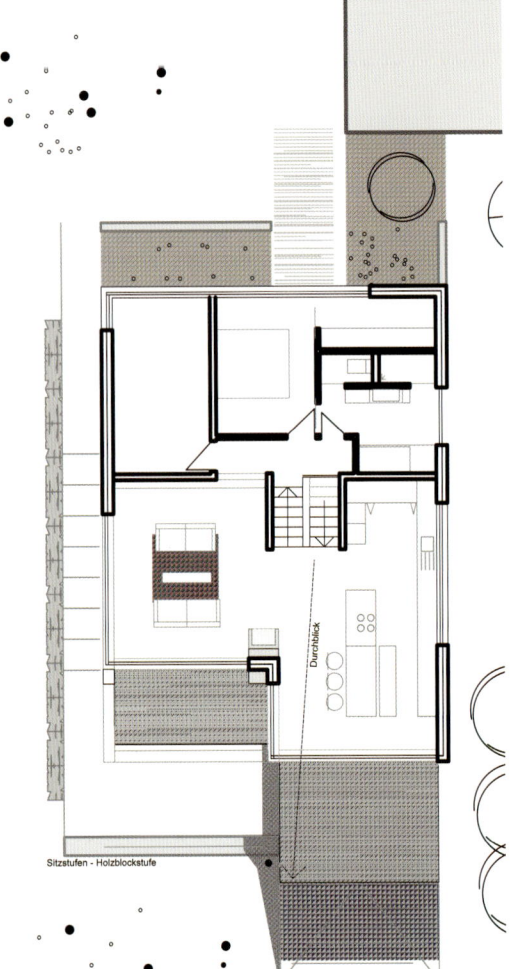

Sitzstufen - Holzblockstufe

left: Ground floor plan_Entrance_Exterior view. right: Garden view_Exterior view_Terrace.
links: Grundriss EG_Eingang_Außenansicht. rechts: Gartenansicht_Außenansicht_Terrasse.
gauche: Plan RdC_Entrée_Vue de l'extérieur. droite: Vue du jardin_Vue de l'extérieur_Terrasse.

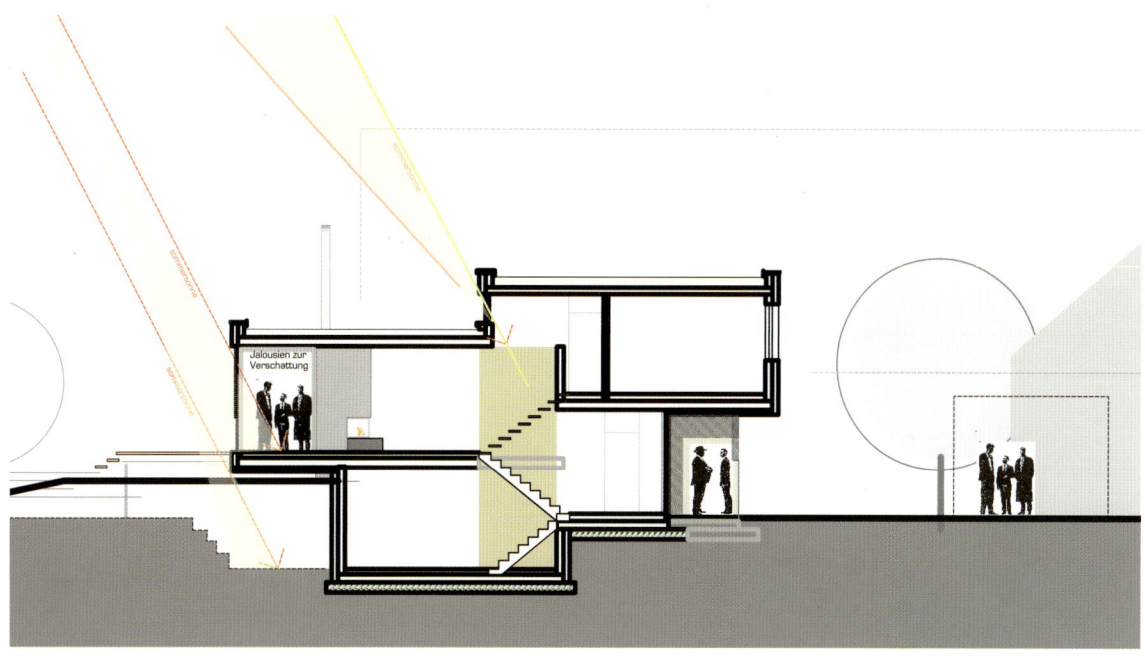

left: Kitchen. right: Section_Stairs_Living room_Office.
links: Küche. rechts: Schnitt_Treppe_Wohnraum_Büro.
gauche: Cuisine. droite: Vue en coupe_Escalier_Bureau.

ROTTERDAM, THE NETHERLANDS **VILLA ROTTERDAM**

ARCHITECTS: OOZE ARCHITECTS
COMPLETION: 2010_**PROPERTY SIZE:** 2,500 M²
GROSS FLOOR AREA: 549 M²_**NUMBER OF ROOMS:** 9
PHOTOS: JEROEN MUSCH & OOZE

The project is a conversion of an already converted villa. The existing villa was composed of a strange architectural patchwork. Ooze architects developed a design in keeping with the spirit of the old house. Due to regulations, the proposal expanded the volume of the house from its original footprint to the maximum space in the form of a skin wrapped around the old house shaping new living spaces. The layout was reorganized around a central void with an additional staircase. Folds and facets additionally benefit the interior space within the permitted volume. This structure sits like a hat on top and acts as a load carrier to reduce the additional weight of the new floors and roofs. Solid timber panels were used for walls, floors and roofs. The external cladding is a reference to old Dutch farms with green sedum roofs.

Da die Villa bereits einmal erweitert wurde, setzte sich der Bestand aus einer eigenartigen architektonischen Mischung zusammen. Der Entwurf von Ooze zielte darauf ab, die Seele des alten Hauses zu bewahren. Aufgrund der Bauvorschriften wurde die ursprüngliche Grundfläche beibehalten. Eine Außenhaut wächst um den Bestand und formt durch Falten und Facetten neue Wohnbereiche aus. So wird das zulässige Volumen maximal ausgenutzt. Die Anordnung der Räume ist um das neue Treppenhaus herum organisiert. Wie ein Hut stülpt sich die Struktur über das Haus. Massive Holzplanken tragen das Gewicht der Stockwerke und Dächer. Die Außenverkleidung und die mit Mauerpfeffer begrünten Dächer erinnern an die traditionelle Bauweise holländischer Bauernhöfe.

Chargés d'agrandir une villa à laquelle plusieurs remaniements avaient donné un aspect « patchwork », les architectes ont travaillé en s'inspirant de l'esprit du bâtiment d'origine. Tout en respectant la législation locale en matière de surface bâtie maximale, ils ont construit une extension conçue comme une enveloppe moderne à multiples facettes qui enrobe la vieille maison. L'espace s'organise désormais autour d'une nef centrale qui accueille un escalier supplémentaire. En dépit de son apparente légèreté, la nouvelle structure supporte les lourdes charges dues aux étages et au toit ayant été rajoutés. Les nouveaux éléments intérieurs (murs, planchers et charpente) sont en bois tandis qu'à l'extérieur, la villa n'est pas sans rappeler les vieilles fermes hollandaises avec toit végétalisé en sédum.

left: Ground floor plan_Exterior view_Hall. right: Detail of the façade.
links: Grundriss EG_Außenansicht_Flur. rechts: Fassadendetail.
gauche: Plan RdC_Vue de l'extérieur_Couloir. droite: Détail de la façade.

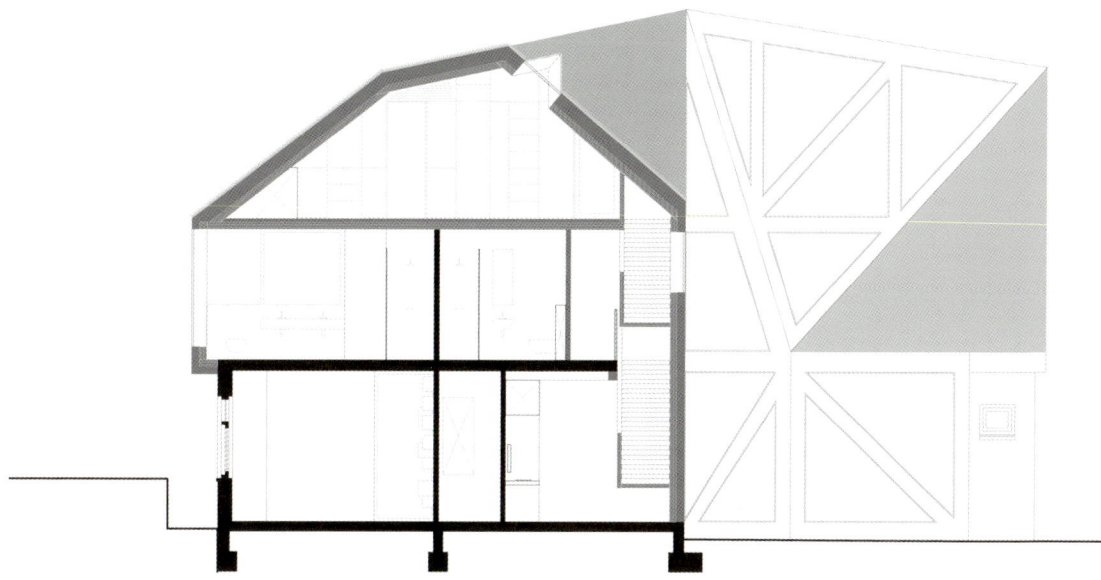

left: Staircase. right: Section_Entrance area.
links: Treppenraum. rechts: Schnitt_Eingangsbereich.
gauche: Cage d'escalier. droite: Vue en coupe_Entrée.

![Interior photograph of staircase and entrance area]

BINNINGEN, SWITZERLAND **PRIVATE HOUSE**

ARCHITECTS: LUPO.ZUCCARELLO ARCHITEKTEN
COMPLETION: 2012_**PROPERTY SIZE:** 900 M²
GROSS FLOOR AREA: 320 M²_**NUMBER OF ROOMS:** 7
PHOTOS: BÖRJE MÜLLER

This generously sized single-family dwelling is located on one of the last empty lots in the quiet city of Binningen near Basle. Cream whitewashed extended cubes form a structure that is concealed from the street side and open towards the private garden. Clear, horizontal lines give the two-floor building a certain degree of rigidity, which is however loosened by the offsetting of the two floors towards each other. This creates overlaps and terraces that create retreat areas and open spaces. The ground floor contains the daytime sections with the entrance area. A large gallery connects it to the upper floor with the bedrooms.

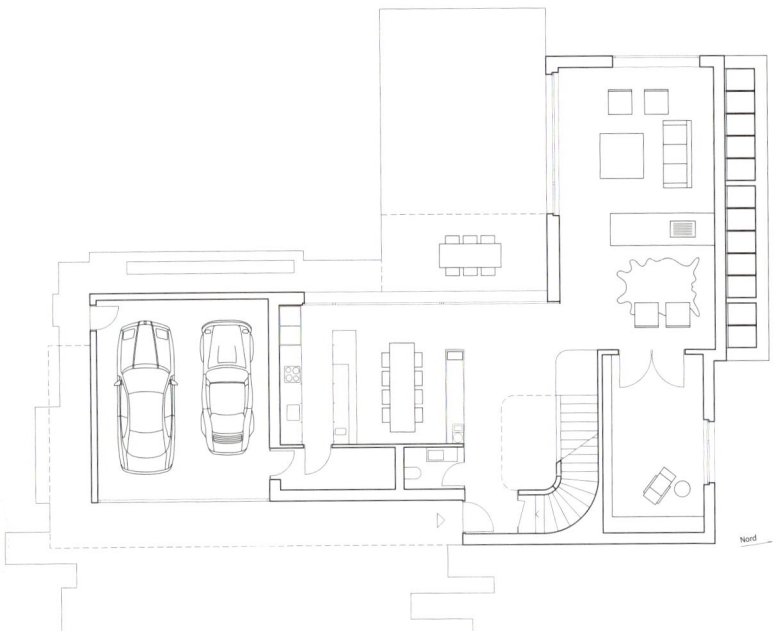

Eines der letzten unbebauten Grundstücke im ruhigen Basler Nachbarort Binningen, war Ausgangslage für dieses großzügige Einfamilienhaus. Cremeweiß verputzte Längskuben bilden einen Baukörper, welcher sich zur Straßenseite abschirmt und zum privaten Garten hin öffnet. Klare horizontale Linien verleihen dem zweigeschossigen Gebäude eine gewisse Strenge, die jedoch durch die Verschiebung der beiden Geschosse zueinander aufgelockert wird. Es bilden sich Überdeckungen und Terrassen aus, welche Rückzugsbereiche und Freiflächen entstehen lassen. Das Erdgeschoss umfasst die Tagesbereiche mit dem Entrée, das sich über die grösszügige Galerie mit dem Obergeschoss verbindet, wo sich die Schlafräume befinden.

Cette villa spacieuse sur deux niveaux se trouve à Binningen, un faubourg tranquille de Bâle. Elle se compose de parallélépipèdes blancs crème fermés côté rue et largement ouverts côté jardin. Des lignes horizontales claires confèrent à l'ensemble un aspect austère, que vient toutefois alléger le décalage du niveau supérieur par rapport au rez-de-chaussée. Le porte-à-faux et les terrasses qui en résultent génèrent plusieurs espaces de repos et de plein air. Le niveau inférieur accueille les pièces utilisées durant la journée tandis que la grande galerie reliée à l'entrée par un escalier dessert les chambres du niveau supérieur.

left: Ground floor plan_Seen from west_Living area. right: Outdoor area.
links: Grundriss EG_Westansicht_Wohnbereich. rechts: Außenbereich.
gauche: Plan RdC_Façade ouest_Séjour. droite: Extérieur.

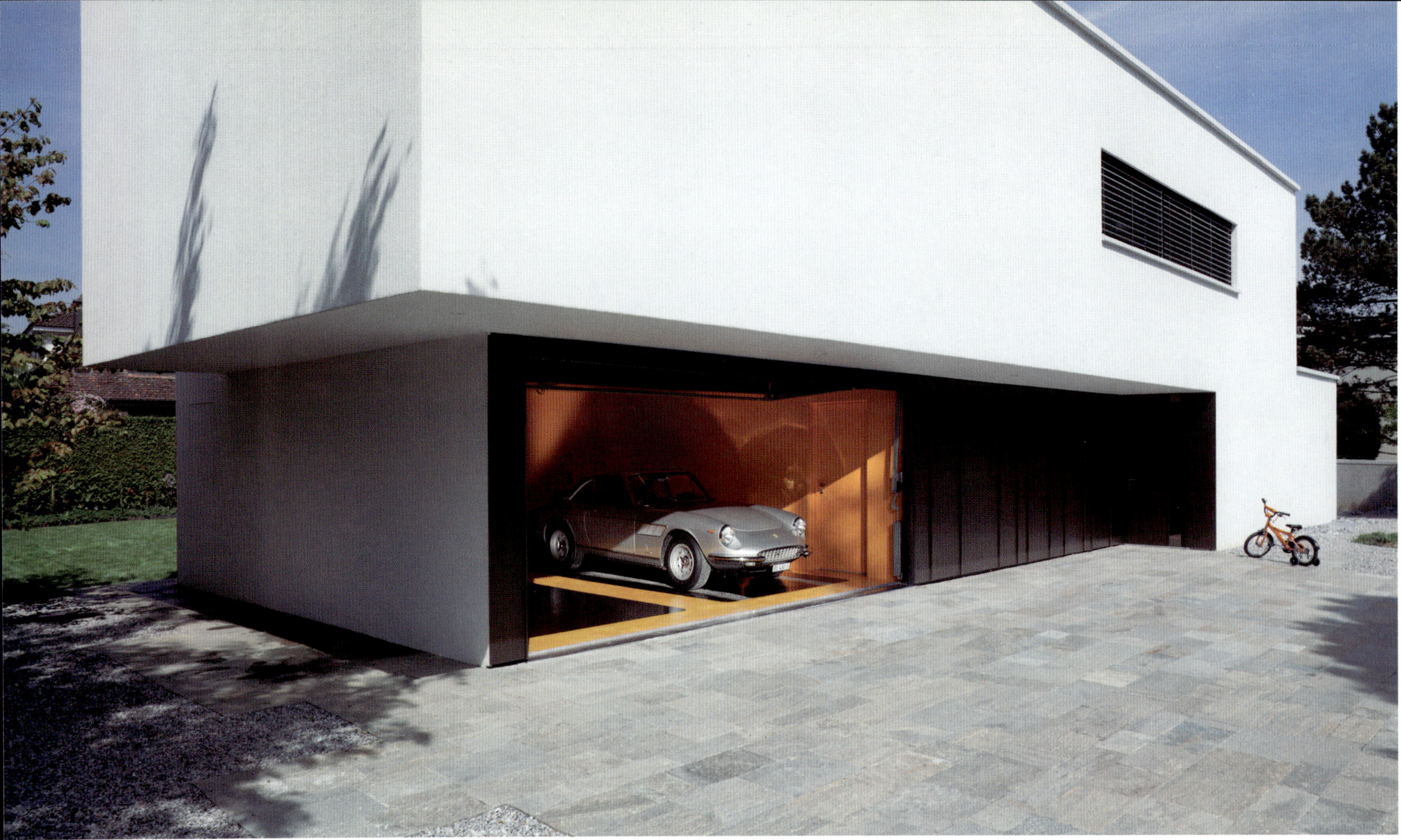

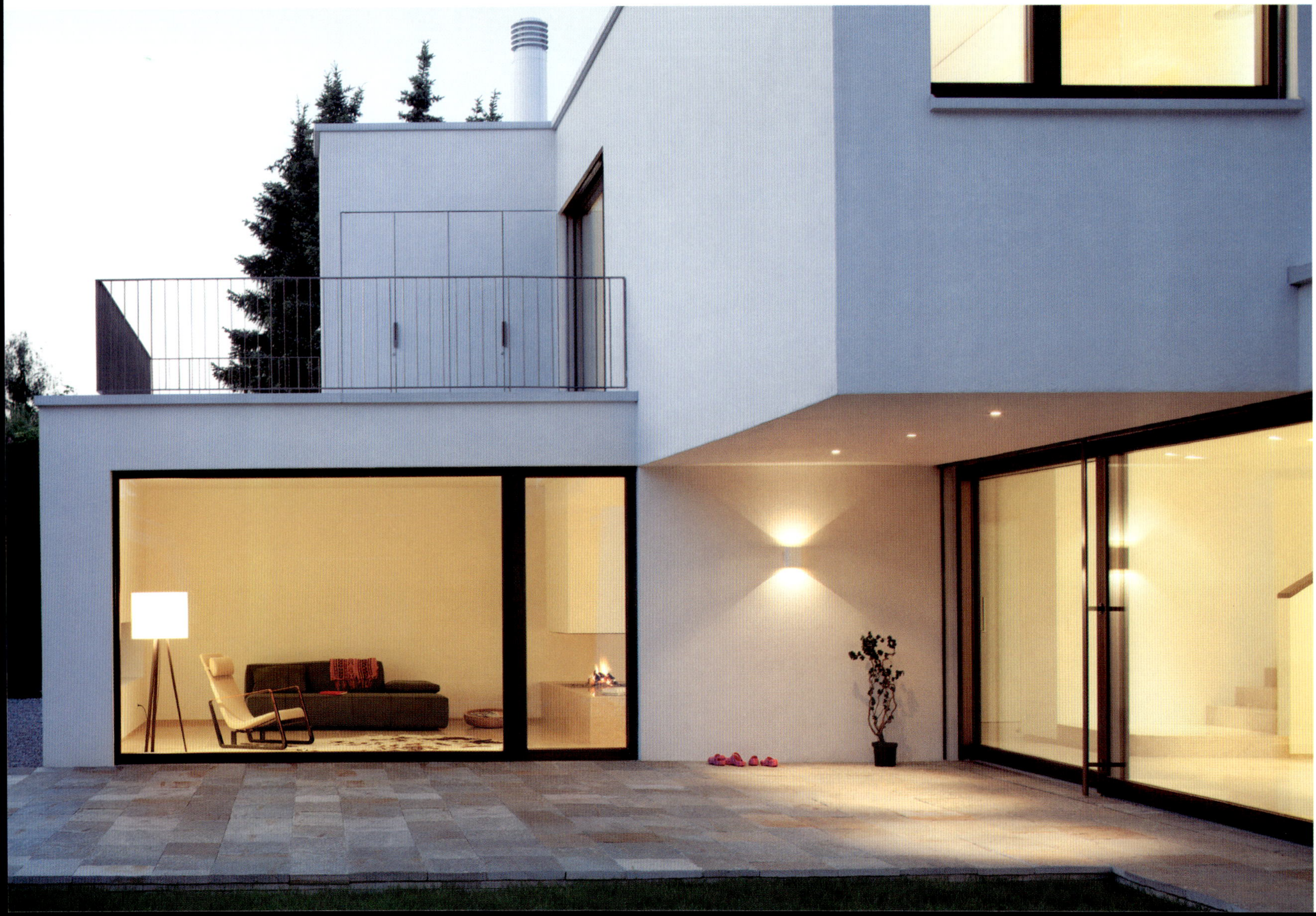

left: Garage_Terrace. right: Elevation_Living area.
links: Garage_Terrasse. rechts: Ansicht_Wohnbereich.
gauche: Garage_Terrasse. droite: Élévation_Séjour.

STONEGATE, EAST SUSSEX, UK **OLD BEARHURST**

ARCHITECTS: DUGGAN MORRIS ARCHITECTS
COMPLETION: 2011_**PROPERTY SIZE:** 28,327 M²
GROSS FLOOR AREA: 433 M²_**NUMBER OF ROOMS:** 4
PHOTOS: JAMES BRITTAIN / ARTUR IMAGES

The two-century old oast house was extensively remodeled, its existing barn and roundels overhauled, and a new annex constructed to provide space for the client's growing family. The building is located in a rural setting in an area of outstanding natural beauty, which has required a unique response to the topography, landscape, history and setting. The project aimed to create a unified series of flowing contemporary spaces, allowing a greater degree of flexibility, linking internal spaces to the rolling fields to the south, and the higher meadow land to the north. Equally, the brief called for a building with character and personality, respectful of the existing oast house, and taking advantage of the views and surrounding environment.

Das Anwesen liegt in einem ländlichen Gebiet von bestechender Schönheit. Die landschaftliche Kulisse, ihre Topografie und Geschichte, verlangten nach einzigartigen Lösungen. Der zwei Jahrhunderte alte Trockenschuppen wurde restauriert und umgestaltet, der Stall sowie die Rundbauten instand gesetzt. Zudem entstand ein Anbau, um Raum für die wachsende Familie des Bauherrn zu schaffen. Ziel des Projekts war ein kontinuierlicher Fluss moderner und flexibler Räume, die in einen Dialog mit den weitläufigen Feldern im Süden sowie den höher gelegenen Wiesen im Norden treten. Der Auftraggeber wünschte ein Gebäude mit Charakter und Persönlichkeit. So setzten die Architekten den historischen Bestand in Szene und nutzten den Standortvorteil in Form schöner Ausblicke.

Le projet consistait à rénover entièrement une brasserie deux fois centenaire et ses touraiiles, et à la compléter d'une annexe afin d'augmenter la surface habitable. Les bâtiments d'origine étant situés dans une zone rurale très pittoresque, il était nécessaire de réaliser les travaux en tenant compte de la topographie, du paysage et de l'histoire du site. Les architectes ont conçu des espaces contemporains homogènes qui offrent un haut degré de flexibilité et sont reliés à la fois aux champs s'étirant au sud de la propriété et aux prairies qui se trouvent au nord. Le bâtiment répond ainsi au souhait du maître d'ouvrage, qui souhaitait un ensemble de caractère respectant les anciens bâtiments et tirant parti des avantages du site.

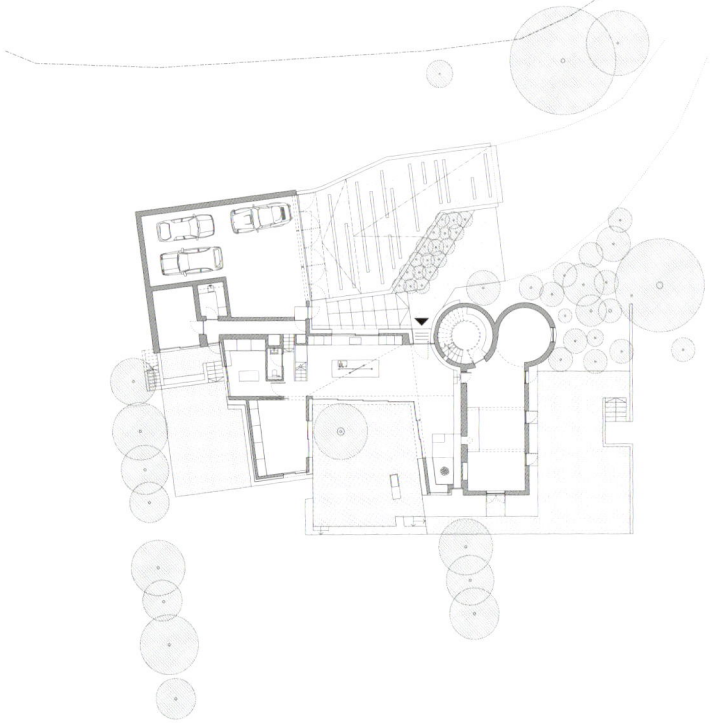

left: Ground floor plan_Annex_Entrance. right: Roofscape.
links: Grundriss EG_Anbau_Eingangsbereich. rechts: Dachlandschaft.
gauche: Plan RdC_Annexe_Entrée. droite: Paysage des toits.

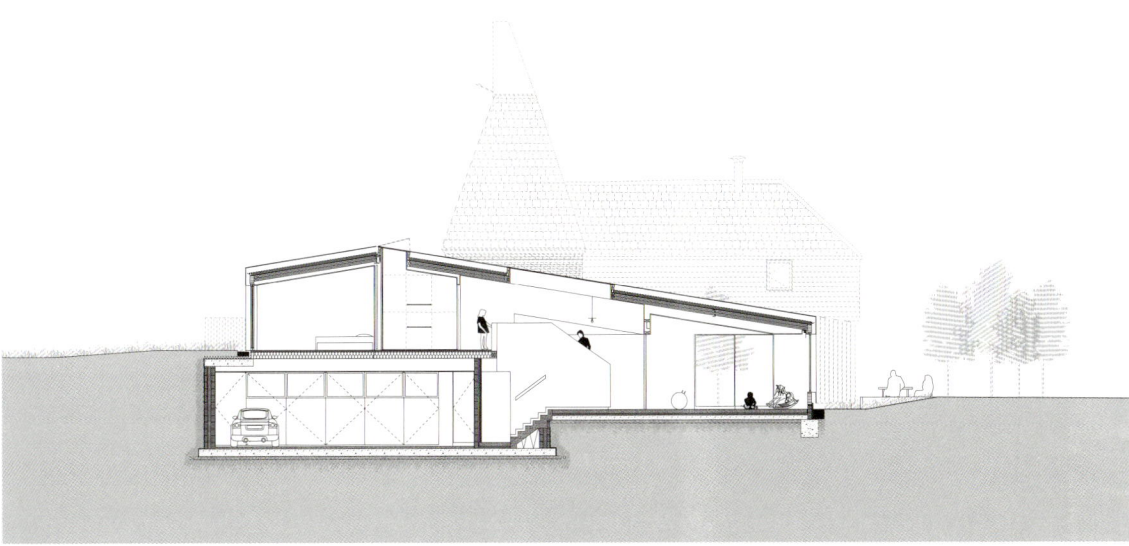

left: Kitchen window. right: Section_Kitchen.
links: Küchenfenster. rechts: Schnitt_Küche.
gauche: Fenêtre de la cuisine. droite: Vue en coupe_Cuisine.

KIEL, GERMANY **HOUSE OE**

ARCHITECTS: SCHMIEDER.DAU.ARCHITEKTEN.
COMPLETION: 2009_**PROPERTY SIZE:** 1,600 M²
GROSS FLOOR AREA: 254 M²_**NUMBER OF ROOMS:** 7
PHOTOS: CHRISTOPH EDELHOFF

The plot of land is located at the edge of town on a slight elevation with an unobstructed view to the south of the hilly end moraine landscape of the Westensee natural preserve. The residence consists of two cubes inserted inside each other that manifest their independence by the use of very different materials, wood and stone. The house opens up towards the south via large glazed sections with terrace spaces located in front. Up to the ground floor ceiling, the building is a solid construction. The top floor is added as a light-weight wooden post-and-beam structure. The façades are covered in untreated giant cedar cladding.

Das Grundstück liegt in Ortsrandlage auf einer leichten Erhöhung mit einem unverbaubaren Blick Richtung Süden in die hügelige endmoränen Landschaft des Naturpark Westensee. Das Wohnhaus besteht aus zwei ineinander geschobenen Kuben, die ihre Eigenständigkeit durch sehr unterschiedliche Materialien: Stein und Holz, manifestieren. Nach Süden hin öffnet sich das Haus mit großflächigen Verglasungen über die vorgelagerten Terrassenflächen in die Landschaft. Das Gebäude ist bis zur Erdgeschossdecke in massiver Bauweise errichtet. Das Obergeschoss ist als leichte Holzständerkonstruktion aufgesetzt. Die Fassaden bestehen aus einer Verkleidung aus unbehandelter Rotzeder.

Cette villa se dresse sur un promontoire des environs de Kiel offrant une vue imprenable sur les collines du parc naturel du lac de Westensee. Elle se compose de deux parallélépipèdes emboîtés l'un dans l'autre, chacun affirmant sa personnalité à l'aide de matériaux différents : la pierre pour le plus petit, le bois pour le plus grand. Sur la façade sud, de larges baies vitrées ouvrent le bâtiment sur des terrasses permettant d'apprécier le paysage. Un socle massif sert de support à une structure légère en bois. Les façades du volume principal sont pourvues d'un revêtement en cèdre rouge non traité.

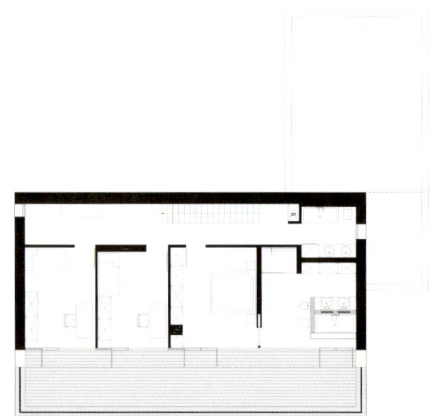

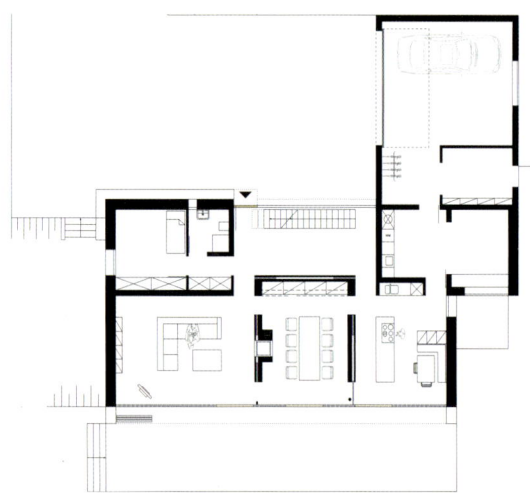

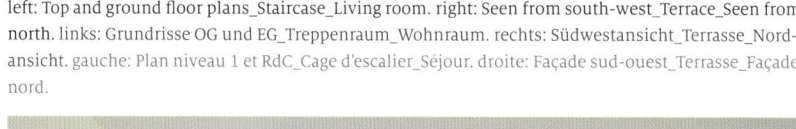

left: Top and ground floor plans_Staircase_Living room. right: Seen from south-west_Terrace_Seen from north. links: Grundrisse OG und EG_Treppenraum_Wohnraum. rechts: Südwestansicht_Terrasse_Nordansicht. gauche: Plan niveau 1 et RdC_Cage d'escalier_Séjour. droite: Façade sud-ouest_Terrasse_Façade nord.

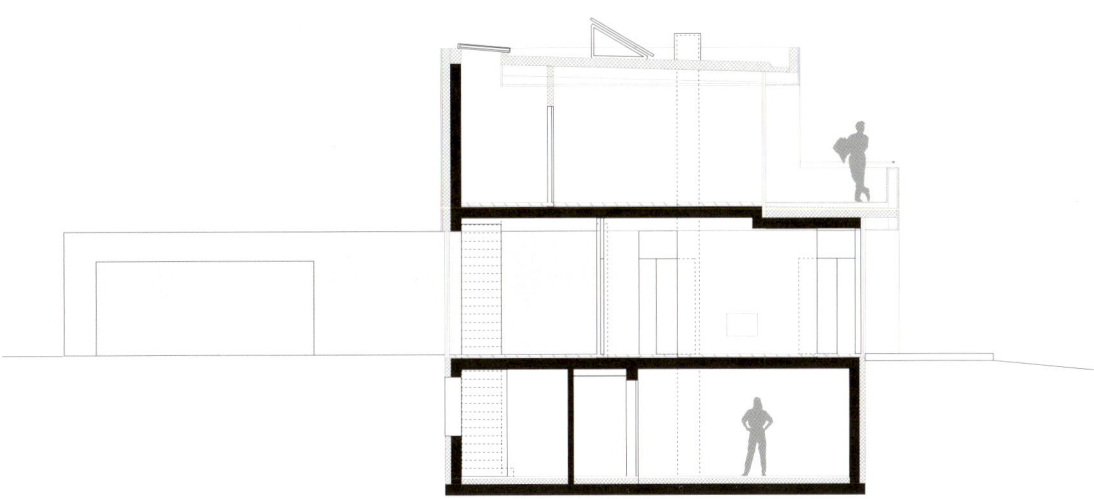

left: Kitchen. right: Section_Bathroom and balcony.
links: Küche. rechts: Schnitt_Bad und Balkon.
gauche: Cuisine. droite: Vue en coupe_Salle de bains et balcon.

MERANO, ITALY **HOUSE M**

ARCHITECTS: MONOVOLUME ARCHITECTURE + DESIGN
COMPLETION: 2012_**PROPERTY SIZE:** 1,200 M²
GROSS FLOOR AREA: 330 M²_**NUMBER OF ROOMS:** 6
PHOTOS: M&H PHOTOSTUDIO

House M is located in the heart of Merano, nestled in a quiet residential area of the Obermais district. The design is based on the interplay between solid and transparent areas, creating various insights, views, and perspectives. The interior merges with the exterior. The terrain flows through the building and is extended in the pool and meadow section. The clever outdoor design and the arrangement of pool, sunbathing lawn, garden, and house make it appear like a single unit with seamless transitions. The ground floor adjusts with steps to the slightly sloping terrain to gain as much garden space as possible.

Das Wohnhaus M befindet sich im Herzen von Meran, eingebettet in eine ruhige Wohngegend des Ortsteils Obermais. Der Entwurfsidee liegt das Wechselspiel zwischen massiven und transparenten Flächen zu Grunde, sodass Ein-, Aus- und Durchblicke entstehen. Der Innenraum verschmilzt mit dem Außenraum. Das Gelände fließt durch das Gebäude und findet dessen Verlängerung im Pool- und Wiesenbereich. Durch die raffinierte Außengestaltung und Anordnung von Pool, Liegewiese, Garten und Haus, erscheint das Ganze als Einheit mit nahtlosen Übergängen. Das Erdgeschoss folgt dem leicht abschüssigen Geländeverlauf in abgetreppter Form mit dem Ziel viel Gartenfläche zu erhalten.

La villa M se trouve à Merano, dans le quartier résidentiel d'Obermais. L'idée de base des architectes était d'établir une alternance entre surfaces pleines et transparentes afin de multiplier les perspectives et d'interconnecter l'intérieur et l'extérieur : le terrain pénètre le bâtiment, qui se prolonge pour sa part grâce à la pelouse et la piscine. La conception et la disposition raffinées de la villa et de ses espaces extérieurs ont permis de réaliser ici un ensemble homogène. Le rez-de-chaussée compense la légère pente du terrain à l'aide de quelques marches afin d'empiéter le moins possible sur le jardin.

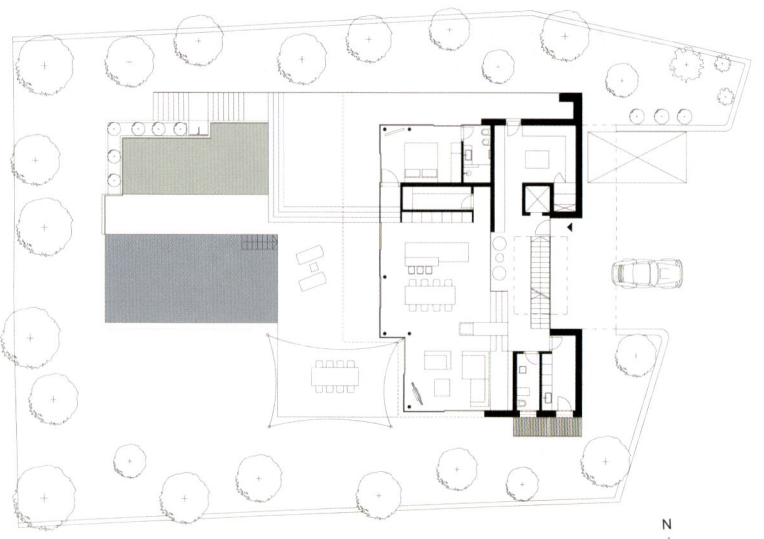

N

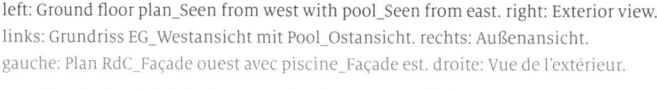

left: Ground floor plan_Seen from west with pool_Seen from east. right: Exterior view.
links: Grundriss EG_Westansicht mit Pool_Ostansicht. rechts: Außenansicht.
gauche: Plan RdC_Façade ouest avec piscine_Façade est. droite: Vue de l'extérieur.

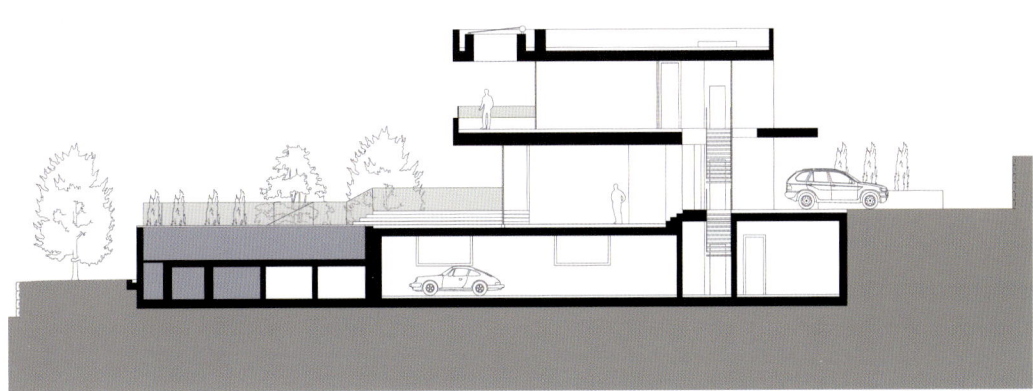

left: Stairs_Living room_Dining area. right: Section_Exterior view_Bathroom_Pool.
links: Treppe_Wohnraum_Essbereich. rechts: Schnitt_Außenansicht_Bad_Pool.
gauche: Escalier_Séjour_Salle à manger. droite: Vue en coupe_Vue de l'extérieur_Salle de bains_Piscine.

LIENEN, GERMANY **HOUSE PELLEMEIER**

ARCHITECTS: PELLEMEIER ARCHITEKTEN
DANIELA UND LARS PELLEMEIER
COMPLETION: 2010_**PROPERTY SIZE:** 8,400 M²
GROSS FLOOR AREA: 425 M²_**NUMBER OF ROOMS:** 12
PHOTOS: ROLAND BORGMANN

House Pellemeier is located on the southern slope of the Teutoburg forest, surrounded by the cherry trees of the historic farmstead. The building evolves around the central hall on the ground floor. Located at the center, the fireplace divides the kitchen, dining and living room. The western wing of the house contains the offices of the architectural firm. Ecological materials such as oak, exposed concrete, steel and clinker were used. The façade is designed in the modern classicist style with windows and façade elements such as pilaster strips and pillars strictly arranged. The small sized clinker brick creates a multifarious play of warm colors that combines with the anthracite colored windows into a harmonious unit.

Das Haus Pellemeier liegt am Südhang des Teutoburger Waldes, umgeben vom Kirschbaumbestand der historischen Hofstelle. Das Gebäude entwickelt sich um die zentrale Halle im Erdgeschoss. Der im Mittelpunkt stehende Kamin gliedert Küche, Ess- und Wohnzimmer. Im Westteil des Hauses befinden sich die Büro- räume des Architekturbüros. Bei der Materialwahl kamen ökologische Baustoffe wie Eiche, Sichtbeton, Stahl und Klinker zum Einsatz. Die Fassadengestaltung zeigt eine moderne klassizistische Architektur mit stringenter Anordnung der Fenster und Fassadenelemente wie Lisenen und Pfeilern. Der kleinformatige Klinkerstein erzeugt ein facettenreiches Farbspiel von warmen Farbtönen, das mit den anthrazitfarbenen Fenstern ein harmonisches Gesamtbild ergibt.

La villa Pellemeier se dresse au sud de la forêt de Teutoburg, sur un terrain planté de vieux cerisiers. Les pièces du rez-de-chaussée sont groupées autour d'une nef centrale. Une cheminée est positionnée entre la cuisine et l'espace séjour/salle à manger. L'architecte, dont les bureaux occupent la partie ouest du bâtiment, a privilégié les matériaux écologiques comme le chêne, l'acier, la brique et le béton brut de coffrage. Les façades réinterprètent l'architecture classique dans un style moderne, notamment en ce qui concerne la disposition des fenêtres et l'utilisation d'éléments tels que piliers et lésènes. Des briques de petite taille et de teintes variées confèrent aux façades un aspect chaleureux en harmonie avec l'anthracite des fenêtres.

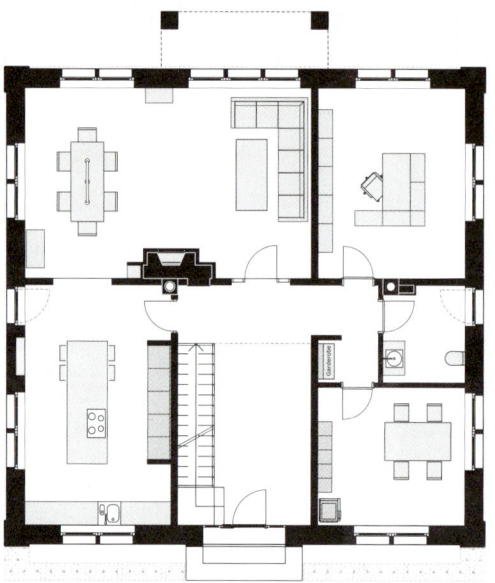

left: Ground floor plan_Seen from north_Seen from south-east. right: Seen from south.
links: Grundriss EG_Nordansicht_Südostansicht. rechts: Südansicht.
gauche: Plan RdC_Façade nord_Façade sud-est. droite: Façade sud.

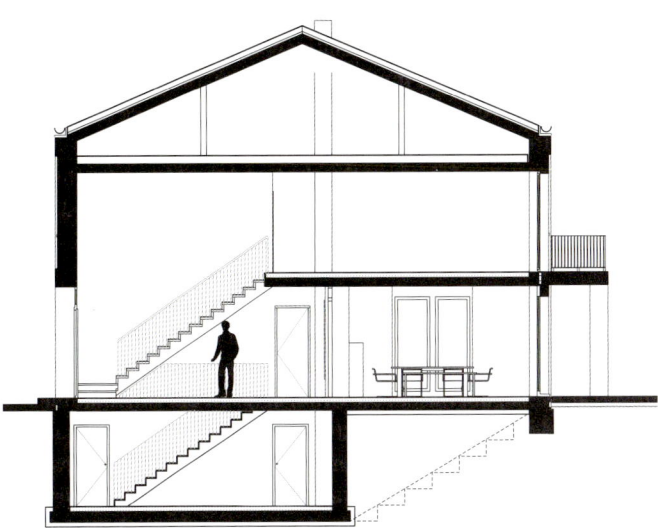

left: Entrance area. right: Section_Kitchen_Bathroom_Living room.
links: Eingangsbereich. rechts: Schnitt_Küche_Bad_Wohnzimmer.
gauche: Entrée. droite: Vue en coupe_Cuisine_ Salle de bains_Séjour.

TOKYO, JAPAN **GROW**

ARCHITECTS: APOLLO ARCHITECTS & ASSOCIATES
COMPLETION: 2012_**PROPERTY SIZE:** 39 M²
GROSS FLOOR AREA: 125 M²_**NUMBER OF ROOMS:** 4
PHOTOS: MASAO NISHIKAWA

This downtown residence, which also includes a working space, is located on an extremely small plot measuring just 65sqm. Its interior brims with a sense of openness that cannot be imagined from the relatively closed facade and its few visible openings. It is distinguished by myriad faces and spatial configurations that can be enjoyed as one moves up and down the cleverly designed different levels of the home. The three floors are flooded in light and the family room on the third floor presents a panoramic view of the sky and downtown area through ample glass panels. In addition, the rooftop garden, which can be accessed through a rooftop structure, is a genuine urban oasis.

Das Stadthaus verbindet Wohnen und Arbeiten auf einem nur 65 Quadratmeter großen Grundstück. Hinter der relativ geschlossenen Fassade, die nur wenige sichtbare Öffnungen aufweist, überrascht die Großzügigkeit der Innenräume. Die erstaunliche Vielfalt der räumlichen Strukturen lässt sich von außen kaum erahnen, doch wer sich zwischen den intelligent angeordneten Ebenen bewegt, erlebt drei lichtdurchflutete Stockwerke und kann dank der großzügigen Verglasung des Familienbereichs im Obergeschoss einen Panoramablick über die Dächer der Stadt genießen. Zusätzlich erreicht man über eine Dachkonstruktion den Dachgarten – eine grüne Oase inmitten der Stadt.

Cette maison doublée d'un bureau se trouve dans un centre ville sur un terrain mesurant tout juste soixante-cinq mètres carrés. Bien que seules quelques ouvertures soient visibles de la rue, le bâtiment est très lumineux et ouvert sur l'extérieur. L'intérieur se caractérise par une configuration spatiale intelligemment structurée aux différents niveaux, tous abondamment baignés de lumière. Le séjour du second étage est pourvu de grandes baies vitrées qui offrent des vues panoramiques sur le ciel et les bâtiments environnants. Le toit en terrasse, auquel on accède par un escalier en colimaçon, constitue une véritable oasis de verdure dans la ville.

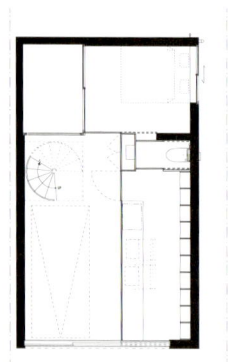
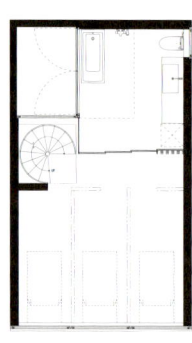
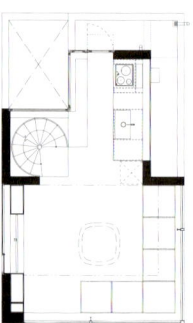

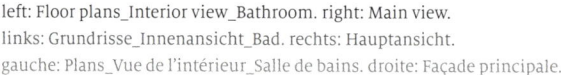

left: Floor plans_Interior view_Bathroom. right: Main view.
links: Grundrisse_Innenansicht_Bad. rechts: Hauptansicht.
gauche: Plans_Vue de l'intérieur_Salle de bains. droite: Façade principale.

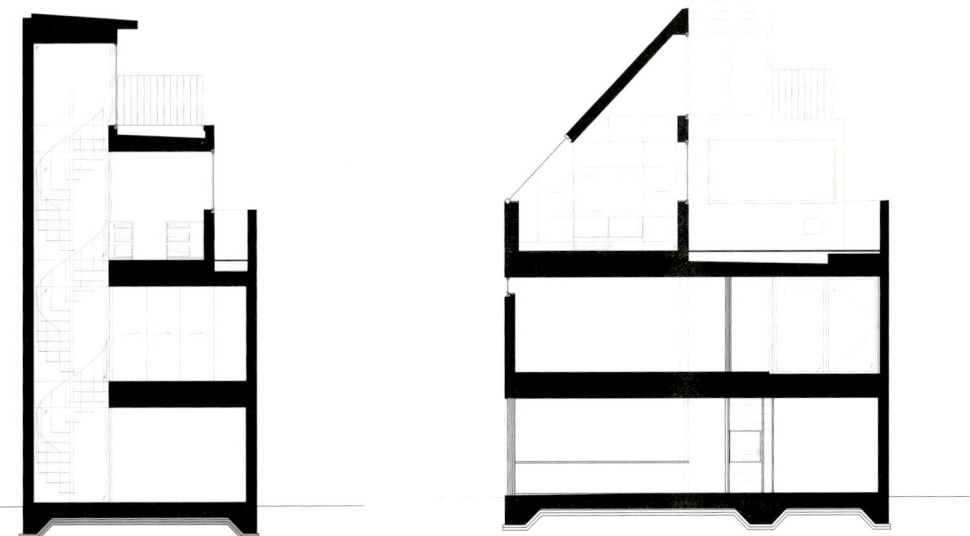

left: Kitchen. right: Sections_Garage_Living area_Stairs_Skylight.
links: Küche. rechts: Schnitte_Garage_Wohnbereich_Treppe_Oberlicht.
gauche: Cuisine. droite: Vues en coupe_Garage_Séjour_Escalier_Éclairage zénithal.

FREIBURG, GERMANY **BUBAT RURAL RESIDENCE**

ARCHITECTS: WEBER + HUMMEL ARCHITEKTEN BDA
COMPLETION: 2011_**PROPERTY SIZE:** 1,867 M²
GROSS FLOOR AREA: 900 M²_**NUMBER OF ROOMS:** 40
PHOTOS: CHRISTINA KRATZENBERG

Built in 1908 by Prof. Hugo Eberhardt on a steep villa plot in Freiburg, the house displays clear conceptual and formal influences of the English country cottage movement. Many interior design details, from the indoor fountain to the fire irons, were designed by the architect and have been preserved to this day. The listed house was carefully renovated and rendered habitable for a young family. This included improving the energy efficiency of the 114 windows while maintaining their original substance, replacing obstructive modern radiators by wall heating, and renewing the bathrooms. The spirit of the 21st century is present in the contemporary lighting design and decidedly modern furniture.

Das 1908 von Prof. Hugo Eberhardt auf einem steilen Villengrundstück in Freiburg erbaute Haus zeigt deutliche konzeptionelle und formale Einflüsse der englischen Landhausbewegung. Viele innenraumgestalterische Details - vom Zimmerbrunnen bis zum Kaminbesteck - stammen aus der Feder des Architekten und sind bis heute erhalten. Das denkmalgeschützte Haus wurde behutsam saniert und für eine junge Familie bewohnbar gemacht. Unter Anderem wurden die 114 Fenster des Hauses unter Wahrung der Originalsubstanz energetisch optimiert, störende neuzeitliche Heizkörper durch Wandheizungen ersetzt und die Bäder erneuert. Der Spirit des 21. Jahrhunderts wird durch zeitgenössisches Lighting Design und dezidiert modernes Mobiliar Einzug halten.

Ce bâtiment de prestige construit en 1908 sur des plans du professeur Hugo Eberhardt s'inspire distinctement du style des manoirs anglais datant de la même époque. On doit également à l'architecte de nombreux détails de la décoration intérieure conservés jusqu'à nos jours, notamment la fontaine et les ustensiles de cheminée. L'édifice, classé monument historique, a été soigneusement rénové à la demande d'une jeune famille. Les travaux ont principalement porté sur l'optimisation énergétique des cent quatorze fenêtres d'origine, le remplacement de radiateurs inesthétiques par un système de chauffage mural, et la rénovation totale des salles de bains. Le XXIe siècle a par ailleurs fait son entrée dans ce bâtiment traditionnel grâce à des dispositifs d'éclairage et un mobilier résolument modernes.

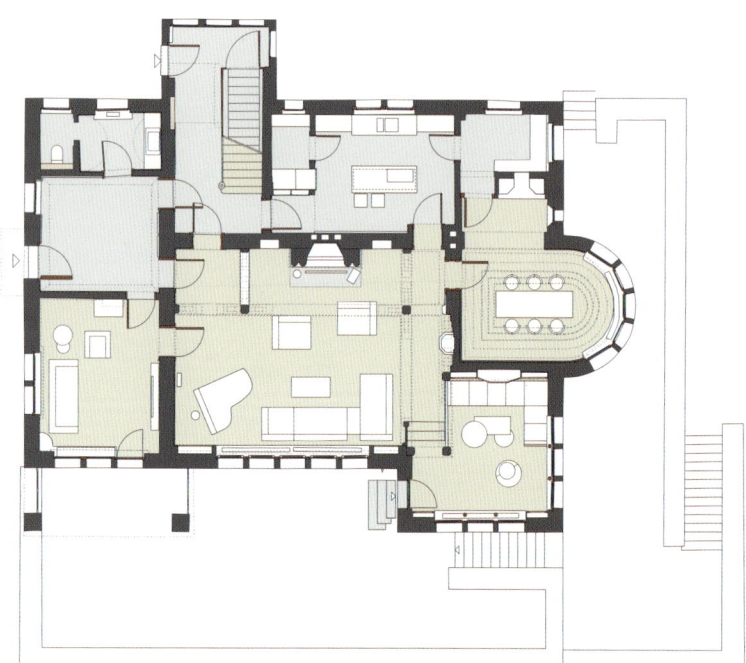

left: Ground floor plan_Street view_Parlour, fireplace. right: Parlour_Studio_Playroom.
links: Grundriss EG_Straßenansicht_Salon, Kaminblick. rechts: Salon_Studio_Spielzimmer.
gauche: Plan RdC_Vue de la rue_Salon, cheminée. droite: Salon_Studio_Salle de jeu.

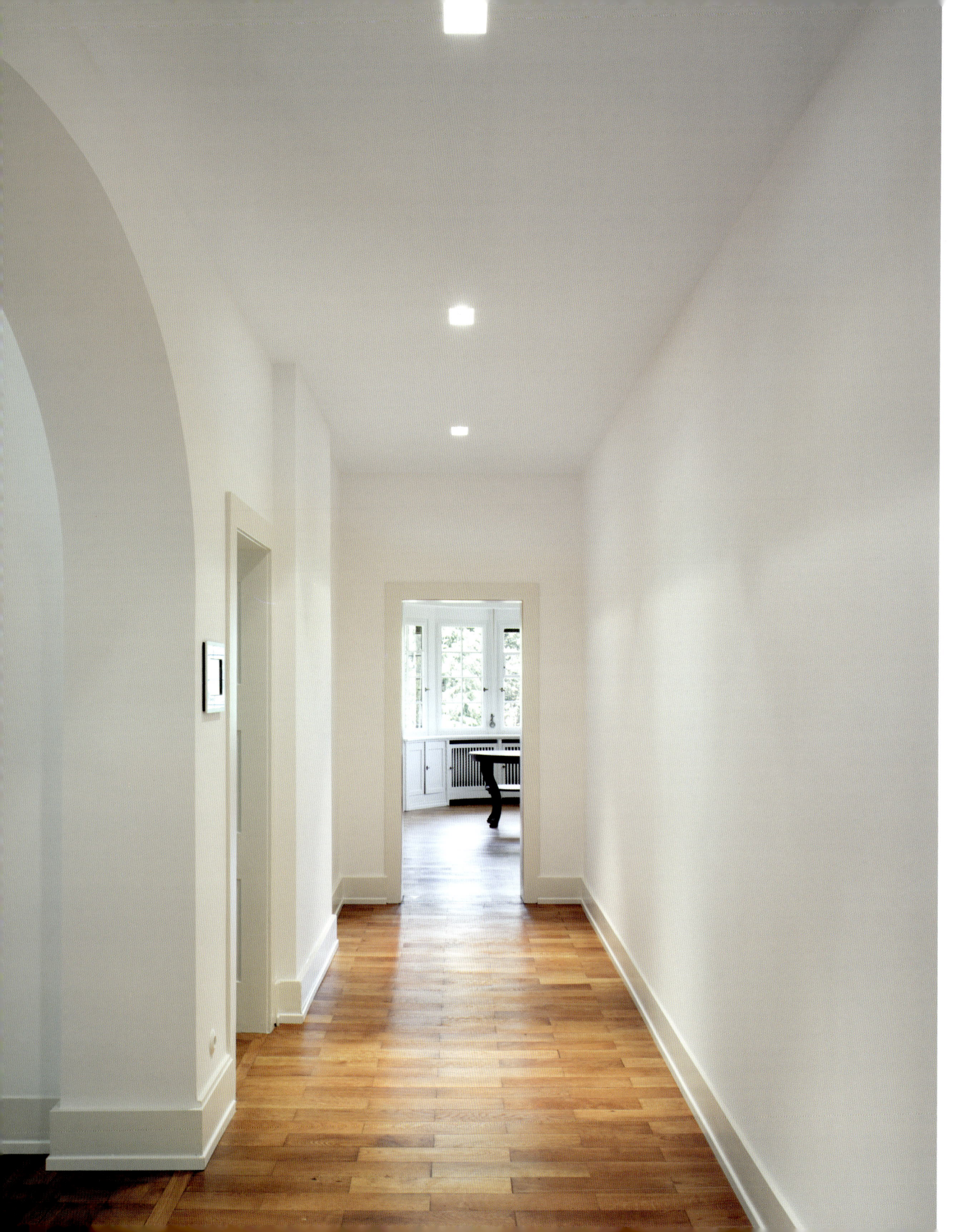

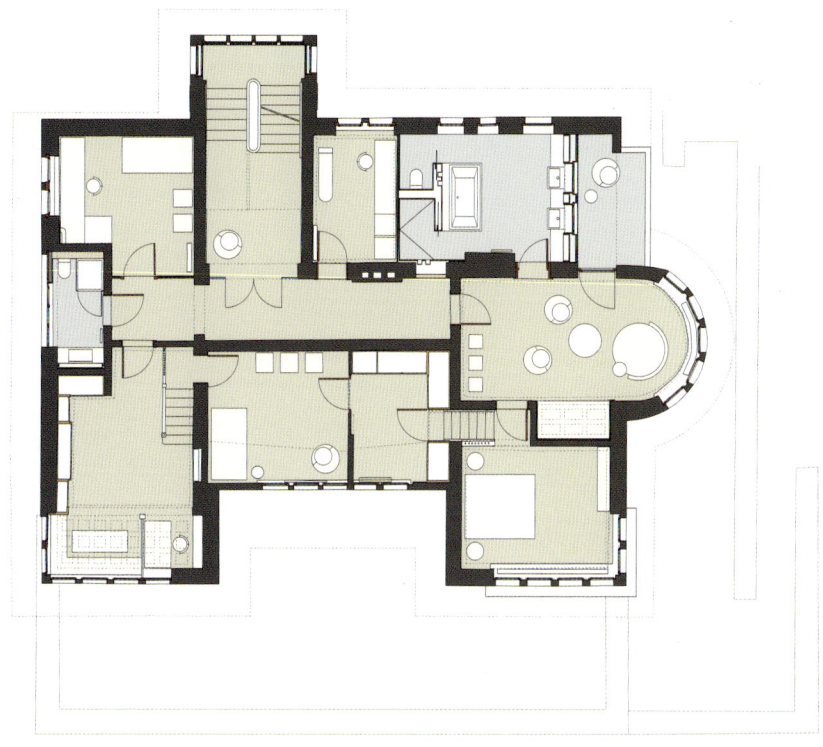

left: Hall. right: Top floor plan_Stairs_Master bathroom_Attic floor staircase.
links: Flur. rechts: Grundriss OG_Treppenpodest_Masterbad_Treppenhaus Dachgeschoss.
gauche: Couloir. droite: Plan niveau 1_Escalier_Salle de bains générale_Cage d'escalier.

LAKE AMMER, GERMANY VILLA COMPLEX AT LAKE AMMER

ARCHITECTS: WIEGAND/HOFFMANN
GESELLSCHAFT VON ARCHITEKTEN MBH
COMPLETION: 2012_**PROPERTY SIZE:** 5,500 M²
GROSS FLOOR AREA: 824 M²_**NUMBER OF ROOMS:** 14
PHOTOS: REINHARD GÖRNER

The family estate, consisting of a villa, a side building for vehicles, and a garden house is grouped around a large forecourt with a driveway. The elevated villa opens up towards the lake through large panoramic windows as well as terraces facing an expansive garden located in the famous natural landscape of Lake Ammer. References to the impressive landscape are found in the staggered façades and roofs of the villa. The interior consists of a cosmopolitan composition, consisting of Italian and French furniture, wallpaper and mosaics in combination with custom-made and fitted elements.

Der Familiensitz, bestehend aus einer Villa, einem Nebengebäude für Fahrzeuge und einem Gartenhaus, gruppiert sich um einen großzügigen Vorplatz mit Vorfahrt. Zum See hin öffnet sich die erhöht liegende Villa durch große Panoramafenster sowie Terrassen zu einer weitläufigen Gartenanlage, die in der berühmten Naturlandschaft des Ammersees liegt. Die Referenz der beeindruckenden Landschaft zeigt sich in den gestaffelten Fassaden und Dächern der Villa. Das Interior definiert sich als kosmopolitische Komposition, die aus italienischen und französischen Möbeln, Tapeten und Mosaiken besteht und mit eigens angefertigten Möbeln und Einbauten kombiniert wird.

Cette propriété se compose d'une villa, d'un garage et d'un pavillon de jardin groupés autour d'une vaste esplanade à laquelle on accède par une allée. Construite sur un promontoire, la villa s'ouvre sur le célèbre lac bavarois d'Ammersee par des fenêtres panoramiques qui donnent sur des terrasses et un vaste parc. La sophistication des toits et des façades répond à la beauté impressionnante du site tandis que l'intérieur, cosmopolite, se caractérise par des meubles, mosaïques et papiers peints français et italiens complétés par divers éléments intégrés à la décoration.

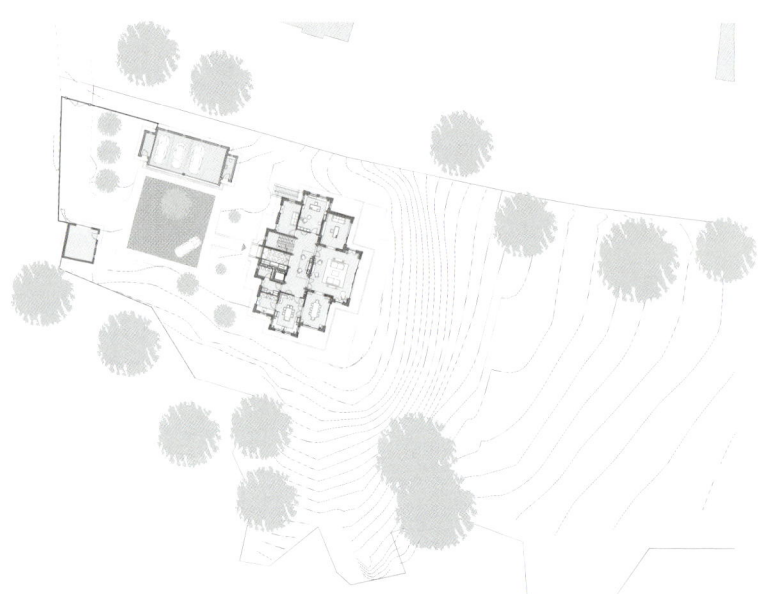

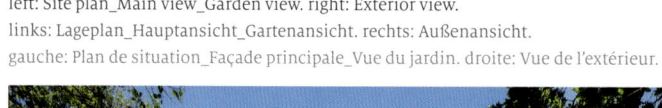

left: Site plan_Main view_Garden view. right: Exterior view.
links: Lageplan_Hauptansicht_Gartenansicht. rechts: Außenansicht.
gauche: Plan de situation_Façade principale_Vue du jardin. droite: Vue de l'extérieur.

left: Hall. right: Section_Dressing room_Living room_Bathroom.
links: Halle. rechts: Schnitt_Ankleide_Wohnzimmer_Bad.
gauche: Nef. droite: Vue en coupe_Dressing_Séjour_Salle de bains.

ACASSUSO, BUENOS AIRES, ARGENTINA **ACASSUSO HOUSE**

ARCHITECTS: REMY ARQUITECTOS
COMPLETION: 2012_**PROPERTY SIZE:** 1,200 M²
GROSS FLOOR AREA: 1,200 M²_**NUMBER OF ROOMS:** 5
PHOTOS: ALEJANDRO PERAL

Located on an irregular lot, this house is an answer to the plot lines, and a very demanding needs program. The V shaped plan connects the different function of the house through glassed bridges. This makes the exterior constantly presence on the inside. The house is developed at three levels – the basement, the main social area on the first floor, and the private areas on the upper floor. The stone path to the entrance surprisingly stops at a risen pond. The pond overflows as a cascade to the basement, copying the rusted metal sheet, where it is surrounded by greenery. This house has an intricate flow of space, forming green terraces overlooking the river, where nature and concrete enter a harmonic union.

Der Entwurf reagiert auf die asymmetrischen Flurlinien und die gehobenen Ansprüche des Bauherrn. Im V-förmigen Grundriss sind die Funktionen des Hauses über gläserne Brücken verbunden, was dem Außenbereich zu steter Präsenz verhilft. Die Villa erstreckt sich über drei Geschosse – vom Souterrain über den zentralen Gemeinschaftsbereich im Erdgeschoss bis hin zu den Privaträumen im Obergeschoss. Der Steinweg zum Eingang endet überraschend an einem erhöhten Teich, der in Kaskaden zum Untergeschoss hin überläuft. Hier wechseln sich die Patina korrodierter Metallplatten und das Grün des Gartens ab. Aus der komplexen Raumstruktur heraus erwachsen grüne Terrassen, die über dem nahen Fluss liegen, so bilden Natur und Beton eine harmonische Einheit.

Les architectes ont conçu cette villa sur un terrain aux formes irrégulières en tenant compte d'exigences complexes. Deux volumes formant un V sont reliés par des ponts vitrés, de sorte que l'intérieur reste constamment en contact avec l'extérieur. Les pièces se répartissent sur trois niveaux : le sous-sol, le rez-de-chaussée abritant les espaces communs et le premier étage où se trouvent les chambres. La rampe d'accès en dalles de pierre longe un bassin surélevé et verdoyant dont l'eau s'écoule en cascade vers un second bassin situé au niveau inférieur. Cette villa se caractérise ainsi par des espaces imbriqués les uns dans les autres et par l'harmonie qu'elle réalise entre béton et éléments naturels.

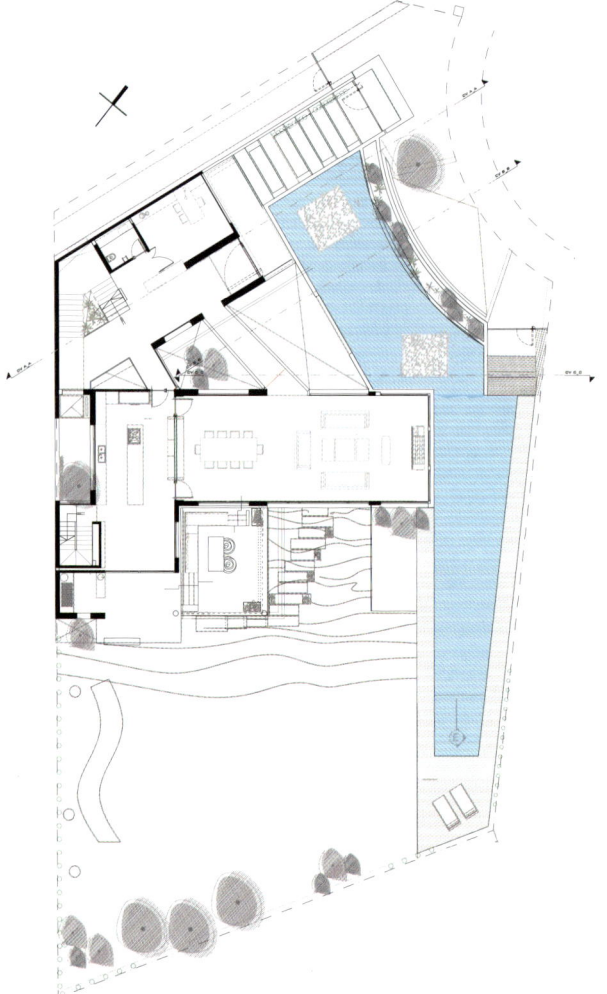

left: Ground floor plan_Street view_Entrance. right: Outdoor area.
links: Grundriss EG_Straßenansicht_Eingang. rechts: Außenbereich.
gauche: Plan RdC_Vue de la rue_Entrée. droite: Extérieur.

left: Pool. right: Section_Exterior view_View_Living room.
links: Pool. rechts: Schnitt_Außenansicht_Ausblick_Wohnraum.
gauche: Piscine extérieure. droite: Vue en coupe_Vue de l'extérieur_Vue panoramique_Séjour.

INDEX

ARCHITECTS ARCHITEKTEN ARCHITECTES

INDEX
PROJECTS PROJEKTE PROJETS

Imprint

The Deutsche Bibliothek lists this publication in the Deutsche Nationalbibliographie; detailed bibliographical information can be found on the internet at http://dnb.ddb.de

ISBN 978-3-03768-158-9
(English edition)

ISBN 978-3-905982-13-8
(Édition française)

© 2014 by Braun Publishing AG
www.braun-publishing.ch

1st edition 2014

Editor: Sibylle Kramer
Editorial staff and layout: Sabine Heußel, Helen Gührer, Maria Barrera del Amo
Text editing (English): Cosima Talhouni
Translation into German: Dagmar Glück
Translation into English: Cosima Talhouni
Graphic design: Michaela Prinz, Berlin